KIDS
TALK

KIDS
TALK

STRATEGIC LANGUAGE
USE IN LATER CHILDHOOD

Edited by

Susan M. Hoyle

Carolyn Temple Adger

New York • Oxford

Oxford University Press

1998

Oxford University Press

Oxford   New York
Athens   Auckland   Bangkok   Bogotá   Buenos Aires   Calcutta
Cape Town   Chennai   Dar es Salaam   Delhi   Florence   Hong Kong   Istanbul
Karachi   Kuala Lumpur   Madrid   Melbourne   Mexico City   Mumbai
Nairobi   Paris   São Paulo   Singapore   Taipei   Tokyo   Toronto   Warsaw

and associated companies in
Berlin   Ibadan

Library of Congress Cataloging-in-Publication Data
Kids talk : strategic language use in later childhood / edited by
Susan M. Hoyle, Carolyn Temple Adger.
p.   cm. — (Oxford studies in sociolinguistics)
Includes bibliographical references.
ISBN 0-19-509892-7; 0-19-509893-5 (pbk.)
1. Language acquisition.   2. Children—Language.
3. Sociolinguistics.   I. Hoyle, Susan M., 1950– .   II. Adger,
Carolyn Temple.   III. Series.
P118.K49   1998
401'.93 — dc21   97-38553

1 3 5 7 9 8 6 4 2

Printed in the United States of America
on acid-free paper

To Deborah Tannen and Deborah Schiffrin
In continuing appreciation of
their generous mentoring

Series Foreword

Sociolinguistics is the study of language in use. With a special focus on the relationships between language and society, sociolinguists analyze the forms and functions of language across social groups and across the range of situations in which speakers and writers deploy their verbal repertoires. In short, sociolinguistics examines discourse as it is constructed and co-constructed in the interactions of everyday life and as it reflects and creates the social realities of that life.

Some professional linguists examine the structure of sentences independent of who is speaking or writing and to whom, independent of what precedes and what follows, independent of the situated discourse in which linguistic form takes shape. By contrast, sociolinguists and discourse analysts investigate linguistic expression embedded in its social and situational contexts. Among observers who are *not* professional linguists, interest likewise focuses on language in discourse—for it is discourse that mirrors the patterns of social structure and strategic enterprise that engage the attention of most language observers.

Oxford Studies in Sociolinguistics offers a platform for studies of language use in communities worldwide. We invite synchronic or diachronic treatments of social dialects and registers, of oral, written, or signed discourse. We welcome studies that are descriptive or theoretical, interpretive or analytical. As with *Kids Talk*, some series volumes report original research, but an occasional one synthesizes or interprets existing knowledge. The series aims for a style that is accessible beyond linguists to other humanists and social scientists, and some volumes may appeal to educated readers keenly interested in the language of human affairs—for example, the discourse of lawyers engaging clients and one another with specialist registers or of patients engaging physicians over the challenges of treating disease and maintaining or regaining health or of kids talking to those around them about their academic and not-so-academic concerns. By providing a forum for innovative studies of language in use, Oxford Studies in Sociolinguistics aims to influence the agenda for linguistic research in the twenty-first century and to provide an array of thoughtful analyses to help launch that agenda.

In *Kids Talk*, Susan M. Hoyle and Carolyn Temple Adger have orchestrated a rich album containing over a dozen fascinating views of kids talking. Readers will hear older kids talking at home and work, in school and on the playground, discussing public and very private matters, having fun with language and using it to strategic advantage in the challenges of ordinary and extraordinary interaction. For decades, infants and young children have won research attention from linguists, and a great deal is known about the early stages of language acquisition and use. By contrast, the older children who are the focus of *Kids Talk* have been a neglected lot, and too little is known about their language. *Kids Talk*, with its varied portraits, adds significantly and spiritedly to our understanding of the talk of older kids. *Kids Talk* combines insights from discourse analysis, sociolinguistics, anthropology, sociology, and education; its pages furnish insight and, coincidentally, considerable joy at the opportunity to hear kids talk about their concerns and display their impressive linguistic skills as they negotiate the sometimes playful and often challenging tasks of this period of their lives.

Kids Talk fills a vacuum that has long been noted, and its chapters offer researchers, teachers, counselors, and parents informative and interesting discussions—by the kids themselves and by the distinguished contributors who have analyzed their talk. We are indebted to Susan Hoyle and Carolyn Adger for their editorial care and to them and the other authors for their contributions to this book. Oxford Studies in Sociolinguistics is pleased to have *Kids Talk* as its most recent volume.

EDWARD FINEGAN

Preface

This volume represents a rich mix of scholarship examining how different groups of children use language to negotiate their place in the world. Analytic approaches draw on conversational analysis, ethnography, ethnography of communication, and interactional sociolinguistics. Data from recorded, naturally occurring conversation and from careful observation of social interaction represent a range of settings (home, school, work, and play), as well as different ages, social classes, ethnicities, and genders.

This collection is the first to draw together scholarship on language behavior in the years between early childhood and adulthood. The chapters reveal unique attributes of language use during these years, when there is an increasing grasp of how participant and social situation define each other and an increasing sophistication at framing speech activities. The role of peer culture as both interactional accomplishment and social venue is illuminated. Contributors examine different discourse types and linguistic practices such as code-switching and register shifting, adoption of newly useful grammatical patterns, and social attitudes toward language differences.

The idea for this volume grew out of a presession we organized, called "Language Practices of Older Children," at the Georgetown University Round Table on Languages and Linguistics, March 10, 1993. We thank James E. Alatis, who was Dean of the School of Languages and Linguistics at Georgetown and Round Table organizer, for extending that opportunity to us. Early versions of Chapters 2, 3, 8, and 9 were presented there. At the time, Susan Hoyle was Visiting Assistant Professor of Linguistics at Georgetown University, and Carolyn Temple Adger was a Research Associate at the Institute for the Study of Exceptional Children and Youth at the University of Maryland College Park. We thank the two universities for their support of early work on this book. We are grateful to the scholars who contributed their work to this book and to each other for the conversations that accompanied its development. We thank Cynthia Read and Deborah Tannen for their early and continuing encouragement. During later stages, we profited immensely from Ed Finegan's insights and advice. Peter Ohlin kindly guided us through manuscript preparation, and Will Moore through the production process. We also thank our families, John and Joshua Hoyle, and John and Jake Adger, for their staunch support.

Bethesda, Maryland   S. M. H.
Silver Spring, Maryland   C. T. A.
October 1997

Contents

Contributors

Editors
CAROLYN TEMPLE ADGER
Center for Applied Linguistics
Washington, DC

SUSAN M. HOYLE
National Library of Medicine

Contributors
DONNA EDER
Department of Sociology
Indiana University

CATHERINE EMIHOVICH
Department of Counseling and
Educational Psychology
State University of New York at
Buffalo

SIGNITHIA FORDHAM
Department of Education
University of Maryland, Baltimore
County

MARJORIE HARNESS GOODWIN
Department of Anthropology
University of California, Los Angeles

ALICE GREENWOOD
Bell Laboratories

SHIRLEY BRICE HEATH
Department of English
Stanford University

LYNN MCCREEDY
Independent Scholar
Alexandria, VA

MARILYN MERRITT
Center for Applied Linguistics
Washington, DC

JENNIFER SCHLEGEL
Department of Anthropology
University of California, Los Angeles

STUART TANNOCK
Department of English
Stanford University

ANA CELIA ZENTELLA
Department of Black and Puerto Rican
Studies
Hunter College, C.U.N.Y.

Transcription Conventions

Each chapter uses those transcription conventions that its author finds most useful. Following Tannen (1993a), the editors have not imposed uniformity, recognizing that transcription and analysis are inseparable (Ochs 1979b, Edwards & Lampert 1993). However, there is a good deal of similarity in the conventions adopted by the contributors; this list includes the most common ones. Any additional or different conventions are indicated in individual chapters.

Sentence-final falling intonation	. or //
Sentence-final rising intonation	?
Continuing intonation	, or /
Animated voice quality	!
Pause	. . or . . . (shorter or longer)
	[3.5] or (3.5) numbers in brackets or parentheses represent pauses in seconds
Transcriber's comments	[comment] or ((*comment*))
Uncertain transcription	(words) or ((*words*))
Inaudible portion	( )
Laughter or breathiness	hh or (hh)
Inbreath	*hh
Lengthened sound	: (extra colons for extra lengthening)
Emphasis	**bold** or *italics*; CAPITALS for extra loudness
Overlap	[or / or // (at beginning of overlapping speech)
Latched or continuing speech (no pause either between speakers or within one speaker's turn)	=
Sound cut-off	-
Point of analysis	→
Unidentifiable speaker	X:
Speaker's identity uncertain	(Name):

Introduction

SUSAN M. HOYLE & CAROLYN TEMPLE ADGER

Studies of language in interaction have usually examined the talk of adults. As more and more scholarly attention focuses on language socialization, we are also learning a great deal about the development of grammatical, pragmatic, and discourse abilities among preschoolers. Only recently, however, has work begun on the language practices of the intermediate group. Attention to school-age children and adolescents is essential to a complete understanding of the dimensions along which language use can vary in the social construction of everyday life across the life span. In bringing together the work of several researchers who have been investigating the linguistic and interactional practices of older children, this volume contributes to our understanding of how members of a society use their language resources.

Between early childhood and adulthood, language users expand and refine their repertoires for managing interaction in social and cultural contexts, although documentation of just how they do so is still rather sparse. Some research on older children's language has investigated their acquisition of the referential and literacy skills central to educational advancement (e.g., Beach & Hynds 1990). Another important dimension, however, is the focus of this collection: how children use oral language in everyday settings—at home, in the community, on the playground, or at school—to organize their interaction and their lives.[1] All the chapters in this volume proceed from the view that the linguistic interaction of daily life constructs cultural and social groupings as well as individual identity—both in the moment and across the life span—and, conversely, that social group membership and individual identity make an imprint on language behavior. All the contributors would agree that language socialization—that is, "both socialization through language and socialization to use language" (Ochs 1986:2)—does not stop at the age of five or six (indeed, it can be argued that it never stops). They share the assumption that naturally occurring discourse reveals a degree of social and linguistic competence at once more complex and more subtle than that inferrable from talk elicited in an experimental setting, revealing much about how language and social life shape contexts for each other. Together, the contributors extend the pool of evidence proving that people construct their social worlds largely through language.

In speculating about what distinguishes the competence of older children from that of both younger children and adults, scholars agree (whether they themselves concentrate on younger or older children) that although syntactic competence continues to develop after the preschool years (Chomsky 1969), the difference between younger and older children is largely attributable to developing communicative competence (e.g., Cook-Gumperz 1977, Edelsky 1977, Garvey 1984, Heath 1983, McTear 1985, Ochs 1988, Ochs & Schieffelin 1979, Schieffelin 1990, Schieffelin & Ochs 1986). Despite such basic agreement, however, important questions arise. First, what does communicative competence look like as it is developing? Older children are undoubtedly in the process of mastering more and more complex interactional and communicative skills, yet it is difficult to tease apart developmental progress and new opportunities for its display. Moreover, the competences displayed by eight-, twelve-, or sixteen-year-olds are not merely immature reflections of those of adults; rather, the nature of those nonadult but well-formed competences is the issue.

A second question concerns the forces that shape the development of communicative competence. Older children are moving from their homes and neighborhoods, with their familiar patterns of linguistic interaction, into a wider social sphere in which they encounter new settings and new participant structures. New experiences challenge their register repertoires, framing capacities, and assumptions concerning appropriateness; at the same time, new challenges create opportunities for innovation as speakers employ their expanding repertoires to create and modify their social worlds. The expectations, beliefs, and habits of peers contribute to the construction of a distinctive group within the larger community: kids.

Third, we must ask whether the language of this age group is theoretically interesting. The age range between, say, seven-year-olds and eighteen-year-olds is very wide, but it is perhaps no more artificial to consider older childhood as a coherent time than to so consider adulthood or early childhood. In early childhood, linguistic structure and basic pragmatic skills are acquired; by adulthood, speakers have for the most part achieved competence in the varieties of language they require to perform a wide range of personal and professional tasks and to present themselves as particular sorts of people. During the years in between, speakers not only refine basic proficiencies but also become increasingly aware of, and able to wield power through, the strategic use of language.

In the pursuit of answers to these questions, we include chapters about many aspects of older children's discourse in a variety of settings and situations, with different interlocutors, for different purposes. All of the analyses are based on naturally occurring oral language in interaction, and each sheds light on the interrelation of linguistic practices and the extralinguistic world. Beyond that, the contributions are diverse, since we believe that cross-cutting methodological stances can illuminate linguistic phenomena in ways that benefit theory building. The contributors come from disciplines that offer complementary methodologies and assumptions—sociolinguistics, anthropology, and sociology. Many of the chapters are discourse analytic, attending closely to the details of language in specific interactions. Others take a wider, ethnographically based view, explicating patterns of language use and variation in particular communities. Some of the authors discuss language during play; some, conversation; some, academic discourse; and yet others, talk at work. Settings include the family, the peer group, and the classroom. Some chapters analyze talk among children of the same age; some, talk among children of different ages; some, talk between children and adults who play significant roles in their lives—teachers, parents, or community leaders. Boys' and girls' talk is heard in same- and mixed-gender groups. Children are Black, Latino, Puerto Rican, and White;[2] middle class and working class; residents of urban, suburban, and rural locations.

Three themes that pervade the growing literature on older children's language and that resonate in the chapters of this volume address the questions posed above. First is the characterization of the development of communicative competence during older childhood (including adolescence). Second is the notion that the peer group is crucially important in accounting for the language practices of older children. Third is the proposal that by examining the language in interaction of older children we can learn much of theoretical interest about language and interaction in general. As background for this first collection of work on older children's language, we provide an overview of what has been said about these themes.

Development of Communicative Competence

Our question about the dimensions of developing communicative competence is addressed by a growing body of research that confirms two related notions: in many ways the communicative competence of older children exceeds what is often expected of them, and their communicative repertoires nonetheless continue to expand at a rapid pace—if not with the striking rapidity of very young speakers. Here we outline some aspects of competence that have received attention: (1) its longitudinal development, (2) register usage and cultural patterning, and (3) competence in different settings.

Development over Time

That older children and adolescents are more adept speakers than younger ones would seem to be self-evident, but the exact nature of their increased proficiency is not well understood. Researchers have focused on various phenomena to suggest some of the answers, including aspects of narrative competence and conversational competence.

Narrative competence has been seen to increase with age in terms of such elements as length and complexity of stories, plot development, provision of needed information to listeners, and effective use of particular linguistic devices. Martin

(1983), for example, found that eight-year-olds, as compared to six-year-olds, used reference and conjunction in elicited narratives much as adults do. Kernan (1977), examining stories told by Black American girls, found that between the ages of seven and eleven, they grew in their ability to supply information about characters, motivations, and events that their listeners needed to understand and appreciate their narratives; among other things, the older girls, but not the younger ones, used the very effective evaluative device of quotation. Romaine (1984), similarly, analyzed the narrative performance of a ten-year-old Edinburgh girl who displayed skillful use of elaboration, including, like the older girls in Kernan's study, much quotation.[3]

In addition to skills manifested primarily in narrative, other conversational skills have been identified as changing noticeably over time; among them are topic development, backchanneling, and the use of discourse markers. Dorval and Eckerman (1984) and Dumesnil and Dorval (1989) noticed age differences in how conversationalists construct discourse topics on a turn-by-turn basis. While the second graders in their study produced a large number of what the authors saw as "tangential" and "unrelated" turns, adolescents tended to tie their talk to the factual details recounted in a previous speaker's turn, and young adults tended to relate their contributions to a previous speaker's expression of thoughts and feelings. Boggs (1990) found that sixth graders' talk showed greater adherence to a single topic over a long stretch of conversation than did the talk of second graders. Reichman (1990) proposed that topical organization becomes more hierarchical with age (that is, the conversations of older speakers have a greater number of embedded topics than those of younger people). Both Boggs and Reichman noted that, for eight-year-olds, wordplay and laughter seem to be enough to sustain engagement in a conversation, with little topic development.

Backchanneling—giving continuation signals that show listenership such as nods, "mm-hmm," "yeah," or longer comments—is done more by older children than younger ones. Corsaro (1977) noticed that three-year-olds did not give backchannels when conversing with adults, and Dittmann (1972), looking at children ages seven to twelve in a laboratory setting, found that not before the age of twelve did subjects produce frequent or consistent "listening responses." Hess and Johnston (1988:319), based on observation of seven- to twelve-year olds in an instructional setting, suggested that "back channel listener responses could be among the last conversational skills acquired"; the oldest listeners in their study gave three times as many backchannels as the youngest ones. Thus, although backchanneling behavior is culturally variable (White 1989), among many middle-class American children, at least, it appears to be a developmental matter.

The use of discourse markers (such as *and, but, then, so, now, though, anyway, because, so,* and *well*) may be another age-related phenomenon.[4] Because the production and understanding of coherent discourse is so complicated, studying the acquisition of discourse markers as resources for its achievement becomes interesting. Preschool children do not control the full range of adult functions for discourse markers (Gallagher & Craig 1987; Peterson & McCabe 1988, 1991; Sprott 1992).[5] Scott (1984) found six-year-olds to use very few "discourse connectivity devices" other than *and* and *but*, but found twelve-year-olds to use a wide variety. Sprott

(1992), examining the talk of children ranging in age from two to nine, found that the youngest children marked only interactional components of speech (using markers at turn boundaries and as preface to directive speech acts), whereas with increasing age, children began to mark the ideational structure of their talk (first by subordinating one proposition to another and later by marking a switch in topic or argumentative tactic). But even the nine-year-olds did not exactly mirror adult usage.

Although this volume does not, as a whole, focus on longitudinal development, some chapters do address the issue of change over time.[6] Heath (Chapter 12) finds that, over the course of collaborative projects with adults, adolescents increase their turns at talk and begin freely using certain syntactic constructions that characterize the talk of their adult mentors. As they perform adult roles, they talk more and more like adults; furthermore, the talk itself constitutes those roles. Emihovich (Chapter 6) shows another aspect of proficiency that presents itself over time: the ability to manipulate the framing of a topic. In her study of a younger and an older group of low-income African American teenage girls, she finds that the older group is much more skillful at this aspect of discourse in both small-group discussion and a public forum. Unlike their younger counterparts, they incorporate adult perspectives into their framing of a situation while at the same time resisting and subverting adult authority. McCreedy's comparison of talk in two elementary classrooms (Chapter 9) demonstrates that, given encouragement and practice in producing academic discourse, even students with learning disabilities gain remarkable proficiency in this genre. When they are encouraged to author their own texts, rather than animate a teacher's script, they do so, and over the course of a school year their performance improves.

Key Issues in Communicative Competence

Register   A major aspect of developing communicative competence is the mastery of a wide range of registers—varieties of language, distinguished by the clustering of linguistic features, that are considered appropriate for and are used in different situations (Biber & Finegan 1994). Much language acquisition after the early stages consists in expanding one's register repertoire.

Andersen's (1990) study was one of the first to examine the acquisition of register skills among children; her work suggests questions about such development not only in children of the ages she considered (four to seven) but also older ones. Role play, as she found, is a fruitful arena in which to look for register competence. Even her youngest children used different registers as they animated puppets representing different characters (mothers, fathers, babies, doctors, nurses, teachers). The older children, though, controlled a wider range of linguistic devices to mark the registers associated with different roles. Whereas the younger ones relied on phonology, prosody, and voice quality, the older ones also freely used lexical and syntactic features and a range of speech act types and were able to sustain register-specific talk for longer periods. Similarly, Halmari & Smith (1994), looking at a slightly older pair of bilingual (Finnish/English) sisters, ages eight and nine, found that in their play the girls marked different registers not only through changes in voice quality but also through the use of particular sentence types and verb tenses, as well as through code-switching.

Quantitative variation studies (many summarized in Romaine 1984) have documented the style-shifting (i.e., register-shifting along a continuum of formality) displayed by older children. Although some early work seemed to indicate that pre- and early adolescents were "close to monostylistic speaker[s] of [their] local vernacular" (Wolfram & Fasold 1974:92), other studies have found them to adhere to the same sorts of patterns first identified for adult speakers by Labov (e.g., 1972b). That is, within a speech community, the frequency with which speakers use particular phonological or grammatical features varies according to the social class of the speaker and the level of formality of the occasion. Reid (1978), for instance, noted patterns of both stylistic and social variation among eleven-year-old Edinburgh boys and found that they could explicitly talk about such variation when asked. Romaine (1984), who also examined the speech of Edinburgh children, reported that ten-year-olds used different phonological variants in a reading task and an interview. Cheshire (1978, 1982, 1991) found working-class British adolescents (ages eleven to fifteen) to use fewer nonstandard forms in the classroom than on the playground, although their classroom language did not consist completely of standard variants. Register variation, it is important to note here, is a matter of degree, especially when different registers are realized by variation between standard and vernacular forms. These forms exist on a continuum, and a speaker's production is rarely a matter of all-or-none; rather, situational constraints may favor the use of more (or fewer) forms from one or the other end of the continuum.[7]

Among bilinguals, register variation can involve code-switching. Zentella (1981a, b, 1985), for instance, studied inner-city New York Puerto Rican children (ages four to sixteen), members of a community that values switching between Spanish and English as a sign of membership. She identified a wide range of discourse-internal functions for switching, including being practical (e.g., speaking to an addressee in her stronger language), modulating affect (e.g., coupling an aggravated command in one language with a mitigated form in the other language), and signaling a change in alignment toward the hearer or toward the speaker's own utterance (e.g., shifting from statement to question or shifting topic). The children she studied displayed a knowledge of register appropriateness: they code-switched much more often outside the classroom setting than during lessons (or during interviews with the researcher).

In this volume, several chapters document the register competence of older children; the kinds discussed include functionally specialized registers and age-graded registers. Hoyle (Chapter 2) shows boys engaged in pretend play using two registers in addition to their ordinary speech style: one specialized to the kind of activity they are performing and another more broadly "adult-sounding." Heath (Chapter 12), on the other hand, examines teenagers acquiring adult registers as they work alongside adults; as the young people assume adult roles, they come to use the kind of language that characterizes those roles. The chapters by Adger and McCreedy both focus on acquisition of an academic register. Adger's investigation (Chapter 8) of an elementary classroom in which the children are native speakers of African American Vernacular English (AAVE) reveals that they shift to the standard variety—their most academic register—to accomplish tasks most related to literacy. McCreedy (Chapter 9) finds that the capacity for academic authorship can flourish among elementary students if it is encouraged. Other chapters, although not focusing explicitly on register, nevertheless address the issue of how particular children suit elements of language to situations they encounter. Emihovich (Chapter 6) shows teenage girls approaching the same topic differently in a private versus a public setting. Fordham (Chapter 11) discusses the strict social prescriptions that teenage speakers of a vernacular discourse style may face as they decide when, or whether, to use the standard variety. The standard may be part of these young people's register repertoire, but it is, for many, far from the most valued part.

Cultural Patterns   Another major aspect of communicative competence is using the patterns of talk characteristic of and valued by one's community. Such patterns can, of course, conflict with those of people from other backgrounds, and intercultural clashes can become more problematic as children move into life outside their own communities. In particular, school can present difficulties: as Boggs (1985:1) has said (in relation to Hawaiian children but pertaining more generally), "success or failure in school is due in large part to the congruence of or incongruence between ways of speaking learned at home and those required at school" (cf. Au 1980). The language of the classroom is often more "literate" than the language of the home, with explicit lexical marking of logical relationships and minimal assumption of shared background knowledge. A large part of what all children learn in school is to lexicalize shared meaning (Cook-Gumperz 1977), as they develop "conscious awareness of the systematic grammatical distinctions between informal talk and more formal narrative prose" (Gumperz & Field 1995:146–47). For some children, the discourse encountered at home provides a means of socialization into academically valued kinds of talk even before they start school (e.g., Ochs, Taylor, Rudolph, & Smith 1992; Scollon & Scollon 1981). For others, however, discontinuity between the types of linguistic interaction encountered at home and at school may be extreme. Philips (1993), for instance, studying patterns of interaction among Native American children living on an Oregon reservation, identified cultural differences in participation structures (patterns of speaking, listening, and turntaking) between home and school that help explain the children's failure to meet the expectations of non-Indian teachers. For instance, these children hesitated to speak when singled out, for they did not share the teachers' expectations about the value of individual performance.

At school, children's acquisition of academic discourse strategies can build on the narrative skills they bring from home, but the process is smoothest when children and teachers share expectations. Whereas children from middle-class homes are likely to be familiar with the sorts of stories favored by their teachers—factual narratives about personal experiences, fictional narratives about storybook characters, and fictionalized stories based on but departing from reality—children from other communities may be unfamiliar with these but accustomed to highly creative stories or stories performed jointly with the audience (Heath 1982, 1983; Scollon & Scollon 1981; Watson-Gegeo & Boggs 1977). Heath (1983) discussed storytelling styles in two working-class communities in the southeastern United States, one White and one Black, and contrasted both of them to that of the "mainstream" townspeople of the same area. Only the mainstream children experienced at home the kind of literacy events that were expected and valued by the schools—those featuring decontextualization of experience and speculation about events in books. The other children encountered severe dissonance at school. Scollon and Scollon (1984) described features of the organization of Athabaskan narratives that negatively affected the way non-Indian teachers evaluated Athabaskan children's stories and general linguistic abilities. Michaels (1981, 1986, 1991) and Michaels and Collins (1984) demonstrated how a teacher's success in helping a child structure a piece of explicit academic discourse depends on whether child and teacher share culturally based narrative conventions and interpretive strategies. White, middle-class children, they showed, who produced the kind of "topic-centered" narrative style that their White, middle-class teachers expected, tended to receive helpful questions and comments. But Black children who used a "topic-associating" style (recounting a series of anecdotes with a common theme and tying them together prosodically but not lexically or explicitly) did not get from the teachers the sort of questions and comments that would scaffold the talk into a literate-style presentation.

Different narrative practices can persist beyond the early elementary school years. Gee (1989) compared a story told by an eleven-year-old working-class Black girl to her peers and one told by a middle-class White girl of the same age to an adult and showed how the girls used different linguistic devices to shape their stories. The Black girl used rhythm, sound play, repetition, syntactic and semantic parallelism, and changes in tempo, pitch, and loudness to create patterns and thus convey meaning. The patterns created by the White narrator, on the other hand, were topic/comment and background/foreground, patterns not primarily of sound but of content.

Besides cultural and subcultural differences in narrative styles, there may be group differences in modes of topic development during more dialogic discourse. Erickson (1984) found that the discussion of a group of inner-city Black teenagers (thirteen to sixteen years old) was characterized by the same sort of "topic-associating" style that Michaels found in the narratives of Black elementary school students. The teenagers' conversation consisted of a series of narrative anecdotes stitched together ("rhapsodized") through a common underlying theme that was never explicitly stated. Hemphill (1989), comparing White middle-class and Black working-class sixteen-year-old girls, found that they developed conversational topics differently. Her work modified the early suggestions of Bernstein (1971) about social-class differences in speech by showing that the more direct influence of class may be on conversational style rather than in availability of linguistic resources. The working-class girls tended to tie their turns grammatically to those of previous speakers (by means of anaphora and ellipsis) and to use backchannels to support a current speaker's turn. The middle-class girls tended not to tie their turns grammatically to the talk of a previous speaker (instead, new speakers re-identified topics by using full noun phrases) and to use backchannels as bids for the floor. Hemphill found the working-class girls' discussion to be more collaborative in style (emphasizing the relatedness of successive turns) and the middle-class girls' more competitive (emphasizing the novelty of an individual's contribution).

In this volume, Fordham (Chapter 11) focuses on cultural norms for speaking. The high school students who are the subject of her study experience a sharp dissonance between the discourse style they value and the communicative style associated with the culture of power—including a variety of English that can open a gateway to academic success.

Settings for Language Socialization

Language socialization includes the acquisition of attitudes, skills, and strategies that are manifested and practiced in a variety of settings—home, community, street, school, work. Not all of these sites have received equal attention, and indeed some of them may not be easily differentiated. Goodwin's (1990a) study of neighborhood talk and play illuminated ways in which language and social life are contexts for and constituents of each other. Heath's (1983) analysis of ways of speaking, knowing, and telling moved from the homes and neighborhoods of working-class White and Black children into their schools, showing how discontinuities between these domains may be overcome. At home, older children playing in pairs or small groups may engage in practices that they do not manifest as clearly in other settings. Hoyle (1989, 1993) suggested that children's experimentation with participation frameworks in dyadic play reveals their recognition that the most meaningful discourse is multi-layered. Several studies have found rich data on older children's communicative repertoire and attitudes by observing them in informal settings at school rather than in the classroom (Eckert 1989a, Eder 1995, Shuman 1986).

But the classroom setting has received much attention. Given the importance of schooling in children's socialization, language at school becomes a crucial research site for witnessing their developing communicative competence, as Merritt (chapter 7, this volume) reminds us. For all children, going to school presents significant challenges that differ from those demanded within the home or peer group (Cazden 1988; Cazden, John, & Hymes 1972; Delpit 1995; Gilmore & Glatthorn 1982; Lucas & Borders 1994; Mehan 1979, 1982; Shuy & Griffin 1981; Sinclair & Coulthard 1975).

Teacher-led classroom discourse has a sequential and hierarchical structure of its own. Such features as students' opportunities to speak (Mehan 1979), the syntactic shape of their contributions (Lerner 1995), and the organization of repair in the classroom (McHoul 1990) are to a great extent orchestrated by the teacher. Classroom talk comprises different sorts of events, bounded by recurring clusters of verbal and nonverbal behavior, each having its own organization and providing a specific set of participation rights. Children are generally expected to recognize such structures and rights without explicit instruction (Mehan 1979).[8] To be credited with academic knowledge, students must discern what normative procedure applies from moment to moment, since a contribution offered at the wrong time is likely to be ignored or negatively sanctioned, whether it contains factually correct information or not. In addition, students must come to recognize other tacit expectations: Lemke (1990), for instance, showed that, in order to understand the content of lessons, high school science students must already have some competence in the linguistic register of science and must be able to discern the information structure favored by teachers in which conceptual relationships are expressed only implicitly.

Students' interactions with each other are valuable sites of learning, too. Cazden's (1988) review of classroom discourse included a focus on peer collaboration as a resource for cognitive growth: a catalyst for problem solving, an arena for taking the perspective of another, and in general a place to practice academic discourse. At the same time, as Streeck (1985) showed, children in peer teaching arrangements organize their interaction in terms of their own categories and interests; for instance, gender and peer ranking become salient, and group members conduct disputes even while engaging in the basically cooperative enterprise of teaching and learning.

It is becoming increasingly clear that in classrooms, as elsewhere, knowledge and competence are co-constructed and that children take charge of their own learning when given the chance (Duran & Szymanski 1995; Gutierrez 1995; Rosebery, Warren, & Conant 1992; Tuyay, Jennings, & Dixon 1995). Cooperative learning environments, for instance, are intended to encourage children's active engagement in academic tasks as they bring multiple perspectives to them. Children working among themselves do actively engage in the task they have been assigned, but they do so on their own terms, revealing their own interests and concerns, which may not be anticipated by the teacher or the curriculum (Gumperz & Field 1995).

Talk at school is central to children's lives, and their interaction with each other and with adults in that setting—successful or not, satisfying or not—is a rich resource for researchers seeking insight into the nature of children's developing communicative competence. In this volume, five chapters, by Merritt, Adger, McCreedy, Schlegel, and Fordham, concern language use at school. They depict children as active agents in their activities there, working to assemble pieces of their own worlds.

Construction of Peer Culture

A central force shaping older children's developing communicative competence is interaction with peers. Labov (1972a: 255–92) first proposed that peer group allegiance is important in predicting the linguistic behavior of older children and showed that, among Black inner-city adolescents in New York, those who belonged to peer groups adhered most closely to the grammatical rules of the vernacular dialect. In Cheshire's (1982) study of working-class British teenagers, the frequency with which speakers used particular nonstandard features reflected the extent to which they shared the norms of the vernacular culture (e.g., liking to fight, stealing, setting fires, and valuing "toughness") and opposed mainstream norms (e.g., school attendance). Some nonstandard features functioned as markers of vernacular loyalty for both boys and girls, some for boys only, and some for girls only. Cheshire (1991) analyzed these adolescents' use of *ain't* in "non-conventional tag questions" such as "You're a girl, ain't you" or "I'm going on holiday, ain't I" (with falling intonation), which do not call for an answer (because it is obvious or the hearer could not know it) and in the context convey hostility. She suggested that in such utterances the use of *ain't* marks an important vernacular norm: aggression. In these tags, the adolescents always used a phonological variant of *ain't* approximating "in't" (and never used *isn't* or *aren't*), whereas in other cases they used several different pronunciations of *ain't* as well as standard English forms. She concluded that the teenagers were conveying a dominant theme of their culture through syntactic and phonological choices.

Eisikovits (1991a, b), who used sociolinguistic interview data from working-class girls and boys (ages thirteen to sixteen) in inner-city Sydney, found regular variation between standard and nonstandard verb forms based on sentence-internal grammatical constraints. She also found that at least one feature, nonstandard *don't* (e.g., *Dad don't*) was used exclusively by boys, whose increasing use of this "marker of group identity, 'maleness' and working-class values" (1991a:239) suggested that as these boys got older they identified more strongly with a male peer group and with the working class.

Eckert's (1988, 1989a) ethnographic study of a suburban Detroit high school showed that adolescent social structure is closely related to linguistic change in the wider society. The way that teenagers organize their lives helps to explain how vowel changes currently in progress in northern U. S. cities spread outward from urban centers and upward through the socioeconomic hierarchy. She identified two opposed focal social categories in the school, the opposition between which structured the adolescent social world. The "Jocks" were oriented to middle-class values, the "Burnouts" to working-class values (although parents' socioeconomic class did not strictly determine category membership). Jocks accepted the hegemony and values of the school and associated mainly with classmates in local networks. Burnouts, rejecting the values of the school, built outside networks, especially in the nearby city. An individual's category affiliation was a significant predictor of variant linguistic usage, with Burnouts adopting the innovative variants while "In-betweens" (students who identified closely with neither focal category) served as a conduit for the spread of change to the Jock end of the social spectrum.

Some studies of code-switching among young people also reveal the importance of peer group affiliation. From an early age, children in bilingual or multilingual settings code-switch (e.g., Youssef 1993), and among older children in-group solidarity is one major situational feature that encourages switching. Hewitt (1986), for instance, discussed the use of West Indian Creole by Black and White British adolescents alike as a manifestation of allegiance to a youth culture. Rampton (1991, 1995) described "crossing" among an ethnically mixed group of British adolescents (of Anglo, Afro-Caribbean, Bangladesh, Indian, and Pakistani descent). Although the non-Panjabi-speakers had a very limited repertoire in that language, Panjabi was important both in managing differences within the peer group and in extending their outlook beyond the neighborhood to a wider youth culture. Whereas use of Panjabi was an expression of sociability. adolescent use of Caribbean Creole forms often signaled opposition to the establishment hierarchy.

Activities in the Peer Group

Few of the daily social tasks of children or adolescents have been described (cf. Garvey 1984). It is clear, though, that children organize their own interactions, often differently than adults would. Sharing and trading, for instance, may be centrally important to children. Mishler (1979) analyzed the negotiation of trades in a group of six-year-old boys. Traders inform each other through their talk as to what speech activity they are engaged in, each expresses the way in which his tradable object differs from another's, and each presents his own object as desirable while downplaying the value of the other's. Katriel (1987) examined ritualized sharing among Israeli children (ages five to twelve), who routinely share bites of their snacks if asked with the appropriate phrase. Meaningfully, it is sweets and other treats that they share (rather than food approved by adults), mainly on the way home from school (on the street, where they are not subject to adult rules). Ritualized sharing, Katriel argued, is a communicative event that functions to "assert the very existence of children's peer group culture as such" (1987:319) and to confer a social identity on those who participate.

Storytelling may be vital to the formation and maintenance of peer culture. Goodwin's (1982, 1990a, b) ethnographic study of Black working-class Philadelphia children demonstrated how they construct participation frameworks through stories that allow them to "construct and reconstruct their social organization" (1990a:33). Stories were embedded in the disputes of both boys and girls; boys used them to engage the audience on the storyteller's side, whereas girls used them to provoke future confrontations. Shuman (1986, 1993) examined "fight stories" (both oral and written) told by inner-city junior high school girls that involved issues of authority, entitlement, intertextuality, and voicing. Stories about fights were integral to ongoing disputes, and in fact these girls spent more time telling such stories than they spent fighting. Storytellers, using reported speech to distance themselves from the responsibility of authorship, demonstrated skillful use of fight stories both to reveal and to conceal information. Because the narrators and their audience shared norms and expectations about this genre, tellers did not have to spell out all the details about a sequence of events; in fact, "to judge the texts according to fixed standards of intelligibility, and thus find the narratives lacking, would be to ignore exactly what makes them successful in the community in which they are told and written" (1986:188).

Arguing, like storytelling, is a popular and important speech activity for maintaining social structure among children (though as Goodwin's and Shuman's work shows, disputing and storytelling are not necessarily separate activities). Argument is valued by children in its own right; they often work to sustain a dispute rather than resolve it (Goodwin 1982, 1990a; Maynard 1985a). Boys, especially, extend arguments as a means of displaying verbal skills and creating or maintaining hierarchical status (Goodwin 1990a; Dundes, Leach, & Ozkok 1986; Labov 1972a: 297–353), but at least some girls are equally interested in and skilled at sustaining conflict for both serious and playful purposes (Eder 1990). Among both preschoolers (e.g., Corsaro & Rizzo 1990, Eisenberg & Garvey 1981, Sheldon 1993) and school-age children (Adger 1984, 1986, 1987; Brenneis & Lein 1977; Emihovich 1986; Lein & Brenneis 1978; Goodwin 1982, 1990a; Maynard 1985a), disputes appear to be an important means of organizing play and negotiating understanding. But among school-age children, disputes take on the additional function of providing an arena in which to acquire and display expertise in specific linguistic forms and sequences (C. Goodwin & M. H. Goodwin 1990, M. H. Goodwin & C. Goodwin 1987). For example, Katriel (1985) described the forms and functions of Israeli children's enactment of a state of deliberate noncommunication (*brogez*), during which they maintain interactional unavailability (e.g., by using third-person pronouns to refer to co-present others). Eventually overtures by one or another child lead to peace (*sholem*), but in the meanwhile children effectively regulate their conflicts by taking time out from intense hostilities. In addition, a *brogez* episode can "serve as dynamic testing grounds for the social organization of the group, for assessing individuals' leadership as well as loyalty potential" (1985:487). Perhaps even more than some, this form of argument is clearly not learned in interaction with adults but is part of children's repertoire in their peer culture.

Children in their peer groups, then, organize a range of activities. In this volume, several chapters show children engineering their own activities and their own socialization. Goodwin (Chapter 1) provides insight into the world of girls' play, by analyzing the way they play hopscotch and showing that (contrary to both popular and scholarly belief) many girls relish both competition and legalistic complexity. Eder (Chapter 4) shows how collaborative storytelling in middle school boys' and girls' groups serves as a means of constructing individual and group identities that are distinct from those of adults. Greenwood (Chapter 3) reports that young adolescents' conversational norms regarding accommodation are not identical to adults' and finds that a conversational group constructs and modifies its own norms on different occasions of talk. Schlegel (Chapter 10) provides an instance where children devise interactional structures in order to perform an academic task; her analysis suggests that when the children abide by such tacit structures, their task is more likely to succeed than when they do not. Heath's and Tannock's chapters (12 and 13) on adolescents working and Hoyle's chapter (2) on preadolescents playing all note that young people rely to a striking extent on talking simultaneously and on finishing and repeating each other's utterances as ways of displaying solidarity.

Contributions to Theories of Linguistic Interaction

Through examining the language in interaction of older children, we can learn a great deal about language and interaction in general. Labov's (1972a: 354–96) classic work on narrative structure, which demonstrated the sophisticated narrative abilities of teenage Black urban vernacular speakers, has long served as a model against which to evaluate the structure and effectiveness of narratives produced by speakers of different ages and social groups. In a different vein, Schleppegrell's (1991, 1992) analysis of interviews with third and sixth graders showed that in spoken discourse, *because* is often not a marker of subordination (either grammatical or ideational) but instead serves interactional and cohesive functions. It is noteworthy that she used the talk of school-age children to claim that notions about linguistic complexity and the function of particular forms in the organization of discourse deserve periodic re-examination. Eckert (1989b) and Eckert and McConnell-Ginet (1995) argued, on the basis of sound changes in progress among suburban Detroit teenagers, that the ways in which a speaker's phonology indexes gender and class allegiances are more complex than is often assumed, for speakers do not construct gender and class as independent sets of practices. Halmari and Smith (1994) argued in their study of children at play that code-switching falls squarely in the domain of register variation, since a shift in code tends to co-occur with shifts in other linguistic features, just as any sort of register change does. In another recent investigation of register use, Rickford and McNair-Knox (1994) quantitatively analyzed the style-shifting of an eighteen-year-old African American girl speaking to different interviewers: one a familiar community member accompanied by her own teenage daughter and one an unfamiliar White woman. The informant's use of grammatical features of AAVE depended largely on addressee and topic, so her vernacular usage was much greater when speaking to the familiar interviewer and when talking about personal (rather than, for example, academic) topics. In previous interviews with the familiar interviewer, however, this girl, at the ages of thirteen and fifteen, had displayed strikingly different degrees of vernacular usage (a great deal in the earlier interview, much less in the second one). Thus, Rickford and McNair-Knox emphasized the importance of register- or style-shifting as "a resource and strategy" (1994:264) as opposed to an automatic reaction to addressee or situation.

Turning to studies of children's arguing, we learn from them that disputes are cooperatively constructed, rule-governed speech activities that serve important interactional functions and that require, exhibit, and develop skills. Arguing is a positively valued sociable activity for adults from some cultural backgrounds (Schiffrin 1984, 1990), but it appears to be positively valued by a very wide range of children, and thus much information about its structure and function comes from them.[9] Maynard (1985a), for instance, showed that any utterance, move, presupposition, or nonverbal activity can be opposed by an interlocutor and that whether or not opposition escalates into a dispute (instead of being treated, say, as a repair or a suggestion) is a matter of contingency. Goodwin and Goodwin (1987) pointed out that argument is both embedded in and encompasses other activities and thus that trying to distinguish it strictly from other types of discourse is not fruitful. Adger (1984, 1986, 1987), whose study of a culturally diverse first-grade classroom showed that cross-cultural communication need not be fraught with misunderstanding, found that while a Black American boy and a Vietnamese boy used different, culturally based styles of arguing, these styles did not clash. Indeed, both children could feel successful because their conversational goals were complementary and compatible. We learn from children, then, that argument is not inherently disorderly, divisive, or disruptive, but rather provides a means of using communicative skills to forge a shared community.

Theorizing about gendered patterns of talk and interaction also benefits from including examination of older children's practices. Cross-gender differences in ways of talking, behaving, and valuing are apparent in very young children (e.g., Ochs 1988, Sachs 1987, Schieffelin 1990, Sheldon 1993), but it is from close study of older children that we see complexities emerge (Thorne 1986). Goodwin (1983, 1990a; C. Goodwin & M. H. Goodwin 1990, M. H. Goodwin & C. Goodwin 1987) noted, for instance, that disputes in boys' groups were extended whereas those in girls' groups were short-lived; nevertheless, boys and girls used the same linguistic resources to construct their arguments, and they performed equally effectively in cross-gender argument. When girls were engaged in practical group tasks, they created through their talk an egalitarian, cooperative social structure (fitting common notions about female patterns); however, when playing house or taking care of younger children, they constructed hierarchical structures, commonly thought to be typical of boys (Goodwin 1988, 1990a). Eckert (1993), analyzing an extended stretch of "girl talk" among high school girls, suggested that such talk about "people, norms, and beliefs" (1993:32) provides a forum in which girls and women balance their needs for independence and consensus. Eder's (1993) examination of another complex speech activity among girls, romantic and sexual teasing, showed that it fulfills several functions simultaneously (such as communicating liking for particular boys, reinforcing group solidarity, managing feelings of jealousy, and experimenting with both traditional and untraditional gender roles). On the basis of girls' teasing, she argued that "children bring traditional and societal concerns to their activities, but primarily as a resource. Their actual behavior reflects these traditional concepts but frequently goes beyond them to include new and creative transformations" (1993:29). Tannen (1990a) also relied on older children's talk as a basis for theoretical hypothesis and generalization. Examining gender differences in the videotaped conversations of pairs of same-gender friends at each of four ages (second graders, sixth graders, tenth graders, and young adults), she found striking differences between the talk of the girls and women, on the one hand, and that of the boys and men, on the other, in the ways they physically aligned to each other, introduced and developed topics, and displayed concern for each other. Males and females of all ages, it appears, may have different norms for showing involvement in conversation.

In this volume, several chapters argue for the importance of examining the details of children's interaction in order not to overlook theoretically significant sources of data. Goodwin (Chapter 1) demonstrates how examining children's play can refute stereotypes about both children and adults—in this case, stereotypes about gender differences in language use. Hoyle (Chapter 2) shows that speaking in a particular register is a collaborative task. Greenwood (Chapter 3) shows that children's conversation reveals details about how accommodation works. Tannock (Chapter 13) helps answer the question of how activity and talk structure each other, modifying previous understanding about the nature and function of collaborative floors. Other chapters make the point, applicable of course not only to children's talk, that language in interaction constructs aspects of the self. Chapters by Goodwin, Emihovich, and Eder attend to the construction of gender; Hoyle shows the construction of imaginary but potential selves; Adger, McCreedy, and Merritt show the growth of academic selves; Heath and Tannock both show how working selves are built.

Finally, many of the chapters in this volume (by Adger, Emihovich, Goodwin, Hoyle, McCreedy, and Merritt) rely on Goffman's (1981) notion of footing—the moment-to-moment alignments that speakers and hearers take toward each other and toward the content of their talk. Just as this concept has been a fruitful one in the microanalysis of discourse generally (Tannen 1993a), it is shown to be valuable for examining the talk of older children.

Contributions to Practice

Although this volume is designed for students of language and language development, each chapter contains insights that can be productively applied within the social organizations that nurture children's growth. At a minimum, adults who help compose the structures in which children and their language mature need to consider language development as an essential aspect of growth, for which they may have some obligation. Those charged with formal attention to language development—including teachers and clinicians—need to know how children's language capacities expand during the school years and what they can do to support this growth.

Given changing demographics throughout the world, most educators are now interacting with students from various speech communities in addition to their own. Knowing how language can vary socially and how aspects of children's language competence continue to build through the school years seems essential for educators dedicated to enhancing children's cognitive and social development. School practices held over from simplistic views of language and language use waste teaching and learning time and alienate children who sense that language is more than teachers say it is. Professional development, standards setting, curriculum design— these and other aspects of the educational enterprise need to accommodate traditional school patterns to emerging understanding of language development in the school years.

It must be acknowledged that the field of education is not solely responsible for buttressing language development. Community institutions—places of worship, employment, social services, and recreation—provide settings and role relationships that contribute as well, although their contributions and attendant responsibilities may not be labeled. Emihovich (Chapter 6), Heath (Chapter 12), and Tannock (Chapter 13) point to some of these. Likewise, interactions in the family (whatever its composition) and around the home continue to provide important sociolinguistic environments past the end of the language acquisition period, as considered in the chapters by Greenwood and Hoyle. The roles of communities, families, and other organizations in supporting language development need to be recognized as interdependent.

All of the chapters suggest foci for critical inquiry into how society supports language development. Such an examination might ask whether the sociocultural structures we live with undergird language socialization adequately and what implications the descriptions presented here may have for practice and policy. The chapters by Fordham and Zentella present particulars.

Overview

The chapters in this volume are arranged according to contextual domain. Chapters 1–6 depict children among their friends; Chapters 7–11, children at school; and Chapters 12 and 13, children at work (a setting that has not previously been analyzed in any detail).

In Chapter 1, "Games of Stance: Conflict and Footing in Hopscotch," Marjorie Harness Goodwin shows how close analysis of a girls' game gives the lie to widely held beliefs that girls' games lack complexity and that all girls value cooperation above all and shun conflict. She shows that, whereas among White middle-class girls opposition is often mitigated, this is far from the case among Latina or African American players, who revel in competition, delight in disputes, and slip easily between serious and playful opposition. Through their play, girls build a repertoire of resources for stating and contesting positions, constructing displays of alignment and affective stance, and constructing themselves as particular kinds of social actors.

In Chapter 2, "Register and Footing in Role Play," Susan M. Hoyle discusses register use as both interactional resource and joint accomplishment. For the boys in this study, register-specific features become building blocks for co-constructing and dramatizing imaginary roles. Imaginary play, it is suggested, gives children the incentive to learn, use, and perfect their skills in different registers, and analysis of children's register competence requires attention to interaction.

In Chapter 3, "Accommodating Friends: Niceness, Meanness, and Discourse Norms," Alice Greenwood analyzes the dinner-table talk of three siblings and their guests, contrasting two instances of successful, friendly conversation with an instance that goes awry. Successful conversation among these children depends on more than shared interpretations, for failure to accomplish friendly interaction results when one participant understands perfectly well what the others expect but refuses to provide it. The group's interactional norms vary from occasion to occasion, established by a majority whose composition shifts.

In Chapter 4, "Developing Adolescent Peer Culture through Collaborative Narration," Donna Eder uses sociolinguistic and ethnographic methods to examine collaborative stories told by middle school students, stories that construct and reinforce friendship and group solidarity and help the adolescents develop complex views of their peer culture. Co-narrators explore individual and group identity, contrast their own attitudes with those of adults, and mock traditional gender roles.

In Chapter 5, "Multiple Codes, Multiple Identities: Puerto Rican Children in New York City," Ana Celia Zentella presents an ethnographically informed overview of code-switching practices among some New York Puerto Rican working-class children who command several dialects of Spanish and English. She also offers a case study of one girl as she grows from a first grader to a teenage mother. For the residents of this neighborhood, language is an integral part of continually experienced conflicts centering around national, racial, and cultural identities, but it is also a resource for the construction of identity. Zentella points out that, although studies of code-switching behavior have demonstrated that bilingual speakers can juggle two grammars, scholars may fail to emphasize the creativity of individual bilingual speakers.

In Chapter 6, "Bodytalk: Discourses of Sexuality among Adolescent African American Girls," Catherine Emihovich shows construction through talk of a complex female identity. She looks at two age groups of teenagers participating in a pregnancy prevention program. The older girls have to a large extent mastered forms of talk that empower them: they can incorporate adult perspectives into their own discourse while at the same time resisting and subverting adult authority. A central task of adolescence, it appears, is acquiring the means to manage competing, and indeed conflicting, discourse demands.

The five chapters by Merritt, Adger, McCreedy, Schlegel, and Fordham investigate older children's talk at school. These chapters, like the others, focus on children's talk, interaction, and attitudes, identifying patterns of and constraints upon language practices in this institutional setting (rather than focusing on the application of such findings for pedagogical purposes). Children in school, as elsewhere, actively participate in the negotiation of meaning, context, and text, using linguistic, social, and cultural resources. The authors show ways in which children at school forge an identity for themselves and ways in which the competence that is displayed there and the learning that takes place are to a great extent interactional accomplishments.

These chapters show that the language of school is just as variable as that of other domains. Classroom talk, for instance, may include patterned dialect shifting (as discussed in Adger's chapter), shifts in stance within a single lesson (as McCreedy shows) or across different activities (as Merritt discusses), and problem-solving techniques that arise only in small work groups (such as those that Schlegel examines). The interactional demands of the school—which may presage such demands in institutional settings of later life—contrast with those of the home and the peer group in important ways. At school, children have an opportunity to develop and demonstrate competence in styles, registers, and speech activities—in particular, those that make up academic discourse—for which they may have little use at home or at play (just as in those other settings they develop and display competences that are not manifested at school). But, as Fordham emphasizes, when home and school language varieties impose conflicting requirements and, indeed, index conflicting identities, students face complicated dilemmas and painful choices.

In Chapter 7, "Of Ritual Matters to Master: Structure and Improvisation in Language Development at Primary School," Marilyn Merritt analyzes broad similarities in classroom interaction around the world. Children work to balance three overlapping and intersecting structures common to (probably all) classrooms—activity structures, participation structures, and modality structures. A major portion of what older children must master in school consists of ritual requirements, and an individual child's access to valued resources in the classroom depends on moment-to-moment construction of alignments.

Chapters 8 and 9 both examine children's talk during teacher-led lessons, an activity in which children are, ideally, afforded practice in academically valued ways of speaking. During lessons, teachers constrain students' contributions, and as they do so, they can provide for different sorts of student alignment to instructional material. In Chapter 8, "Register Shifting with Dialect Resources in Instructional Discourse," Carolyn Temple Adger finds that, in a classroom where both teacher and children are sensitive to local norms of dialect appropriateness, children take advantage of opportunities for practice in the variety of speech and the type of stance that are academically valued. Dialect constitutes a register resource by which speakers signal their footing with respect to the task at hand. The children, who use their vernacular much of the time, adopt an authoritative footing when they are engaged in discourse tasks closely connected with writing.

Lynn McCreedy's "The Effect of Role and Footing on Students' Oral Academic Language," (Chapter 9) contrasts lessons during which children merely animate their teachers' scripts, by providing a single word or phrase in response to an elicitation, with lessons that afford students opportunities to speak at length on academic subjects. When students participate in both small-group activities and whole-class discussions in which they are encouraged to author texts, their oral academic language can flourish.

Chapter 10, Jennifer Schlegel's "Finding Words, Finding Meanings: Collaborative Learning and Distributed Cognition," is, like McCreedy's, set in a classroom where children work together in small groups. She analyzes how fifth-grade work groups carry out word searches in fulfillment of an assignment. The children devise a three-part collaborative structure for this task, a structure that appears to be crucial for the successful completion of the search. Their collaboration consists of both talk and gesture.

Chapter 11 is Signithia Fordham's "Speaking Standard English from Nine to Three: Language as Guerrilla Warfare at Capital High." This chapter, like Adger's, discusses issues related to dialect shifting among students whose home language is AAVE, but from a broader perspective, based on ethnographic observation in a high school and the surrounding community. Fordham argues that speaking standard English—by which she means also stylistic features and other behaviors associated with the language of the dominant society—involves adopting a wide range of attitudes that implicitly denigrate speaking, and speakers of, nonstandard varieties. The adolescents face a conflict between home and school language that threatens their cultural identity.

In Chapter 12, "Working through Language," Shirley Brice Heath looks at teenagers working in youth organizations in collaboration with adults. Adolescents engaged in meaningful work, she finds, are afforded extensive, natural practice in linguistic structures appropriate to adult roles: they learn new ways of talking and, through talking, ways of planning, strategizing, and collaborating. On the other hand, the young people distinguish themselves from adults, adopting only those grammatical and discourse structures that they find appropriate for their own (adult-like yet not fully adult) enactment of work roles.

In Chapter 13, "Noisy Talk: Conversation and Collaboration in a Youth Writing Group," Stuart Tannock examines data from a project in which teenagers and adults work together to produce a brochure. The teenagers' talk, always lively, is marked by much laughter, loudness, and simultaneous and overlapping speech. This "noisy talk" is central not only to the development of a cohesive group identity but also to the actual writing process. Rather than being disruptive, noisy talk is an important component of their collaboration. It functions not only as a side sequence or time-out from an official agenda but also as task-driven talk used by the group to further its agenda.

Taken together, the chapters show older children as strategic language users, dynamic actors who are often concerned with defining themselves as a distinctive group, different from adults, yet who just as often display proficiency at the sophisticated discourse activities that characterize their ages and stages and presage those of adulthood.

NOTES

Thanks to Patrick Gonzales and Donna Christian for very helpful comments on previous drafts of this Introduction.

1. One likely reason for the relative scarcity of research on the naturally occurring talk of older children is a practical one: school-age children and teenagers are simply harder for researchers to observe and record than are younger, more docile children. They often play and talk out of the monitoring range of adults, and they are aware when they are being watched or tape-recorded. Another reason may be the difficulty of identifying a unit of analysis relevant to the study of older children's talk. For instance, as McTear (1985:201) points out, there is as yet no "model of the skilled adult conversationalist" against which to contrast the skills of children who have already mastered such basics as securing an inter-locutor's attention, taking turns, introducing and developing topics, asking for and provid-ing repair, and performing a variety of speech acts. Nevertheless, such in-depth studies of young people's talk in interaction as those of Goodwin (1990a), Eckert (1989a), and Eder (1995) demonstrate that analysis of naturally occurring talk among older children is indeed a feasible goal and can illuminate categories and patterns that are meaningful for the young participants themselves. Heath (1983), although focusing primarily on language socializa-tion among young children in their homes and communities, traces the consequences of this socialization for the children's linguistic performance once they start school. Moreover, she provides a blueprint for careful data collection and analysis of children's talk.

2. We adopt the convention of capitalizing Black and White in referring to ethnic groups, except where chapter authors desire not to do so. In addition, following current practice, we use both Black and African American.

3. The importance of quotation itself as characteristic of adult narratives in particular is worthy of further examination.

4. As Schiffrin (1987) shows, adult conversationalists use discourse markers to signal which plane of discourse is the focus of attention at any given moment: the plane of ex-change (on which participants coordinate turns at talk), action (on which they coordinate sequences of speech acts), ideation (on which they encode propositions), information (on which they modify one another's cognitive states), and participation (on which they form and change alignments to one another).

5. It is not surprising that certain markers that encode cognitively more difficult con-cepts are acquired later than others.

6. The question remains as to whether these differences represent language develop-ment per se or derive from new opportunities to display expertise.

7. Our thanks to an anonymous reviewer for emphasizing this point.

8. Even the teacher may be unaware of how social order is achieved: Dorr-Bremme (1990) demonstrated that a teacher's contextualization cues (Gumperz 1982) are a power-ful means of retaining children's attention at context boundaries, although the teacher, of course, produces such cues unconsciously rather than purposely.

9. An interesting question for future investigation is whether children from families and communities that do not highly value extended argumentative exchanges come to devalue disputing as they get older.

Games of Stance

Conflict and Footing in Hopscotch

MARJORIE HARNESS GOODWIN

Recent work in the social sciences has reified stereotypes of gender differences in children; girls are reputedly more interested in cooperative interaction and a morality based on principles of relatedness, relationships, care, equity, flexibility, and responsibility, whereas boys are concerned with dominance and an ethic based on principles of objectivity, individual rights, and rule-governed justice. For example, psychologists Miller, Danaher, and Forbes (1986:543) write that while boys are "more concerned with and more forceful in pursuing their own agendae . . . girls are more concerned with maintaining interpersonal harmony."[1] Sociologists Adler, Kless, and Adler (1992) find that in contrast to boys' "orientation of autonomy" (1992:183), girls seek a "culture of compliance and conformity" (1992:184) that lacks assertiveness. Linguist Jennifer Coates (1994:72)[2] argues that "[t]here is a great deal of evidence to suggest that male speakers are socialized into a competitive style of discourse, while women are socialized into a more cooperative style of speech." Recently within communication studies, Barnes and Vangelisti (1995), building on Sheldon's (1992, 1993) notion of double-voice discourse, have argued that girls often employ a strategy that simultaneously asserts one's position while maintaining relational solidarity. Through mitigation (modification of expression to avoid creating offense [Labov & Fanshel 1977:84]) of opposition, girls demonstrate their concerns for "affiliation, reciprocity, and *efforts to protect others' face*" (Barnes & Vangelisti 1995:354; emphasis added). Such positions, built on studies of middle-class White girls' talk, implicitly accept the collaborative model of women's speech (Coates 1991, 1994; Falk 1980; Troemel-Ploetz 1992) and resemble the "two cultures" view of language differences postulated by anthropologists Maltz and Borker (1982).[3]

While celebrating support, cooperation, and nurturance, the dichotomies that shape current research often imply that females lack the specific language and social abilities required to pursue conflict.[4] As researchers such as psychologists Hare-Mustin and Maracek (1988) and linguists Bing and Bergvall (1996) have argued, dichotomous categorizations such as these contribute to perceptions of women and men as essentially and invariably different. Girls' games, reputedly devoid of strategic forms of interaction and the negotiation of rules, are viewed as lacking the intellectual complexity and intricate division of labor characteristic of boys'.

Researchers stake their claims on hypothetical studies of conflict—work by Piaget (1965:77), who argues that "the legal sense" is "far less developed in little girls than in boys," and Gilligan (1982), who states that because girls are primarily concerned with maintaining relationships within intimate social groups, they avoid negotiation. Gilligan's studies, cited in almost all social science studies of women's experience, make use of sociologist Janet Lever's studies of girls' games. Relying primarily upon verbal reports, Lever (1978:479, 472) argues:

> Because girls play cooperatively more than competitively, they have less experience with rules per se, so we should expect them to have a lesser consciousness of rules than boys.

> The play activities of boys are more complex than those of girls, resulting in sex differences in the development of social skills potentially useful in childhood and later life.

Despite the tremendous scope of such statements, they are not based on close, ethnographic study of what girls actually do as they play games. Research has relied on *interviews about* children's activities rather than *records of* naturally occurring events. In addition, it has concentrated on the *forms* of games (for example, a comparison of the rules and team structure of jump rope versus football) rather than the interaction through which a game is accomplished in situ (Evaldsson 1993, Goldstein 1971, Goodwin 1985, Hughes 1993). When, instead, sequences of interaction are investigated, a very rich social world of the female child is observable—one in which conflict is as prevalent as cooperation.

In this chapter I challenge popularly held beliefs about the lack of complexity in girls' games, based on close analysis of videotaped sessions of girls playing hopscotch, and I argue for the importance of conflict. The data are drawn from fieldwork I conducted among elementary school girls in several different communities: (1) bilingual Spanish/English-speaking working-class girls in grades 2–5 (primarily second-generation Central Americans) in an elementary school located in the Pico Union/Koreatown district near downtown Los Angeles in spring 1993 and (2) fifth-grade African American female children of migrant workers in a federally sponsored summer school program in rural Ridge Spring, South Carolina, during summer 1994.[5] For purposes of comparison, the group on whom the generalizations in the psychological literature are based, White middle-class girls, is briefly examined as well. I looked at their play in an integrated public school and private summer day care program in Columbia, South Carolina, during May and June 1994.

Social Organization within the Game Setting

Hopscotch provides a prototypical example of a girls' game. Generally its rules are described in terms of a simple pattern of rotation, as one girl after another tries to move her token and her body through a grid without hitting a line. According to Lever (1978:479), games such as hopscotch and jump rope are examples of eventless turn-taking games: "Girls' turn-taking games progress in identical order from one situation to the next. Given the structure of these games, disputes are not likely to occur."

This view of hopscotch is seriously flawed. First, in this model rules are viewed as mechanical instructions, but the girls whom I observed treated rules as resources to be probed and played with and actively competed for first place in a round of hopscotch.[6] Second, by focusing only on the actions of the jumper, the model ignores the work of other parties who act as judges, checking to see if any fouls have been committed.

The Moves in Hopscotch

In hopscotch a player systematically moves through a grid of squares drawn in chalk or painted on the sidewalk, street, playground, or other flat surface. The marks on the grid construct a visible field for action, which orients those who know how to read it to the sequence of moves through space that must be traversed while playing the game. Though there are many different types of grids, the one painted on a cement school yard used in Pico Union looked like Figure 1.1.

One person jumps at a time through the grid. She is expected to move from square to square, in the pattern displayed by the numbers in the diagram. (Frequently the numbers are not actually written in the squares.) The object of the game of hopscotch is to be the first player to advance her token, commonly a stone or a beanbag, from the lowest to the highest square and back again. From behind the start line (below square one), a player tosses her beanbag into a square and jumps from one end of the grid and back again on one foot, without changing feet and without jumping on squares where beanbags lie. Where there are two unoccupied squares next to each other, the jumper's feet should land in the two adjacent blocks. If a person falls down, steps on a line, or steps outside the appropriate square, she must forfeit her turn.

Girls patrol the boundaries of their play space from boys' intrusions, delimiting their territory through what Thorne (1993:64–88), following Barth (1969), has called "borderwork." When boys intruded into girls' space, girls from Pico Union would sanction boys by yelling, "Get out of the way!," while in similar situations African American girls prevented intrusions by yelling, "Go back! Go back!"

The Role of Judges within the Situated Activity System

The game of hopscotch can be viewed as a form of situated activity system (Goffman 1961); it entails the coordinated activity of movement of a player through the playing field and commentary on that player's performance during her turn. Wittgenstein's notion of a language game as a "whole, consisting of language *and* the actions into which it is woven" (1958:¶7) is appropriate in considering talk

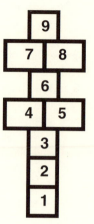

Figure 1.1 A hopscotch grid

that occurs within this frame. Girls playing the role of judge frequently provide critiques of the player's actions, stating their opposition and providing accounts for their position.

A particular social organization of attention is required to construct a point of common focus. Girls evaluating performances attend not only to a particular place (a geographic space), the game grid, but also monitor for particular types of events that are supposed to occur in that place (a form of conceptual space). The grid makes possible the forms of action and local identities[7] that constitute the game: for example, throwing one's token or stepping on or outside a line counts as a consequential event, an "out" in which the hapless player loses her turn. The situated activity provides both a place *to look* and a particular category of event *to look for*.

Onlookers do not passively watch as someone takes her turn. Rather, hoping to detect mistakes, to call "outs," girls intensely scrutinize a jumper's body as she moves through socially inscribed space. Both African American (AA) and Latina (L) girls playing judge use the term "Out!" to call a foul. In each of the following examples, the player acknowledges her error following the out call. (In transcription, English translations appear in italics in parentheses under Spanish text.)

(1) AA
     Alisha: ((*steps on a line while jumping*))
     Joy: Out!
     Vanessa: You out.
     Alisha: ((*moves out of grid*))

(2) L
     Paula: ((*steps on a line while jumping*))
     Rosa: Out! Out! Out!
     Paula: ((*smiles widely, then moves out of grid*))

Rita: Out! Out! Out!
         Tú estás out!
         (You're out!)

Rather than consisting of a series of isolated jumping episodes, the game of hop-scotch is constituted through the play-by-play analysis of a jumper's moves. In what follows, I analyze the ways in which players negotiate the status of moves in the game through their commentary. The first part discusses the shape of judges' foul calls and shows that they are crucial to the achievement of the activity. Through intonation, gesture, or positioning of turn elements, turns may either downplay opposition or highlight it. In that fouls can be ignored or pardoned, turns that display a clear orientation toward a position of opposition demonstrate the importance of conflict in the play of some girls.

The second part shows that, rather than slavishly following rules, girls transcend the framework that the game provides, to play with, pull apart, and resist the very structures that make the activity possible. While the game is played with the intent to win, it is richly overlaid with multiple types of framings and textured nuances, including laughter, tricking, joking, and bicultural puns. I discuss some examples of reframing by showing how having the last laugh, by outwitting those in the audience judging one's performance, seems as important as finishing first for some girls.

The Structure of Out Calls

Because play takes the form of embodied movement through a publicly visible space, propelling one's token onto a line or stepping on a line or into a space occupied with a token can be identified as a "social fact," something that can be independently seen by separate observers while remaining open to negotiation and challenge. Often, as in the next set of examples, two referees converge to produce a simultaneous assessment of the player's move, enthusiastically challenging the player:

(3)   AA
      Lucianda: *((puts foot in square with token))*
      Joy: You ⌈out. *((pointing toward jumper))*
      Crystal: ⌊Out!
      Lucianda: I'm out.

(4)   L
      Carla: *((throws the token and it hits a line))*
      Gloria: Ou⌈t! *((claps hands))*
      Sandra: ⌊Out! *((claps hands))*
      Carla: AY! *((smiles, tosses head, picks up token))*
      Gloria: **I'm** next!

Frequently the judge demonstrates that her call is the product of rule-governed analysis by adding a reason for it.

(5)   AA
    Lucianda: ((*steps on a line while jumping*))
    Vanessa: Ah: ⌈Lucianda.
    Crystal: ⌊Out!
    Vanessa: →   Out- You step be**tween** the line.
                Not **in** it.

(6)   AA
    Alisha: ((*jumps putting two feet in square 4*))
    Joy: →   All right honey. You put both foot in fou(hh)r.

(7)   AA
    Crystal: ((*steps on a line while jumping*))
    Joy: →   You hit that line.
                Sorry to tell you that.
                But you hit that line right there. ((*tapping on line*))

(8)   L
    Sandra: ((*steps on a line while jumping*))
    Carla: →   Out! Repítalo porque pistaste la de acá. ((*tapping line*))
                (*Out! Try it again because you hit this line.*)

(9)   L
    Rosa: ((*hops with one foot outside grid, one foot on line*))
    Carla: Out.
    Maria: Out.
    Rosa: Ay:::!
    Carla: →   ¡Pisistes la raya! ((*hops on the line where Rosa stepped*))
                (*You stepped on the line.*)

(10)   L
    Rosa: ((*throws beanbag and it lands on a line*))
    Maria: →   Ah: tocastes. ((*points to square*))
                (*Ah: you hit.*)

In these instances the girl acting as referee or judge provides either an "out," a "response cry" (Goffman 1978) such as "Ah:" (in both Spanish and English), or an "All right" or "Sorry," accompanied by an account of what the foul was.

Highlighting in Embodied Accounts in Out Calls

As examples 5–10 demonstrate, a range of diverse practices is used to call somebody out. In most argumentative moves, the very first thing said, the turn preface, occupies a particularly important position. Retrospectively it classifies the action being opposed, and prospectively it provides a guide for interpreting the position being stated in the accounts and embodied demonstrations to follow. The following provides an example of an "out call." After Sandra steps on two lines while jumping, Carla cries "OUT! OUT!" (line 2). This is followed by an account for her foul call, "PISTASTE LA DE AQUÍ, Y LA DE ACÁ" (lines 3–4).

Figure 1.2 Carla: OUT! OUT!

(11) 1 Sandra: ((*steps on two lines while jumping*))
      2 Carla: OUT! OUT!
      3   PISTASTE LA DE AQUÍ,
                   (*You stepped on this one,*)
      4   Y LA DE ACÁ.
                   (*and this one.*)

In producing an out call, a participant playing judge may take up different types of *footing*, defined by Goffman (1981:128) as one's "stance, or posture, or projected self." Intonation, body positioning, and turn shape are all critical in the construction of alternative types of stance. In example 11 the word "OUT!" is accompanied by a quite vivid embodied affective alignment (Ochs 1993:288) as the finger of the judge points accusingly at the offender (while the player laughs at her own attempt to pull something over on the girl acting as judge). Figure 1.2 illustrates the accusatory point of the judge and the humorous stance of the player.

Pitch Leaps

The foul call itself states unambiguously without doubt or delay that a violation has occurred. Moreover, the foul call is spoken in a very distinctive fashion, as seen in Figure 1.3.

Although the normal pitch of the girls is between 250 and 350 Hz, here Carla's voice leaps dramatically to 663 and 673 Hz over the two tokens of "out." Like the accusing finger, such pitch leaps provide a way to highlight and make especially salient the speaker's stance, here gleeful opposition.

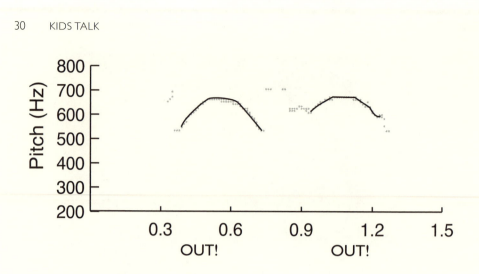

Figure 1.3 The pitch of "OUT! OUT!"

Change in pitch can be shown more clearly if the action being opposed is itself talk. In Figure 1.4 an argument develops between Carla and Gloria over whose turn it is. When Carla states, "Ya voy" (*I'm going now*), Gloria counters "*N'ai::* Ya voy YO!" (*No. I'm going now*). First speaker Carla's pitch is between 300 and 400 Hz. The opposition turn "Nai::!" leaps quickly and dramatically to 600 Hz, displaying in her preface her strong oppositional stance.

Pitch leaps thus provide one way of vocally highlighting opposition in the turn preface.

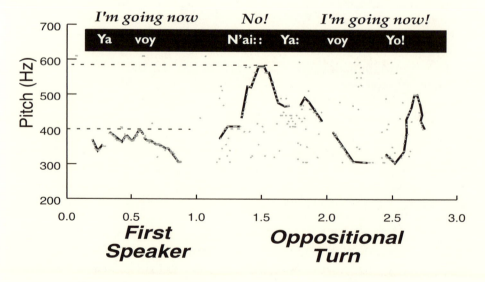

Figure 1.4 Change of pitch in opposition

Figure 1.5 Carla: PISASTE LA DE AQUÍ,

Demonstrations in Embodied Accounts

Rather than simply providing a verbal account, a judge may *show how* an "out" occurred by dramatically using her own body and the grid to "replay" the activity just seen. In much the way that a speaker can report another's speech, in example 11 the feet of the judge, Carla, both replay and comment upon the errors made by Sandra's feet (see Figures 1.5 and 1.6).

(11)	Sandra:	((*steps on two lines while jumping*))	**Problematic Move**
	Carla:	OUT! OUT!	**Out!** ((*finger point*))
		PISTASTE LA DE AQUÍ,	**Explanation**
		(*You stepped on this one,*)	((*demonstration*))
		Y LA DE ACÁ.	
		(*and this one.*)	

Judges not only state verbally their objections to a player's moves in the game. In addition, in conjunction with their talk, they may provide nonvocal accounts that consist of replaying of past moves, to add further grounding for their positions. In challenging player Sandra's move, Carla animatedly provides a rendition of Sandra's past mistake. As she states that Sandra had stepped on "this one" (*la de aquí*) and "this one" (*la de acá*), Carla re-enacts Sandra's movement through space, challenging the player's prior move. The demonstration—involving a fully embodied gestural performance in an inscribed space—could not have been done without the grid, as it provides the relevant background for locating violations.

Figure 1.6 Carla: Y LA DE ACÁ

Playful Transformations of Out Calls

Players watching the game provide a running commentary on a jumper's actions, congratulating her, mimicking a particularly difficult move, or critiquing her. Girls playfully tease players, lightly pushing them, and in other ways trying to unnerve them. For example, Latina girls point to a player's feet and shout "¡Un ratón! ¡Un ratón!" (*A mouse! A mouse!*). To distract a player, African American girls may make barking dog noises ("Rerrruff") or scream someone's name in a falsetto tone that imitates a rooster crowing: "Barbara! Barbara! Barbara!" For these African American girls, the last square is the "Quiet Box," and they try to make jumpers laugh or speak when they land in that square, thereby disqualifying them. A player frequently seems to get as much delight out of her role as a commentator on activity as she does from actually jumping through the grid.

Humorous ways of responding to a referee's out call are possible as well. Not only may players demonstrate an alignment that either ratifies a categorization or challenges it; instead, players may invoke an alternative participation framework, for example, a playful interlude, which closes down the dispute.

One such form of playful transformation occurs in example 12 in which a bicultural pun occurs. The player's high-pitched response cry (Goffman 1978) "Ooo::" and laughter key the interaction as humorous; this results in a transformation from a foul call into a word play exchange. In lines 2 and 3 "Out" and "Sorry" (an alternative way of calling a foul) are spoken by two different evaluators at the same time (lines 4, 5). The action begins as Carla throws her bag outside the grid:

(12)   L
    1 Carla: ((*throws bag and hits outside grid*))
    2 Sandra: ⌈Out.
    3 Gloria: ⌊So⌈rry. ((*clapping hands*))
    4 Carla: ⌊Oooo:: (hh) ((*laughing, moving off grid*))
    5 Sandra: **Sorry.**
    6 Carla: So**rillo. Sorilla tú.**
    7 Sandra: *h heh!=
    8 Gloria: =¡¡¡SORILLA!!! ((*singing*))

In this sequence the girls collaborate in turning the calling of a foul into a form of wordplay. The jumper, Carla, who is "out," transforms the judge's "sorry" into "sorillo" (pronounced [so ri yo]) (line 6). This word, a bicultural pun, has two meanings. First, the word "zorillo" (pronounced [so ri yo]) means 'skunk.' Second, the addition of the affix *-illo* (a diminutive) transforms the English word "sorry" into "sorillo"— 'a little bit sorry.' Carla then further transforms "sorillo" into the feminine "sorilla" [so ri ya] and uses it as a form of name-calling. By adding a subject pronoun, she targets one of the judges as the explicit addressee of her epithet: "¡Sorilla *tú* !"(line 6). Subsequently a third girl changes "sorilla" through singing it (line 8). The sung modality indicates that the word is no longer being treated as an insult addressed to a particular target, and the sequence is closed down. Wordplay and other playful transformations provide players less oppositional ways of keying the interaction.

Displaying Stance in Opposition Turns

In alternation to keying an exchange as playful (as in example 12), turns may display other types of alignment or footing—for example, a serious orientation toward forms of "aggravated correction" (Goodwin 1983). The shape of turns in which children clearly signal opposition contrasts strongly with what has been described in the literature about the preference for agreement in adult conversation. Yaeger-Dror (1986) notes that intonation over disagreement is frequently nonsalient. Sacks (1987 [1973]) and Pomerantz (1984) find that in adult polite conversation disagreement is a dispreferred activity, which is minimized through various features of turn design, including delays before the production of a disagreement and prefaces that mitigate the disagreement.

(13)   A: She doesn't uh usually come in on Friday, does she.
       B: Well, yes she does, sometimes,

Here disagreement is mitigated by both the hesitant "Well" that precedes it and the qualifier "sometimes" that follows it.

By way of contrast in the game of hopscotch, in an out or a foul call, opposition occurs immediately.

(14)   Gloria: ((*jumps from square two to one changing feet*))   **Problematic Move**
      Carla: ¡NO CHIRIONA!   **Polarity Expression +**

(No cheater!)	**Negative Person Descriptor**
YA NO SE VALE ASÍ.	**Explanation**
(That way is no longer valid.)	

(15) Gloria: *((takes a turn out of turn))*   **Problematic Move**

Carla: ¡AY: TÚ CHIRIONA!   **Response Cry +**
(Hey you cheater!)   **Negative Person Descriptor**
EH NO PISES AQUÍ   **Explanation**
(Hey don't step here.)
¡PORQUE AQUÍ YO VOY!
(Because I'm going here.)

(16) Gloria: *((Jumps from square 3 to 2 changing feet))*   **Problematic Move**

Carla: ¡EY::! ¡CHIRIONA!   **Response Cry +**
¡MIRA!   **Negative Person Descriptor**
(Hey! Cheater! Look!)
¡TE VENISTES DE AQUÍ ASÍ!   **Explanation**
(You came from here like this.)
*((demonstrating how Gloria jumped
changing feet))*

In constructing an opposition move, the preface is critical, because it states quite literally a stance or *footing* (Goffman 1981) with regard to the current action. Affective intensity (Bradac, Mulac, & Thompson 1995) or highlighting (Goodwin 1994) is indicated through pitch leaps, vowel lengthening, and raised volume. Unlike the delayed disagreement in adult conversation, the girls, through their intonation and gestures (such as extended hand points) display in no uncertain or mitigated terms that opposition is occurring. Thus, in example 14 Carla begins her turn with a strong polarity marker "¡NO!"[8] followed immediately by a negative person descriptor, "¡CHIRIONA!," and then an explanation for why the move is illegal. Variants of this same pattern are found as well in examples 15 and 16. Here the turns begin with response cries or exclamatory interjections, not full-fledged words, which take up a position with regard to a prior action (Goffman 1978): "AY:" and "¡EY::!"

With negative person descriptors referees argue not simply that an infraction has occurred but that what the player is doing is something morally wrong. Girls use the term "chiriona" meaning 'cheater,' derived from the English word "cheat" and "ona," a Spanish agentive nominalizer (or intensifier).

cheat + ona
English verb + Spanish agentive nominalizer (intensifier)[9]

"Chiriona" provides an explicit characterization of the person who produced the move being opposed. By using such a term, a judge argues not simply that an infraction has occurred but that the person who committed the foul is accountable in a very strong way for its occurrence. Following the opposition preface, a referee further explicates why the move is invalid by providing a reason, often through a demonstration. Unlike the delayed disagreement in adult conversation, intonation and gestures (such as extended hand points) display in no uncertain or mitigated terms that opposition is occurring.

Thus, to summarize, characteristic features of opposition turns in hopscotch include the following:

1. Opposition is signaled immediately through an *expression of polarity* (Halliday & Hasan 1976:178) such as "No!"
2. Alternatively, opposition is signaled through a *response cry*: nonlexicalized, discrete interjections such as "AY:!," "EY!" (in Spanish).
3. *Dramatic pitch leaps* that provide emphasis and contrast with surrounding talk. The work that they do here displays salience and highlights opposition.
4. *Negative person descriptors* follow the polarity marker or response cry and provide a third component of opposition turns. Terms such as "chiriona" (*cheater*) are used by Spanish speakers.
5. Following the opposition turn, participants provide *explanations* for their positions.
6. *Embodied demonstrations* may accompany explanations.

In contrast to what has been written about them in the social science literature on girls' games, these players not only pay close attention to what can and cannot count as infractions of rules but also have the resources to strongly state and contest positions. These same sequential resources can be deployed to build powerful displays of alignment and affective stance. Indeed, they are part of the grammatical resources through which power is constructed through language. In playing games such as hopscotch girls develop a repertoire of language practices that can be used to build and display themselves as social actors with specific embodied characteristics, a habitus of power.

A Second Instance of Authoritative Stance

Working-class African American girls, children of migrant workers in the rural South, use many of the same practices for highlighting opposition and building explanations. The following provides an example:

(17)	1	Lucianda:	((*takes turn jumping twice in square two and possibly putting her foot on the line of square one*))
	2	Joy:	You out.
	3	Lucianda:	⌈ No I'm **not**. ((*shaking head no*))
	4	Joy:	⌊ You hit the line.
	5	Crystal:	**Yes** you did.
	6		⌈ You hit the line. ((*with hand pointing at line*))
	7	Joy:	⌊ You hit the line.
	8	Lucianda:	I AIN'T HIT NO LINE! ((*leaning toward Crystal*))
	9	Alisha:	**Yes** you did.
	10	Crystal:	((*smiling, shaking head, goes to the spot*)) You did. You s-
	11	Lucianda:	**No** I didn't.
	12	Alisha:	Yes you did.
	13	Crystal:	Didn't she go like this.
	14	Lucianda:	((*does a challenge hit toward Alisha*))
	15	Alisha:	You hit me.
	16	Crystal:	You did like this. ((*stepping on the line as she replays the jump*))
	17	Lucianda:	Shut up with your old-fashioned clothes. ((*to Alisha*))
	18	Crystal:	You did like that.

19	Joy:	Yeah you hit that line right there honey. ((*as she goes up and uses her foot to index it, tapping it twice*))
20	Lucianda:	((*throws the rock and it lands outside*))
21		My feet.
22	Vanessa:	Y- you out now!

In this game of hopscotch, referees state unequivocally, "You out" (line 2), followed by an explanation ("You hit the line") (lines 4, 6, 7). As in oppositional sequences in the talk of African American working-class girls in Philadelphia (Goodwin 1990a), here polarity markers such as "No" (lines 3, 11) and "Yes" (lines 5, 9, 12) preface opposition moves. The foul call—"You hit the line"—is emphatically opposed by the player with "I AIN'T HIT NO LINE!" This utterance is produced at an extremely high pitch range, 780 Hz, as shown in Figure 1.7, and accompanied by a strong body stance—a challenge position in which the player extends her chest toward one of the judges.

Here the larger number of persons present can ratify the observer's point of view, and multiple judges counter the player's position about her move. Explanations or demonstrations of positions are presented by girls re-enacting the moves of players committing fouls. For example, replaying a player's stepping on a line, Crystal states, "You did like this" (line 16) as she re-enacts Lucianda's prior move. Judges' positions are also highlighted by stomping feet on the place where the line was touched (line 19). Here, as in the previous example, the grid is used as an area that can be tapped (line 19), pointed to (line 6), and jumped upon (line 16) to further explicate the

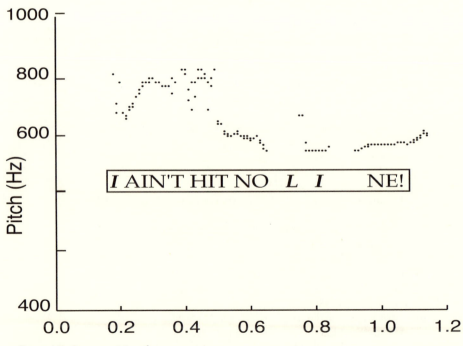

Figure 1.7 An oppositional turn

proofs judges are offering. Girls formulate their logical proofs by making use of a number of components in an integrated manner—the material game grid, their own bodies, and accounts. In the midst of this sequence, the player produces a personal insult with a challenge gesture toward one of the referees (line 17). However, despite rather direct oppositional moves, girls do not break up the game.

Mitigated Stances toward Fouls

In the data presented so far, girls work to forcefully construct salient opposition while holding each other accountable for deviations from rules. However, with other language choices it is possible to construct actors, events, and social organization in a very different way. I found one group that did not use the participation possibilities of hopscotch to enact forceful positions: middle-class White girls from Columbia, South Carolina.[10]

(18) 1 Linsey: ((throws stone and hits line))
      2 Liz: Oh! Good job Linsey!
      3   You got it ⌈all the way on the seven.
      4 Kendrick: ⌊((shaking head)) That's-
      5   I think that's sort of on the line though.
      6 Liz: Uh- your foot's in the wr(hhh)ong-
      7   ⌈sp(hh)ot.
      8 Kendrick: ⌊Sorry.
      9   That was a good try.

(19) 1 Linsey: ((throws token))
      2 Cathleen: You **did** it!=
      3 Linsey: Yes! ((falsetto))
      4 Linsey: ((jumps on line))
      5 Cathleen: ⌈Wh-
      6 Kendrick: ⌊You- accidentally jumped on that.
      7   But that's okay(hh).

The working-class girls above highlight opposition and definitively categorize moves as fouls.[11] Here, however, the girls acting as judges use a variety of language structures to *mitigate* their foul calls. Hedges such as "I think" and "sort of" (18, line 5) display uncertainty about the accuracy of the call. The force of a fault-finding word such as "wrong" is undercut by embedding laugh tokens within it (18, line 6). Whereas expressions such as "chiriona" attributed strong responsibility to the party who committed the foul, here agency is removed from the offender's action through use of terms such as "accidentally" and divorcing the foot that lands on the line from the actor controlling that foot. Moreover, committing a foul may have no real consequences. Girls assert that a violation of the rules has occurred when they state, "You- accidentally jumped on that" (19, line 6). However, they note that within their version of the game this is permitted: "But that's okay(hh)." Rather than articulating strong stances in calling fouls, these girls let actions they deem violations pass as acceptable moves. It's "okay" if someone "accidentally" jumps on the line. Finally, even a failed attempt is praised as "a good try" (18, line 9). The game of hopscotch can thus be played drawing upon diverse notions of acceptable forms of accountability for one's actions.

A range of language choices (as well as embodied stances and affect displays) is available to speakers. Through the way in which players *select from* a repertoire of linguistic possibilities—alternatively making opposition salient or masking it—they construct themselves as quite different types of social actors.

Probing Rules

The model of girls' play in the current literature argues that turn-taking games such as hopscotch progress in identical order from one situation to the next, thus proposing that they operate within what Hart (1951:125) has called a world of "mechanical jurisprudence." To the contrary, when actual play is examined we find that girls regularly test the rules, disputing what can count as a proper application of one and seeing how far they can extend certain rules to work to their advantage. Rather than following rules, they learn how to work and play with them.

In the next example Paula is learning how to do "ABC"—taking three baby steps before throwing her beanbag into a number above six on the grid. Looking toward the other players and laughing, Paula persistently takes a slightly larger third step, playfully probing what she can get away with. The referees counter her tests with polarity markers "NO::" (lines 2, 4), response cries "AY:::" (lines 3, 11), opposition turns containing negative person descriptors: "NO CHIRIONA!" (line 4) and "cheater" (line 7), as well as explanations: "AY:: QUE TIENES QUE METERTE EN LA RAYA DE AQUÍ LOS DOS JUNTITOS AL OTRO PIE NIÑA" (*Hey you have to place yourself on this line with both feet very close together to the other foot Girl!*). The verbal statement is accompanied by enactments of how precisely to place one's feet one behind the other in small steps on the grid.

(20)   ((*Paula, a newcomer, has just been instructed in how to take baby steps in ABC, putting her heel to the toe of her shoe. She is now trying to take larger steps than permitted.*))

1	Paula:	A(hh), B, C(h) ((*smiling*))
2	Rosa:	NO⌈:
3	Risa:	⌊AY::: ((*spanking Paula*))
4	Rosa:	¡NO CHIRIO⌈NA!
5	Paula:	⌊Okay.
6		⌈A
7	Rosa:	⌊Cheater!
8	Paula:	B, C.= ((*taking big steps*))
9	Risa:	NO::: ((*body lowers dramatically*))
10	Paula:	((*smiles widely*))
11	Risa:	AY:: ((*pushing Paula out of the way so she can demonstrate the correct foot patterns*))
12		⌈QUE TIENES QUE METERTE
		(*You have to put yourself*)
13	Paula:	⌊Hih hih!

14	Risa:	EN LA RAYA⌈ DE AQUÍ
		(on this line)
15	Paula	⌊ Okay!
16	Risa:	LOS DOS JUNTITOS
		(with both feet very close together)
17		AL OTRO ⌈PIE NIÑA
		(to the other⎥ foot Girl!)
18	Paula:	⌊A,

In the midst of play the referees take up a very complicated stance toward the rule. While they counter the player's large steps with response cries (lines 3, 11) and subsequently accounts and a demonstration about how one's feet should be placed (lines 12–16), their action is keyed with laughter by the jumper, who laughs about her own thwarted probes of the rules in the midst of her turn (lines 1, 10). By playing with the possibilities provided by the game in this way, girls are developing the ability to resist the rules that are simultaneously providing structure for the events that they are engaged in.

What happens here raises another issue as well. Social scientists (Gilligan 1982, Lever 1978, Sutton-Smith 1979) have argued that conflict is so disruptive to girls that they are incapable of continuing to play when it emerges. However, as examples 17 and 20 show, these girls do not treat conflict and play as mutually exclusive alternatives. Conflict about rules and fouls is embedded within a larger participation framework visibly constituted through playfulness and laughter. Instead of breaching relationships, the disputes engendered by the game are a central part of the fun of playing it. Rather than treating conflict and cooperation as a bipolar dichotomy, the girls build complex participation frameworks in which disputes, with their rich possibilities for cognitive organization and the development of a habitus skilled at visibly taking powerful stances, are embedded within a larger ethos of playfulness.

Playing with the Structure of Attentiveness

Such probing of the structures organizing the game can be applied not only to its rules but also to the frameworks of attentiveness that sustain it. Not only do referees monitor players, but players for their part can monitor the watchfulness of their referees; when they can discern that referees are less than fully engaged in scrutinizing the game, they can try to advance their tokens without referees knowing it—thus playing with the participation frameworks within which the game is conducted.

In the following example Sandra tricks the other players who are involved in their own side conversation about boyfriends. While invisible to the referees, Sandra's movements (as well as a collusive eyeball roll) display to the ethnographers the trick she is attempting. She sneaks across the grid, advances her beanbag to the next square, and then dances back to her place with a Charlie Chaplinesque walk. The following frame grabs (Figure 1.8) show the sequence of moves she makes to advance her token before returning home to her place.

Of course, the trick would not be any fun were the referees not to eventually discover that they had been tricked. After Sandra has moved her beanbag while Glo-

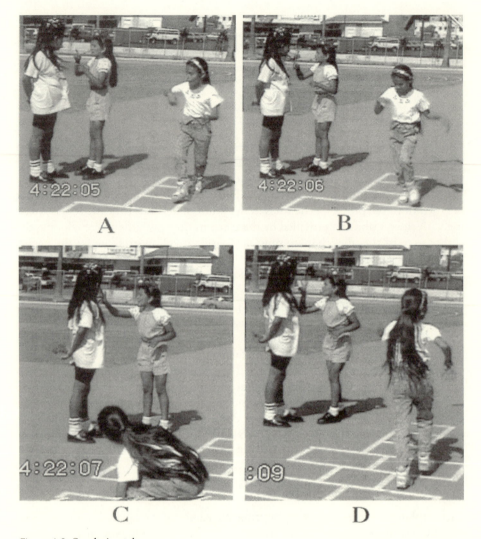

Figure 1.8 Sandra's trickery

ria and Carla have been talking, she states, "Perdí. Sigues tú" (*I lost. Your turn*), pointing to the square where her token has been moved. She then chants "Eh YEI!" (line 4) as she claps her hands. Sandra's posture with hands on hips, and slight bouncing up and down, visibly keys the possibility that something special is going on. In the midst of jumping, as Carla comes to realize that all is not okay, she moves through a sequence of embodied stances. She first puts her hands on hips, in a challenge position (Figure 1.9).

Then Carla uses her extended arm to make an accusatory point as she states "Tú no has pasado *este* número" (*You haven't even advanced to this number*), with the movements shown in Figures 1.10 and 1.11.

Figure 1.9 Carla's challenge pose

During "este número" she advances to the square in question and leans toward Sandra (in another challenge posture) as she stomps on the square she is referring to. The following provides a complete transcript of the interaction in question.

(21)   ((*While Gloria and Carla have been talking about boyfriends, Sandra*
                   sneaks to advance her token.))
1   Sandra: Perdí. ⌈Sigues tú.
              (*I lost.*⌊*Your turn.*)
2   Gloria: ⌊Whew:::!!! ((*twirling around*))
3   ⌈Esto es . . otro problema.
              ⌊(*This is another problem.*)
4   Sandra: ⌊Ey YEI! ((*clapping hands*))
5   Carla: ((*jumps and discovers Sandra has cheated, assumes challenge pose with*
              arms akimbo))
6   Tú no has pasado ((*finger point*))
7   **este** número. ((*stomps on square*))
              (*You haven't gotten past this number.*)
8   Sandra: *hhhh hih-hih-hih! ((*wringing hands*))
              hih-hih-hih-hih! ((*kicks bag to lower square*))
              eh hih-hih-hih-hih-hih-hih

Figure 1.10 Carla: Tú no has pasado (line 6 of example 21)

In this sequence stance is displayed through both language and the vocal and nonvocal organization of the body. The party who has been tricked uses her pointing finger and leaning body to display her outrage at the wrong done her. In contrast, Sandra, who has successfully exploited a lapse in monitoring to play with the participation structures that frame the game, punctuates the entire exchange with gleeful, playful laughter (line 8). Keyings of many different forms occur, as coparticipants transform their affective alignment toward the game in different ways throughout its course. Within hopscotch, stances are displayed through language choices, intensified intonation contours, gestures, and embodied performances, within the built social world of the game grid as a framework for the interpretation of action.

The Relevance of Conflict for Models of Girls' Interaction

While concern for face-saving has been a major theme in research about female speech, one line of thinking in contemporary social theory stresses the importance of the pursuit of conflict[12] for the organization of social life. Anthropologists argue that "interpersonal conflict, disagreements, and moral dilemmas are at the heart of social life" (White & Watson-Gegeo 1990:3). According to developmental psychologists Shantz and Hartup (1992:11, 2), "the virtual 'dance' of discord and ac-

Figure 1.11 Carla: este número (line 7 of example 21)

cord, of disaffirmation and affirmation . . . is critical to the comprehension of de-velopment. . . . No other single phenomenon plays as broad and significant a role in human development as conflict is thought to. Many different functions—cogni-tion, social cognition, emotions, and social relations—are thought to be formed and/or transformed by conflict."[13] However, most contemporary feminist scholar-ship has not only avoided analyzing conflicts between women but also actively pro-moted a view of women as essentially cooperative.[14]

Not only do we view conflict and cooperation in dualistic terms (Mukhopadhyay & Higgins 1988) but we also omit competitive interactions among women from ethnographies. As anthropologist Victoria Burbank (1994:100–01) has noted, women's aggressive interactions with other women are rarely a topic of academic in-terest.[15] According to feminist philosopher Helen Longino, "Our conceptual linking of competition with domination, hierarchy, and scarcity prevents us from appreciat-ing the value of competitive challenge in developing skills and talents, and ulti-mately undermines our potential to change ourselves and our worlds" (1987:256).

In a similar vein Flax (1990:181–82) has warned: "We need to avoid seeing women as totally innocent, acted upon beings. Such a view prevents us from seeing the areas of life in which women have had an effect, are not totally determined by the will of the other, and the ways in which some women have and do exert power over others."

Feminist sociolinguists argue that we need to move the diverse experience of women of different backgrounds from the periphery to the center of social theory (Freed 1995, Henley 1995, Houston & Kramarae 1991, Kramarae 1990, Morgan 1995). For example, hooks (1989) has contended that while for WASP (White Anglo-Saxon Protestant) women confrontation is viewed negatively, African American women are powerful actors in many different kinds of interaction. Houston (1990:31) notes that gender is frequently perceived as separate from ethnicity and class; as a consequence gender is treated "as if it is experienced in the same way by all women, that is, according to white middle class women's experience."

Contrary to the notion that females attempt to avoid conflict, here I have shown through the ways in which elementary school girls construct opposition that they are actively seeking it out. Positions are highlighted not merely through words, but also through intensified intonation contours and embodied performances—marking the spaces stepped on with physical tapping and jumping—within the built social world of the game grid. Girls intently scrutinize players' actions to produce judgments about the jumpers' moves. As these girls play, they do not simply rotate through various positions, but animatedly and playfully dispute, resist, and probe the boundaries of rules as referees and players together build the game event—without the development of physical fighting. Though research (Lever 1978, Sutton-Smith 1979) has used hopscotch to build a deficit picture of girls who lack the ability to use and contest rules, ethnographic study of how the game is actually played reveals just the opposite.

This analysis of preadolescent girls' language practices has obvious relevance to theories of women's language and social organization. Strong claims about female cooperative language styles fall apart under close scrutiny. However, it *is* possible to systematically describe the reciprocal shaping of alternative language choices and the structures for the organization of participation in social activities. Study of these practices would not be possible if my only data were reports to an anthropologist about such events. Instead, analysis requires accurate records of precisely how talk was produced in the midst of the activity itself as an embodied performance addressed to another consequential actor. Talk, social organization, and context are deeply intertwined with each other. To incorporate agency into studies of female interaction and to avoid dichotomies that essentialize gender differences, we need to look ethnographically at the diverse ways that language is used in a range of natural settings—that is, if we want our notions of gendered aspects of linguistic stance and footing to be on solid ground.

NOTES

Earlier versions of this paper were presented at the Symposium on Conversation, Linguistic Institute, University of New Mexico, July 14, 1995; the 10th Annual Visual Research Conference sponsored by the Society for Visual Anthropology, American Anthropological Association Annual Meeting, Atlanta, November 29, 1994; and colloquia at Indiana University and UCLA during April 1995.

Salomé Santos and Carla Vale assisted in translating portions of text used in this paper. Roberta Chase-Borgatti, Patrick Gonzales, Sally Jacoby, Pat Mason, Norma Mendoza-Denton,

Alicia de Myhrer, Marjorie Faulstich Orellana, Manny Schegloff, and Malcah Yaeger-Dror provided many useful comments. Chuck Goodwin helped in all stages of the development of this paper. This research would not have been possible without Lori Cronyn, who introduced me to the teachers, principal, and children of the school where this research was conducted. I have benefited in countless ways through talks with her about children, schooling, language, and community in Pico Union.

1. Similarly, according to Leaper (1991:798), while boys seek "independence, competition, and dominance" in their interactions with others, girls strive for "closeness, cooperation, and interpersonal harmony" (see also Maccoby 1990).

2. Coates (1994:72) cites Kalcik (1975) and Coates (1989, 1991, 1996). Her model builds on the work of Falk (1980) and Troemel-Ploetz (1992).

3. Harding (1982:235) argues that women and men have very different rationalities: for women a rational person is one who "values highly her abilities to emphasize and 'connect' with particular others and wants to learn more complex and satisfying ways to take the role of the particular other in relationships." Men base the idea of a rational person on one's "ability to separate himself from others and to make decisions independent of what others think."

4. For example, Oliver (1991:345) argues that by de-emphasizing women's rationality we propose characterizations that "have permitted women to be seen as lacking the skills and characteristics which might allow them to become adequate leaders."

5. In addition, cross-gender interaction was observed and videotaped among African American working-class girls and boys during a summer day camp sponsored by the Columbia Department of Parks, Recreation and Tourism.

6. Boasting is generally considered more characteristic of boys than of girls (Best 1983: 93; Goodwin 1990a:39–46, Whiting & Edwards 1973:184). However, during the course of hopscotch girls in Pico Union openly brag about their successful playing, sing-chanting, "Qué bueno. Yo voy en el último!" (*How terrific! I'm going to the last square!*) or "Voy ganando! Voy ganando! !EY:::::::::::!" (*I'm winning! I'm winning! Yeah!*). Similarly, when someone skillfully maneuvers a difficult trajectory, an African American girl openly acknowledges her success, shouting "Hallelujah!," followed by joyful hand claps above her head (as if proclaiming herself a winner), and announcing that she is on the last box: "Number *nine*! I'm on *nine* y'all."

7. On membership categorization devices in children's games, see Sacks (1992b).

8. On the multifunctionality of "no" in turn preface position in the contentious speech of Spanish-speaking Latina girls in Northern California, see Mendoza-Denton (1995).

9. Norma Mendoza-Denton (personal communication) points out that this example shows how the bilingual phonology of the children operates, taking the English word "cheater" and code-switching in the middle of it at a morphological boundary by changing the /t/ of "cheat" to /r/. Although the vowel quality is primarily Spanish, the word has an English phonological process operating within it, with the intervocalic flapping of /t/.

10. In her study of working-class children in the Piedmont region of South Carolina, Heath (1983) found that African American girls incorporated more assertive and mocking cheers in their playsongs than White girls. In a study of ritual insult, Ayoub and Barnett (1961) found that while White high-schoolers may know how to use ritual insult, they frequently deny such knowledge. For a discussion of literature on ritual insult among American subgroups differing in ethnicity and social class, see Eder (1990).

11. Much more work needs to be done to sort out the effect of ethnicity and social class on norms of speaking. Working-class White children in the Baltimore community studied by Miller (1986) are socialized to be assertive when needing to defend themselves. Eder (1990:82) similarly argues that for the working- and lower-class White girls she studied,

"'toughness' is more highly valued and there is less concern about 'politeness'." By way of contrast, the principal of the Columbia school where children's mitigated responses were observed actively promoted an ideology of conflict avoidance; such an ideology was consistent with the norms of the Unitarian Universalist Church, which two of the White middle-class girls whose actions are reported here attended.

12. Shantz & Hartup (1992:4) distinguish *aggression*—"behavior aimed at hurting another person or thing"—from *conflict*, defined as "a state of resistance or opposition between (at least) two individuals."

13. For an analysis of the role of conflict in children's friendship development see Corsaro (1994), Corsaro and Rizzo (1990), Eder (1990), Maynard (1985b), and Rizzo (1992).

14. However, see Eder's (1990) analysis of conflict exchanges among working- and lower-class White adolescents in the Midwest and Shuman's (1986, 1993) analysis of disputes among African American, White (Polish American and Irish American), and Puerto Rican inner-city junior high school students. When conflict in young girls has been examined, it has been in terms of face-saving strategies that young (White) girls utilize to mitigate conflict (Sheldon 1992, 1993).

15. However, see Schuster and Hartz-Karp's (1986) analysis of women's aggression on an Israeli kibbutz.

2

Register and Footing in Role Play

SUSAN M. HOYLE

The pretend role play of school-age children has attracted relatively little attention. It deserves scrutiny, though, because through such play older children can
develop and display some of their most intricate linguistic and interactional abilities. During role play, children have an opportunity to practice skills in a variety of
registers, some of which they may otherwise not need and thus not display. Furthermore, role play that involves more than one child is subject to complex constraints as participants closely monitor one another's performance. The register
display that sustains children's pretense provides the analyst with a window into
their microlevel interactional practices, illuminating their sometimes underesti-
mated communicative competence and underanalyzed interactional skills.

In this chapter I show how some preadolescent boys enact imaginary roles by as-
sembling alignments out of register-specific resources. Investigation of linguistic registers is often accomplished by examining completed texts (e.g., Biber & Finegan
1994). However, the children in this study demonstrate talk in register as clearly an
interactive endeavor. Not only do they exhibit their command of the different ways
of speaking associated with different roles, but they also actively use the features of
different registers to build coherent and engrossing play episodes.

Playing a role (pretend or otherwise) involves (at least) two major tasks accomplished through language. First, the performer must display mastery of the appropriate register by producing the sorts of linguistic forms and the speech actions typical of the role: both what is said and how it is said are aspects of any register.
Second (and simultaneously), the performer must attend to any co-participants.
The first of these tasks might be thought of as a cognitively based individual one
and the second as an interactional one. But the children's play that I examine here

illustrates that in fact both of these tasks are interactive and intertwined. The sometimes exaggerated ways in which children enact imaginary roles can illuminate the more general relation between these tasks, a relation that we might expect to obtain in all kinds of role performances.

Tannen and Wallat's (1993) discussion of the interplay between *interactive frames* and *knowledge schemas* helps to capture the way that roles (imaginary or actual) are played out. Knowledge schemas, as they define them, are cognitive entities; they consist of "participants' expectations about people, objects, events and settings in the world" (1993:60). Interactive frames, on the other hand, are the ways in which participants signal and interpret an activity that they are jointly constructing. A frame is constructed through participants' signaling their own and recognizing each other's *footing*, Goffman's (1981:128) term for "the alignment we take up to ourselves and the others present as expressed in the way we manage the production or reception of an utterance." Thus, an individual's assumptions about how to perform a role (including, centrally, what register to use) constitutes a knowledge schema, whereas the detailed means by which performers orient to one another make up an interactive frame. When knowledge schemas are not shared, the flow of an exchange can be disrupted and the interactive frame of the moment modified, as Tannen and Wallat show. When schemas are shared, however, as in the material presented here, invoking them can be part and parcel of the fun. Invocation of a shared schema allows children at play to sustain interactive frames by jointly enacting pretend roles associated with distinctive registers.

Older children, not surprisingly, are more adept than preschoolers at producing the linguistic register called for by a particular task or situation (e.g., Martin 1983). As Hymes (1974a:112) points out, though, registers "are not chosen only because a situation demands them; they may be chosen to define a situation." Indeed, during pretend play, choice of register is a primary means of defining the situation. Older children control a wide range of linguistic resources for constructing register in pretend play. Both Andersen (1990) and Cook-Gumperz (1986, 1995), for instance, find that preschoolers rely primarily on phonological and prosodic features to mark the registers deemed appropriate to different roles, adopting different voices to indicate which character they are animating or who is being addressed. But Andersen (1990) finds that children older than six additionally exploit lexical and syntactic means of signaling pretend roles. Halmari and Smith (1994) provide support for this finding with their analysis of the play of a pair of eight- and nine-year-old Finnish-English bilingual sisters. The girls used two registers—everyday talk as opposed to in-character talk attributed to dolls—each characterized by a cluster of features. These included not only prosody and voice quality but also grammatical elements (e.g., sentence type, verb tense, presence or absence of deictic terms) and code-switching (the dolls spoke English, the girls' second language, but negotiation of the play was usually carried out in Finnish). Older children's play, then, can be expected to evince a wide range of role-enacting procedures, strategies, and styles.

The Children

The children whose talk and play provide the data for this chapter are three eight- to ten-year-old middle-class, White American boys—my son and his friends.[1] I audio-recorded them as they were playing competitive games and, at the same time, acting as various characters involved in a sportscast: sportscasters, interviewers, and interviewees. Their sportscasting play was almost always dyadic (my son and one or another friend). I recorded it under two different conditions: first, as they produced it spontaneously, and, later, as I elicited it. The spontaneous version arose as the boys played Ping-Pong, indoor basketball, or a computer game; they would begin to announce the action, acting like sports announcers on television or radio. I recorded this kind of play from time to time over a period of fifteen months. The second set of episodes was elicited after I had finished collecting the spontaneous data and had identified sportscasting as a naturally occurring (and recurring) speech activity; the boys agreed eagerly to my request that they play a game and announce the action as I recorded them. This chapter is based on a total of approximately two and a half hours of each version.

The two versions were not identical. In the spontaneous one, two boys shared the speaking role of sportscaster, and, at the same time that they were announcing the action, they were competing against each other. In the elicited version, on the other hand, the boys did not share the sportscaster role, nor did they compete against each other. Instead (by their choice), they always set up a computer game, one of them playing against the computer while the other acted as announcer. But the play-by-play report was punctuated by frequent "interviews with the player," during which the erstwhile announcer would act as interviewer and the player would take the part of interviewee. At the end of each game, the boys would switch positions (literally and figuratively) so that the one who had been the announcer got a chance to play against the computer and vice versa.

Whether the boys are collaboratively enacting the part of the sportscaster or collaboratively staging an interview, they define and sustain their play by doing two things: producing a role-appropriate register and aligning to each other's pretend selves. Despite the convenience of separating these activities for analysis as I do here, they are tightly interwoven: it is by displaying attention to the features of a register that the boys ratify each other's contributions to the play and thus frame their performance as a lively, joint, imaginative venture.

Role Requirements

The Role of Sportscaster

Sportscasters have a two-fold task. They are expected, first, to use linguistic forms and constructions that are conventional to the specialized register of sports announcing (Ferguson 1983) and, second, to confine themselves for the most part to reporting the action of the game in progress. The boys not only display their knowledge of these expectations but enthusiastically embrace them and use them as the basis for their performances. The following excerpts, typical of their spontaneous sportscasting, show how they perform it as a joint monologue. Two boys share the sportscaster role, together addressing an imaginary audience:

(1)   [playing indoor basketball; Josh is "the Lakers," Matt is "the Celtics"]
 1 Josh: It's eighty-two t' seventy-six here,
 2   the Lakers have the ball.
 3   Byron Scott has it.
 4   [3.0]
 5   Scott controlling.
 6   Inside to Worthy.
 7   Worthy shoots!
 8   Worthy misses.
 9   Worthy misses the rebound!
 10   And it's eighty-two t-
 11   And Kareem puts it back in.
 12   And it's eighty-two: t' seventy-eight.
 13 Matt: McHale with the ball.
 14 Josh: McHale has the ball.
 15 Matt: Outside shot.

(2)   [playing Ping-Pong]
 1 Ben: He's comin' back man.
 2   He's comin' back, four four [he's comin' back.
 3 Josh: [Four four.
 4   [4.0]
 5 Ben: Ya-hoo! Five four.
 6 Josh: Five four, Ben Smith's lead.
 7   Will he try and slam it.
 8 Ben: Yeah-ho!
 9 Josh: (He's excited) it's six four Ben Smith's lead.
 10   He serves=
 11 Ben: =Oh::!
 12 Josh: Ben Smith hits- gets it over
 13   and it's six five Ben Smith's lead.
 14   Hoyle's service!

(3)   [indoor basketball; Ben is "Big Fry," Josh is "Small Fry"][2]
 1 Ben: Big Fry.
 2   Trying t' get it in.
 3 Josh: Shoots over Small Fry!
 4   But he misses!
 5   But he gets the rebound and he puts it up and in!

The boys have a good deal of productive competence in the register of sportscasting (Hoyle 1991), which is characterized by forms and constructions that are unusual or inappropriate in other forms of standard English (Crystal & Davy 1969, Ferguson 1983, Green 1982, Leech 1971, Weber 1982). The most frequent and salient register-marking feature in the boys' performance, as in that of adult professionals, is the use of simple present action verbs (e.g., "Worthy shoots!," "But he misses!").[3] Announcers use the simple present to give the impression that their announcement of an action is simultaneous with the action itself, so that the remote audience (especially a radio audience) can experience the game along with the physically present audience. Other register-marking constructions are seen in example 3 at line 2, where Ben's "Trying t' get it in" lacks both a subject and an auxiliary verb, and at line 3, where Josh's "Shoots over Small Fry!" lacks a subject. (The antecedent of the missing subject, of course, is identified at line 1.) Omission of an auxiliary occurs at line 5 of example 1 ("Scott controlling") and omission of a main verb at line 13, "McHale with the ball." Finally, Josh's "Inside to Worthy" (example 1, line 6) and Matt's "Outside shot" (line 15) exemplify another typical omission (Ferguson 1983), that of an initial phrase such as "it is" or "there is." In all of these types of syntactic reduction, sports announcers use simplified constructions for two reasons: partly because they assume that their audience shares knowledge about the sort of action taking place, but also and probably more importantly (Ferguson 1983, 1985), because these forms have become conventionalized markers of the register. Matt, Josh, and Ben have learned how and when to use them.

Along with using a specialized register, sportscasters are expected to restrict the sorts of speech actions that they perform. For some roles, of course, most notably that of "ordinary conversationalist," it would be impossible for an analyst to delimit allowable or even typical speech acts. But for the role of sportscaster (and as discussed below, for the roles of interviewer and interviewee), such a delimitation is plausible. Sports announcing is an "activity type" in which there are "rather special relations between what is said and what is done" (Levinson 1992:70), for the announcer's task is to give a play-by-play account of the action taking place on the field or court. Occasionally announcers may voice a guess or query about what will happen next, but for the most part they confine themselves to reporting the action that they see. Thus, examples 1–3 show the boys reporting the actions taken by the official players, and what the boys say about these figures is restricted by what actions the figures in fact take, with what results. In example 1, Josh and Matt, playing basketball, are each taking the part of an entire team. Although it is not actually "Worthy," "Scott," or "McHale" who is acting, the boys who embody these roles are in fact doing the things reported. In example 2, Josh and Ben, playing Ping-Pong, announce what they are doing (e.g., "He serves," "Ben Smith hits- gets it over"), with what resulting score (e.g., "Five four, Ben Smith's lead"), along with a general comment about the action from Ben ("He's comin' back," lines 1–2) and a speculation from Josh on what Ben will do next ("Will he try and slam it," line 7). (This summarizing and speculating, of course, does not report particular actions and is used only occasionally, but such utterances do contribute to the announcing line and, as Crystal & Davy [1969] note, are present in adult sports announcing.) In example 3 Ben and Josh report the attempts of "Big Fry" to get the ball in the basket. When they speak as announcers, then, the boys' topics and speech actions are limited.

The boys thus fulfill the register requirements of the sportscaster role: they use appropriate forms and constructions, and they issue the appropriate sorts of speech acts. The same general requirements hold for the reciprocal roles of interviewer and interviewee.

The Roles of Interviewer and Interviewee

In the elicited version of their sportscasting, the boys take on the additional roles of interviewer and interviewee. In each episode where these figures appear, one boy is playing basketball against a computer, manipulating the on-screen figure "Larry Bird," while the other boy acts as announcer, reporting to the imaginary audience the actions taken by Larry Bird and his computer-controlled opponent, "Doctor J." In the course of each game, though, the announcer interrupts his play-by-play description several times in order to conduct "interviews" with the player. The interviews, then, are dialogic exchanges embedded within the sportscaster's monologue, as shown in example 4, where the interview occupies lines 4–18. Josh, who has been doing the play-by-play announcing (lines 1–3), takes on a new role as interviewer; Matt, who has been the (nonspeaking) player, speaks as the interviewee. At the end of the interview, Josh switches back to speaking as announcer (line 19).

(4)   [Josh is sportscaster/interviewer; Matt is "Larry Bird"]
1   Josh: He takes a three pointer it i::s . . no good!
2   And Doctor J gets the rebound,
3   and we'll have a halfti- a first quarter interview with Larry Bird.
4   Well Larry how d' you feel about your performance.
5   Matt: Well I'm just sick about it.
6   Y'know . . . that . . . I shot that ball,
7   and it was halfway t' the basket,
8   and they called a violation.
9   I don't know what's wrong with these people!
10   Josh: Neither do I!
11   But at any rate,
12   you certainly did not play very well that quarter though.
13   Matt: Well I had- I- my main game plan for that quarter was t' try t' keep . . . him so he couldn't clear the ball,
14   and it worked for a little bit,
15   but I still didn't do that well in the uh long run.
16   Josh: Yeah you played great defense,
17   but you didn't have very much offense.
18   Now let's go back t' the game.
19   Okay and Doctor J has it,
20   drives by Larry Bird.
21   And he scores.

Like the role of sportscaster, the reciprocal roles of interviewer and interviewee involve the use of certain forms and a rather restricted range of speech acts. However, although both sports announcing and interviewing are typically adult roles, the register of announcing, as we have seen, is characterized by unusual grammatical forms, and it is a fairly straightforward matter for the boys to use them. The forms that characterize (adult) interviews are not as easily specified. I suggest, though, that while enacting the roles of interviewer and interviewee the boys use their version of a "general adult register." They freely use forms that they use only sparingly, if at all, in other talk. For instance, the terms *performance* (as in example 4, line 4), *at any rate* (line 11), *certainly* (line 12), and *in the long run* (line 15) appear in many of their interviews and lend an adult-style flavor. But even more frequent are the discourse markers *well* and *now*. Example 4 contains three tokens of *well* (lines 4, 5, 13);[4] examples 5 and 6 show the use of both *well* and *now*:

(5)   [Ben is sportscaster/interviewer; Josh is "Larry Bird"]
    1   Ben: We're gonna have a (ref's) time out here.
    2   And we just called Larry Bird over to talk to us.
    3   →   Now Larry, you have a one hundred and
    4   [3.5]
    5   you have *over* a one hundred point lead.
    6   How do you feel about that.
    7   Josh: →   Well y'know Vince, I- I just feel great about that,
    8   and I like the way I'm playin' ball,
    9   and I think I- I'm gonna score
    10   over three hundred points today.
    11   [interview continues]

(6)   [Josh is sportscaster/interviewer; Matt is "Larry Bird"]
    1   Josh: That's the end of the quarter.
    2   And we're having an interview with Larry Bird right now.
    3   →   Now are you pleased with your performance so far?
    4   Matt: →   Well not really I gotta get into the-
    5   →   well I'm still leading by three,
    6   but I hafta get psyched for this game
    7   and do some rebounding.
    8   [interview continues]

Well and *now* appear during practically all of the interviews that the boys stage, but never (in the case of *now*) or seldom (in the case of *well*) in a corpus of these same children's casual conversation (Hoyle 1994). It seems apparent, then, that the boys are using them as register-marking forms, to index an adult style appropriate for the speech event of interviewing. Andersen (1990), similarly, found that children who were pretending to be adults—parents, doctors, or teachers—used *well* and that children taking the part of a teacher used *now*, whereas children playing the part of children rarely used these forms. Furthermore, the six- and seven-year olds in her study used *well* when playing adult parts more often than did the four- or five-year-olds, suggesting increasing sensitivity over time to the term's appropriateness in adult speech. Josh, Matt, and Ben, at the ages of nine and ten, use both *well* and *now* throughout their interviews, and these discourse markers, along with the other lexical items and phrases mentioned above, mark their interviews as at least approximating a general adult register.

More easily specified are the speech acts or turn types expected of interviewers and interviewees. Interviews differ from ordinary conversation in that they consist of pre-allocated turn types (Clayman 1992; Greatbatch 1988, 1992; Heritage 1985; Heritage & Roth 1995; Schegloff 1992). An interviewer's main task is to ask questions, whereas an interviewee's is to provide answers, and it is largely the succession of questions and answers that defines a stretch of interaction as an interview. This is as true for the interviews that the children stage as for real ones conducted by adults. And just as for adult interviewers (Heritage & Roth 1995), most of the child interviewers' utterances are syntactically interrogative (e.g., "Well Larry how d' you feel about your performance," "How do you feel about that," "Now are you pleased with your performance so far," "Now Larry what is your strategy for today's game").

The interviewer is also expected to open and close the interview (Greatbatch 1988). In part, of course, this responsibility follows from the task of asking questions, since without a first question the interview cannot proceed, and when the questions stop, the interview stops (Heritage & Roth 1995). In the boys' performances, then (as in adults'), the person acting as interviewer takes the first and last turn. And like an adult, rather than plunging in with his first question, he usually prefaces it with an remark or two. Each of the initial questions in examples 4–6 is prefaced: "and we'll have a halfti- a first quarter interview with Larry Bird," "We're gonna have a (ref's) time out here. And we just called Larry Bird over to talk to us," "And we're having an interview with Larry Bird right now." The introductory comment in example 7 is similar (if a bit abrupt):

(7)   [Matt is sportscaster/interviewer]
    1   Matt: →   Okay now a pre-game interview with Larry Bird.
    2   Now Larry what is your strategy for today's game.
    3   Josh: Well y'know Pat, I'm just- Irv, I'm just gonna um . . . go in and get my good shots.

The interviewer's last turn closes the interview, as in example 4 where Josh says, "Now let's go back t' the game" (line 18) and as in examples 8 and 9:

(8)   [interview is in progress]
    1   Matt: I think I'm gonna hafta try t' outrebound him.
    2   And try t' block some of those outside shots that he gets.
    3   Josh: →   You heard it, straight from Larry Bird.
    4   [Josh resumes announcing]

(9)   [continuation of (7)]
    1   Josh: Well y'know Pat, I'm just- Irv, I'm just gonna um . . . go in and get try t' get my good shots.
    2   Matt: →   O:kay. You heard it straight from Larry.
    3   [Matt resumes announcing]

So in addition to asking questions, the interviewer issues introductory remarks that provide a transition away from the play-by-play announcing and final comments that provide a transition back to it.

The interviewee, for his part, provides answers. In examples 5–7 each second speaker specifically marks his utterance as an answer by prefacing it with *well*, a "marker of response" (Schiffrin 1987:102):[5]

(5) 6 Ben: How do you feel about that.
      7 Josh: →   Well y' know Vince, I- I just feel great about that.

(6) 3 Josh: Now are you pleased with your performance so far?
      4 Matt: →   Well not really I gotta get into the-
      5   well I'm still leading by three,
      6   but I hafta get psyched for this game
      7   and do some rebounding.

(7) 2 Matt: Now Larry what is your strategy for today's game.
     3 Josh: →   Well y'know Pat, I'm just- Irv, I'm just gonna um . . . go in and get
                       my good shots.

So besides functioning as a general indicator of register (an "adult-style" one), *well*
functions more narrowly to mark a particular speech act type (an answer) that is recurrent in and typical of the interview register.

In sum, whether enacting the role of sportscaster or the roles of interviewer and
interviewee, the boys exploit their knowledge of the forms and acts that characterize typical performances, thus ensuring that their productions approximate those of
their adult models. In the adult world, both sportscasting and interviewing on radio
or television are public displays intended to engage an audience. For children at
play, the requirements are slightly different but perhaps even more intricate, because the players must sustain their pretense as well as a connection to an (imaginary) audience. In the next section I turn to the ways in which the children turn
the elements of linguistic registers into vehicles for lively performances.

Alignment Displays

Besides displaying mastery of the registers of sportscasting and interviewing, the
boys use that register proficiency as the basis for alignment displays. They define and
sustain their play by aligning to each other's imaginary selves and, by so aligning,
ratify each other's contributions. Despite differences in the spontaneous and elicited
versions of their play, in both cases alignment is manifested through (1) use of reference and address terms, (2) joint construction of propositions, and (3) exhibition
of continuing involvement.

The Sportscaster's Footings

The spontaneous sportscasting (the version in which two boys share the sportscaster
role) is remarkable for the fact that the participants orient to each other while not
addressing each other—which would be contrary to the spirit of the activity. Although they do lapse into direct address from time to time, they do so only as brief
out-of-frame side sequences (Hoyle 1989, 1993). Tannen's (1990a) distinction between *directly aligning* to a conversational partner and *orienting* to a partner captures
what is going on. As she points out, it is typical of boys (and men) not to align directly (either physically or linguistically) to their interlocutors, even though they
are attending to them. The boys here capitalize on the difference between direct
alignment and orientation: the whole point of acting as sports announcer is not to
address your playmate.

In jointly enacting the role of sportscaster, the boys form and display alignment in three ways: (1) they refer to each other in the third person while addressing an imaginary audience in the second person, (2) they jointly construct
propositions describing the action, and (3) they continue to orient to the activity despite distractions.

Using Reference and Address Terms   The most obvious alignment marker in this activity is the use of reference and address terms. The boys use third-person forms to talk *about* themselves and each other and the second-person pronoun to speak *to* the imaginary audience. In example 1, for instance, in which Josh and Matt are each taking the part of an entire basketball team, they refer to all of the characters on both teams in the third person, not resorting to the first person at all. That the addressee is the audience is apparent in the excerpts presented so far, but it is especially clear in examples 10 and 11:

(10)			[playing computer basketball]	
	1	Josh:	Larry Bird for three points.	
	2		Misses bu::t . . .	
	3		He jumps and gets the rebound back on the floor!	
	4		And he sco:res.	
	5	Matt:	Instant replay.=	
	6	Josh:	=And it's an instant replay here	
	7		[at Whatchamacallit [Stadium.	
	8	Matt: →	[For you	[for you people at home.

(11)			[playing indoor basketball]	
	1	Ben:	Rebound.	
	2	Josh:	And it's forty [eight	
	3	Ben:	[Forty-eight forty-eight.	
	4	Ben: →	Five minutes t' win this game folks.	

Matt, in example 10, addresses the audience as "you" (claiming that the "instant replay" generated by the computer program is for the benefit of "you people at home"). Ben, in example 11, addresses the audience as "folks" (implying that the announcement of the score is for the audience). Treating the audience as addressee creates and reinforces the activity-appropriate footing toward the playmate: it is precisely by not addressing each other that the boys orient to each other.

Jointly Building Propositions   A second way of mutually aligning while co-creating the role of the sportscaster is through joint (and enthusiastic) construction of propositions, like the "duetting" described by Falk (1980) or the "cooperative sentence building" depicted by Tannen (1984) as an aspect of "involvement." The statements that the boys construct jointly (like those that they produce individually) fulfill the announcer's task of describing the action. In the simplest sort of joint proposition building, two boys construct a single proposition over two turns. In example 3, Josh's predication builds on Ben's mention of an actor:

(3)			[indoor basketball]
	1	Ben:	Big Fry.
	2		Trying t' get it in.
	3	Josh:	Shoots over Small Fry!

Likewise, in example 12, reference and predication are divided between two speakers. Josh starts to say something about Larry Bird but hesitates with a filled pause (drawing out the /r/ in "Bird," probably waiting to see what happens on the computer monitor), and Matt joins in to complete the proposition:

(12)   [computer basketball]
    1   Josh: And Larry Bir:::d
    2   Matt: He gets a two: pointer.

In example 13 the first speaker produces a reference and part of a predicate, and the second speaker completes the predicate. Ben is announcing what happens to "Bird"; when he hesitates, Josh offers a phrase that is propositionally appropriate (and syntactically acceptable, if not perfect)—"A serious injury"—and Ben accepts it by repeating it:

(13)   1   Ben: Bird falls down!
       2   Bird is having . . .
       3   Josh: A serious injury.
       4   Ben: A serious injury!

Notice too that in example 10 Matt's "for you people at home" is built onto Josh's utterance:

(10)   6   Josh: And it's an instant replay here
       7   [at Whatchamacallit [Stadium.
       8   Matt: [For you   [for you people at home.

Josh's "And it's an instant replay here" is potentially complete as is; that is, Matt's contribution comes initially at a transition relevance place. But the phrase that Matt adds, "for you people at home," shows alignment to Josh's concerns and, moreover, offers evidence of proper alignment to the (pretend) audience.

Besides such cases in which two boys construct a single proposition over just two turns, they may construct a series of propositions over several turns, as in example 14. All the names refer to characters whose parts are being played by Matt:

(14)   [indoor basketball]
    1   Josh: But, Parrish gets the rebound and sends it out t' . . .
    2   Matt: Johnson.
    3   Josh: Johnson passes it t' McHale,
    4   Matt: McHale t' Bird,
    5   Josh: McHale passes it [t' Bird,
    6   Matt: ['n Bird- Bird makes a bad shot.
    7   Josh: And Bird misses a shot.

When Josh (line 1) fails to say who the ball is (supposedly) being passed to, Matt (line 2) supplies the name ("Johnson," who is a teammate of "Parrish"). Josh accepts this suggestion and incorporates it into his announcement of the next action ("Johnson passes it t' McHale"). Matt in turn accepts that "McHale" is now involved and names him as the agent of the next action, "McHale t' Bird." Josh repeats this with a slight variation at line 5. Both boys then go on to say what happens next: Bird fails to score. Josh's way of expressing this at line 7 is a variation of Matt's at line 6, and again Josh's version adds no information; rather, it serves to ratify what Matt has said. The boys thus synchronize their talk both rhythmically and syntactically to jointly produce a series of announcements.

The boys not only finish, overlap, and repeat each other's sentences; they also repair them—a different type of joint proposition building. Examples 15 and 16 show

a second speaker repairing a first speaker's utterance, with the first accepting the repair, so that together they construct a coherent statement. In example 15 Matt accepts Josh's repair:

(15)   [playing computer basketball]
    1   Matt: And Larry Bird comes back,
    2   And Dr. J comes back with a few points.
    3   Josh: Two!
    4   Matt: Two of 'em, I should say.

Josh's repair (line 3) corrects Matt's announcement about the score (line 2): the
player in fact scored only "two" points, not "a few." (The correct score is visible on
the computer monitor.) By using the phrase "I should say" (line 4), Matt treats the
correction almost as a self-repair, incorporating it smoothly into his announcement.

In example 16 Josh is announcing the actions of various players, and Matt repairs
one of his statements:

(16)   [indoor basketball; Josh is "the Lakers"; Matt is "the Celtics"]
    1   Josh: Magic Johnson has the ball.
    2   Magic Johnson misses.
    3   Now Dennis Johnson has the ball.
    4   Dennis Johnson shoots.
    5   Dennis Johnson misses.
    6   But Larry Bird gets the rebound.=
    7   Matt: →   =Parrish.
    8   Josh: Parrish gets the rebound.

After a miss by "Dennis Johnson" (played by Matt), Josh says that "Larry Bird" (also
played by Matt) gets the ball (line 6). Matt, however, suggests that this action be attributed to "Parrish." There is no basis in actuality for this correction, since Matt is
playing both parts, but Josh agrees and corrects his utterance to "Parrish gets the rebound." This repair does not make the announcement factually or externally true,
but it makes it accord with Matt's idea of which player is doing what.

Examples 15 and 16 show that other-repair is not a dispreferred action in the
boys' sportscasting, as it is in much of adult conversation (Pomerantz 1984; Schegloff, Jefferson, & Sacks 1977). Rather, it is readily accepted and is incorporated
smoothly into the reporting, so that the activity can proceed without a break for
argument. A preference for other-repair has been identified in children's talk (e.g.,
Adger 1986; Goodwin 1990a, chapter 1, this volume; Maynard 1985a) and a preference for argument as a form of "sociability" among some adults (Schiffrin 1984).
But whereas some conversationalists (including many children) may engage in
other-repair and argument for the sake of sociability, other-repair in the present
data serves a practical function: a more mitigated form of repair would require
breaking into the sportscasting activity. If repair is called for, the way Matt and
Josh do it in examples 15 and 16 is the efficient, reasonable way to accomplish it.

Displaying Continued Orientation   A third manifestation of the boys' alignment as
joint announcers is their continued display of orientation toward the activity even
in the face of threatened disruption. One source of disruption is the failure of one

participant to contribute: a sportscasting episode tends to die down after about five minutes of solo announcing. The boys, however, guard against premature termination. One speaker may carry most of the announcing burden as long as the quieter participant makes an occasional contribution, as illustrated in the following (an expansion of example 10):

```
(17)                    [computer basketball; Josh is "Doctor J," Matt is "Larry Bird"]
      1   Josh:    And Doctor J runs in,
      2            and he sco::res.
      3            Thirty-seven t' thirty-three here at Whatchamacallit Stadiu:m.
      4            Larry Bird for a three pointer!
      5            He misses!
      6            Bu::t . . . and . . . Doctor J gets it.
      7   Matt:    But Larry Bird is in: very good position.
      8   Josh:    But Doctor J comes i:n,
      9            he shoots and he sco::res.
     10            Thirty-nine t' thirty-three here at Whatchamacallit Stadiu::m.
     11            [4.0]
     12            Larry Bird for three points.
     13            Misses bu::t . . .
     14            He jumps and gets the rebound back on the floor!
     15            And he sco:res.
     16   Matt:    Instant replay.=
     17   Josh:    =And it's an instant replay here
     18            [at Whatchamacallit [Stadium.
     19   Matt:    [For you          [for you people(h) at home.
```

In this segment Josh is doing most of the announcing, but Matt chimes in with appropriate lines. First, he announces that a player is in "very good position" (line 7); in referring to himself in the third person (as "Larry Bird"), he addresses the audience and thus identifies with the sportscaster role. Second, he announces an "Instant replay" (line 16), a contribution immediately ratified by his playmate that leads to the co-constructed lines (17–19). Matt's contributions, though few during this stretch, are not negligible interactionally.

In example 18, too, Josh has been the main announcer for several minutes, with only scattered contributions from Matt, as in line 3:

```
(18)  1   Josh:          And Dr. J comes in for a layup
      2                  and it's forty-seven t' forty in Whatchamacallit Stadium in Dr. J's
                         favo:r.
      3   Matt:   →      And I don't know if this announcer . . . this- he's getting hoarse.
      4   Josh:          A:nd . . . Larry Bird makes a layup, forty-seven t' forty-two in
                         Whatchamacallit Stadiu:m.
```

Here Matt contributes a comment that is not, strictly speaking, the sort expected from the sportscaster: rather than report an action by a player, he says that the announcer is "getting hoarse" (in fact on tape a change in Josh's voice quality is evident). But in offering this comment, Matt ratifies Josh's identity as sportscaster by referring to him in the third person and thus ostensibly addressing the audience. As in example 17, then, it is a manifestation of the boys' alignment toward each other that even a quieter participant contributes to keeping the activity going as a joint production.

Another likely source of disruption is the boys' need to deal with literal concerns such as the rules of the game, the score, or injury. When such matters come up, the participants sometimes step out of the sportscaster role and speak as themselves. In example 19, Ben and Josh shift out of the sportscaster role during a dispute:

```
(19)                        [indoor basketball; Ben is "Doctor J," Josh is "Larry Bird"]
      1    Ben:             Two shots for Doctor.
      2                     Doctor puts up one and it's oh:::
      3                     bounces off the rim all the way t' (    )
      4                     The Doctor sets up another one.
      5    Josh:    →       Ben you can't slam it off the wall.
      6    Ben:     →       I wasn't trying to, I was trying t' make it go up.
      7    Josh:    →       Yeah I know but you still [can't
      8    Ben:                                       [And the Doctor. . . . still has not taken
                   his shot.
```

Ben has been announcing the action when Josh interrupts to voice a protest (line 5), addressing Ben by name and with the second-person pronoun. Ben defends himself in the first person (line 6), and Josh repeats his protest using "I" and "you" (line 7). The dispute ends when Ben does not pursue it but resumes announcing, marking his return with a shift back to the third person (line 8). In this example, then, the boys step out of the sportscaster role to handle a conflict.

But often when disputes or other outside concerns arise, the boys do *not* step out of role. Instead, they avoid derailment by treating untoward occurrences as if they were official, reportable actions: they continue to address the audience and report what is happening. In averting interruption to the sportscasting, they display their alignment toward each other's imaginary selves and toward the ongoing activity, as in examples 20 and 21:

```
(20)                        [indoor basketball; Ben is "Big Fry"; Josh is "Small Fry"]
      1    Ben:             Small Fry is down!
      2                     He gets back up with the ball!
      3                     And he misse::s!
      4                     Big Fry moves back.
      5                     Big Fry comes around.
      6    Josh:    →       It's traveling but there isn't any call.
      7    Ben:     →       The officials didn't see it.

(21)                        [indoor basketball; Josh is "Magic," "Worthy," and "Kareem"; Matt
                            is "the Celtics"]
      1    Josh:            But Magic Johnson gets the rebound.
      2                     [2.5]
      3                     Magic, in t' Worthy!
      4                     [3.0]
      5             →       There's a lot of pushing going around
      6             →       but the refs do not see it.
      7    Matt:    →       hhh The ref has a gnat up his nose.
```

8   Josh: →   Y(h)eah. The ref has a gnat up his n- Kareem!
9   Oh! And it's almost a tied ball game.

In example 20 Josh declines to complain directly about Ben's ("Big Fry's") violation ("traveling," or carrying the ball). Instead, he reports a foul by the official player, and Ben joins in with "The officials didn't see it." The question of whether Ben is guilty of a violation, then, is eclipsed by the boys' common task of announcing what his character "Big Fry" has done. In example 21, Matt (who does not have the ball) appears to be guilty of "pushing," but there is no accusation. Instead, the boys collaborate in incorporating the "pushing" into the sportscaster's announcements. They also account officially for the fact that this violation has been continuing for some time (during the silence at line 4): "the refs do not see it" because "The ref has a gnat up his nose." In both of these examples, by announcing the violations as official actions, the boys continue to align to each other's imaginary selves and deflect the need for lodging complaints against each other's real selves, complaints that would threaten the ongoing announcing. Once again, they ensure that the activity will keep going without interruption.

Interview Footings

So far we have seen that when jointly enacting the sportscaster role the boys not only produce register-appropriate forms and speech actions but at the same time vigorously display their alignment. The same is true when they enact interviews. The details are different, since interviews are quintessentially dialogic whereas sportscasting is monologic (albeit in their case jointly produced). Interview footings are nevertheless assembled out of the same sorts of resources as is the joint sportscasting: address terms, joint proposition building, and dramatic display of continuing orientation.

Using Address Terms   The most obvious alignment marker is the use of address terms. In interviews, the boys address each other (rather than refer to each other) for the benefit of an (imaginary) overhearing audience. To initiate the interview in example 4, for instance, Josh switches from referring to "Larry Bird" in the third person to addressing him by name:

(4) 3   Josh: and we'll have a halfti- a first quarter interview with Larry Bird.
     4   Well Larry how d' you feel about your performance.

The participants continue to address each other until, after directing a final remark to the interviewee (lines 16–17), Josh shifts back to addressing the audience:

(4) 16   Josh: Yeah you played great defense,
     17   but you didn't have very much offense.
     18   Now let's go back t' the game.
     19   Okay and Doctor J has it,
     20   drives by Larry Bird.
     21   And he scores.

Besides addressing each other as "you," the boys, as interview participants, call each other by name—but never by their real names. This helps to create and signal the imaginary participation framework by indicating both to each other and to the imagined audience who is talking to whom. In practically all of the interviews, the boy speaking as interviewer addresses his playmate as "Larry" or "Larry Bird" (perhaps more often than is usual in real interviews). In example 5 we have seen the interviewee address the interviewer as "Vince," and in example 7 as "Irv."[6] In example 22, which shows the beginning of an interview, Josh addresses "Larry Bird" by name at line 5; before that, however, he addresses the character of the interviewer (i.e., himself) as "Howard":

(22) 1 Josh: Bird has extended his lead to six points,
      2   and we're gonna have an interview with Larry Bird.
      3   Let's go down to Howard.
      4   Howard?
      5   Well hi, Larry Bird, how d' ya feel about your performance.
      6 Matt: Well if they didn't call that twenty-four second violation [answer continues]

In all these cases, address terms help create the alignment that is crucial to the imaginary participation framework. Not only do the participants—the imaginary characters—speak to each other, but the boys dramatize the case by having the characters call each other by name, and often.

Jointly Building Propositions   As we have seen, the children's interviews consist, appropriately, of questions and answers. Question-answer pairs may also be looked at as jointly constructed propositions, with the answerer supplying that part not given by the questioner. But an interviewer's turn need not consist of (or only of) a syntactic question in order to be treated as a pragmatic question. Just as in adult interviews (Clayman 1992, Greatbatch 1988, Heritage & Roth 1995), even when a strict question/answer format is departed from, the children nonetheless orient to that format. In doing so, they are orienting to the pretend situation, keeping it going in more than a mechanical way. For one thing, as Heritage & Roth (1995) point out, interviewers may embed assertions within questioning turns, as Ben does in example 5 and Matt does in example 23:

(5)   [Ben is interviewer]
      3 Ben: Now Larry, you have a one hundred and
      4   [3.5]
      5   you have *over* a one hundred point lead.
      6   How do you feel about that.
      7 Josh: Well y'know Vince, I-
      8   I just feel great about that,

(23)   [Matt is interviewer; interview is in progress]
      1 Josh: I was real tired cause I . . .
      2   worked real hard on those turnaround jumpers in the early goin',
      3   but I still managed t' come out with a seven point lead.

```
4   Matt:   Yeah you are very (active).
5           How d' ya feel about the ref is doin' today.
6   Josh:   Well he made one bad call,
7           but I- well a couple bad calls,
8           but . . . I . . . I think he's a good ref.
```

Ben opens in example 5 with a statement to "Larry" that he has "*over* a one hundred point lead" and then proceeds to ask his question, "How do you feel about that." Josh, as interviewee, does not start speaking until the question has been asked. In example 23, when Matt, as interviewer, takes his turn at lines 4–5, he first agrees with what the other has just said by issuing a statement, "Yeah you are very (active)," and only then goes on to ask a question, "How d' ya feel about the ref is doin' today." Again, the interviewee treats the interviewer's statement as a preliminary: Josh refrains from taking his turn until the question has been issued.

Even when an interviewer's turn does not include a syntactic interrogative, the interviewee treats it as a question and provides a reply. Examples 24 and 25 show interviewer turns that consist solely of comments about the player's performance:

```
(24)            [Matt is interviewer; interview is in progress]
      1   Matt:   If he only scored five points
      2           and you scored eleven,
      3           that's pretty good,
      4           but I saw you gettin' tired at the end,
      5           you couldn't jump real high.
      6   Josh:   hhh No I couldn't.
      7           I was real tired cause I . . .
      8           worked real hard on those turnaround jumpers in the early goin','
      9           but I still managed t' come out with a seven point lead.

(25)            [Josh is interviewer; part of (4)]
     11   Josh:   But at any rate,
     12           you certainly did not play very well that quarter though.
     13   Matt:   Well I had- I- my main game plan for that quarter was t' try t' keep . . . him
                  so he couldn't clear the ball,
     14           and it worked for a little bit,
     15           but I still didn't do that well in the uh long run.
```

The interviewers' utterances here are not interrogative in form, but they receive replies. In example 24 Matt's statements that the player has been "gettin' tired" and "couldn't jump real high" concern matters about which only the addressee has first-hand knowledge. They thus can be heard as requesting confirmation (Labov & Fanshel 1977), which the addressee provides: Josh, as "Larry," says, "No I couldn't. I was real tired. . . ." In example 25 the interviewer's remark that the player "certainly did not play very well that quarter though" also gets in response a confirmation ("I still didn't do that well in the uh long run"). In each case, the interviewee treats his interlocutor's utterance as if had been a *why* question and gives a reason for his poor showing: in example 24 Josh explains that he was tired because he "worked real hard on those turnaround jumpers in the early goin.'" In example 25 Matt explains his unsuccessful "main game plan for that quarter."

By treating one another's utterances as questions and answers, then, and thus jointly constructing propositions, the children align toward each other in their interview-specific roles. The actions of both participants are necessary and meaningful. When the interviewer embeds an interrogative within a longer turn, it is up to the interviewee to delay his answer until the question has been asked; when the interviewer issues a pragmatic question that is not interrogative in form, it is up to the interviewee to interpret it as a question.

Displaying Continued Orientation   I have said that the boys use *well* and *now* to index the adult register in which they conduct their interviews. But these discourse markers have another function, too: they pointedly display the boys' orientation to a participation framework different from that of the surrounding monologic discourse. As elements that indicate speakers' attention to interlocutors (Schiffrin 1987), these markers are resources that the children employ to create an imaginary situation in which characters' talk is central.

Well, as a signal of a speaker's "interactional presence in talk" (Schiffrin 1987:127), is an especially appropriate form for the interviews, for it dramatizes their dialogic nature. We have seen that the boys use *well* when speaking as interviewees to mark answers to questions. But they also exploit a broader function of this marker, that of displaying any sort of contribution as a response to whatever precedes it (Schiffrin 1987). Such usage is shown in example 26:

(26)			[Josh is sportscaster/interviewer; Matt is "Larry Bird"]
1	Josh:		LARRY BIRD WINS!
2			THIRTY-SIX THIRTY-THREE,
3			WHAT A SHOT BY LARRY BIRD!
4			Now let's go down t' Irv Cross for an interview.
5		→	Well Larry what d' you think about that.
6	Matt:	→	Well I had planned t' do that,
7			because today I've been shooting pretty good three pointers.
8			So I decided I'd call time,
9			be nice and fresh,
10			right off the bench,
11			and try t' get the lead in the last second.
12	Josh:	→	Well you certainly did that, Larry Bird.
13	Matt:	→	Well I'm *still* mad about a couple of those calls.
14			I wouldn't've had t' even even *think* about that- trying something like that,
15			if any of those calls were not called.
16	Josh:		Okay and there's another game going on right now.

Only one of the four tokens of *well* in this example (at line 6) prefaces an answer to a question. At lines 12 and 13 *well* marks two utterances in a row by different speakers. Both are displayed as responsive, though not to questions. Josh's comment as interviewer at line 12 responds to the preceding utterance, which is the interviewee's description of what he had been doing ("try[ing] t' get the lead in the last second"). Matt's ("Larry's") comment at lines 13–15, on the other hand, is responsive not specifically to the immediately preceding utterance but to a more global concern: he is responding to the interviewer's expressions of interest in his reactions to the entire game that he has just won.

At line 5 *well* prefaces the interviewer's first question, thus marking it as responsive to previous talk even though it is the beginning of the interview. The interviewer ("Irv Cross") has been invited to talk (line 4), and his doing so is in response to that invitation. Examples 4 and 22 are similar:

(4)   [Josh is sportscaster/interviewer]
   3   Josh: and we'll have a halfti- a first quarter interview with Larry Bird.
   4   → Well Larry how d' you feel about your performance.

(22)   [Josh is sportscaster/interviewer]
   3   Josh: Let's go down to Howard.
   4   Howard?
   5   → Well hi, Larry Bird, how d' ya feel about your performance.

In each case Josh helps to signal that a new character is talking by using *well*, an element that specifically identifies an utterance as responsive to an interlocutor.[7]

A boy acting as interviewer is also likely to preface his initial question with *now*, which "marks a speaker's progression through discourse time by displaying attention to an upcoming idea unit, orientation, and/or participation framework" (Schiffrin 1987:230):

(5) 2   Ben: And we just called Larry Bird over to talk to us.
      3   → Now Larry, you have a one hundred and
      4   [3.5]
      5   you have *over* a one hundred point lead.
      6   How do you feel about that.

(6) 1   Josh: That's the end of the quarter.
      2   And we're having an interview with Larry Bird right now.
      3   → Now are you pleased with your performance so far?

(7) 1   Matt: Okay now a pre-game interview with Larry Bird.
      2   → Now Larry what is your strategy for today's game.

By using *now* to mark a first question, a boy not only directs his playmate's attention toward the interview that is coming up and displays his own attention to it; he also dramatizes the shift in footing being enacted, in that *now* marks the entrance of a new speaker.

Using *now* and *well*, then, helps to create and dramatize the participation framework of the interviews. The interviewee who prefaces his answers with *well* emphasizes his interactional presence in contrast to his lack of an interactional role during the sportscaster's announcing. For the interviewer, using both *well* and *now* emphasizes his alignment to the interviewee (rather than just to the audience).

So, like the jointly constructed monologues of the spontaneous sportscasting, the interviews are constructed not only by using a recognizably appropriate register but also by using its features as the building blocks of footing. In both activities, the children attend to one another's pretend selves. Throughout their role play they rely centrally on three techniques: using address terms (which indicate which character is speaking and to whom), jointly constructing propositions (which requires and displays close attention to the playmate), and pointedly displaying an orientation toward the activity at hand.

Conclusion

It has long been recognized that acquiring register variation is integral to language development, for from a very young age children vary their speech for different addressees (e.g., Andersen 1990, Ervin-Tripp 1977, Garvey 1975, Mitchell-Kernan & Kernan 1977, Sachs & Devin 1976). I suggest that play itself gives children the incentive to learn, use, and perfect their skills in different registers—to put into practice the notion that propositions can and should be expressed in different ways in different situations. Children create these very situations simply by speaking as if they were in the midst of them.

Any activity requires participants to orient to one another, but the details of what, specifically, is necessary vary from one activity to another. I have looked here at a few children's construction of joint pretense, a very different sort of activity from, for instance, casual conversation, academic discourse, or competitive games. Their schemas of typical ways in which sportscasters, interviewers, and interviewees talk give them the linguistic resources to perform these different roles. Simultaneously, they create lively joint performances by manipulating interactional resources. They play with linguistic features as they take and ratify particular footings toward each other—as they strategically use address and reference terms, continuously co-construct a text, and continuously put on a show of commitment to the activity. Their pretense is structured by schemas, brought to life by mutual invocation of them, and sustained by constant attention to the details of alignment.

Children's talk in register is an interactional accomplishment and an interactional performance, sometimes exaggeratedly so. When they are playing roles, children do not just produce the forms, constructions, and actions that are appropriate for particular roles: they do those things, but they do them *together*, in synchrony. Roles are sustained not only by using their associated registers but also by taking an appropriate footing toward co-participants. When the roles are pretend ones, they are sustained through the participants' aligning to each other's pretend selves. Although the details of role enactment in the real, adult world are no doubt different, we can expect the same sort of interweaving of register knowledge and alignment display.

NOTES

Earlier versions of this chapter were presented at the presession on Language Practices of Older Children, Georgetown University Round Table on Languages and Linguistics, March 1993, and at the Developments in Discourse Analysis Conference, Georgetown University, February 1995. I thank audience members for their comments, and Carolyn Adger, Ed Finegan, Carolyn Kinney, Branca Ribeiro, and anonymous reviewers for comments on subsequent drafts.

1. In previous work I have discussed these children's competence in a specialized register (Hoyle 1991), their layering of participation frameworks (Hoyle 1993), and their use of discourse markers in the management of frame shifts (Hoyle 1994). Here I focus on the interactionally emergent nature of talk in register and the tight bond between linguistic form and interactional alignment.

2. "Big Fry" and "Small Fry" are names that Ben and Josh used for the duration of this particular afternoon, which they spent playing basketball in Josh's basement. As indicated by these names, Ben was a much bigger child than Josh.

3. In example 2 at line 12 the simple present appears in both a repairable and the following self-repair ("Ben Smith hits- gets it over"): even when Josh repairs his initial choice of lexical item, he has no need to repair its form.

4. *Now* at line 18 of example 4 functions as a temporal adverbial rather than a discourse marker (cf. Schiffrin 1987).

5. Compared to adult usage, the boys' use of *well* in responding to *wh*-questions in the interviews is tremendously high (Hoyle 1994; cf. Schiffrin 1987). The boys are thus dramatically displaying their talk as responsive.

6. He repairs his choice of name: "Irv" is the name of a real sports interviewer, while "Pat" does the play-by-play announcing.

7. The children do not adopt a different voice quality in order to speak as the interviewer (or interviewee). Besides semantic content, the discourse marker is the clearest signal of role shift.

3

Accommodating Friends

Niceness, Meanness, and Discourse Norms

ALICE GREENWOOD

Preschool children, with grand insouciance, are able to explicitly announce whom they are "friends" with and whom they "hate," as well as whom they want to play with and whom they don't. Such alliances and allegiances are often created on the spot, simply by virtue of the spoken declaration. For example, in saying, "We don't want to play with you," a group bands together, asserting a common goal of ousting the "other" to nongroup status. Or, in saying, "We're friends, right?" (Corsaro 1985), individual children seek to claim or reinforce their solidarity with one another. Thus, language itself can create an immediate sense of friendship.

Older children of school age are somewhat less explicit and more subtle about defining their group identity. Yet they are even more preoccupied than younger children with establishing friendships, aligning with their peers, and identifying their place in their complex social world. They still announce who their friends are, especially their "best friends," and identify, via label, the "creeps," "dweebs," and other undesirables they wouldn't be caught dead interacting with. But beyond such labeling it is not clear how older children verbally encode friendship—or enmity— or how they "play" together in conversation or employ language in creating and supporting these relationships.

In analyzing children's language use, one should not assume that the norms and values of the children are reflections, albeit immature and sometimes awkward ones, of an adult worldview or that child language involves nothing more than a steady progression toward mature language skills. Assuming that children are little adults in the making ignores the profound need of children, especially older ones, to de-velop and adhere to their own peer-group norms, which may have unique, distinct, and not particularly adult characteristics (Cicourel 1970, Fine 1981). More and more research on the verbal interaction of adults has pointed to the need to examine the specific context in which each communication situation occurs (e.g., Eckert & McConnell-Ginet 1992) and to be wary of generalizing from one communicative situation to another (e.g., Tannen 1993b). Children's talk, then, should not be extracted from social context, and particular care must be taken to ground its analysis in the children's own standards and values (Eder 1993, chapter 4, this volume; Thorne 1993). To this end, for instance, researchers who are reluctant to impose preset criteria on the social and linguistic practices of children can ask the young speakers what they themselves think is going on in their own interactions and let their replies direct attention to the values they place on particular pieces of social and linguistic behavior.

As an adult researcher of children's conversation, I discovered that my own children and their friends were only too happy to explain their social encounters to me. When my three children had what they called a dinner party during their preadolescent years, they always had something to say, afterward, about their various dinner guests. They used much the same language as they had when they were younger. One person was "really nice"; someone else "mean." Someone, they "could just tell," "didn't like" them; another they never wanted to see again because he was "*so* boring." Since the social interaction of the children and their guests had been almost exclusively verbal (dinner was generally eaten in three minutes, but the table talk lasted up to an hour), I surmised that the criteria they used to infer these interpersonal qualities must have been embedded in conversational behavior.

This chapter explores the conversational criteria that these older children used to make such social judgments and the correspondence that they drew between conversational behavior and social identity. I show how the children use properties of discourse to orient to each other and how they signal friendship or hostility by means of this orientation. In particular, I offer examples to show that successful, friendly conversation results when all the conversational participants endorse the particularized norms that arise during their encounter. On the other hand, unfriendly and unsuccessful conversation results when not all the members of the group accept the same norms. For these preadolescents, the crucial social concepts of meanness and niceness are defined and instantiated within conversation; their verbal exchanges serve to constitute their social relations.

Table Talk among Friends

During a period of two years, I audio-recorded Dara and her twin brother David, age thirteen at the time of the conversations analyzed here, their sister Stephanie, age eleven, and their dinner guests while they conversed at the dining table.[1] In each case, there were no adults present in the room with the children, and the recorder was out of sight on a countertop. In the three excerpts presented here, the family members are entertaining a male friend of David's. Thus, each conversational group consists of two female and two male preadolescents—three family members and one male nonfamily member—within the age range of eleven to fourteen.

Before these recordings were made, I had asked each of the children to answer some questions and found that they were able to explicitly articulate what they hoped to accomplish in various social situations.[2] I asked about their friends, whom they liked and why, and whom they liked visiting or eating dinner with and why. They all had clear and decided opinions about what a "good time" consisted of, and, remarkably, all the children stated exactly the same goal for their dinner interactions: to "have fun" with their friends, where fun was defined as laughing, joking, and feeling as if they were "liked." The goal for the social situation thus established, the children were easily able to evaluate its success.

Adam

In example 1, Dara, David, and Stephanie are having dinner with David's friend Adam, age twelve, whom they have known all their lives. The interaction takes place after the children have been at the table for about fifteen minutes. Just prior to this exchange Dara and Stephanie have been singing a song that they have made up about potatoes. With no preamble, David introduces the new topic of "Betty."

(1) 1   David: ((his mouth full of potatoes, and in a barely audible voice)) Betty.
     2   Dara: What?
     3   David: ((more clearly)) Betty.
     4   Dara: Okay. Watch this, Adam.
     5   Stephanie is pretending to be our piano teacher, named Betty
              Rosenblum. I'm pretending not to know her last name.
     6   David: ((aside to Stephanie)) Did you call her up?
     7   Steph: ((to David)) Yup.
     8   David: ((in a funny voice, as if pinching his nose) Did you say, are you Betty?
     9   Dara: Okay, Adam. Watch . . .
    10   Watch.
    11   David: Look, Adam. Watch.
    12   Steph: Waaaatch!
    13   Dara: ((in funny voice)) Excuse me, miss. Are you Betty?
    14   Steph: ((in falsetto)) Yeeees.
    15   Dara: ((in same funny voice)) Betty, who.
    16   Steph: ((very rapidly)) Bettybitabitofbitterbutter...
    17   Dara: ((laughing)) Her lips are moving faster than the words are coming out.
    18   ((All the children laugh.))

Here, Dara, David, and Stephanie are united in their desire to share their joke with Adam, a parallel, I think, of engaging in a group game. Like offering a favorite toy or initiating some make-believe, the family's attempt to draw Adam into their world is an overture of friendship, one that involves verbal play. Their "Betty" routine is a frequently enacted, stylized speech event with specific parts, characters, and set phrases. It has a beginning ("pretending"), a punchline (the tongue twister), and a goal (laughter). Part of the funniness comes from the special voices that all three adopt as part of their characters. It is the voices that mark the "play" aspect of the talk; they signal that the children are not being themselves but are dressing in a verbal costume. The cast always remains the same: Stephanie plays Betty, and Dara or David inquires as to who she is. The family thinks the tongue-twister conclusion, coupled with the coincidence of their knowing a real Betty, is hilarious; as many times as they perform the joke they are amused. Thus, they function as audience as well as performers. Adam, as audience, has a responsibility to react, and his reaction becomes an indication of his involvement in their game.

The children do not offer Adam any verbal enticement on the order of, "Did you hear the one about . . . ?" or even cue him as to what is going on with something like, "This is so funny." Instead, they attempt to provoke his interest by repeatedly insisting that he "watch" (lines 4, 9, 10, 11, 12). Since there is nothing especially visual about this routine, no body language or funny faces, the demand to be "watched" is a demand for active attention and a way of signaling that a performance is coming. Although Adam does not say a word throughout this exchange, he is clearly the focus of the group's conversation; all the talk is directed toward him. In a nonverbal way, he controls the topic (Sattel 1983). As long as he is not attending to them, the family members are invested in engaging him. When he "watches," that is, becomes an active although silent participant, they are free to continue with their lines. Adam's role here is by no means passive. The hearer of a narrative or joke is jointly responsible with the teller(s) for making a performance successful; she or he must behave appropriately and appreciatively, exhibiting what Goffman (1974:504) calls a "receptive stance." Here, Adam laughs with the performers at the end, and the joke succeeds.

The family members make use of a very elliptical "in-group" style (Tajfel 1978); when David initially says the word "Betty," Dara and Stephanie know exactly what he is talking about and what he is inviting them to do. Such a nonelaborated family style is typical of speakers of shared background and frequent interaction (Bernstein 1972), and its use preserves the in-group nature of a particular speech community (Milroy 1980). In performing the Betty routine, David, Dara, and Stephanie are inviting Adam to join their group; by endorsing their speech activity, simply by laughing with them, Adam aligns himself with them and becomes a participating member of the group (cf. Eckert 1993). Adolescent peer relations are often marked by exaggerated communal behavior (Fine 1981), whereby conforming to group behavior indicates allegiance, and small deviations from group practices are unacceptable. Through his response, Adam joins in the "collective identity" (Corsaro 1985:65) of the children's peer culture.

In these terms, then, a communicative event can be said to be interactionally successful if all the participants embrace the peer group's norms. Each member of the group needs to accept not only the local norms for *interpreting* specific discourse events—in this case, the joke—but also, and perhaps more important, the norms for *displaying appropriate discourse behavior*, in this case, laughter. Joining the group is enacted through discourse, by appropriating the group's norms for both interpretation and behavior. Adam's willingness to participate as audience to the family's performance indicates not just an understanding but a willing acceptance of the group agenda (Gumperz 1982); he cooperates with their goal and in so doing enhances the solidarity of the group and his connection to it. In addition, by laughing and thereby acknowledging a shared sense of what is humorous, Adam protects the positive face needs (Brown & Levinson 1987) of the group, that is, their desire to be liked and admired. To this group of children, the sharing of discourse norms and discourse behavior defines "friendly." When interviewed later, they all said they had had a wonderful time together; they were "good friends" and knew how to "have fun together" because they found the same things funny. In other words, and with an echo of the playground, they liked being together because they knew how to play together well.

Max

The Betty routine was repeated several days later when another friend of David's, Max, age fourteen, joined the family for dinner.[3] The children's relationship with Max is quite different from their relationship with Adam. Max has only been to their home a few times; he is David's school friend. He is also older than David and Dara and much larger in size. He is an only child of actors and has been performing on stage for most of his life; compared to their other friends, his speech style is unusually self-possessed and confident. Example 2 occurs after the children have been eating for about five minutes. Their exchanges have not been successful; they seem to be having trouble agreeing on a topic for friendly discussion. The long extract of conversation presented here reveals how these children are unable to successfully collaborate with each other.

They have been talking about current events, and Max has been bragging that his family is "best friends" with actress Olympia Dukakis. Dara, changing the topic, uses her "Betty" voice and addresses Stephanie:

(2) 1   Dara: ((in her Betty voice)) Betty what.
    2   Steph: ((in her Betty voice)) Betty Bup.
    3   ((giggles.))
    4   Dara: I hear Mrs. Rosenblum.
    5   Max: Sooooo?
    6   Dara: Are you Betty?
    7   Max: Do you know what, uh, whatever his name is, Dukakis's is?
    8   Dara: But that's not half as important as who=
    9   Max: =Katie
    10 Dara: That's not half as important as uh who dropped out of=
    11 Max: =I know that too.
    12 Dara: So why did you say "more importantly."
    13 Max: Because it is more important.
    14 Steph: To Dukakis maybe.
    15 Max: I told you, they dropped out of the race. Who cares about them anymore.
    16 Dara: It's important to know who was in it.
    17 Steph: It's more important to Dukakis who's who=
    18 Max: =What? You're afraid I'm gonna vote for someone who dropped out or something.
    19 Dara: ((screechy)) Nooo. I don't vote. I'm sorry. I'm not eighteen yet but=
    20 Max: =You look it.
    21 Dara: Ah. Thank you. That is the highest compliment. I look more like it than=
    22 Max: =Yeah, actually.
    23 Steph: There's a nice relation going between six and eighteen.
    24 Dara: ((funny voice)) Yes. Six times three. Ya know and uh, uh- . . .
    25 Dara: Stephanie, do it.

26	Max:	It used to be fun here. You guys didn't beat up on me.
27	Dara:	Stephanie, come on. Before he gets mad at us.
28	David:	*((in a special voice of another routine))* Come on. Don't be such a stupid idiot.
29	Dara:	Listen to this. Max, listen.
30	Dara:	*((in Betty voice))* Stephanie, are you Betty?
31	Steph:	I am not Betty.
32	Dara:	Stephanie. Do it!
33	David:	No. Come on. Do it, Steph.
34	Steph:	You say to me "Stephanie, are you Betty?"
35	Dara:	*((in Betty voice))* Ste- No. Are you Betty?
36	Steph:	*((in Betty voice))* No.
37	Dara:	Stephanie, do it.
38	Steph:	No.
39	Dara:	Come on.
40	Steph:	No.
41	Dara:	*((whining))* Stephanie.
42	David:	It's so funny, Steph.
43	Dara:	It's sooo funny. Listen.
44	Steph:	All right. All right.
45	Dara:	All right.
46		Watch this.
47	Max:	Is it as funny as a . . .
48		*((David laughs.))*
49.	Dara:	Our piano teacher is named Betty Rosenblum. She's an idiot. She's prim and proper. So I go *((in Betty voice))*, Excuse me, are you Betty?
50	Steph:	*((in a voice from yet another routine))* Yes.
51	Dara:	Stephanie, don't talk like Clu.
52	Steph:	Oh, yes.
53	Dara:	*((in Betty voice))* Betty who.
54	Steph:	*((in Betty voice))*: Bettybitabitofbitterbutterbut . .
55		*((David, Dara, and Stephanie laugh.))*
56	Max:	Whaaaat?
57		*((David, Dara, and Stephanie laugh.))*
58	Dara:	I said, Betty who, like you say Betty Cohen. Then she says, Betty-bitabitofbitter.
59	David:	*((aside))* Did anyone eat from this yet?
60	Max:	*((aside))* No. Actually, what I was going to say was can I try that soup? It looks quite good.
61	Dara:	Listen, listen, listen, listen.
62	Max:	Say it in slow motion, okay?
63	Steph:	Betty bought a bit of bitter butter and she said this butter's bitter. If I put it in my batter, it will make my batter bitter. So Betty bought a bit of better butter to=
64	Dara:	=You never heard that before?
65	Max:	No. Never.
66	Dara:	Max, seriously?
67	Max:	Seriously.
68	Dara:	It's like the famous to=
69	Steph:	=tongue twister.

70	Max:	No. The famous tongue twister is: Peterpiperpicked=
71	Dara:	=Same thing. It's like that. It's like that one.
72	Max:	You keep interrupting me.
73	Dara:	It's like saying . . . It's like saying, Peter Who. Peter piper picked . . . It's like her last name.
74	Max:	It doesn't make any sense at all.
75	Dara:	It's funny.
76	Max:	What is Peter. Who is anything.
77		((David and Steph laugh.))
78	Dara:	Listen to this. We'll do it in slow motion. Come on. Watch.
79		((David laughs.))
80	Dara:	David, shut up!
81		((David laughs.))
82	Max:	Stephanie who.
83	Dara:	Stephanie, just Stephanie.
84		((Dara, David, and Stephanie laugh.))
85	Dara:	Stephanie is pretending to be our piano teacher, Betty Rosenblum and I'm pretending to be someone who doesn't know her last name. So I say ((in Betty voice)): Excuse me. Are you Betty?
86	Steph:	Yes.
87	Dara:	((in Betty voice)) Betty who.
88	Max:	But if you don't know who she is, how are you asking her name.
89	Steph:	Maybe I have a nameplate on me that says "Betty."
90	Max:	Okay.
91	Dara:	Okay. Watch. ((in Betty voice)) Excuse me. Are you Betty?
92	Steph:	((in Betty voice)) Yees.
93	Dara:	((in Betty voice)) Betty who.
94	Steph:	It's no fun in slow motion.
95	David:	It's not good in slow motion.
96	Dara:	Okay. Are you Betty?
97	Steph:	Yes.
98	Dara:	Betty who.
99	Steph:	Bettyboughtabitofbitterbutterbut=
100		((Dara laughs.))
101	David:	((laughing)) I love it.
102	Dara:	((in Betty voice)) I thought you were Betty Rosenblum.
103	Steph:	No. That's my sister.
104		((pause))
105	Dara:	Do you get it?
106	Max:	((fake loud laughter)) Ha! Ha! Ha! Ha! Ha!
108		((Steph laughs.))
109	David:	Max, you don't seem to be enjoying=
110	Max:	=Oh, it's real fun.

This interaction is unsuccessful in several ways: the participants fail to establish a common topic as Max repeatedly interrupts the girls, the "Betty" routine fails to engage Max, and the children display hostility to each other. Dara and the other family members have trouble introducing the "Betty" routine, partly because Stephanie seems reluctant to pursue it without Max's cooperation. Max turns his verbal back on their attempted performance by first saying "Sooooo" (line 5) with a marked lack of curiosity and then ignoring the repeated mention of "Betty" (lines 1, 2, 6) to return to the previous discussion of the Dukakis family (line 7). Dara and Stephanie are unable to hold the floor because of Max's frequent interruptions and his attempts to control the conversational topic.

In the first few moments, Max interrupts Dara four times (lines 9, 11, 20, 22) and Stephanie once (line 18). Max exclaims that the girls are "afraid" that he will vote for a noncandidate (line 18), but they have not, in fact, been talking about Max at all, and his remark appears to be gratuitously contentious. Dara then says she is not old enough to vote, and again Max interrupts with a snide "You look it" (line 20), to which Dara responds sarcastically that she is highly complimented. Thus, interruptions, conflict around topic control, and a sarcastic, mocking tone reflect conversational trouble.

The children explicitly acknowledge that this exchange is not friendly. Dara asks Stephanie to perform the routine "before he gets mad at us" (line 27). Her phrasing identifies "us" as a group, with "he," Max, outside it. Although Max has not overtly expressed anger or raised his voice, Dara senses that he is "mad" because his discourse behavior is unfriendly. By changing the subject away from "Betty" and by vying for floor control through frequent interruptions, Max, she intimates, is refusing to join their group; on the contrary, his discourse stance distinguishes himself from them. Max, for his part, also makes overt reference to the tension. He says, "It used to be fun here. You guys didn't beat up on me" (line 26). His use of "you guys" again underlines the family as the group, with him as the outsider. He feels "beat up on," as if the others have been antagonistic and hostile toward him. Since the interaction has been completely verbal, he, like Dara, must interpret hostility as stemming from the discourse trouble. Although all the participants in the conversation are aware of tension, none is willing, or perhaps skillful enough, to accommodate the other(s) conversationally. The result of this lack of accommodation is a sense of conflict and unfriendliness.

Dara's solution to the conversational tension is to try to enlist Max in the family joke: "Listen to this. Max, listen" (line 29). According to Dara (as she explicitly stated in several interviews), if everyone is laughing together, they are all friends and are having a good time. Dara wants to dissipate the tension between her and Max ("before he gets mad at us") and wants Max to laugh with them. So she pursues the Betty routine ever more aggressively. Her request that Max "listen" (line 29) is echoed by David (line 33), who joins her in trying to enlist the reluctant Stephanie to "do" her routine because it is "so funny" (lines 42–43).

Although repeatedly asked to do so, Max resists participating; he does not want to "watch this" (line 46). The family members proceed with the Betty routine, overriding Max's attempt to once again control the topic. At its conclusion they laugh (line 55). But Max, unlike Adam in example 1, does not play his part. He does not join in their laughter; rather, he keeps himself aloof and separate. After the tongue-twister punchline and the group laughter, Max, who has been silent, says, "Whaaat?" (line 56). Dara, determined to proceed with her agenda to get Max engaged and amused, tries again, demanding of Max that he "listen listen listen listen" (line 61). Max asks them to "say it in slow motion" (line 62), which would take the fun away. When Dara and Stephanie explain that it is a "famous tongue twister" (lines 68–69),

Max takes the reins and once again attempts to reroute the talk so that he is in control (line 70). When Dara interrupts him to draw him back to the original joke (line 71), Max protests that she "keeps interrupting" him (line 72).

It is curious that Max feels as if he has been repeatedly interrupted when this is the first time that his turn at talk has been prematurely intruded on.[4] Until this point all the interrupting has been done by him. Bennett's (1981) observation about interruption and conversational rights illuminates Max's accusation. When a speaker protests about being interrupted, the speaker is explicitly claiming that her or his conversational rights have been neglected or violated. Interruption, as Max uses it in this context, may have more to do with floor control than with turntaking violations (West & Zimmerman 1983), because he has not been allowed to pursue his own topic or control the conversation. Here Max interprets the others' refusal to allow him to control the floor as a form of rudeness, as if he has not been taken good care of conversationally.

The interaction proceeds with Max's claim that he doesn't understand what is required of him because "it doesn't make any sense" (line 74). But since it has been explicitly stated that it is "so funny" and "pretend," his lack of response seems disingenuous, underlining his unwillingness to participate in the verbal game. Finally, after the girls do the routine for him yet another time and he still doesn't react, Dara questions, "Do you get it?" (line 105). Max's fake laugh, "Ha! Ha! Ha! Ha! Ha!" (line 106), indicates that he knows quite well what is required of him here. His disdain for their joke is insulting. For Dara (who states that she knows who her friends are because they laugh together at the same things and share a sense of fun), Max's behavior is, by definition, unfriendly. He is communicating that he doesn't "like" her, or, since the siblings constitute a group, any of them. As David points out at the conclusion of this exchange, Max does not "seem to be enjoying" himself (line 109).

After Max left, Dara talked about how awful she felt about him, saying that she hated him and that he was "mean" and "a boring pig." These very strong feelings were engendered by the children's lack of success in managing this conversation, rather than from any preexisting antipathy. The children interpreted their conversational misalliance as conflict and hostility. But I do not believe hostility was the communicative intent of either Dara or Max. They were unable to adjust their discourse styles so as to form a group (Eckert 1993), and consequently they did not feel that they had been friendly toward each other.

Discourse Accommodation

It is generally accepted that successful communication depends on the shared interpretation of conversational norms, what psychologists call "interpretive competency" (Clark & Shaefer 1987, Krauss & Fussell 1988). But example 2 shows that there must be more than shared interpretations among speakers for communication to be successful, at least for this group of school-age speakers. Discourse norms and behaviors need to be both understood and positively *accepted* for communication to be successful, for "conversational cooperation" (Gumperz 1982:17) to occur. Max has interpreted the requirements of the discourse event correctly: Dara is trying to amuse him. The failure of this exchange occurs precisely because Max understands the requirements of the discourse event, as signaled by his fake laughter (line 107), but he rejects them. In not playing the family's game, he separates himself from their group. As Sheldon (1993:86) points out about preschool children's conflicts, "successful resolution requires the participants to adapt to each other." The requirement is the same for these older children. Of course, it is not only Max who failed to accommodate; Dara, too, was unable or unwilling to modify her conversational position in a way that would accommodate Max. Because neither Dara nor Max adapted to the other's style of discourse, they did not resolve their conflict. Max was never invited to dinner again. In effect, the potential for friendship evaporated because the children couldn't play together well.

The children's interaction is illuminated by notions of peer group solidarity and accommodation. Adherence to group norms signals loyalty to children's peer culture, an insight that first arose from studies of phonological variation (Cheshire 1982, Labov 1972b, Milroy 1980) but, as demonstrated here, applies equally to discourse behavior. Communication accommodation theory (CAT) offers a social psychological interpretation of how language behaviors forge alliances among interactants (Giles, Coupland, & Coupland 1991). Early studies of accommodation (e.g., Giles & Smith 1979; Thakerar, Giles, & Cheshire 1982) showed that interactants who desire to ally with one another or to signal in-group identity converge on each other's style of talk—for instance, using the same phonetic variants, syntactic constructions, or specialized vocabulary—and that, conversely, styles may diverge to signal distance. Convergence to the group style identifies a speaker's desire for social integration and identification with the group. It also serves as an expression of a desire for the social approval of the group. Divergence marks the speaker's desire to distinguish herself or himself from the others, to accentuate the difference, and to mark a lack of desire for approval. Divergence may be seen as "insulting, impolite, or downright hostile" (Deprez & Persoons 1984, quoted in Giles et al. 1991:28). The CAT extension of this theory recognizes that discourse-level choices and behavior may also signal convergence or divergence. The conversations considered here, besides offering supporting evidence for this theory, demonstrate that discourse accommodation can involve endorsing shared criteria for fun and funniness. Adam adhered to the group's norms for the role of audience in a family joke, and he accommodated to the group by laughing at their joke. Max, on the other hand, linguistically enacted a lack of friendship (what Dara calls "meanness") by flatly rejecting—in fact, mocking—the discourse norms of the group. He increased the distance between himself and the family (i.e., he diverged) by refusing to participate in their routine and separating himself from their fun.

I do not suggest that being competitive is "mean" or that being passive is "nice" in all cases for all speakers. The discourse norms for each conversation must be interpreted within the particular social dynamics of the context. But once local norms are established, there must be an active accommodation to those norms if friendly conversation is to ensue. There is no reason to assume that Max desired to be perceived as angry or mean or boring; it is just as likely that he failed to realize the social import of his lack of accommodation to the group's norms. It is certainly possible, for example, that in many of Max's conversational groups, or within his family style, competition for the floor and frequent interruptions signal active participation and friendship (Tannen 1982a), perhaps with mockery seen as a form of acceptable teasing. In the case examined here, however, such strategies were unshared and unsuccessful in promoting rapport, and the conversation was considered unfriendly by all. Indeed, it may well be the participants' unfamiliarity with each other's discourse habits that caused the social failure. It is even possible that Max was displaying a form of male "otherness," stressing his difference from Dara as a form of gender play (Thorne 1993); Dara, however, did not respond to his opposition as flirtatiousness. The point is not that these children equate a particular bit of discourse behavior with a specific social interpretation. Competition for the floor or interruption is not automatically a sign of hostility.[5] Rather, lack of mutual agreement on local norms for discourse behavior (whatever they are) results in lack of verbal encoding of friendship.

Jihad

Example 3 shows how it is the acceptance of the group's norms as they evolve within the conversation, rather than any particular preexisting, external norm, that is interpreted as friendly conversational behavior. This conversation occurred when the dinner guest was Jihad, age fourteen, David's friend for the previous six years and frequent family visitor. This excerpt shows that competition for the floor and interruption, the discourse behaviors that isolated Max from the family group, are not always defined as unfriendly.

(3) 1   Steph: We were talking about recycling paper because we have this thing in our school about recycling paper.
    2   Dara: Ah!
    3   Steph: And=
    4   Jihad: =So does my mom.
    5   David: Really? Really?
    6   Jihad: Um hum.
    7   Dara: Oh, recycling. We put all our cans in one garbage and off of our boxes.
    8   Jihad: You do?
    9   Dara: You have to put all your tin or aluminum in one garbage can.
   10   Steph: You know what? You know what?
   11   Jihad: We throw it down the table and whatever can it goes to.
   12   Dara: Where do you sit.=
   13   Steph: =Listen!
   14   Jihad: At a long table at the end, so I just slide it down.
   15   Dara: It's at the door, right at the door. There's two yellow garbage cans.
   16   Jihad: But I don't do that.
   17   Dara: Oh, well, usually people don't have cans. . . . Why was it so full of soda the other day. Were they selling soda? The whole thing was full of lots and lots of soda.
   18   Jihad: Maybe it's from a few weeks.
   19   Dara: Maybe it's from the teachers.

20   Steph: Well, anyway, so he was telling us what we could put in it and what we
             couldn't and he said we could put tissues ((*and she tells a long story*))

Group alliances form and reform continuously within dynamic social occurrences like these children's conversations. This flexibility requires that the members of the conversational group carefully monitor what is going on. In example 3, unlike examples 1 and 2, it is not the three family members who form the group that establishes the norms for appropriate discourse behavior. Instead, here the three older children form the in-group, and Stephanie, who is younger, becomes the outsider. As in the previous two examples, the "other" is expected to accept the group's conversational norms in order to be defined as nice and friendly. Stephanie is the other here, the little sister.

Stephanie attempts to get the floor in order to tell her story, but Dara, David, and Jihad jointly manage to keep her from speaking. Stephanie introduces her topic, recycling (line 1); then, having gotten an acknowledgment from Dara ("ah!"), she attempts to develop it. When Stephanie and Jihad speak almost simultaneously, David responds to Jihad, with the result that Stephanie does not complete her incipient contribution:

3   Steph: And=
4   Jihad: =So does my mom.
5   David: Really? Really?

Dara joins the conversation, addressing her comments to Jihad. Stephanie tries to reclaim the floor after Jihad and Dara interact (lines 7–9), asking: "You know what? You know what?" (line 10), but she is completely ignored. Then she and Dara speak almost simultaneously:

12   Dara: Where do you sit.=
13   Steph: =Listen!
14   Jihad: At a long table at the end, so I just slide it down.

Jihad answers Dara's question while Stephanie's plea for them to "Listen!" goes unheeded. In this subtle way, by taking control of the floor and passing it back and forth to each other over Stephanie's head, as it were, the in-group is established. Each of the older children validates the others' control of the floor, refusing to be interrupted by Stephanie.

Dara and Jihad continue discussing the topic together, and it is not until they finish (line 20) that Stephanie is able to recapture the floor and their attention. Her "Well, anyway" is a continuation of her earlier attempt to talk. Dara does not seem to find Jihad's control of her sister's conversational space particularly troublesome; he is, after all, taking good conversational care of her, being very responsive and engaged. Previously Dara had reported that Jihad is very "cute," so an element of flirting may be a part of their joint topic development. If so, it further supports the notion that the sharing of conversational behavior is what is interpreted as friendly, as a way of being together.

Here Stephanie's conversational needs are being neglected, but, unlike Max, she does not protest the others' lack of attention to her by highlighting their frequent interruptions. In fact, she accommodates to their controlling the topic, waiting until they give her (back) her turn. When I interviewed her later, Stephanie revealed no bad feelings about this interaction; on the contrary, she said they all had had a good time and were good friends.

It is impossible to know whether the reason Stephanie does not overtly protest being ignored is idiosyncratic to her personality, a sign of feeling inadequate as the younger sister in this group, or a result of immature conversational skills. It might even be a sign of mature conversational skill that she is able to wait for their attention. But what is evident in this example is that the social interaction is considered successful, indeed friendly, by all the participants: there has been no hostility over rights to the floor, and there has been an accommodation by all the members of the group to the in-group's norms. Stephanie relinquishes her right to hold the floor when she realizes that she is not going to get it; her accommodation seems to ally her with the group. No matter whether it is unwillingness or inability to strongly contest the control of the floor, the fact that she does not do so makes her much more socially attractive to the others than Max, who aggressively pursued his agenda and ignored the norms of the larger group. Stephanie, like Adam and unlike Max, is "nice" because her discourse behavior shows group loyalty.

Conclusion

For these older children, social concepts such as meanness or niceness are not only evidenced but are actually defined through discourse; verbal exchanges are used to constitute social relations, especially peer-group loyalty. Within each encounter, an in-group—the inner core sharing local norms—establishes acceptable conversational norms for the entire group. Those who want to be identified with the group have to accede to those norms. Adam did so, if somewhat passively; he indicated that he wanted to be with the family, to be their friend. Max actively, explicitly, and repeatedly refused to accept the group's norms. He was perceived as unfriendly and not nice; his divergence certainly appeared to Dara as "downright hostile." Finally, Stephanie allowed the group to align together and ignore her, and her acceptance of their behavior allowed her to remain within the group.

It is possible that it is immature social skill evidenced in these conversations, a kind of midway development point between young children's insistence on playing exactly the way they want and an adult tolerance of styles different from one's own. More simply, these children may be unaware of the needs of the other speakers or unskilled at accommodating them. For instance, Dara may be insisting on a kind of family friendship style of shared alliances, whereas Max may want to call attention to his otherness for social reasons. I suspect that as older children become young adults they learn to tolerate conversational styles that differ from their own and interpret conflicting norms as something other than a lack of friendship; they find ways other than being alike for establishing peer relations. Perhaps their own conversational style becomes more flexible and varied too, and they learn to adapt themselves to other styles without feeling socially compromised. Or, as conformity becomes a less compelling badge of peer-group friendship, notions of friendship and hostility may become more complex. On the other hand, it is worth considering

that the so-called conversational maturity of adults may be a grown-up way of masking our notions of what "playing nicely" together feels like.

NOTES

1. These recordings were part of a much larger project on early adolescent conversational behavior (see Greenwood 1989). The children and their friends knew that I was involved with a project about talk, and I had recorded them so frequently, with tape recorders
running in various places in the house over such a long period of time, that I am convinced
that the data from these conversations are examples of natural and unconstrained speech

2. A sociolinguist interviewing her own children and their friends has an apt opportunity to function simultaneously as a parent and as a researcher. Since I knew the children so
well, and certainly knew their speech habits and styles, I was able to direct my questions effectively. For example, when each of my children agreed (separately) that they wanted to
have "fun" with their friends, I was able to encourage them to explain what "fun" meant to
them. It is, for many children, a kind of cover term for feeling good. I think, because they
were talking to their mother (or to their friend's mother), they were not self-conscious about
their speech. Certainly their speech sounded very natural to me. I was able to question
them, not as a researcher or a linguist, but just as a normal question-asking parent.

3. Extracts from the dinner with Max have been discussed by Tannen (1990b).

4. Intrusion into another's turn at talk is the definition that West & Zimmerman (1983)
use and one widely accepted in discussions of conversational dominance between female
and male speakers.

5. In another conversation (Greenwood 1996), Dara and a female friend interrupt each
other very frequently, but they are sharing this discourse behavior equally.

4

Developing Adolescent Peer Culture through Collaborative Narration

DONNA EDER

Narrative discourse offers the opportunity for expressing and evaluating multiple points of view and especially for contrasting one's own perspective with that of others as one selects, recounts, and dramatizes the details of an episode from the past. Through both self-presentation and altercasting—that is, projecting an identity for others (Weinstein & Deutschberger 1963)—storytellers propose a particular outlook on their situation, distinguish themselves from other people, and indicate the values they share with their audience.

In this chapter I examine the narratives produced by young adolescents during lunchtime in a middle school setting. Through their stories they contrast their own views with those of their parents, teachers, and other adults, as they explore their attitudes toward various behaviors and values. The stories told by these middle school students are mainly collaborative ones, rather than monologues with a single narrator. Collaborative narratives, I argue, are a highly flexible form of discourse that allows participants to develop relatively complex notions of their shared culture.

In one sense, of course, all narratives are collaborations between the speaker and the audience, in that the audience's response is critical to the development of the narrative (Goodwin 1987). Here, however, I focus on stories that are collaborations *among speakers*, stories in which two or more speakers describe what happened and elaborate that description. Although one narrator may predominate, the other(s) contribute substantially to advancing the story line and evaluating its contents. Although both boys and girls on occasion told solo stories, there seemed to be a strong preference for collaborative ones among the groups that I studied. Typically, solo stories about personal experiences were of less interest to peers than were stories about experiences that had been shared by group members; solo stories did not hold the interest of others nearly as well as did collaborative ones and were consequently both shorter and less frequent.

Because shared participation in creating a story allows for active, immediate negotiation of norms and concerns and because collaborative stories often draw on common experiences and interests of the group, collaborative narration among these adolescents plays a major role in the development of peer culture. Students often waited to tell a story until friends who had shared the experience were present. Often, they explicitly invited others to share in both the memory and telling of an experience by introducing narratives with the phrase "Remember when." As they jointly produced an account of a salient experience, the adolescents created a mutual orientation toward it. In many cases its meaning was actively negotiated, and in all cases the attempt to arrive at a mutual orientation reinforced their bonds, in a way that offering solo stories on the same theme would not have. Many of the stories were repeated, each time evoking the themes of the local culture in modified form. Sometimes these retellings were for the benefit of group members who had not been actively involved in the first telling, providing a clear excuse for exaggeration and embellishment to add greater interest. Thus, collaborative narration served to recreate the local adolescent culture by socializing members into its thematic bases.

The fact that collaborative narration was more prevalent than monologic narration does not mean that tellers lacked opportunity to develop their individual performance skills. Skill at storytelling, especially the ability to describe humorous or entertaining events, was highly appreciated by peers. Generally, however, individual performances were nested within collaborative ones and were aimed at enhancing the group's experience rather than at competing for social goods. Students who could use humor to mock themselves were particularly admired. In fact, the leader of one of the male groups, who gained most of his status through his strong performance skills, did just that, as will be shown later. Although girls were less likely to actively seek leadership roles in their groups, collaborative narration offered them opportunities to strengthen their performance skills. Unlike solo stories, these stories allowed them to get attention from the group without standing out too much, since the performer role was shared with others.

Since telling stories, especially humorous ones, was a source of status in these groups, there were occasional cases in which friends vied for the chance to tell a particular story or reprimanded a co-narrator for talking too much. At the same time, though, the adolescents were sensitive to the importance of providing opportunities for co-narration as a way to sustain the interest and involvement of other group members.[1]

The Nature of Collaborative Narration

Despite considerable research on the structure of solo narratives, only recently have scholars begun to study storytelling as a collaborative performance. According to Jefferson (1978), stories consist of segments of talk by the teller interspersed with segments by the recipients. Tellers often indicate appropriate places for recipients to respond by pausing, gazing in their direction, and asking tag questions such as "Right?" (Duncan 1972, Goodwin 1990a, Jefferson 1978). In some cultures the role of a responder is clearly defined. For example, in Mayan culture one audience member is identified as the responder, who is expected to provide agreement and acknowledgments throughout the story as well as ask questions of the storyteller (Burns 1980).

Studies of performances with co-narrators, which are less common, note that they show a range of differences from more monologic narratives. They are more loosely structured than solo stories and tend to progress from one climax to another rather than build to a single high point (Kalcik 1975, Watson 1975, Watson-Gegeo & Boggs 1977). Polanyi (1989) finds co-narration to be more common in stories concerning friendship between the narrators than in "diffuse stories" that include extensive negotiation between the narrators about what actually took place and why. Goodwin (1990a), comparing the participation structure of narratives with that of disputes, notes that switching to a story expands the opportunities for participation in that all recipients can offer evaluative comments. Thus, stories allow all group members to take part and allow them leeway in selecting the timing of their turns. In this respect they are like gossip episodes (Eder 1995, Eder & Enke 1991). Unlike gossip, however, co-narration as performed by the adolescents in this study imposes an important constraint on full participation: to take part in the description of a past event as well as the evaluation of it, one needs to have taken part in the original event.

The Research Setting

The study reported here is part of a larger investigation of adolescent peer relations and interaction in a middle school setting (Eder 1995). Located in a medium-sized midwestern community, the school enrolled students from a range of socioeconomic backgrounds, including working- and lower-class families as well as middle-class ones. Approximately 250 students were enrolled in each grade. Some of the students came from surrounding rural areas. A small number were African American; the rest were European American.

Four researchers (three female, one male) observed peer-group interaction during lunch periods on a regular basis over a three-year period. The students in the groups we observed were between the ages of ten and fourteen. At the beginning of the study, students were informed that we were interested in what they liked to do at school and in what they talked about. We were not asked to supervise them in any way, nor did we record notes in their presence. Thus, we behaved as onlookers rather than as authorities. Within a week or two, students started to swear in our presence, and when no action was taken they reassured other students that we were "okay." Since we spent between five and nine months observing each group, we eventually developed excellent rapport with most students. After observing groups for a minimum of three months, we audiotaped and/or videotaped four to eight lunchtime conversations in eleven (out of a total of fifteen) groups. All of the audio-recordings were made in the lunchroom. However, since it would have created too much chaos to take the video camera into the lunch room, we did the video-recording in the media center, a room to which students were free to go during lunchtime. At times students paid explicit attention to the tape recorder or camera, shouting humorous remarks into the microphone or showing their muscles to the camera. These sections of the tapes were not included in our analysis. Instead, we focused on those sections in which their attention seemed to be focused on more routine activities such as the storytelling episodes examined in this chapter. All of the narratives analyzed here were new to at least some of the group members and thus were told primarily to them and not to us as researchers. (Since we attempted to adopt very low-key roles within the groups, few stories were told explicitly for our benefit.)

The analysis presented here concerns the recorded conversations, although ethnographic information gathered during the field study is used in interpreting these data. There are a number of reasons for combining discourse analysis and ethnography in a study. Given the complexity of informal talk, a sociolinguistic analysis of tape-recorded talk allows identification of the detailed patterns of speech through which peer culture can be seen to be actively constructed. At the same time, by including ethnographic information it is possible to draw on a larger context in determining the meaning and significance of specific utterances. Since this is what speakers naturally do in conversation, this approach makes the sociolinguistic analysis more valid (Corsaro 1985).

The prior events to which the narratives refer are an important aspect of the data that lies outside the conversations. In the boys' groups, many stories and performances were based on experiences that the entire group had shared. Stories about athletic events were common in three of the male groups, and because membership in those groups was based on participation in athletics, most members had shared the experiences on which the collaborative stories drew. In another male group, many of the collaborative performances were based on media, in particular movies seen through Home Box Office.[2] Because most boys in this group watched these movies, they, too, had shared experiences to draw upon. As a result, collaborative performances among males promoted the solidarity of the entire group. At the same time, boys were less likely than girls to engage in other modes of collaborative talk and more likely to engage in competitive styles of talk such as insult exchanges (Eder 1995). For them, collaborative narration appeared to be a key way to reduce group tensions stemming from competition.

In contrast, girls were less likely to form groups based on common experiences in athletics or other school activities; they also drew less on media for collaborative talk. In fact, participation in choir was one of the few activities members of girls' lunchtime groups had in common that could serve as the basis for group co-narration. Thus, collaborative stories were more likely to be told about experiences that two or three girls, rather than the whole group, had shared.[3] Since among these adolescents, engaging in collaborative narratives required prior participation in the events recounted, girls' storytelling tended to involve fewer participants than did boys'. For girls, then, storytelling served to solidify specific friendships rather than strengthen groupwide solidarity.

Narration as a Means to Challenge Adult Perceptions

A major theme of adolescent peer culture developed in collaborative narration is an opposition to adult views about teenagers. One way in which storytellers voice such opposition is by incorporating imagined adult dialogue into a narrative to dramatize the gulf between their own perceptions and those of salient adults in their lives. In discussing the common storytelling strategy of quoting both oneself and others, Goffman (1974) distinguishes between "animator" (the person producing the dialogue) and "figure" (the person whose words are being repeated). In the process of animating someone's words, speakers convey their attitude toward the figure (Goffman 1974, Goodwin 1990a). By animating both themselves and adults as figures, the adolescent narrators are able to contrast adult and adolescent perceptions and thereby convey their attitudes toward adults.

By animating their real or imagined dialogue with adults, the girls, in particular, would offer positive, sophisticated evaluations of themselves and in contrast portray parents and other adults as overly protective and naïve. In the following episode, two sixth graders jointly describe a comedy routine they saw with their parents. Of particular interest to them are some of the more sexually explicit aspects of the skit and their parents' reactions to their having seen this routine. This particular episode is the eighth routine to be described by these two girls from the concert that they both attended. Although most of these routines have been jointly described, the girls nonetheless vie for the chance to describe especially humorous details such as those found in this episode. (All names are pseudonyms. In transcribed excerpts, onset of overlapping talk is marked by either [or //; when the latter symbol is used, only the first speaker's talk is marked at the point where the next speaker begins.)

1	Andrea:	He goes, um, he was talkin' and he goes uhm what'd he say about the-
2	(Marla):	Oh, gross.
3	Andrea:	I was gonna tell you about ((pause)) right, oh the balloons!
4	Marla:	Oh yeah! Shish.
5	Andrea:	Okay, he goes
6	Marla:	He reached down [his pants
7	Andrea:	[( ) pop it. Oh shut up! He reached down, he reached down his pants and he pulled out a balloon=
8	Marla:	=Ooooh! ((laughs))
9	Andrea:	And he goes- (Marla shut up!) and uh he goes "Shit you gotta test these things that woulda been a, that woulda been two babies!"
10	Marla:	He's dirty!
11	Andrea:	I couldn't get over that. Oh (it was funny.)
12	Marla:	My mamma was sittin' there goin', "Oh my God!" ((laughs))
13	Andrea:	My dad, I'll bet you he goes, "Oh my God, my little girl's here." ((laughs)) I would've said listen, I wo- wo- would've said, "Listen honey, I know all about it already."

Although Andrea invites Marla to help her tell the skit by asking "uhm what'd he say about the" as she starts the story, she later sanctions her for describing how "he reached down his pants" (see turn 7 in which Andrea tells Marla to "shut up"). It appears that she wants to tell the key details of this sexually explicit and humorous skit. After Andrea finishes, Marla sums up the skit by saying, "He's dirty!" She goes on to animate her mother, casting her in the role of an overly concerned and protective parent. Marla's attitude toward such a position is conveyed by her laughter over her mother's concern. Andrea immediately mirrors this perspective by animating her father as showing a similar degree of concern for his "little girl." She, too, laughs at this excessively protective stance. Andrea goes on to animate herself, taking on the role of a sophisticated adolescent talking to a naïve adult, "Listen honey, I know all about it already." Through these animations, these girls are displaying a shared view of normative behavior for adolescents (sophisticated, unshockable), in contrast to the norms they perceive adults as having for their children (naïve, innocent).

Collaborative stories are also used to resist adult views positing that normative behavior for girls consists of being cooperative and acting like "ladies." In the following example three choir members tell a highly collaborative story in which there is no main narrator. The story is primarily about an event in which the sopranos got in trouble with the choir director; it is told in response to a question about why this occurred. Although a nonsoprano begins the story, most of the narration is by the two group members who are sopranos and also happen to be best friends.

1	Penny:	She was sayin' how *three* sopranos were fighting about it.
2	Karen:	There's *only* three sopranos.
3	Penny:	You weren't gonna sing that song in the snotty way you were sayin' it. ((laughs))
4	Mardi:	She goes yesterday=
5	Karen:	=It's a good thing she didn't see me give her the finger when they were sitting behind the piano and I go ((makes gesture))
6	Mardi:	Yesterday she said, "I'm not gonna play it for you ladies." 'Cause she said we said we weren't going to be able to sing it. Then she goes, "Well, I'm not gonna play it. I'm not gonna *baby* you anymore."
7	Karen:	We only sang it for Karla and Terri and Lori. We should walk up there and go "We didn't sing it for you, we sang it for them."
8	X:	She didn't hear it.
9	Karen:	I know. I didn't sing it for Cindy 'cause I hate her, I can't stand her guts. ((Unclear section))
10	Penny:	And then she says . . you guys begged her . . . to do [that.
11	Mardi:	[Yeah, we got down on our knees and actually just tore her dress and said, "Please let us sing it."
12	Karen:	We didn't want to sing it to begin with. . . . We just [sang so everybody'd stop
13	Mardi:	[sang
14	Karen:	so everybody'd stop naggin' at [us.
15	Mardi:	[gripin' at us.
16	Karen:	I just loved that one time when she goes, "I have nothing else to say to you girls. Good *night*." ((in a high voice)) ((laughter))
17	Mardi:	(She) goes out that door and goes, "Good *night*!" ((in a high voice)) ((laughs))

18	Karen:	It's a good thing she didn't hear what we said after she got out the door. [You would've
19	Mardi:	[Oh God. ( )
20	Karen:	She probably heard that. It was awfully loud.
21	Mardi:	How 'bout (butt?) . . .
22	Karen:	You nasty (worded girl.)
23	Mardi:	I only told Mom the good parts. I didn't tell her=
24	Karen:	=I know. ((*laughs*)) Me too. My mom, "You're the only one of my daughters ever gonna be arrested." ((*in a high voice*))
25	Mardi:	Probably so. ((*laughter*))

Here Penny sets up the story by describing a scene in which the choir director is complaining about the behavior of the sopranos to another teacher. Her complaints—that the girls "were fighting about it" and "weren't gonna sing that song"—reveal the teacher's view (as animated by the girls) that girls are expected to be cooperative and accommodating. Mardi's animation of the teacher's talk in turn 6 explicates the strategies used by the teacher to encourage this normative behavior. By referring to them as "ladies," she demonstrates her expectation of how they should behave. To further prompt their conformity to this desired view of appropriate female behavior, she taunts them by saying, "I'm not gonna *baby* you anymore." As animated by these girls, the teacher offers them the choice between being babies or ladies in order to discourage them from defining girlhood on their own terms.

The girls use this collaborative story to demonstrate and reinforce their perceptions of girlhood, which contrast sharply with those of the teacher. In turn 5 Karen offers an example of her own actions (i.e., "giving her the finger"), which does not fit the teacher's desired norm of "lady-like" behavior. Later Karen describes her intense feelings toward Cindy—"I hate her, I can't stand her guts"—which abnegate the cooperative attitude that the teacher expects from girls. Still later the girls contrast the teacher's polite, though angry, "Good night" with their own less polite conversation after she left the room (turns 16–21). This leads to Karen's description of her friend as a "nasty (worded girl)" in turn 22. The girls conclude the story by juxtaposing their self-identities as girls with those of their mothers, who can't be told the whole story since it might conflict with their expectations and hopes for their daughters. In fact, Karen goes on to mock her mother's imagined distress about her potentially deviant behavior ("You're the only one of my daughters ever gonna be arrested"), which Mardi supports with a flippant "Probably so" (see turns 24–25).

This story, focusing on the girls' battle with a female authority figure, enhances their friendships as they jointly retell it. However, since other group members are not sopranos and some are not even in choir, it does not unite the entire group against an adult authority. Again, because girls shared fewer experiences as a group than did the boys, most of their stories illuminated and strengthened friendship ties between a few individuals rather than groupwide bonds.

These two stories told by the girls show why narration is so well-suited to collaborative culture building. Collaborative narration is highly flexible. In these two stories, participation involves a range of actions: co-narrators offer pieces of the description, repeat or embellish the description, provide evaluative comments, and offer exclamations throughout. Furthermore, the structure of a collaborative story is quite open-ended. Although the time sequence of the reported events places some ordering constraints on the stories, the primary structural requirement is simply that a specific contribution be linked to the previous one with some connecting word or device (Eder 1988). In contrast, the structure of other speech activities such as gossip and insulting is much more strictly defined. Those activities offer fewer ways to participate; for instance, often a previous utterance greatly limits the opportunities for subsequent participation (Eder 1995, Eder & Enke 1991, Goodwin 1990a).

Girls mine the flexible nature of collaborative stories to reveal conflicts between the views that significant adults hold regarding girlhood and their own views. These stories allow them the opportunity to define themselves in contrast to adult perceptions as well as to further develop a shared perception of alternative notions of girlhood. For these girls, the alternative notions include greater sexual sophistication as well as conflictual, defiant, and "impolite" behavior.

Use of Stories to Mock Traditional Roles

The flexible nature of collaborative narration allowed adolescents to detach from traditional gender roles by making fun of their own behavior or that of significant others in their lives. The girls in this middle school used both collaborative teasing and collaborative narration to mock feminine roles, whereas the boys, in mocking masculine roles, relied much more on collaborative narration (Eder 1991, 1992, 1993, 1995). A central difference between these two types of activity was that teasing involved directing mocking comments at others, whereas storytelling involved more self-mocking. Storytelling may have been less threatening to males, who, because they were generally more competitive within their peer groups, may have tried to avoid the greater vulnerability inherent in teasing.

In the following story, Bobby makes fun of his coach's behavior by animating him as someone who gives the same advice in all situations ("Bunt, Bobby, bunt"), including at the most critical point in a championship game. But even more strongly Bobby mocks his own behavior, which fails to meet the traditional expectation that males are athletically competent.

1	Bobby:	Baseball man. That's all I do is strike out. Um. My coach'd tell me to bunt, wouldn't he? ((to Johnny)) ((laughter)) "Bunt, Bobby, bunt," ((in a deep voice)) is all he said to me. These two ((referring to Mark and Johnny)) were on my team. That's all he wanted me to do because it was the only thing I could do, but ((laughter)) I, I told him once, I go, "Maybe I should try to hit it sometimes." An' he goes, "No, bunt." ((laughter)) That's all I did was to bunt.
2	Johnny:	I know, I know.
3	Bobby:	An' then there was the championship game. At the championship=
4	Johnny:	=Oh two outs, you wanna tell 'em ((referring to the other group members)) or you want me to tell 'em?
5	Bobby:	I'll tell 'em. But there's uh=
6	Johnny:	=This is funny. This is hilarious.
7	Bobby:	There's uh=

8	Johnny:	=Two outs and the bottom of the ninth
9	Ken:	I think I heard this but=
10	Bobby:	=No, not the bottom of the ninth- we didn't have nine innings=
11	Ken:	=Bottom of the fifth.
12	Johnny:	Oh, bottom of the sixth.
13	Bobby:	Oh, the play-offs, the play-offs.
14	Ken:	Sixth? You guys had six innings? That's right.
15	Bobby:	And um, it was the tournament, and, uh, it was my turn to bat ((*laughter*)) and he goes and we had two outs, and=
16	Johnny:	=It was bases loaded too.
17	Bobby:	Yeah, it was bases loaded. ((*laughter*)) So I get up there and I'm ready to hit ((*holds imaginary bat*)) an' he goes "Bunt, Bobby! bunt!" ((*in a deep voice*)) ((*laughter*)) So, so, I have to bunt// and bases loaded ((*laughter*)), so I bunted one, and it, and it was fair, you know, and uh, and uh, I ran to first but they called it foul, and so then I struck out of course.
18	Johnny:	((*to Mark*)) Remember that? ((*laughing*)) Didn't, I thought, I thought a guy touched home ( ).
19	Bobby:	Nuh-uh, see I was up and I bunted and like here's the foul line ((*illustrates on the table*)) and it rolled like this. And it was fair you know the ref [called it
20	Ken:	[the umpire ((*giggles*))
21	Bobby:	I mean the umpire called it, oh god, that's in basketball ((*giggles*)) and he, he called it foul, a foul ball. ((*Johnny laughs*)) So then I got up there again and then they pitched a strike. It was kinda low, I thought. ((*laughter*)) But hey, I blew the game of course. ((*looks down and slumps a little*))
22	Johnny:	Not really you.

Bobby's presentation of himself as an incredibly unskilled athlete is in direct contrast to the general view that males should be skillful athletes. Even though athletic skills were highly valued in this school, Bobby and other boys in this peer group sought to minimize the pressures to perform athletically. The laughter that follows many of the references to his limited ability (see turns 1 and 17) suggests that this type of self-mocking helped to relieve the pressure that accompanies the concern with excelling in sports.

Although Bobby does not accept Johnny's request to tell the part of the story about the championship game, he does allow Johnny several opportunities to participate in the storytelling. Goodwin (1987) has noted that a narrator's pauses, "uhs," and other hesitancy markers provide opportunities for others to add to the narration. After Bobby first hesitates (turn 5), Johnny adds to the performance by offering an explicit evaluation about the humorous nature of this story: "This is funny. This is hilarious." When Bobby hesitates again (turn 7), Johnny adds some details to the narration ("Two outs and the bottom of the ninth"), although these turn out to be partially incorrect (turns 8–10). Although participants debate, modify, and expand upon the facts presented, the only challenge to the identity being developed by Bobby is Johnny's attempt in the last turn to upgrade it by countering Bobby's claim that he blew the game. Whatever status Bobby might lose for pointing out his own athletic limitations is more than made up for by his storytelling skills and his ability to make others laugh: he takes on different voices, uses repetition for humorous effect, and laughs at himself. It is thus not surprising that he was unwilling to let someone else tell the story for him. At the same time, allowing some participation by other group members enhanced their interest in the story-telling event and ensured him the opportunity to display his performance skills. In fact, Bobby's strong performance skills were the main basis for his leadership role in this group.

Mirroring Bobby's use of these skills to make fun of his own limitations, other group members also told stories pointing out ways in which they failed to live up to the ideal of being competent and tough athletes. Shortly after Bobby's bunting story, Johnny tells a story about a large pitcher who frightened him with his fast throws.

1   Johnny: There's this big guy about Ken's size. There's this big guy, against T.C. we were playin' G.A. last year. His name is Kevin Klinton 'n he's about as big as Ken, 'n he goes RRRRRROOOOMMM ((*mimics throwing a wild ball*)) an' he throws (mean). ((*mimics throwing ball again*)) He threw me a strike, then he goes sour 'n he walked me. // I was lucky. He goes ((*gestures*)) RRRROOOOOMMM and the ball goes WHOOOMMMM. ((*mimics motion of whizzing ball with his hands*)) The guy's fast!
2   Bobby: Yeah ((*nods his head*))
3   Johnny: ((*pause*)) He's not really fast, he just scares you=
4   Mark: =(   )
5   Johnny: He's so big and that little=
6   Bobby: =He's huge man. ((*shakes his head*))
7   Johnny: Kevin Klinton, that little ball comes so close= ((*Bobby mimes huge pitcher winding up*))
8   Ken: =Yeah ((*also mimes huge pitcher*))

The other participants' responses offer support to Johnny by confirming the fearful nature of the large pitcher Johnny animates. Both Bobby and Ken imitate a huge and fearsome pitcher winding up to throw a ball that will be hard to hit. Through both their verbal comments ("Yeah," "He's huge man") and nonverbal behaviors (head-nodding, miming the pitcher), the boys collectively recreate a frightening situation. In the process they allow themselves to express their fear, they relieve some of the tension inherent in this situation, and they distance themselves from the expectation that males should be fearless under all circumstances.

Collaborative Narration as an Ongoing Negotiation of Peer Culture

Since storytelling offers such a range of opportunities for developing culturally de-fined identities and themes through both self-presentation and altercasting, form-ing a shared peer group orientation through storytelling can be a highly complex process. Within a single performance, central concerns of peer culture may be sub-ject to ongoing negotiation and refinement. For example, one day Sam told a story in which he presented himself as tough because he was capable of continuing to play despite sustaining a serious injury during a football game. However, his friends

counter this identity, casting him as failing to achieve a different aspect of toughness, that is, never crying.

1	Sam:	Hey Joe, remember when I told ya, I go, "My finger hurt so bad I can't even feel it"? He goes, "Good, you won't feel 'em hit it." ((laughter)) He didn't know I'd broke it, man. You remember, in the Edgewood game, I broke my finger?=
2	Hank:	=I called him a big pussy when he told me that. "Hey, you big pussy, get out there 'n play."
3	Sam:	He goes, "Don't worry, you won't feel it when they hit it."
4	Hank:	Sam goes, Sam goes "Look at my finger." ((in a high voice)) I said, "Oh, you pussy cat, you can't play."
5	Sam:	You liar.
6	Hank:	I did too=
7	Sam:	=Well I did, I played the whole game.
8	Tom:	((to Sam)) You was cryin' too.
9	Sam:	Yes I did man.

After Sam offers a positive, tough identity for himself (playing with a broken finger), Hank presents a different type of tough identity for himself. Hank reports himself as having said, "Hey, you big pussy, get out there 'n play"—that is, as using
"coach-like" talk to intimidate and thereby "toughen up" players who are not willing to give their full effort under every circumstance. He is implying, then, that Sam
was in need of more toughness than he was demonstrating. However, Sam chooses
not to pick up on this negative implication and instead picks up Hank's casting of
himself as a "tough coach." Sam says of Hank, "He goes, 'Don't worry, you won't feel
it when they hit it.'" Hank, though, returns to the theme concerning Sam's weak,
negative identity by casting Sam as a whiner, using a high intonation to convey his
negative view of this role. He also expands on his own tough, coach-like role by
adding additional taunts to Sam, "Oh, you pussy cat, you can't play." At this point
(turn 5) Sam opposes this line, calling Hank a liar. Now Tom (turn 8) joins in, reinforcing Sam's weak persona—someone who cries when in pain. In acknowledging that he cried (turn 9), Sam confirms the view that he is not "tough" as defined
by some boys in this peer group.

Through this brief but complicated co-narration, these boys reveal the way in
which their peer culture interprets several aspects of toughness. Through taking on
different identities and casting others into various roles, these boys demonstrate
their orientation toward different dimensions of this valued characteristic. Sam portrays himself as measuring up in some ways in that he did sustain a serious injury
during an athletic event yet continued to play. At the same time, Hank faults Sam
for needing some form of intimidation to carry out this tough behavior. Sam was not
able to mask his pain sufficiently: he drew undue attention to his injury and he
cried—two behaviors portrayed as not tough or masculine enough. Thus, Sam's attempt to portray a tough identity turns into a lesson in the ways in which he still
lacks toughness. This example suggests that although all the boys in this group may
agree on some meanings of toughness, they may not share other meanings that will
require further negotiation.

An important function of storytelling among these boys, then, was to explicate and negotiate a unified and unifying understanding of such cultural peer values as toughness. Even though toughness was highly valued among most boys in this school, there was less than full agreement about the range of behaviors and attitudes that should be regarded as evidence of toughness, as this episode indicates. Because storytelling was one of the few speech events that allowed the complex nature of concepts such as toughness to be revealed and thus negotiated, it is an essential research site for studying the complexity of adolescent peer culture.

Conclusion

Collaborative narration contributed to the formation of peer culture among the adolescents in this study by providing a forum for two major and closely intertwined concerns—negotiating individual members' identities and verifying adolescent culture as distinct from adult culture. Through storytelling, group members clarified their perspectives and values.

Developing and openly negotiating individual identities through joint storytelling helped clarify the group culture. Often the identity being negotiated was that of one of the narrators, with co-narrators either supporting or challenging the developing identity. By comparing and contrasting an individual's developing identity with the values of the group, members clarified both the group's values and the extent to which individuals personified those values. For example, Sam found that he met his group's standards for toughness only partially in the broken finger story: he was tough enough to continue playing while injured, but not tough enough to conceal his pain. At the same time, the reality that both aspects of toughness were valued in this group was displayed. Johnny found that his fear of large pitchers matched his group's general concern about facing daunting athletic situations, and all group members saw that this fear was considered normative in the group.

A second function of collaborative storytelling with respect to clarifying group perspectives was showing how an individual's behavior deviated from adult norms, especially norms about gender-specific behavior. Including in a story details about an adolescent's deviation from adult expectations foregrounded the contrast between the group's values and adult societal norms. By describing cases when they got in trouble with adults or they imagined adults being critical of their behavior, adolescents clarified the extent to which their views of being male or female differed from (or conformed to) views held by adults. Although some collaborative stories did reinforce traditional gender concerns, such as the value of toughness among boys, they were also used to mock and detach from traditional concepts of gender. Boys used humorous stories to mock male concerns with being competent and fearless athletes. Girls made fun of adult notions of appropriate female behavior, such as the expectation that girls should not be interested in or knowledgeable about sexuality and should be cooperative and polite.

Collaborative narration is more flexible than other activities common among these adolescents. Unlike insulting, which requires the target to respond with another insult (Kochman 1983, Labov 1972a: 297–353), storytelling provides for a wide variety of ways to participate: adding to the story line, asking questions, evaluating the experience being recounted, and evaluating the telling of the story itself. And in comparison to gossip (Eder & Enke 1991), storytelling imposes less pressure to conform to the group's developing evaluation. Furthermore, insulting and gossip are used by these adolescents to promote *only* traditional gender views (Eder 1995).

At the same time, collaborative narratives may require more resources or skills than do some other speech events. If a story concerns a real experience, co-narrators need knowledge of or familiarity with the experience being described. One has to be willing to be the focus of attention, something that may be difficult for shy adoles- cents and more problematic for females in general who have developed negative views about "standing out" (Eder 1985, 1995). And to be successful at storytelling, one needs to know how to get and maintain the interest of the audience by making humorous or colorful remarks.

Many collaborative stories allowed for the collective development of humor as part of the development of a particular perspective. Displaying a shared sense of what is funny and how humor is to be conveyed affords both culture building and shared enjoyment. Thus, the flexible nature of collaborative narration makes it ideal for clarifying the content of adolescent peer culture, both in terms of its simi- larity to and difference from that of adult norms, while simultaneously strengthen- ing bonds within the peer group.

NOTES

An earlier version of this chapter was presented at the American Sociological Association Meeting, Pittsburgh, August 1992. I would like to thank both Carolyn Temple Adger and Susan Hoyle for their helpful comments. I am also grateful to Cathy Evans, Steve Parker, and Stephanie Sanford for their assistance in collecting these data and to Cathy Evans, Joyce Owens, and Stephanie Sanford for their help in transcription. This research was sup- ported by NIMH Grant No. 36680.

1. A similar phenomenon has been found among a group of younger children who also engaged in frequent collaborative stories (Watson 1975, Watson-Gegeo & Boggs 1977).

2. Due to space limitations I will examine collaborative narratives only among the ath- letic male peer groups. For an extensive analysis of the use of collaborative narratives on media in male peer groups, see Milkie (1994).

3. These same girls did engage in other modes of collaborative talk that did not, for them, require common experiences, such as gossip and teasing. In both of these activities, many members of a group tended to participate actively, since they were not constrained by prerequisite need for participation in a prior event (for instance, one could engage in gossip whether one knew the people being gossiped about or not). Gossip and teasing, then, tended to reinforce groupwide bonds (Eder 1993, 1995).

5

Multiple Codes, Multiple Identities

Puerto Rican Children in New York City

ANA CELIA ZENTELLA

Discussions of multicultural diversity often stress differences and similarities among groups at the expense of intragroup diversity. Latinos in the United States number 22 million and have roots in twenty nations. In New York City, where the children who are the subject of this chapter live, 50% of the city's 1.7 million Latinos are Puerto Ricans, but Dominicans and Colombians have been growing at a faster pace over the last decade. There are also significant numbers of Cubans, Ecuadorians, Mexicans, Salvadorians, Hondurans, and Nicaraguans, each with distinct immigration, geographic, racial, and economic patterns. Latinos constituted 24% of the city's population in 1990; that proportion is expected to reach 30% in the year 2000 with Latinos outnumbering African Americans and other minorities by the year 2010 (Bouvier & Briggs 1988). A similar diversity exists throughout the United States, yet constant media references to "*the* Hispanic community" obscure significant differences, for instance in voting patterns, high school completion rates, and attitudes toward abortion. Studies that purport to represent "the Puerto Rican community" or "the Mexican community" are similarly obscuring and sometimes seriously damaging in their one-sidedness. For example, Oscar Lewis's award-winning best seller *La Vida* (1965) portrayed Puerto Ricans on the island and in New York as trapped in an unalterable subculture of poverty and prostitution. Contemporary fascination with "the underclass," particularly focused on unwed teenage mothers on welfare, has taken *La Vida*'s place (Chávez 1991).

The truth is that even within one New York Puerto Rican lower-working-class neighborhood like *El Barrio* (lit. 'the neighborhood', Manhattan's East Harlem), groups with the same ethnic, class, and racial background are separate communities because they identify with a specific block or blocks, a particular period of immigration, a distinct mix of neighbors, and a unique set of dense and multiplex social networks. And even within the same network, individual children have experiences that shape their identities in different ways within a larger multicultural reality. Focusing on linguistic codes and language practices highlights the individual diversity that flourishes amid intragroup diversity, thus providing a more accurate meaning to the term "multicultural children."

Introducing *El Bloque*

My observations of *El Bloque* ('the block'), one lower-working-class community in *El Barrio* (East Harlem), began in 1979. The heart of *El Bloque* was three five-story walk-up tenements that had been abandoned by their landlords. Cracked walls, unreliable plumbing, lack of heat, mailboxes with private locks, and unlocked main doors characterized the buildings that more than fifty families—nineteen of them with thirty-seven school-age children—called home. The old-timers who had lived there for two decades, since their arrival from Puerto Rico in the huge wave of post–World War II migration, helped ease the way for newcomers, many of whom were their relatives. Eleven of the families were linked by blood or marriage, and those links, as well as extensive sharing—of Spanish, memories of Puerto Rico, customs, skills, material goods, and aspirations—made *El Bloque* like one big supportive family. *El Bloque* was on the brink of disruptive changes due to Reagonomics and cuts in the city's social services, but none of us knew it at the time.

Intermittently over the next thirteen years I observed the effect of those changes on five girls who formed a primary school-age network, and I gained new respect for the diversity that resulted within one community, within one group of close friends, and within each member of the group as the children of immigrants confronted the old ways and adapted the new. This chapter begins with an overview of *El Bloque* as it was in the early 1980s, when most of the children were in elementary school, with emphasis on those aspects of community life that shaped the children's language. Of particular interest are the ways in which language intersected with conflicts around national, racial, and cultural identities. The chapter ends with a case study of Paca, one member of the schoolgirl network, and of the ways in which she confronted those conflicts by pursuing, rejecting, and transforming alternative identities in her teens.

When I first met Paca, she was six years old. She and her four closest friends (Isabel, eight years old; Lolita, eight-and-a-half; Blanca, nine; and Elli, eleven), all of whom had been born on or near the block, spent a lot of time under the watchful eyes of parents, older siblings, and ever vigilant neighbors. They were required to remain on the sidewalk in front of the tenements or to ask permission to go to the play area of the public housing directly across the street. Their activities and range of action were much more restrained than those of the boys, who were often out of sight. When Paca complained that her brother Herman, who was two years older, got to go more places, her aunt responded, *Déjalo, que él es macho* ('Let him, because he's a male'). Girls were expected to help women with chores for which Spanish was appropriate, such as taking clothes to the laundry machines several blocks away, and with social or religious obligations, such as cooking for visitors from Puerto Rico or attending nine nights of prayers for the dead. As a result, girls were more likely than their brothers to be fluent in Spanish, although the usual gender-linked pattern of language exposure—girls to Spanish, boys to English—sometimes was overridden by individual differences in family language practices, access to bilingual schooling, trips to and visitors from Puerto Rico, and so forth (Zentella 1990). For example, Herman got to practice his Spanish with age-mates when several boys came to the block from Puerto Rico.

Despite the customary gender restrictions, the girls' activities were more rough-and-tumble than those their mothers had participated in while growing up in poverty in Puerto Rico, and, unlike their mothers, most of the girls learned how to roller-skate, ride a bicycle, and swim. In order to get an accurate record of their speech as they whirled about, playing with whatever showed up on their street—from abandoned cars to fiddler crabs—I had the children wear backpacks that carried a tape recorder and a microphone clipped to the front of their clothes. They accepted the tape recorder in their lives with the same ease and interest with which they accepted "boom boxes" (the oversized radio-tape machines that the young dudes of *El Bloque* carried around) and any other new technology that came their way. Over the years, the range of data collected with the aid of telephone-answering machines, beepers, three-way calling, and video recorders provided a more expanded linguistic portrait than that which emerges from the traditional tape-recorded sociolinguistic interview. I was also able to see how the new communications equipment and other gadgets that entered children's homes facilitated their integration into an English-speaking world via their advertisements, packaging, and instruction booklets.

Most important, the combination of ethnographic observation, interviews, letters, telephone recordings, and videotapes helped me appreciate the multiple ways of what Peter Auer (1984:7) has called "doing being bilingual," ways that are not unearthed if Spanish and English are treated as monolithic codes or if a bilingual person is treated as if he or she were two monolinguals stuck at the neck. Saying that a community is bilingual or that a certain member speaks Spanish and English reveals nothing about the boundaries of their linguistic codes or about how community members use bilingualism to construct their ethnic, racial, gender, or class identities.

Multiple Codes and Linguistic Insecurity

Growing up in *El Bloque* was not only a bilingual experience but also a multidialectal experience. Unfortunately, most community members did not appreciate the extent of the linguistic resources they commanded, and many suffered from linguistic insecurity. Children were raised hearing at least four dialects of Spanish and five of English; they understood them all but usually limited their production to the ones spoken in their immediate networks, which changed over time. The dialects of Spanish included varieties that distinguished Puerto Rican residents according to their educational and class backgrounds and other varieties that identified speakers from different parts of the Spanish-speaking world:

1. Standard Puerto Rican Spanish (SPRS),
2. Nonstandard PRS,
3. Nonstandard Dominican Spanish, and
4. Standard Ecuadorian Spanish.

Members of *El Bloque* who were fortunate enough to have completed high school in Puerto Rico—for example, Lolita's father—spoke SPRS in formal settings. More frequently, he used a more informal, more nonstandard Puerto Rican Spanish when he chatted with others leaning on parked cars, during domino games, and in the Puerto Rican–owned *bodega* 'grocery store'. Dominicans and an Ecuadorian were the owners of two other *bodegas* that were less frequented; these were the only locales where Dominican and Ecuadorian Spanish were spoken in the community. In the mid-1980s, as Paca and her friends left elementary and junior high school, two other sources of Spanish language variation entered the neighborhood: Cuban Mariel immigrants were moved by the city into *El Bloque*'s abandoned tenements, and nonstandard Mexican Spanish speakers became part of the surrounding neighborhood.

Like all dialects throughout the world, these Spanish dialects vary principally in the way certain vowels and consonants are pronounced and in regional vocabulary items. They are mutually intelligible and more similar than different, but their colonizers' roots in distinct regions of Spain and the political, racial, and economic history of each group since colonization confer greater status on some. The Spanish of the Caribbean, the oldest in the new world, is traced to Andalucía in southern Spain, with vestiges of the languages of the Taíno Indians and Africans who were enslaved by the Spanish colonizers. Its elimination of some syllable-final consonants, particularly the aspiration or deletion of /s/ (e.g., *Las costas de las islas* > /lah kohtah de lah ihlah/ 'the coasts of the islands') contrasts with the Spanish varieties of the interior highlands of Central and South America, which have their roots in northern Spain and were influenced by different Indian languages. The latter varieties, which are accorded greater prestige, conserve syllable-final /s/, although they may aspirate initial /s/ and/or eliminate unstressed vowels (e.g., *Sí, estamos* > /hi, stams/ 'Yes, we are here').

Speakers of Caribbean Spanish learn—via direct criticisms and indirect jokes—that their variety of Spanish is stigmatized (Zentella 1990). The Ecuadorian *bodeguero* 'bodega owner' could not contain his disdain for the neighborhood and the way Puerto Ricans spoke, but he was not alone. Lolita's father and other community members also made negative comments about the way the community spoke. The children often heard that Puerto Ricans speak not "real" or "pure" Spanish but a dialect. Those critics, including teachers, were ignorant of basic linguistic truths, for example, that no language is "pure" and that everyone, including the King of Spain and the Queen of England, speaks a dialect. Attitudes toward Puerto Rican Spanish in the United States and the history of language policies on the island provide classic evidence that invidious comparisons among dialects have more to do with politics, economics, and race than with linguistic validity.

United States language policies in Puerto Rico after the takeover of the island in 1898 insisted on the inferiority of Puerto Rican Spanish as part of an overt policy of Americanization (Zentella 1981b). The first commissioner of education expressed his linguistic prejudices bluntly when he described Puerto Rican Spanish as "an al-most unintelligible patois" with "little value as an intellectual medium" (cited in Osuna 1949:324). Changing the language of the people from Spanish to English was characterized as "doing them a favor." United States officials imposed various versions of an English-only policy on Puerto Rico's schools and courts for fifty years. The primary result was to contribute to an 80% school dropout rate, the ravages of which have lasted up to the present.

Despite the policies that have favored English, island Puerto Ricans continue to speak Spanish, but it is influenced by English in ways that become the source of fur-ther censure. Words are borrowed from English all over the Spanish-speaking world and by many other languages, because of its link to economic power and because of the internationally known objects or activities linked to it, for example, /béisbol/ 'baseball', /šo/ 'show', /computadora/ 'computer', /printer/ 'printer'. In New York, the new or distinct realities encountered encourage borrowings like *estín* 'steam heat', *la renta* 'the rent', *lanlor* 'landlord'. Linguistic insecurity that has been pro-voked on the island by Castilian Spanish biases and English-only policies is exac-erbated in the United States when borrowings are rejected as *barbarismos* 'bar-barisms' and ridiculed in the media (Fernández 1972). Second-generation children, whose intense contact with English results in grammatical as well as lexical inno-vations in their Spanish, are accused of talking *mata'o* 'killed'.

The psychological harm and educational detriment that Puerto Rican children suffer because of negative attitudes toward their Spanish has not been studied di-rectly, but research on troubled children indicates that language harassment can be a significant source of friction and distress. As reported in one such study, a ten-year-old Puerto Rican boy in New York underwent psychological counseling when he became belligerent in school after teachers ridiculed his Spanish and forbade him to speak it (Montalvo 1972). The child's attempts to "correct" his pronuncia-tion by imitating the sibilant syllable-final /s/ of radio newscasters led to ostracism by his classmates, who reacted negatively because in the Caribbean that pronunci-ation communicates aloofness and superiority when it is employed in informal con-versations. (Imagine the following analogous scenario: an American child is made to feel ashamed of her English because she pronounces words like "water" and "but-ter" with a flap sound in the middle of the word instead of the British /t/, when adoption of the British pronunciations would earn her ridicule.) Understandably, the Puerto Rican boy reacted violently to the double bind. As this example suggests, the extent to which feelings of linguistic inferiority contribute to school failure and dysfunctional behavior cries out for further study.

The Shift to English

Leaving Spanish behind and shifting to English does not resolve the linguistic inse-curity of Puerto Ricans in New York, because their English dialects also are a source of scorn in the dominant community. In *El Bloque*, immigrant parents spoke His-panized English as a second language, a variety heavily influenced by Spanish phonology and grammar. Children knew that this dialect was ridiculed in popular stereotypes, for example, by the comedian Bill Dana's introductory "Mai ney Ho-sey Hee-men-es" 'My name is José Jiménez'. The children spoke the dialect known as Puerto Rican English (PRE), which shares many grammatical features with African American Vernacular English (AAVE), but their phonology identified them as second-generation Puerto Ricans. Just as Wolfram (1974b) found, some who were close friends with African Americans learned to talk just like them. Either way, the youngsters could end up the object of a linguistic-racial epithet: "You sound like a SPIC" or "You sound like a nigger." As they began to travel beyond the confines of their block, children encountered the working-class English of Italian Americans who still lived on the fringes of El Barrio, the "accents" of other immigrant shopkeepers, and negative attitudes toward their ways of speaking. Elementary school teachers provided young children with the most consistent praise of and exposure to standard English, albeit tinged with the sounds and words of many New York ethnicities. A few college students in the community had learned Standard New York City English in their jobs and schools beyond El Barrio, but they rarely used it on the block, and it was never spoken consistently in any of the children's primary networks.

Notwithstanding the disdain for their English dialects, loss of Spanish fluency and shift to English were accelerated by the low status of Spanish, especially Puerto Rican Spanish, when compared to English. Lolita reported that her fourth-grade bilingual class for intellectually gifted children groaned whenever Spanish lessons began and cheered when they were canceled, and years later a young woman who had been raised on the block with Paca and Lolita said that she had opted to "let Spanish go" because she feared it would "hold me back." The loss of Spanish proficiency among El Bloque's children was significant. In 1980, most (61%) of the twenty-six children who were between three and twenty years old, four of whom had been born in Puerto Rico but arrived in New York before they were eight years old, were more proficient in English than Spanish, while 16% were more proficient in Spanish and 23% were fluent bilinguals (see Table 5.1).[1] Only one boy, Paca's nephew—the only third-generation child—was an English monolingual.

By 1993, the children in the original group and thirty-six more of their siblings and children had moved conclusively toward the English end of the language proficiency spectrum: 93% were dominant in English. Only 7% might be considered balanced bilinguals—all of whom had been born in Puerto Rico—and no one was more proficient in Spanish than English. The percentage of English monolinguals ranged between 17 and 34. Sadly, shifting to English dominance did not guarantee economic or educational success. In 1993 most of the former residents of El Bloque still lived in poverty, and even though most of them commanded a more varied verbal repertoire than their teachers, 55% of the second generation had dropped out of high school.

Talking Both

When I first met the children in 1979, they were full of bilingual promise. By the age of four or five, Paca and her friends, all born in El Bloque, had learned how and when to alternate between at least two dialects of two languages—usually non-

Table 5.1. Language Proficiency Spectrum of *El Bloque*'s Children, 1980 – 1993

	SM	SD	SB	BB	EB	ED	EM	Eng?
1980 (n = 26)	0%	8%	8%	23%	38%	19%	4%	0%
1993 (n = 62)	0%	0%	0%	7%	22%	37%	17%	17%

SM	=	Monolingual in Spanish, limited English comprehension.
SD	=	Spanish dominant, weak English [limited vocabulary, tenses].
SB	=	Spanish dominant bilingual, fluent English.
BB	=	Balanced bilingual, near equal fluency in both languages.
EB	=	English dominant bilingual, fluent Spanish.
ED	=	English dominant, weak Spanish [limited vocabulary, tenses].
EM	=	English dominant, limited Spanish comprehension.
Eng?	=	Either English dominant or English monolingual (based on the evaluation of others).

standard PRS and PRE. Switching began in response to the need to accommodate interlocutors who spoke different languages. Traditional norms of *respeto* 'respect' required children to speak when spoken to and in the language in which they were spoken to, which meant they were expected to address a person in that person's strongest language. Because of their frequent contacts with speakers who occupied different positions along the community's bilingual and multidialectal continuum, children learned to switch from one system's phonological, morphological, syntactic, and lexical rules to another at the drop of a hat. In the following example, Lolita alternates between English and Spanish in rapid succession:

Context: Lolita (L) was in the bodega with another eight-year-old, Corinne (C), who barely spoke and understood Spanish. The two-year-old daughter of a recent migrant, Jennie (J), followed them into the store. The bodeguero (B) belonged to Lolita's father's network of Spanish-dominant men.

C to L:	Buy those.
L to C:	No, I buy those better.
L to *bodeguero*:	*Toma la cuora.* ('Take the quarter.')
L to C:	What's she doing here? [referring to Jennie]
L to J:	*Vete pa' dentro.* ('Go inside.')

The three switches in rapid succession in this excerpt accommodated the linguistic abilities of three different addressees. Lolita spoke to her nearly monolingual English friend in English, to the Spanish-dominant male in Spanish, and to the child of a recent immigrant in Spanish. Her control of the pronunciation, grammar, and vocabulary of each segment was native: she sounded like a native Puerto Rican Spanish speaker in Spanish and like a native New York PRE speaker in English. It was precisely this ability to switch without hesitation from one language to another that was required of members of *El Bloque* if they interacted with members of different networks, and it became a mark of in-group community membership. The ability to switch became a distinguishing characteristic of second-generation children, and they extended the practice to conversations with fellow New York Puerto Ricans at turn-taking points (as in A below), within the same turn at sentence boundaries (B), or within the same sentence (C):

A.   Code-switching and turn-taking
    Paca to ACZ: *Dame una cura.* ('Give me a bandaid.')
    ACZ to P: *¿Pa' qué?* ('For what?')
    P to ACZ: For my hand.

B.   Full sentence switching
    Isabel: Yeah, *me regaña y todo.* I hate her. *Ella e(s>h) mala.*
            ('She scolds me and everything.') ('She's bad'.)

C.   Intrasentential code-switching
    Paca: *¿Por qué la gente en español tiene* funny names?
           ('Why do people have funny names in Spanish?')

Attitudes toward this switching ability vary considerably. Many people refer to it pejoratively as Spanglish, as if it were a deformed linguistic mishmash, a corruption of both English and Spanish. One teacher of Puerto Rican children in Massachusetts believed her students spoke a "hodgepodge" that hindered logical thought and blamed it on their parents:

> These poor kids come to school speaking a hodgepodge. They are all mixed up and don't know any language well. As a result, they can't even think clearly. That's why they don't learn. It's our job to teach them language—to make up for their deficiency. And, since their parents don't really know any language either, why should we waste time on Spanish? It is "good" English which has to be the focus. (Walsh 1991:106)

This assessment is neither unusual nor limited to teachers. Ignorance of the forms and functions of code-switching even extended to the renowned linguist Uriel Weinreich (1968:73), who warned that an "ideal bilingual" would never mix languages "in unchanged speech situations, and certainly not within a single sentence." In contrast, cultural studies scholars who study bilingual poets or rappers rhapsodize about "the vanguard of polyglot creativity" that language mixing represents for them (Flores & Yudice 1990). Paca and her friends, though, were nonjudgmental: they referred to switching between dialects in two languages as "mixing," or "talking/speaking both." For them and for members of other communities like *El Bloque*, it is precisely the ability to switch languages intrasententially that identifies second-generation members and bonds them to each other.

In an effort to counter the categorization of code-switchers and speakers of nonstandard dialects as linguistically and cognitively deficient, sociolinguists have responded by stressing the rule-governed nature of nonstandard dialects and of language alternation. We replace disparaging terms like Spanglish and its southwest equivalent Tex-Mex with the neutral, if bloodless, linguistic term code-switching, and we conduct statistical analyses of speakers' adherence to syntactic rules to show that code-switchers are not creating a hodgepodge, but are, instead, juggling two grammars impressively (Poplack 1981). My quantitative and qualitative analysis of more than 2,000 code-switched sentences produced by *El Bloque*'s children proved that they honored the grammatical rules of English and Spanish, and it documented the pragmatically valuable nature of code-switching (Zentella 1981a, 1982). I also showed that the children knew how to say approximately 85% of their code-switched utterances in both languages, so that, contrary to popular belief, they were not always using one language as a crutch to fill in gaps in the other. Switching was primarily an in-group behavior that served as a badge of identity, but children also switched to accomplish two dozen or more discourse strategies, for example, to realign the speaker-hearer relationship via various types of emphasis, clarification, appeal, and control (Zentella 1997).

Sociolinguistic analyses have rehabilitated nonstandard dialects and the mixing of codes in the minds of some gatekeepers such as teachers and counteracted the linguistic insecurity that frustrates the social and academic development of many bilinguals. But, in the process, the focus on rules and rehabilitation has stressed the integrity of the bilingual's codes at the expense of appreciating bilingual innovations. One frequently cited study that was conducted half a mile from *El Bloque* trumpeted the "overwhelming stability in the systems of tense, mood, and aspect in the PR Spanish spoken in the United States" (Pousada & Poplack 1982:232) when compared with a centuries-old Castilian model and found no evidence of convergence with English. But all twelve of their speakers were born in Puerto Rico, most of them had attended school on the island, and all but three planned future resettlement there. In the Spanish of the U.S.–born and –raised adolescents of *El Bloque* such as Paca and her friends, many verb forms beyond the present, preterit, and imperfect tenses were erratic in formal Spanish interviews (Zentella 1997). They patterned in ways similar to the implicational scale described by Silva-Corvalán (1989) for second- and third-generation Chicanos in Los Angeles: the simple tenses learned first are maintained more than the compound tenses learned last. Some forms modeled on English were also edging out Spanish alternatives; for example, the present progressive was preferred in sentences like *Qué estás leyendo?* ('What are you reading?'), although Spanish allows either the present progressive or simple present (*Qué lees?*) (Klein 1980). Additionally, the influence of AAVE on the Spanish grammar of New York Puerto Ricans appeared in translations of past perfect sentences that I requested of *El Bloque*'s children when they were adolescents. In keeping with what Theberge and Rickford (1989) call "preterit had," AAVE speakers can say "He had gave me the book" to mean 'He gave me the book' with no anterior meaning. Analogously, Lolita and others who used "preterit had" in their English translated "She had given me the book" and "I had read the book" with the simple preterit *Me dió el libro* and *Leí el libro* instead of the past perfect *Me había dado el libro* and *Yo había leído el libro*.

It is not always easy to distinguish transfers from AAVE or transfers from Standard English, on the one hand, from language learning errors in second-generation bilingual speech, on the other hand. But insisting that English has not had any effect on the community's Spanish is akin to maintaining that the experience of being born or raised in the United States has had no impact, as if the young "passively inherited instead of actively created" (Ochs 1992) their culture. In fact, English has affected their Spanish, primarily in the lexicon, Spanish has had an impact on their English, and language alternation has helped to blur the lines between the codes. Similarly, the blurring of the cultural boundaries between island Puerto Rican and New Yorker is captured by the term "Nuyorican."

A purely quantitative approach misses capturing how community members define and get defined as "a minority," "a bilingual," "a Puerto Rican," or "a Nuyorican" and misses the individual and group meaning of Spanish-English mixing in those definitions. As an alternative, Susan Gal (1988:247) has urged "a comparative analysis that interprets code-switching practices not only as conversational tools that maintain or change ethnic group boundaries and personal relationships, but also as symbolic creations concerned with the construction of self and other within a broader political economy and historical context." The code-switching of *El Bloque* and the second generation's increasingly unembarrassed acceptance of the terms Spanglish and Nuyorican are attempts to construct a positive self within a broader political economy and historical context that defines them as semilinguals, dropouts, the underclass. Perhaps the most lethal label, in terms of the damning stereotypes it conjures up, is that of "teenage welfare mother." The difficulty of constructing a positive identity in such an environment is captured by Sandra María Esteves (1984:26), in her bilingual poem "Not Neither" (translations of the Spanish parts are in parentheses):

Being *Puertorriqueña Americana*,	(Puerto Rican American)
Born in the Bronx, not really *jíbara*	(Puerto Rican peasant)
Not really *hablando bien*	(speaking well)
But yet, not *Gringa* either	(American)
Pero ni portorra, pero sí portorra too	(But neither Puerto Rican, yet Puerto Rican)
Pero ni qué what am I? . . .	(But neither what)

The pain and strain of inhabiting what another bilingual poet, the Chicana Gloria Anzaldúa (1987), calls the "uncomfortable territory" of "the borderlands" has led some analysts to interpret a wide range of behaviors, including low literacy skills and dropping out of school, as forms of "resistance" (Walsh 1991). Others posit an "oppositional identity" to explain why some people "dis," or put down, group members who speak standard English for "acting White." Ogbu (1988) contrasts four caste-like groups in the United States (Puerto Ricans, Mexicans, African Americans, and Native Americans) with immigrants, who see themselves, he believes, as merely "different" and whose trust in the temporary nature of their adjustment problems allows them to succeed academically because they have a nonoppositional identity. For Ogbu, the crucial difference lies in the voluntary nature of the initial incorporation of immigrants into this society, in contrast to the involuntary integration of the castes, who were forcibly incorporated via enslavement or imperialist expansion. One result, in Ogbu's view, is that "involuntary minorities may negatively, albeit unconsciously, sanction or oppose speaking Standard English because it is 'white'" (1988:24).

Despite the validity of the historical-political distinction that Ogbu makes, observing Paca and her friends made me conclude that the caste versus immigrant categories are painted with too broad a brush stroke. They allow for no intergroup differences—after all, the ninety-seven-year-old colonial relationship between Puerto Rico and the United States differs from the Native American, Mexican, and African American experience. They also obscure intragroup differences, of which I found many within a small network of five females, two of whom graduated from high school and three of whom did not. The most unfortunate aspect of "opposition" or "resistance" analyses is that they make conquered peoples synonymous with opposition, as if both accommodation and resistance were not part of their daily lives. As the following case study of Paca demonstrates, the linguistic and cultural influences of the home, school, block, and surrounding communities helped children develop a bilingual and multidialectal repertoire that allowed them to display multiple identities not necessarily in opposition to each other.

Paca

The youngest of the girls in *El Bloque*'s schoolgirl network, Paca was tiny and anemic, with black hair and dark skin of the kind that Puerto Ricans call *tipo indio* ('Indian type'). Her parents had been in the United States for six years when they moved to the block with newborn Paca and her brother Herman. When we met, Paca was about to enter a monolingual English first grade in the local Catholic school and Herman was in the public school's third-grade bilingual class. Their twenty-eight-year-old mother Magda, who knew very little English, worked as a home attendant for an elderly Puerto Rican woman in another part of *El Barrio*, and their father lived on a nearby block in a building where he was the janitor. Magda was the principal support of her children, her twenty-three-year-old pregnant niece Dylcia, and Dylcia's nineteen-month-old daughter Jennie, both of whom had arrived from Puerto Rico six months earlier. The language of the adults at home was entirely Spanish, but Paca and Herman spoke more English than Spanish to each other.

During the first months of taping, Paca rated herself a better Spanish than English speaker, "or both a little." Schooling accelerated Paca's increasing dependence on English and the world it represented, and this became evident in the first weeks of class. The nuns sent Paca home with a preliminary progress report that indicated she was about average in most areas, although she had not kept up with all homework assignments. This paper became the only wall adornment in the apartment; it was taped to the entrance wall and visitors commented on it. Paca's given name as it appeared on her birth certificate was written at the top of the sheet—Ivón.[2] A few months later Paca said she preferred Yvonne /ivan/ with its English spelling and pronunciation. On the block, everyone continued to call her by her nickname, Paca, with its Spanish pronunciation. On the one occasion when a nine-year-old jokingly used exaggerated English phonology, [pʰaːka], Paca looked amazed and acknowledged the strangeness of the pronunciation by repeating it in a disbelieving tone. But she continued to prefer the English /ivan/ over the Spanish /ibon/, just as her friends Lolita, Isabel, Blanca and Elli preferred the English pronunciations of their names. It was toward the end of that year that Paca commented on the Puerto Rican custom of giving almost everyone a nickname: "*Por qué la gente en español tiene* funny names?" ('Why do people in Spanish have funny names?'). As was obvious from her remark, her code-switching was increasing along with her awareness of different cultural norms and her distancing from those of the home culture. By the summer after first grade, she usually greeted me and other bilingual adults in the street in English, and she did not always switch to Spanish if it was directed to her, unless the addressee was a Spanish-speaking monolingual.

When Paca was nine years old, her family had to leave their first floor apartment on the block after the building was devastated by two fires (which may have been instigated by the absentee landlord for insurance purposes). The family moved twelve blocks away to the sixteenth floor of a huge, poorly maintained, and heavily African American project on the border between *El Barrio* and Harlem. After three years in Catholic school, Paca changed public schools twice, because "I was having too much fights." She had Spanish-speaking friends in her bilingual classes from fourth to sixth grades, which she rated "a perfect ten," and she still spent some weekends with relatives from *El Bloque*, but she oriented more and more to African American language and styles.

In her junior high school, which had a preponderantly Black student population and a focus on performing arts, thirteen-year-old Paca perfected her steps in all the latest African American dances; she dreamed of being a famous singer-dancer. She took great pains to be up on all the latest clothes styles, which she called "dressin' baggy," "the loaf," and "freestyle," and she bragged that one Black girl told her she was "the only Puerto Rican who knew how to match." She admired Black fashions, including jewelry like large gold bamboo earrings and pendants that spelled out an entire name, rope chains (necklaces), and "fo-finga" rings. In Paca's opinion, "They BAAD!" By the time she completed junior high at fifteen, Paca had a cool style of talking that was peppered with African American phonology (e.g., "fo" for 'four'), syntax (e.g., "They bad"), expressions (e.g., "I'm not down with that" 'I don't go along with that'), discourse markers (e.g., "Know what I'm sayin?"), and lexicon (e.g., "bad" 'good' and "They mess" 'They're lovers'). For good measure, she could reel off unintelligible "righteous talk" (Black Muslim litanies in run-together Arabic). Expressive gestures, such as eye rolling and sucking teeth, and body movements typical of her African American friends were an integral part of Paca's impressive style, so much so that once her friend Kitty, a younger New York Puerto Rican from *El Bloque*, tried to tie her hands down while she was talking.

With her dark skin completing the picture, someone who did not know her could easily assume Paca was African American. But when Kitty observed that Paca "acted Black," Paca not only denied it, she attacked those who did act Black, although she said she understood why it happened: "There's lots of kids who were raised with Black people surrounding them and that's why they're like that. I don't like that, when a Puerto Rican tries to be Black." Paca claimed a strong Puerto Rican, not American, identity, because in her view, "Americans are White people."

Paca's speech and fashions contradicted her "I don't act Black" disclaimer to Kitty, and other attitudes contradicted her defiant pro–Puerto Rican stance. When she moved across the street from one of the last remaining enclaves of Italians in *El Barrio*, Paca learned to love pizza and zepolle, which she pronounced /sepóye/—as if it were Spanish. She also loved Italian boys and the way Italians talked: "I've always wanted to be Italian, 'cause the way they talk. Their accent, they make it so byuteeful!" I never heard Paca talk like an Italian American, but it wouldn't have surprised me if she could. Her usual dialect had the phonology and syntax that reflected her New York Puerto Rican roots; when she said "byuteeful" and "I stick wi' mostly Puerto Ricans though, tha's who I hang out wid," she sounded like other second-generation working-class New York Puerto Ricans.

The verbal behavior that distinguished Paca from her African American and Italian friends and from other Latinos, and identified her with *El Bloque* and other working-class New York Puerto Rican communities, was her code-switching between nonstandard Puerto Rican Spanish and a dialect of English, sometimes AAVE but usually PRE.[3] Her attitudes towards code-switching were positive. She was convinced that switching languages was not incorrect, if the speaker knew when and with whom to switch. When she was fifteen I asked her if she mixed languages and she said, "Yes, when I'm talking to a Puerto Rican and they know both, but not talkin' to a Black person. When you're gettin' excited you put both of them together." When she was nineteen, she elaborated on her conviction that code-switching was a skill and not incorrect:

> Depends who you're talkin' to. If you're talkin' to- if you're talkin' to someone that really understands it, it's not [incorrect], not if you know the difference. . . . Because I can speak to you mixed up because I know you [ACZ: Yeah] so I got that confidence. Now if someone [*sic*] I don't know, I will impress them. I'll talk the language of intelligence. [ACZ: Okay] 'Cause I know you I'll talk to you how I WANNA speak to you, 'cause I know you. Like, for example, right now I'm talkin to you how I WANNA speak to you. [ACZ: Right] But if I don't know you, I'll give you that RESPECT.

Paca's references to understanding, confidence, intelligence, and respect reveal her grasp of the linguistic, interpersonal, and communicative aspects of code-switching, and her ability to exploit them because as she said, she "knows the difference."

It was apparent that Paca was keenly aware of the way in which language could be used to accomplish what Douglas Foley (1990) refers to as "impression management," akin to "getting over" in Harlem and *El Barrio*. At the same time that she was perfecting her AAVE, Paca was accumulating a formal English phonology and lexicon that diverged from that of the majority of her friends and neighbors. Her pronunciation of the first vowel in 'water' and 'chocolate' was so far removed from the high back sound that stereotypes New York's working classes of a variety of ethnic backgrounds that I found it impossible to comprehend her version of these words. Paca said something akin to "what-uh" and "chac-lit," suggesting that she might be participating in the contemporary far-reaching vowel shifts occurring across the northern United States, which young middle-class Anglo women are leading (Labov 1994). Her repertoire also included erudite vocabulary items that she sprinkled in her formal English, like "provoke" and "de-virginize." She did not always employ them correctly, as when she said, "When I get aggravated I provoke to do something. I provoked myself," but she thought she spoke "good English" because she could avoid "slang talk" and, in her words, "I know how to use the right words like 'coping with this' or 'being belligerent.'"

Other evidence of impression management surfaced when Paca talked about books. Once she said mysteries were her favorite novels, and I asked who her favorite author was. She said "Stefen [Stephen] King," but could not recall any title. When I asked where she got her books, she said "Bonz [Barnes] and Noble" but could not recall where the store was located. Later she admitted offhandedly, "I haven't REALLY read them." Just like those of us who have discussed a book based on a movie or a review, Paca understood full well the role of big words and talking about literacy in a convincing display of "the language of intelligence," which she locates in her English repertoire.

The Spanish part of Paca's verbal repertoire was varied too, but less so than the English part. To her parents she spoke nonstandard Puerto Rican Spanish. For her friends she could imitate Dominicans who, in her opinion, "like to curse a lot" and have "weird names" and an "accent" that she hated. She also could imitate Colombians, whose Spanish she liked. She mimicked a snobby Colombian intonation and a strongly articulated /s/ in her example, *Pero yo no he SIDO nada* ('But I haven't BEEN anything')—although she may have meant *hecho* 'done', instead of *sido* 'been', and probably meant to capture the Colombian pronunciation of syllable-final /s/ (which all varieties of Caribbean Spanish delete or aspirate) instead of syllable-initial /s/. Paca's low opinion of Dominican Spanish and high opinion of Colombian Spanish reflect common stereotypes in New York City (Zentella 1990). As for Puerto Ricans, in her opinion "[s]ome talk the right language and some talk it mixed up." Paca thought her own Spanish was good, as good as her English: "Just some words I don' understand—they too high educated!" In fact, Paca's Spanish showed a limited verb system with predominantly present, perfect, and imperfect tenses, and it was influenced by English lexicon. But the Spanish she spoke and her extensive comprehension skills were adequate for the demands made upon her in that language and explained why she rated herself a "good" speaker.

Paca's positive self-evaluation was also prompted by the cultural importance she placed on Spanish. She insisted that Spanish was an important part of Puerto Rican identity: "If you Puerto Rican, you SHOULD know it, because that's their blood, because that's what they are. They should learn." But she did not criticize her younger nephew Eddie for not knowing Spanish or exclude him from being Puerto Rican because he was the only English monolingual in *El Bloque*. For Paca and all of *El Bloque*'s second generation, you could be Puerto Rican without speaking Spanish—in contrast to what most island Puerto Ricans and first-generation immigrants believe—but the variety of English you spoke identified you as an insider or outsider. When her former neighbor Pedrito visited the block after living in a foster home on Long Island for several years, Paca told Kitty that Pedrito "acts like a White boy." Three years later she made a similar comment about one of my students, a New York Puerto Rican who lived not far from her in *El Barrio* but who had studied upstate. Paca said, "I thought she was White because the [sic] way she talks." In both cases, however, when it became clear that neither Pedrito nor my student acted as if they felt superior, their dialect was no longer an issue. After all, Paca herself used what she called "too high words" in her English "language of intelligence," so it is unlikely that she would have been critical of others on language grounds alone.

Paca's seemingly contradictory statements and dialectal shifts may be viewed as signs of internal racial and ethnic identity conflicts or as manifestations of Paca's fascination with language and culture and with the dramatic possibilities of trying on different dialect outfits and identities—particularly given her dream of becoming a famous singer-dancer—or merely as the inevitable result of her participation in diverse social networks. Whatever the source(s), and they probably were multiple, her bilingual and multidialectal repertoire enabled her to interact with a wider range of people than most Americans can effectively interact with. But the opportunity to expand her repertoire to include oral and literate control over Standard English and Spanish, and to get a high school diploma, was cut short. At sixteen, she quit school because of a difficult pregnancy, and by seventeen she was raising two baby boys in her mother's apartment. Soon after, she voiced more concerns about the color of their skin and the size of their lips than about their language development or her dashed plans to become a star.

In sum, just as they say they "speak both," second-generation New York Puerto Ricans increasingly say they *are* both, meaning Puerto Ricans and Americans, or more specifically Nuyoricans—an identity that incorporates cultural patterns and linguistic codes from their parents' homeland, outright adoptions and penetrating influences from African Americans and other members of their primary social networks, and their own unique contributions. Accommodation and opposition coexist in their daily lives, and their reaction to people who sound White is oppositional only if they have to defend themselves because those people *act* superior. The same is true for many other young Latinos, including those from what Ogbu calls the "non-caste immigrant" groups, who are growing up in New York's dense and multiplex inner-city communities. They cannot understand why affirmation of pride in their Puerto Rican or Dominican or Colombian identity, primarily reflected in their maintenance of their region's Spanish phonology and lexicon, is interpreted as a rejection of the United States or Anglos. The rap group Latin Alliance speaks for all these youths when they rap: "Don't be misled. We're not trying to put any ethnic group down, we're just tryin to bring ours UP. *Latinos unidos*! 'Latinos united'." Their pro-Latino stance reflects a stronger identification with a pan–U.S. Latino identity than their parents have, and that unity is reflected in their indistinguishable second-generation Latino English. Finally, code-switching is their way of saying, "We belong in both worlds, don't make us give up one for the other, it's too high a price to pay."

The Need for an Anthropolitical Linguistic Approach

The members of the community called *El Bloque* communicated a different reality in up to five dialects of Spanish and English as they decided when, why, and how to alternate among them. Community members got defined as "a minority," "a Spanglish speaker," "a Puerto Rican," and so forth, but they re-defined those terms, sometimes adhering to group patterns and sometimes going their separate ways to create individual identities. In their re-definitions, accommodation and resistance were not necessarily polarized but were both made a piece of the pattern.

Despite such linguistic skills, which are revealed by long-term participant observation, language is singled out in many studies of Puerto Ricans to explain their high rates of economic and educational failure. Report after report, including a U.S. Commission on Civil Rights study (1976), cites lack of English as the root of Puerto

Rican problems, from high dropout rates to lack of political power. Yet many Puerto Ricans, like Native Americans and African Americans before them, have ended up with English only, and little else. In 1980, Puerto Ricans in New York spoke twice as much English as "other Hispanic" persons, but they earned $4,200 less (Mann & Salvo 1985). In 1990, almost 10% of New York's Puerto Ricans were monolingual in English, but the average Puerto Rican income continued to lag far behind that of other Hispanics who knew less English. Cubans in the United States—21.5% of whom are Spanish monolinguals—have the highest income and college graduation rates of all Latinos (Bean & Tienda 1987). In *El Bloque*, the dropouts were more dominant in English than were some who graduated from high school. Confronted with these challenges to the "You're failing because you don't know English" refrain, gatekeepers in government offices and local schools brush them off by calling upon notions like "correct English," "pure Spanish," "limited linguistic input," and other rehashings of the "verbal deprivation" theory of the 1960s. Such popular but harmful myths about language and language minorities cannot be challenged adequately without an anthropolitical linguistic perspective.

An anthropolitical perspective, based on observation of actual speech in natural settings, is essential to unearth what Gal (1988:247) calls "the political economy of code choice" at work in a community, that is, how bilinguals use language(s) to "construct and display multiple identities, to understand their historic position, and to respond to relations of domination between groups." Such a perspective is needed to amend both the methods and objectives of sociolinguistics and anthropological linguistics. Methodologically, anthropolitical analyses profit from joining the qualitative ethnographic methods of anthropological linguistics with the quantitative methods of sociolinguistics. Both are necessary to uncover stigmatized groups' attempts to construct a positive self within an economic and political context that relegates them to static and disparaged ethnic, racial, and class identities and that identifies them with static and disparaged linguistic codes. Furthermore, both anthropological linguistics and sociolinguistics, despite their significant contributions to our understanding of the links among language, social structure, and world view, often fall short of capturing the way language is linked to issues of survival in multiracial, multiethnic societies. Missing is the *multiple codes for multiple identities* dynamic that permeates verbal behavior in oppressed ethnolinguistic communities and is so often misunderstood by the gatekeepers of institutions crucial in children's lives. Most important, both anthropological linguistics and sociolinguistics, with significant exceptions,[4] fail to champion change in those institutions and the larger society. A primary goal of an anthropolitical linguistics should be to repudiate crippling notions such as dialectal inferiority, true bilingual, alingualism that contribute to a group's subjugation and to participate in the community's challenges of the policies and institutions that dominate its members.

Language use is only part, though a crucial part, of the picture. In poor Puerto Rican communities like *El Bloque*, children experience conflicting messages about fundamental aspects of their identity. From the moment they are born, comments about their color, hair, and facial features teach them the importance—indeed the primacy—of racial classification and the superior status that comes with being classified as White. They come to learn that in the United States one is either Black or White and that, although their families include people in each group, many of them are not accepted by Blacks *or* Whites. Some questionnaires and applications that their parents fill out give the option of selecting Hispanic or Puerto Rican as a third category, thereby converting culture and national identity into a race.[5] However, in Latin America, unlike the United States, not only is a wider range of racial identification recognized, but, in addition, cultural/national identification supersedes racial identity. The inversion experienced in the United States, then, exacerbates the racial aspect of the identity struggles that second-generation Puerto Ricans experience. In response to the conflicting pressures they feel as a result of their parents' identification with Puerto Rican culture, the denigration of Blackness in the United States, and the African Americans' affirmation of racial pride, many mainland-born or -raised Puerto Ricans of all complexions choose to identify themselves as "non-white" (Rodríguez 1980), thus rejecting the Black-White racial dichotomy that denies their heterogeneity.[6]

The racial aspect of the identity crisis is shared by many other Latin Americans, but other aspects, principally those that stem from the political status of Puerto Rico, are unique to Puerto Ricans. Whereas Dominicans, Mexicans, Cubans, and others are citizens of their respective countries until they apply for and are granted U.S. citizenship, Puerto Ricans are citizens of the United States at birth whether they are born here or in Puerto Rico.[7] As a result, American citizenship conflicts with Puerto Rican identity even in the native land. Most parents raise their children to believe that those who were born in Puerto Rico are Puerto Ricans and those who were born in the United States are Americans. This cleavage within families, often based purely on accidents of birth given the back-and-forth migration pattern, contributes to the confusion of the children, especially when they find that they are rejected by other "Americans." The first time I explained my interest in Puerto Rican children to the block, eight-year-old Lolita claimed she wasn't Puerto Rican because she had been born in *El Barrio*. Ten years later, she staunchly proclaimed a Puerto Rican identity. Thus, in addition to confusions about race, the Puerto Rican second generation is subjected to too simplistic a link between culture, place of birth, and nationality.

An anthropolitical linguistics must incorporate the economic, racial and political realities that shape the language and culture of a community. For the children who were born and raised in *El Bloque*, those realities are reflected in their Spanish/English/Spanglish ways of communicating their Puerto Rican/African American/Nuyorican and White/Black/Latino identities. They are continually building bridges with different groups and incorporating the diversity around them into their lives. This is obvious in the complexity and shifting nature of the interrelationships between their linguistic codes and their ethnic, racial, and class identities. In my view, these children are courageously navigating through cross-cultural waters, just as their Taíno, Spanish, and African ancestors did in the encounters between the Old and New worlds over 500 years ago. If only they were met halfway by the gatekeepers they encounter in schools, hospitals, employment and social service offices, they could be among the future captains of a country united in its respect for diversity.

NOTES

1. The children's relative language proficiency was based on their own assessment and that of their relatives, as well as on my analysis of their speech on 103 hours of tape recordings.

2. All of the names are pseudonyms that approximate the phonology of community members' real names.

3. As is true for AAVE in the African American community, not all Puerto Ricans speak PRE, and not only Puerto Ricans speak it. The English of all second-generation working-class Latinos in New York sounds alike, blurring the national origin distinctions that they maintain in their Spanish dialects, no matter how weakened.

4. Among the scholars whose work in language has been concerned with significant social and educational change are William Labov (e.g., 1972a), Shirley Heath (1983), Dell Hymes (e.g., 1974a), Geneva Smitherman (1986), and Walt Wolfram (e.g., 1974b, 1991).

5. Unlike in the U.S., where genotypic theories classify persons with any Black blood as Black and all others as White, the Latin American color spectrum considers those at one end who have white skin and features *blancos* 'whites' and those at the other end whose features are African *negros* 'blacks', but the more prevalent combinations of these groups and others, for example, Indians and Asians, are also recognized. In Puerto Rico some of the labels that identify these mixtures are *trigueño, moreno, jabao, grifo, mulato, indio.*

6. The 1990 census provided evidence that many other Latinos are joining with Puerto Ricans in rejecting racial dichotomies: the largest percentage of Latinos in New York City, close to half (47%), responded to the census question on race by checking off the "Other" category (Institute for Puerto Rican Policy 1992:3).

7. This has been the case ever since a few weeks before the United States began drafting Puerto Ricans to fight in World War I, although the United States has had control of the island since 1898.

6

Bodytalk

Discourses of Sexuality among Adolescent African American Girls

CATHERINE EMIHOVICH

Sociolinguistics has always emphasized the critical importance of the social context in which language use is embedded (Hymes 1974a). Recently researchers have begun to emphasize that language not only reflects context but indeed creates it (e.g., Duranti & Goodwin 1992). Of particular relevance to this chapter is the contention by Gumperz and Cook-Gumperz (1982) that social categories, such as race, gender, and class, are constructed through social interaction. Here I extend this notion to sexuality through examination of data from a teen pregnancy prevention program for African American adolescent girls in a low-income, rural community. I examine how two age groups of teenage girls use language in a counseling group to construct an understanding of their emerging sexual identity and to solidify their relationships. The older group, additionally, participates in a cultural event where they comply with adult expectations as to how the event should be framed yet subtly resist these same expectations by continually renegotiating the frame. Two contrasting settings are analyzed: one a private, small-group setting where the girls met on a weekly basis and the other a public event in the form of a panel discussion where the older girls talked to an audience of younger girls about the problems of being teen mothers. I show that, as they use language in highly sophisticated ways, these girls negotiate the social power to tell their own stories and to choose to what extent they orient to adult expectations.

Language and Social Power

Since language is a potent means of constructing a social identity, the ability to match forms of talk and context can confer social power upon the user. In any interactive context, social power is linguistically negotiated with respect to what forms are appropriate, who has the right to speak, how the event will be framed, and so on. One way to analyze the role language plays in relation to issues of social power and control derives from Foucault's perspective that power is "a force and an effect which exists and circulates in a web of social interaction" (Cameron, Frazer, Harvey, Rampton, & Richardson 1992:19). Foucault (1980:98) notes:

> Power is employed and exercised through a net-like organization. And not only do individuals circulate between its threads; they are always in the position of simultaneously undergoing and exercising this power. They are not only its inert or consenting target; they are always also the elements of its articulation. In other words, individuals are vehicles of power, not its point of application.

One example of how individuals use language to acquire social power is evident in Cameron's (1992) study of young Afro-Caribbean women in London who were able to use their bidialectal skills to mediate between family members and speakers of mainstream English. Their families often asked them to speak to people in authority because the girls' speech was less heavily marked as Caribbean and they were thus less likely to be perceived as inferior. Although the "ability of these girls to speak a more socially acceptable English was crucial to the families' institutional negotiations" (Cameron 1992:125), the girls were torn between resentment at having to play this role and distress over their families' inability to communicate effectively with people in power who controlled access to outside resources. Cameron's work demonstrates that viewing language behavior from the standpoint of the ways in which it creates power and control is especially relevant for examining the language practices of older children, who are developing their place in the social structure and acquiring the means of using language to define a social identity within and across contexts.

Several other theoretical perspectives inform the work described in this chapter. One is the ethnography of communication (Frake 1977, Heath 1983, Hymes 1974b). The language data come from an ethnographic evaluation of a teen pregnancy prevention program. The relationships that I developed with the teenagers and their families over three years enabled me to situate their comments to each other in the counseling groups within a richer context. Thus, the work draws upon detailed knowledge of the cultural meanings given to events by the participants.

A related perspective incorporates the concepts of frames and footing as proposed by Bateson (1972) and Goffman (1974, 1981). Building upon this work, Tannen and Wallat (1993:59–60) suggest that the "interactive notion of a frame refers to a definition of what is going on in interaction, without which no utterance (or movement or gesture) could be interpreted." Framing incorporates the notion that people continually renegotiate their relationships to one another to events, as displayed through their shifts in footing.

Gee's (1990) work on multiple discourses contributes to the analysis as well. He views Discourse (with a capital *D*) as "a socially accepted association among ways of using language, of thinking, feeling, believing, valuing, and of acting that can be used to identify oneself as a member of a socially meaningful group or 'social network', or to signal (that one is playing) a socially meaningful 'role'" (1990:143).

Two aspects of Gee's work are central to this analysis: (1) Discourses are inherently ideological and "crucially involve a set of values and viewpoints about the relationships between people and the distribution of social goods" (1990:144), and (2) because Discourses are closely linked to the distribution of social power and to social hierarchy, "control over certain Discourses can lead to the acquisition of social goods (money, power, status) in a society" (1990:144). Hudson's (1984:33) work suggests that both femininity and adolescence can be conceived of as Gee proposes because of the "interrelationship of themes, statements, forms of knowledge and positions held by individuals in relation to these discourses." Thus, femininity is constructed by young women as they learn to use language to display their sexuality and to define what it means to be a woman; adolescence is constructed as girls begin to acknowledge the conventions of adult forms of talk and to occasionally subvert them to resist authority.

The Community Setting

The data considered here were collected in a community of green pastures dotted with the rusting trailers and abandoned cars that typify rural poverty in northern Florida. The majority of the residents are African Americans, many of them descendants of former slaves of the owners of the vast plantation holdings in the area. Although this community is located only twenty-five miles from the state capital, few residents are able to seek jobs there because of the lack of public transportation. At the same time, there are few well-paying jobs in the community itself. The predominant employment is agriculturally based: many residents work in the local fruit and vegetable packing factories. The educational picture is equally depressing: inadequate curriculum offerings and lack of certified teachers prepare students neither to graduate with employable skills nor to continue with postsecondary education.

Family life is difficult in this community. Infant mortality rates are among the highest in the state. Approximately 35% of the population have income below the poverty level. Over 25% of the county's population of 41,626 are children under the age of 18, and 10% live in families that receive Aid to Families with Dependent Children (AFDC); the average monthly AFDC caseload includes more than 1,300 families. Many of these families include teen mothers who are served through their own mothers' AFDC. Proportionally, a very large number of young girls become mothers every year. In 1989, for example, 17% of all teen pregnancies in the county were to girls sixteen and younger (Florida Center for Children and Youth 1990).

To begin to address the multitude of problems that young women face in gaining access to comprehensive information about contraception, prenatal and postnatal care, and other reproductive services, a local agency, the Community Citizens for Healthy Babies,[1] was founded by an African American woman who had grown up in the community, earned a nursing degree and master's degree in public health, and returned to establish a number of health services programs using state and federal grants. Two of these programs were intended specifically to prevent either a first or second pregnancy among adolescent women: the New Strivers Club and the

Brighter Horizons Club. The language data presented in this chapter are drawn from my ethnographic evaluation of these programs over three years.

The Discourse

Two kinds of data are examined here. One is the girls' talk about sexual behavior taken from participant observations of the groups' meetings. I have tried to preserve an accurate rendering of the talk there. A verbatim transcription of extended discourse was not possible since the girls did not agree to audiotaping because of the intimacy of the topics discussed.[2] Both for this reason and because my focus is on the content and thematic development of the girls' talk rather than on the details of its production, the text of their talk (even from the videotape discussed below) is presented as ideal text (Gee, Michaels, & O'Connor 1994), from which many false starts and repairs, as well as prosodic features associated with Black speech, have been removed.

While conducting this research, I had to consider a critical issue, my relationship to the young women in this study: I was neither poor nor Black nor Southern. Trust was not gained overnight; I had to spend a considerable amount of time in this site (almost eighteen months) before the girls really began to talk to me. I am still troubled by the question of reciprocity. In choosing to write about these girls' lives, I was especially concerned about bell hooks's (1989:43) assertion:

> Even if perceived "authorities" writing about a group to which they do not belong and/or over which they wield power, are progressive, caring, and "right-on" in every way, as long as their authority is constituted by either the absence of the voices of the individuals whose experiences they seek to address, or the dismissal of the voices as unimportant, the subject-object dichotomy is maintained and domination is enforced.

My intention is to present the girls' voices as honestly as I can while keeping in mind the "conundrum of how not to undercut, discredit, or write-off women's consciousness different from our own" (Stanley 1984:201).

A second data source is a videotaped panel discussion by the Brighter Horizons girls for the members of the New Strivers Club on the problems of teen motherhood. The counselors had organized this discussion in the belief that the younger girls could benefit from hearing firsthand about the parenting experiences of the older ones. This presentation occurred after both groups had been meeting separately for about eighteen months, by which time the older girls were well aware of the community's expectation that their difficult experiences as teen mothers would serve as warnings for the younger girls.

Group Discussions among Younger and Older Girls

New Strivers Club

The New Strivers program served girls between the ages of eleven and fourteen who had been recruited because they were considered at risk for early parenthood and school dropout. The program's goals were to ensure that girls delayed pregnancy until after completing high school or vocational training; to help the participants self-determine a future that included goals such as careers; to encourage girls to practice birth control methods, including abstinence; and to develop successful peer discussion group models that could be replicated at other sites within the community. The groups met with a trained counselor for an hour each week in community churches. During each session they either planned a field trip or a special event (e.g., a picnic) or discussed their problems with boys, peers, family, or school, as well as their concerns about their rapidly changing bodies and emerging sexual feelings. The girls were encouraged to "ask the counselors anything" and to raise questions about sexual matters such as masturbation, bodily concerns, and so forth. Because the discussions were quite frank, it was not uncommon for girls to share accounts of traumatic events such as rape and other forms of sexual abuse. The counselors' role was to listen and to provide adult guidance, especially in stressing abstinence or, if necessary, the use of contraception. They also emphasized the importance of developing a strong sense of self-esteem that did not depend upon male approval. Approximately twenty-five girls attended the club on a regular basis; all of the participants, including the counselor, were African American.

Brighter Horizons Club

The Brighter Horizons Club was designed for girls ages fourteen to seventeen who already had one child. The primary goal was to prevent a second pregnancy, but other goals of the program were to encourage the girls to remain in high school and plan a career, to increase their self-esteem, and to help them develop social and leadership skills. Like the New Strivers group, the Brighter Horizons Club met weekly under the leadership of a trained counselor. The discussions focused on problems with parents or guardians, peers, and boyfriends; child care and parenting concerns; family planning options; vocational plans; and problems within the group. Approximately sixteen girls, all African American, regularly attended meetings held in two different locations.

Talk among New Strivers Girls

The first vignette comes from field notes of a New Strivers meeting approximately six months after the girls began meeting. Six girls attended this meeting: Katrina, Iresha, Natalie, Tasha, Keesha, and Roslyn. The group leader was Cathy, who was working on a master's degree in counseling at the state university nearby. This vignette illustrates this group's use of talk to enhance peer solidarity, their hesitation to engage in frank discussion of sexual behavior, and their awareness of the power of negative talk to influence perceptions. By contrast with the older girls' talk presented later, this example reflects the younger girls' less developed sense of power and control and stronger acceptance of social conventions regarding sexual behavior.

The group meeting began with Katrina's reading of two poems she had written about the boy she was dating. After this reading, the girls teased Katrina about her boyfriend and engaged in lively talk about various concerns—peer problems, par-

ent problems, and school problems—and related stories about them. This functioned to convey the girls' regard for each other. As Eder (1993:21) notes, "[T]eas-
ing can be an indirect way of expressing positive affect and through the experience
of shared humor and the enjoyment of that humor can increase positive feelings
among group members."

The solidarity that had been built up over time allowed the girls to work through
difficult stretches, such as when Cathy focused on the explosive topic of sex. A regular feature of each meeting was Cathy's monitoring of the girls' sexual activity.
These were always uncomfortable moments: the girls knew that to acknowledge
sexual activity meant that they were disappointing the counselors' hopes that they
would refrain from it. The following example from my field notes shows how these
girls smoothly shift from teasing to comforting Katrina, who has been falsely accused of being sexually active. (Where possible, direct quotations are provided from
field notes. Paraphrased material or a comment by the observer is placed in brackets
and italicized.)

Cathy: Now for a really hot question. How many of you are sexually active?
           [At the time Cathy asks this, Katrina is not in the room. Keesha and Iresha leave to go
           get her, partially, I surmise, to avoid answering Cathy's question. Katrina walks in and
           Cathy repeats the question. The girls begin laughing and Cathy says they need to tell
           her the truth.]
Katrina: [as she gets up to leave the room again] Let me tell you something. I don't have to
           have sex with my boyfriend to let him know I love him. [She leaves.]
Cathy: All of you (are sexually active)?
Tasha: [emphatically] Not me.
Cathy: Are you using something? [Three members of the group say "yes." Keesha doesn't
           want to talk about it. None of them will say what birth control method they are using.]
Cathy: [looks at Keesha] What?
Keesha: Same they're using. Talk to me after. I'm uncomfortable with this.
Roslyn: Pills my mother gave me. My Christmas present. I take it because of my side and
           the pills help my pain with my time of the month.
Iresha: I don't want them because of the Pap smear.
Cathy: What is your method?
Iresha: Condom.
           [Roslyn begins talking about the doctor examining her "down there."]
Cathy: What's "down there"? You mean your vagina?
Roslyn: Yes, my vagina area. The exam doesn't hurt. You just get undressed and there's a
           nurse in the room the whole time. Then, he put the thing in you to stretch you
           and he gets another thing—a stick—and he takes the Pap smear.
           [Katrina returns to the room.]
Cathy: If you're uncomfortable asking things, it's okay afterwards to ask. What's your
           method, Katrina?
Katrina: I don't do it at all. [The rest of the girls begin laughing at this remark.]
Keesha: I've heard a lot of things. I don't believe everything, but it's surprising [that Kat-
           rina is not sexually active]. Before I got to know you, I thought you was wangin'
           and bangin'.
Katrina: I talk to you calm. This is how I feel. Listen to me. Since I hit seventh grade, I'm
           breaking out. I found out I had the measles. They all clapping at me. Find out I
           had the claps, then syphilis. Syphilis leads to gonorrhea, gonorrhea leads to her-

pes, herpes leads to AIDS, AIDS leads to dykin'. Those things hurt but my grandmother says don't listen. [*As Katrina tells this story she looks and sounds genuinely
upset. The strong impression is that she is telling the truth, that these stories did circulate
about her, and were in fact, mostly, if not totally, untrue. The other girls relate further
stories about Katrina's supposed sexual misconduct and then begin to comfort her.*]

Roslyn: My momma say don't judge Trina. She not like the others say. That's why I
           talked to you and got to know you.

Keesha: I feel this way. I was honest with you. I heard things but I like you. I don't believe
           what they say. [*As this talk goes on, Katrina is sitting quietly and looking hurt. Her
           body posture shifts to a very closed position, with arms crossed and trunk hunched over.*]

Katrina: Why they say that? I don't go nowhere. I'm always there [*in the neighborhood*]. I
           don't bother no one. I sit on the step in the neighborhood by myself. I don't go
           to dances, games, I'd rather stay home. I can do things if I ask. How in the
           world? I'm in the house always unless I'm at church. So how in the world? I don't
           hang around because when I had the chicken pox? What they call that? Oh,
           that's when I got the herpes. But I don't go to their level. I got a boyfriend. My
           boyfriend sticks up for me. Now let me tell you something. There's a boy in my
           class, he stinks. You can take care of your personal hygiene. If girls can, with
           more holes in our body, boys got no reason to stink. [*The other girls laugh and clap
           at this remark and agree with Katrina. Cathy moves to close the meeting.*]

Cathy: All right. Any specific questions you want answered before we go?

In several ways this vignette is typical of interaction that I witnessed among the
New Strivers. First, the girls express solidarity through both teasing and expressions
of concern for one another. They are able to shift their footing from teasing to
showing care once they realize that Katrina is genuinely hurt by their comments.
Miller's (1986:200) observation about teasing among White working-class children—that the "high value placed on interpersonal skills of self-assertion and
self-defense" is related to the "ability to stand up for oneself, to speak up in anger,
and to fight if necessary"—holds true for these African American girls as well.
These Black females engage in teasing similar to that among Black males (Labov
1972a), teasing that does not end in fights. I saw this pattern repeated over and over
in many counseling sessions; at key moments when the girls were teasing each
other, they pulled back to reconstruct the bonds of friendship. The counselor's role
at such moments was to provide linguistic cues for recalling that the purpose of their
meeting was to help one another cope with problems endemic to their social situation, saying, for example, "You got to help one another. Talk to each other. Don't be
pickin' on each other."

A second aspect of the younger girls' discussions is evident in Katrina's reference
to the adult conceptualization of responsible sex. Counselors put considerable emphasis on encouraging girls to abstain as an issue of female control: they were not
obligated to provide sexual services upon boys' demand. However, it was an inescapable reality that many of these girls were sexually active by the age of twelve.
Thus, many of the discussions centered on the need for the girls to take control so
that when sexual activity did occur, it was because the girls chose it as an expression of love in a meaningful relationship.[3] Katrina's remark about not needing to
"have sex with her boyfriend" animated the philosophy that the counselors hoped
to encourage.

A third feature of their talk is the contrast between the information that they appear to have about sex and that which the counselor expects them to evince. Katrina's poignant account of how she was shunned by her peers because she came down with measles (or chicken pox—it was not entirely clear which one she meant) and how the resulting spots were perceived as evidence of a sexually transmitted disease illustrates the girls' and their peers' lack of knowledge in this area. The comment that "AIDS leads to dykin'" reflects the stereotyped attitudes about homosexuality that were also prevalent among the older girls in the Brighter Horizons groups. The hesitation to refer to sexual parts of the body in medical terms was also common. The counselors made a special point of always using the medical names, which often led to intense embarrassment among the girls when they were asked to do the same. My belief is that although some of these girls were sexually active, they had not yet come to terms with the idea of presenting themselves as sexual beings in such a forum. Their difficulty was compounded by the fact that to do so would have been a violation of community norms concerning the sexual behavior of preadolescents.

These younger girls, then, express group solidarity, as the counselors are hoping, though they do so through teasing and consoling rather than through serious discussion of issues. They are relatively compliant with the counselor, and they may echo her views on appropriate sexual behavior (as Katrina does). When they show resistance to the adult's demands, they do so passively, by withdrawing (leaving the room) or showing embarrassment.

Talk among Brighter Horizons Girls

In contrast to the younger girls, the Brighter Horizons girls displayed more power over the discourse of sexual counseling. One way in which this power was manifested was in resisting the counselors' suggestions about how they should interpret certain sexual practices occurring in media presentations or in their community. The following vignette is taken from field notes of a Brighter Horizons group meeting. Ten girls were present, though in this exchange only three of them engage in conversation with the adults: Lena and Yolanda, who are sisters, and Tina, their closest friend. The two counselors present were Cathy, who also counseled the New Strivers Group, and Naomi, the head counselor who worked primarily with these older girls.

The group meeting began with a discussion of the movie *Fatal Attraction*, which Naomi had shown them in order to spark discussion of sexual behavior and gender relations. The plot involves a married man and a single woman who engage in sex after meeting at a party; the woman later threatens the man's family when he refuses to continue a relationship with her. The counselors intended to raise concerns about the dangers of becoming sexually active without developing an emotional relationship and without using protection. However, the conversation takes an entirely different turn:

Naomi: What's your reaction to this movie?
Tina: The relationship's normal.
Lena: Men do cheat on their wives.

Naomi: It's OK for men to screw around? [*Several girls shrug their shoulders. Naomi comments that the movie characters "fooled around" after one meeting and didn't use a condom.*]

Naomi: Is this a relationship of love or lust? [*Several girls agree it is lust.*]

Naomi: How many of you feel you have been close to this kind of situation? [*Several girls say yes. At this point Cathy enters the discussion and mentions the lack of condom use.*]

Cathy: How could this relationship be done differently?

Lena: If they had just talked the man could have seen her mind was strange.

Naomi: When you're angry do you take time to think? [*Several girls chorus "no."*]

Lena: He didn't think; he just wanted it.

Naomi: Was this relationship all the woman's fault? [*Most the girls say yes. Naomi comments that they tend to blame women for problems with men. During a discussion of this point, Yolanda mentions lesbianism. Naomi immediately focuses on this issue.*]

Naomi: Are you girls curious about what two women do together? Do you think lesbians have never had sex with a man? What about women satisfying women better? [*The immediate reaction among the girls to these questions is extremely negative. Several girls remark that no matter how bad their man treats them, it's still better than being with a woman. A few girls comment that only a "real man" could satisfy them. None of the girls indicate any acceptance of female homosexuality.*]

Naomi: Do you think there are any lesbians in the Black community? [*Most of the girls say there are more male homosexuals. Almost all of them admit to knowing a male homosexual, but only two say they know a female one.*]

Yolanda: Men dress up to please other men. Lesbians don't.

Lena: They [*male homosexuals*] dance good. [*In the ensuing discussion, Naomi steers the conversation to the topic of homophobia and gay bashing and attempts to link these experiences to the girls' experiences of being discriminated against because of race. She says, "We live in a homophobic culture. Think of homosexuality as a Black/White issue. We know the hardships of being judged as Black—gays are the same way." Other topics in this meeting are alternative lifestyles, communal living, open marriage, androgyny, and masturbation.*]

This example illustrates how these older girls are able to control discussions of sexuality and to choose not to animate the counselors' views. Despite Naomi's best efforts to establish the movie characters as equally responsible for the resulting trauma, the girls do not see the man in *Fatal Attraction* as carrying any blame; they see the woman at fault for encouraging him. This same view was expressed in another meeting, when the girls agreed that "women have to build their men up." Although they often refer resentfully to being pressured for sex, they also hold the belief that this is "a real man's" behavior. One girl noted that her friends "be pickin' at me because my boyfriend don't pressure me [for sex]—they think he's gay." When the counselor asked, "What do girls do when boys try to act cool?" one girl responded, "Most girls like the cool boys. If they see a nice clean boy they won't have nothing to do with him." The counselor replied, "There's prestige to get girls pregnant, and we allow that to happen. There's just a handful of boys that girls run behind. Girls get right up in their face and say 'do me like that too.'" Even though these girls resent the males who treat them badly, they are unwilling to accede to the older women's demands to present these men in negative terms. They have not yet adopted the counselor's discourse that positions them as women entitled to sexual satisfaction from men who desire them and do not treat them badly.

In this excerpt, too, the girls resist the counselors' attempt to elicit a range of views on homosexuality. Naomi raised the topic of homosexuality in several meetings to make the girls aware of the silencing of alternative sexual choices in the African American community and to have the girls acknowledge that they can support one another in emotional and physical ways that do not lead to undermining their own sexual orientation. However, the girls seem to guard their gender identities, reluctant to take positions that could be construed as favorable to homosexuality. Discussions of sexual choices, of alternatives to the norm (including the mention of masturbation as a way of avoiding AIDS), which almost never occurred either in the girls' families (most admitted they could not discuss these issues at all with their parents) or in school, were subverted here too. Although adults offered a protected space where the girls could begin to raise these issues and work out their feelings about them, the girls resisted these topics.

The older girls were more assured than the younger ones in discussing their sexuality, and their talk reflected their ability to engage in a "discourse of desire" (Fine 1992). In addition, they were more willing (and able) to disagree forcefully with the adult counselors and thus to assume more control over the content and direction of the discussion.

The Older Girls' Talk in a Public Presentation

The older girls' competence in manipulating the framing of a speech event, so as to balance adult expectations with their own viewpoints, is displayed even more strikingly during a public presentation. The excerpts that follow are drawn from a videotaped panel discussion, made at a community center, in which some of the older girls spoke to the younger ones about their experiences as teen mothers. Five girls from the Brighter Horizons program (Angie, Rana, LaKeya, Tamisha, and Patty) sat on a dais at a long table with microphones. Attending the presentation were approximately thirty girls from the New Strivers club, along with several mothers, program counselors, and me. The moderator was Gina, a twenty-one-year-old college student who worked in the Brighter Horizons program as a junior counselor. The excerpts illustrate not only these older girls' degree of mastery over a public discourse form—an adult genre—but also their mastery of techniques that allow them to keep reframing the event to suit their own purpose, which is, in part, to resist the adult sponsors' wish that they adhere to a conventional morality tale.

Framing and Reframing the Event

The panelists and the moderator, although sharing general expectations about how the presentation will go, nevertheless are at odds in some respects. The moderator's intention, it appears, is to frame the event as one in which personal narratives are linked to a broader message about prevention of pregnancy and adherence to a traditional moral code. The panelists, not totally opposed to conveying such a message, balance it, however, with their own more ambivalent and more personal perspectives. They thus construct, for the audience of younger girls, a complex female identity.

Gina's opening statement signals an expectation that this event will be a rather academic presentation. (In the transcription, / indicates a pause for breath and // the end of an utterance.)

Gina: I want to start out by talking a little/ about teen pregnancy. It's considered a problem/ because of the potential adverse health, economic and psychosocial consequences//

Through this introductory remark she in effect proposes to frame the event as a formal discussion, to be conducted at a relatively abstract level. A single participant, however, cannot unilaterally impose a definition of a situation on others (Tannen 1993c). Framing of an interactive event is continuously negotiated and renegotiated, as successive speakers choose either to accept or to modify previous speakers' implicit framing proposals. This element of choice is reflected in Patty's comment following Gina's introduction. By offering personal testimony, Patty proposes to reframe the event as one that blends abstractions with personal stories. Picking up on the comment about teen pregnancy as a "problem," Patty says:

Patty: For me being a teenager meant uhm/ it's a lot of responsibility and/ like when at school you want to try out for different types of sports or cheerleading you can't do that because/ sometimes your baby is sick and when you want to cheer that night but you can't/ because your baby's sick and it causes a lot of problems/ so I just say it's a lot of responsibilities//

Although Patty begins and ends by offering a general, abstract answer to Gina's question ("it's a lot of responsibility"), she illustrates her claim by offering personal details from her own experience.

Gina, tacitly accepting the reframing of the situation to allow for personal narratives and opinions, begins to ask personal questions of the panelists, inviting them to share their stories about pregnancy, motherhood, and their effect on school and social life. In their responses, the girls voice a view that contrasts with Gina's: they acknowledge the problems but at times minimize them.

Gina: What were your experiences as far as/ did you ever have any sicknesses/ body changes/ or complications during pregnancy// Is it difficult/being pregnant/ going through the pregnancy for nine months/delivering//

Rana: About the first impressions that I encountered while I was pregnant was/ late night sickness/early morning sickness// When I tried to eat breakfast I couldn't hold anything in my stomach until around noon// That happened for like/ the first three months of my pregnancy// After that/ it was a normal pregnancy// I had no problems having the baby// My attitude was also bad/ but I didn't blame anybody else cause I knew/ it was **my** fault and the baby's daddy's fault//

Gina: Has having a baby now changed/ has it changed your social life or your school life or has it affected homework// [*As she begins speaking, Tamisha's baby, who had been sitting quietly on her lap, begins banging his bottle on the table. People in the audience laugh, and Gina murmurs to Tamisha, "That's all right." Not surprisingly, Tamisha is the one who chooses to answer this question next.*]

Tamisha: Well for **me**/ it changed my school/ work school and homework/ because it's like/ when I come home/ and like now/ I have a lot of homework and like/

when I come home/ I try to do my homework/ and my baby's begging for me
and *[unintelligible]*// and tearing up my homework and stuff/ and I be like **Stop
boy** let me do my homework// And I be like/ I got to wait and stop and I do it
late at night when I do my homework/ cause it takes me longer in putting him
to sleep// But other than that/ fine//

Gina: You *[addressed to Angie]* mentioned one time about running for Miss
          Homecoming/ how that's caused a problem//

Angie: Well I wasn't running for Miss Homecoming/ I was running for First Attendant
          and it's nowhere in the book that you can't run for those things at school be-
          cause you have a baby// But/ sometimes it's the teachers or maybe the principal/
          well the principals and the teachers/ some of the teachers don't want you to run
          because you have a baby when that's not/ one of the rules that you can not run
          for anything out there because you have a baby/ it's just the way a lot of teach-
          ers felt about it// And uhm/ they took my name off the ballots because I have a
          baby/ so I couldn't run for First Attendant like I wanted to// So it takes a lot of
          those kinds of activities away//

In their responses the panelists seize the opportunity to express, in a public forum,
the complications and subtleties of their views. They demonstrate that they (with
the adult sponsors) assume that their responsibility on this public occasion is not
just to share stories, but to tell stories that have an identifiable moral purpose (Postman 1992)—to prevent younger girls from becoming pregnant. Rana tells about
morning sickness, admits that her "attitude was bad," and accepts partial blame for
her condition. Tamisha speaks of trouble getting her homework done with a baby
in the house. Angie acknowledges the negative effect of motherhood on her social
life. None of these speakers, however, presents her condition in a totally negative
light. Rana says that she had a "normal pregnancy" with "no problems" at delivery.
Tamisha, after recounting the conflict between child care and schoolwork, adds,
"But other than that, fine," suggesting that her life has not really changed much.
(Ironically, during most of her beginning statements, the restless behavior of her
child—whom she eventually had to put down so a woman in the audience could
watch him—effectively undercut her comment, and it was this behavior that supported the adult idea that having a baby created problems.) Angie, an especially accomplished speaker, simultaneously expresses her disappointment at not being able
to take part in Homecoming and her grievance over the fact that the teachers acted
without formal sanctions (as she correctly notes, the school handbook had no stated
prohibition against teen mothers participating in social activities). In effect, she
sends a mixed message to the audience: if you don't play by the rules for being a
"good girl" and you get pregnant, your social life will suffer, but people in authority
don't play by the rules either. This sixteen-year-old girl voices a piece of social commentary as she locates herself within a social nexus that is contradictory in nature.[4]
The panelists, then, simultaneously accept and resist the adult expectation that
they will discuss only the problems of teenage motherhood. They agree that teenage
motherhood brings problems, but they also present themselves as individuals, not
just "negative role models." They interweave their own teenage viewpoints with
their acknowledgments of adult concerns and in doing so show themselves to be
adept at handling the linguistic elements of demonstrating their identities.

    The brief stories that the Brighter Horizons girls tell throughout the presentation may be characterized as "mediate" or "immediate," to use the terms proposed by Shuman (1986, following Schutz 1970) in her discussion of storytelling in a group of urban adolescent girls. In immediate storytelling, Shuman (1986:55) says, "a story and the occasion on which it is told are explicitly connected such that the story is *about* the current occasion" (emphasis in orginal). A "mediate relationship," on the other hand, "presents stories as stored over a long period of time, as part of a storyteller's repertoire." Mediate stories are more distant from both teller and audience; immediate stories are alive in the ongoing situation, contain more dialogue and personal details, and focus less on an abstract message.

All of the panelists are well aware that their stories in this situation are expected to serve a purpose: to mediate their experiences through a moralistic lens. But their stories do not do so consistently—different stories place greater or lesser emphasis on a traditional moral lesson—and they do so in different ways. More mediate stories tend to sustain the moderator's attempts to frame the event as a relatively formal one. More immediate stories tend to resist the "formal" framing and to define the ongoing event as one of personal give-and-take. The responses given by Angie and Tamisha to a question from one of the younger girls about how they felt when they learned they were pregnant illustrate the difference. Whereas Angie restricts herself to listing her own and her mother's reactions, Tamisha launches into a dramatic account of what she and others said and did:

Q: How did you feel when you first heard you were pregnant//
Angie: When I first found out that I was pregnant/ well I had missed my menstruation and/ I went directly to my mother and told her about it// And as soon as I told her she set me an appointment to go to the doctor/ and/ when they called to give me the results I answered the phone and heard the doctor tell my mother and it was Friday when they called/ and she went all weekend wondering why they hadn't called/ and/ she called them back on that Monday/ and they told her they had called// And then she came and asked me a lot of questions and stuff// She was very disappointed because/ a lot of my friends was also disappointed because I/ I wasn't a very loud student [*meaning she was very quiet in school*] at the time/and I did make good grades/ I still am making good grades but/ everyone was disappointed// So after my mom found out about it/ we just talked it through and everything/ she took it kind of hard because I disappointed her very badly but/ she didn't/ fuss or you know/ or anything like that 'cause that wouldn't have settled a thing/ we just talked it over//
Tamisha: Well/ for **me/** it was like/ I didn't tell my mom// I knew I was pregnant but I still didn't tell my mom// Like/ she kept asking me/ she said/ Tamisha/ your menstruation/ had it come on yet/ I said No Mama/ I believe I got blood clots 'cause my legs they hurt l:ong// She took me to the doctor and I came out and was waitin in the yard [*the next section is unintelligible as she speaks very rapidly*]/ she said/Tamisha/ come in the house and take a bath and put on some clothes/ I'm gonna take you to the county [*the County Public Health Unit, where most of these girls received medical care*] first/ she said/ 'cause I called and I told them what you said/ and the lady said/ they said it could be very serious// So she took me down there and they gave me a pregnancy test/ they didn't check my legs [*audience laughs*]/ and then/ the man the doctor came in and said/ Uh you know why your legs be hurting right/ I said No/ he said you pregnant/ you kind of figured that didn't you/ I said No/ he said you want me to tell your mama or

are you gonna tell her/ I said you can tell her/ then he said you want to be in here/ I said No/ so I left and he called in my mama and he told her// So when I was at home my mama was like/ she said Tamisha why didn't you tell me/ she said this is bad because I kept asking you and you kept telling me you weren't pregnant/ that you had blood clots/ I said I was scared to tell you because I didn't know what to do//

Although the two stories deal with the same topic, the speakers use very different rhetorical strategies. Angie offers a summary of what happened (she went to the doctor and subsequently got the results of her pregnancy test) and of people's reaction to it (they were "disappointed"). Her report supports the "formal public presentation" frame by giving a calm, straightforward, undramatic answer to a question. Tamisha, in contrast, gives an animated blow-by-blow rendition of her visit to the doctor. She includes direct quotation (using he-said-she-said patterns characteristic of African American adolescents interacting with their peers [Goodwin 1990a]) and a joke; in addition, she embellishes her account with expressive facial expressions and gestures. Her performance gives the impression that the power of the story is so strong that she cannot distance herself from it and is compelled to recreate her emotions. She follows a similar pattern in her next narrative, not included here, about how her boyfriend reacted to the news. Of all the girls, she is the one who least often responds positively to Gina's repeated efforts to maintain the formal frame.

Different modes of presentation may also be seen within a single panelist's turn. As Shuman (1986:59) notes, "Mediate stories have the potential for immediacy, and the transition is accomplished by the shift in focus from a story that presents another reality to a story that somehow happens to the listener." In the following excerpt, Tamisha's focus as she responds to a hypothetical question shifts from mediate to immediate:

Gina: If any of you could do it all over again what would you do differently//
Rana: For starters// If I had to do it all over again I would wait until I had graduated from high school/ college/ with a degree in law/ married/ in my own house/ **then** I would think about kids//[5]
Gina: Anybody else want to answer that// Things you'd like to be doing//
Tamisha: If I had to do it all over again at least a year I would wait// Because it's har::d/ it's hard trying to take care of a child while you still in school [*She stops to put her son, who has become increasingly restless sitting on her lap, down on the floor, where he begins walking around the room*] // Then you want to be doing other things that your friends be doing// They be like/ Well, I'm going out tonight/ are you going to be able to go/ I go/ well let me see if my mama can keep the baby first/ and then you be all upset when your mama say like/ No not tonight/ maybe another time//

Tamisha begins her answer by summarizing a position, "I would wait because . . . it's hard trying to take care of a child while you still in school," which echoes the statement that Rana has just given ("I would wait. . . ."). But then she shifts to setting up an imaginary dialogue with a parent. She thus voices in two ways the message that motherhood brings with it practical problems. Whereas the first part of her answer does so by simply stating the existence of problems, the second part does so by dramatizing one kind of problem (rather than making a generalization, e.g., that getting a babysitter can be difficult).

At the opposite end of the spectrum from very personal narratives are remarks by panelists that fully uphold the framing of the occasion as a formal public presentation. Following the girls' answers to her hypothetical question ("what would you do differently?"), Gina shifts to a new topic that has the effect of moving the discussion away from personal stories and back to the moral message:

Gina: I want to talk about pregnancy prevention/ and any advice y'all have for the group how to **prevent** pregnancy//

Rana: If anybody/ is engaging in sex without protection/ take precautions and use a condom/ contraceptives/ Norplant/ whatever it takes for you **not** to get pregnant while you're still in school// 'Cause that's a hard job to do/ very hard/ take care of yourself//

Gina: I noticed that the first thing you did mention is condoms// Why is that/ so important to use condoms//

Rana: It's important to use condoms because it will **stop** you from having sexually transmitted diseases for one// And it's another way to try and help prevent pregnancy/ not 100% but/ it will do//

Gina: What do you think is the best way to prevent pregnancy/ or the 100% proof way to prevent pregnancy//

Rana: Abstinence

Gina: That's not having sex at all [*laughs*]// If anyone else has questions you can address the group now//

Here Gina and Rana return to the more formal framing of the event as one in which the girls in the audience receive information on how to prevent pregnancy, with the stress placed on the "best" way not to get pregnant. Their exchange is so well-coordinated in terms of underscoring the message about abstinence the mothers in the audience wanted to hear that it almost seems rehearsed.

Resisting Authority

In responding to the moderator's opening questions, as we have seen, the panelists offer accounts that blend abstraction and detachment with expressions of affect and details of individual speakers' situations and histories. They thus tacitly resist the counselors' expectations that they will consistently convey a strong moral message. As the discussion is opened to questions from the audience (about the panelists' feelings when they learned they were pregnant, reactions to the first sexual experience, peer pressure to have sex, and relations with boyfriends), the mixing of frames becomes more pronounced, as the panelists shift at times to the kind of talk I often heard in the more private counseling sessions. A measure of resistance to authority is seen in the following example, in which the girls are asked to discuss the effects of peer pressure on sexual experimentation. In the counseling sessions, the counselors of both groups stressed the idea that the girls should be free to act upon their own choices; they should not engage in early sexual activity because of peer pressure. The intent to elicit a statement to this effect is evident in a question asked by one of the New Strivers counselors:

Q: Did any of you feel pressured to have sex at that age/ or was it a spiritual thing/or was the feeling that you thought you didn't have any self-esteem/ that you thought everybody else was doing it/ so you were going to do it//

Rana: Well/ I didn't have any peer pressure or substance [*meaning she hadn't taken any drugs*] or other stress or anything/ I was just curious// I wanted to know what it was about// I wanted to try it out to see/ y'know/ what it was about//

NS Girl: 'Cause everybody else was do you feel that. . . . .

Rana: Well/ all of my friends/ they were having sex/ but they were going about it the wrong way//

NS Girl: Did you know for a fact that they were having sex/ or were they telling you. . . .

Rana: [*very decisive tone*] Yes I knew it for a fact//

NS Girl: 'Cause a lot of them braggin' ain't/ a lot don't say anything and they be doing everything//

Angie: A lot of young girls that are having sex now/ the only reason they're doing it is because they are afraid 'cause many of their friends are for it// Many times/ their friends trick them into doin' something they don't really want/ and they end up with a disease or pregnant// 'Cause your friends could just be tellin' you that to get you to do something/ so don't listen to your friends about sex/ listen to your parents 'cause your parents aren't gonna tell you anything wrong//

This exchange illustrates how the discourse easily slips away from the message the counselors hoped to promote, and back again. Here Rana (who throughout most of the presentation cooperates with adult expectations) gives the "wrong" answer: that she opted to have sex because she was "curious." She has to be rescued by Angie, who grasps what the audience, particularly the mothers and counselors, want to hear, especially the idea of listening to your parents. Another answer by Rana to a question from one of the mothers likewise shows resistance to presenting sex in a totally negative light:

Mother: I guess sometimes we need something to really put/ give y'all something to do with your minds instead of wondering about what sex is going to do/ and how it's going to be when I do this/ and how it's going to be when I do that// I know your hormones are movin' around that's common/ that's human/ but find something else to do with your hormones besides havin' sex// So what advice could you give to the ladies out here/ besides wanting to have sex//

Rana: Find something you really like doing/ reading/ playing basketball/ running track/ just find something other than havin' sex/ 'cause it's not all that fun// It all depends/ I take that back/ it all depends/ but you got your whole life ahead// Wait/ it'll come to you//

Watching this event live, and later on the tape, I was struck by how Rana paused briefly after she delivered the line that sex is "not all that fun," then immediately qualified it by saying "it all depends." As she is saying "not all that fun," the rest of the panel begin smiling and giggling. Rana's talk in her small group had indicated she was very much aware of the pleasures of sex, and it appears that she is unwilling to deny her feelings in public—especially, perhaps, in the presence of her peers who have heard them. She does, however, temper her views by ending with the advice, "Wait, it'll come to you."

In the following example, it is Angie whose unsatisfactory answer is supplemented by the next speaker, Rana. Both Gina and the mothers of New Strivers in the audience occasionally interject questions about the official purpose of the event—discussing ways of preventing pregnancy. One mother poses the following question:

Mother: I'm just wondering if you girls could share with these young ladies maybe some circumstances to avoid// I mean/ not all girls want to go on the birth control pill/ but were there conditions or circumstances// Was this your first time/ or were you feeling in any way insecure/ or y'know/ what are some other things they can do other than take the birth control pill to prevent pregnancy// Are there circumstances or any other/ or anything you can say to them about avoiding//

Angie: If you don't want to take birth control pills/ well/ I wasn't taking any birth control pills before I got pregnant// After I had my baby I got on birth control pills/ and I took them for a couple of months/ and the reason that I got off them was that I never wanted to go back and get more// I used to forget how many packs I had or whatever/ and I got tired of just going back to get more/ so I just stopped taking them// And now I have a Norplant[6] and I've had my Norplant now for like a year and almost two months//

Gina: Is there any way they can avoid getting pregnant besides taking birth control pills// When you say they can practice abstinence . . .

Rana: Say No// Tell him No// If he loves like he claims he do/ he can wait//

Angie: 'Cause he's not respecting you if he force you to have sex and you're not ready for it//

Gina recognizes that Angie's answer is not completely satisfactory from a parent's point of view, since her solution is to use birth control that allows her to be sexually active without worrying about pregnancy. So Gina smoothly interjects her own question, and this time Rana and Angie both pick up on her cue.

Throughout the presentation, then, the girls create and display their awareness of overlapping frames (cf. Tannen 1993c). Their responses to questions about prevention of pregnancy reveal that they are very aware of the broader social context in which this event was situated, particularly with reference to how sex education was promoted in the local high schools with its focus on abstinence and slogans of "Just say No." On the other hand, the girls' adherence in this public setting to promoting the value of abstinence is undercut by talk that echoes their discourses within the small-group sessions, where they were free to discuss issues of sexual pleasure.

Public and Private Personas

A constant theme that dominated the talk in the small-group sessions was the idea that teen pregnancy meant the end of the girls' goals and aspirations. By telling the girls that they could choose not to have a second baby (Brighter Horizons) or that they could become high achievers in school and community (New Strivers), the counselors reiterated the theme that the girls could carve out a new future for themselves, one in which they controlled their own sexual behavior and one in which they could have a "house of their own." The panel discussion, as we have seen, contained different sorts of contributions, from intensely personal narratives to adult-sponsored moral messages. On some occasions the personal message and the official message are juxtaposed in the contributions of two subsequent speakers—as in the instances when Angie and Rana "rescue" each other. On other occasions the personal and the official are melded in the contribution of a single speaker. In fact, the moderator Gina offers just such a melding at the end of the panel, as she shares a secret about herself:

Gina: Anyone have a question or a comment// [*No response*] Well/ I just want to add to some of the things they were talking about// My mother had me as a teenager/ so as I was growing up she was always open with me/ and talking to me about preventing teenage pregnancy// Of course/ she wanted me to wait to have sex until I got married and finished school and everything/ but she always let me know if by chance I did decide to have sex/ that there was ways to prevent getting sexually transmitted diseases/ and to prevent getting pregnant/ and I was glad to have that open communication// And I went to my mother and I was able to talk to her/ and a lot of these times you think you think you can't talk to your mother/ but you'd be surprised/ you'd really be surprised// If you just sit down and let her know/ well Mom/ I really . . . /please listen to me/ I didn't have anyone else to talk to and I want your advice/ or I want to talk to you about it// And with **me**/ I had a problem at first talking to her/ so I wrote her a letter// I wrote her a letter and I left it on the dresser and went to school/ but we still had a chance to communicate// I didn't go and try to talk to some of my friends and get their advice/ and let them lead me the wrong way/ and talking to my mother got me this far/ and we still have open communication// [*Looks at panelists*] You want to add something//

Gina becomes the ultimate role model by revealing that her mother had been a teen mother, yet she was able to communicate with her daughter and prevent her from making the same mistake. During her speech, Gina skillfully incorporates themes mentioned by the panelists: she blends Angie's comment that your parents "won't tell you anything wrong" with her account of not letting "friends lead me the wrong way"; she notes that while abstinence is preferable, contraception is a responsible choice; and she states that open communication with your "Mom" (a noticeable departure from the typical African American appellation of 'Mama') is possible on sexual matters. As an older, more accomplished speaker, Gina knows exactly what the mothers in the audience want most to hear—that the New Strivers girls in the audience should not make the same mistake that the Brighter Horizons girls and the mothers themselves had made. This statement is effective because it conveys that moral message but in a more "immediate" way than Gina's previous contributions. Here, rather than speaking as the detached, impersonal moderator, Gina adopts a narrative style very much like that of the panelists; she offers a vignette from her own history.

Gina's story may have been especially significant to the girls, since a major conversation topic in the Brighter Horizons group centered on how much the girls admired her for her poise, attractiveness, and educational achievement as an honor student in a local historically Black college. Not surprisingly, her comments were immediately echoed by Rana, the girl who strove to imitate her the most:

Rana: Well/ today one of my friends/ she's not a close friend/ but she came/ she wrote me a letter for some advice about how she's in love with this guy// This guy's telling her that he love her and he wants her to have a child// So I told her that I would give her the best advice that I could give her// Don't let him fool you into having a child// He's not going to be there always/ she's a senior/ and I think he's a freshman or a sophomore/ or one of those/ and I told her if he love her he would wait// They should graduate from high school first/ get a job/ further their education or something/ but don't// Just taking care of a baby's not fun// I explained to her about buying Pampers and milk and all that/ and it's still going up [*the price*]/ especially formula/ and I tried to tell her all that I can// Don't have a baby just 'cause he wants one//

Rana, too, skillfully blends the official message to the younger girls with a vignette, presenting herself as having offered advice to a friend that itself blended the message ("Don't let him fool you into having a child") with concrete reasons ("I explained to her about buying Pampers and milk and all that").

The older girls, then, in this public setting, show themselves to be skilled at integrating adult concerns with their own values. Their contributions, which range from lively personal anecdotes to more matter-of-fact accounts of personal experience to sobering advice, express a complex point of view. As in the small-group sessions, the young women negotiate aspects of their sexual identity partly in collaboration with and partly in resistance to adults.

Conclusion

The excerpts presented in this chapter illustrate how adolescent girls can define, negotiate, and create their sexuality, an aspect of their gender identity. As they engage in adult-sponsored discussions, they struggle to articulate a view that combines both adult and teenage values. The older girls, in particular, show that they are becoming skilled at constructing their identity through discourse, even when faced with conflicting demands, by manipulating frames and interweaving personal concerns and community values.

Despite living in a society where sexual gratification is relentlessly promoted through the media, young women (of all social class backgrounds) have few opportunities to engage in multiple discourses that allow them to voice their feelings and concerns about their reproductive options, their relationships with men, their conflicting desires, and their self-esteem and worth. Creating contexts for such discourses to emerge is, as feminists argue, critical if young women are to take control of their sexuality and their health by making informed choices. Through engaging in such "discourses of desire" (Fine 1992), under the direction of caring adult women in their community, the young women in this study learned in a protected space to articulate their beliefs about teen pregnancy and sexual concerns and to demonstrate that they understood how to frame these issues in both public and private speech events.[7] Moreover, they took advantage of the opportunities, private and public, to use discourse as a tool for synthesizing their own views and those of the adults around them.

Race, class, and gender, of course, constrain life opportunities; the options open to these girls are severely curtailed by virtue of their being poor, Black, and female. But as Lois Weis (personal communication, September 27, 1995) notes, "people's lives are not so codable," and sometimes a focus on language variation can have the effect of magnifying differences among social groups instead of allowing us to recognize commonalities. Only recently have scholars begun to focus on the talk of women and girls of color in situated discourse (cf. Merritt, chapter 7, this volume), for instance in mediating disputes (Goodwin 1990a), acting as cultural brokers in the community (Zentella 1987), and building social relationships (Robins &

Adenika 1987). Still, we lack substantial discussion of similarities between discourse practices of African American women and those of women in other cultural and ethnic groups. Robins and Adenika (1987) found that a repeated theme in the conversations of lower-middle-class Black women is how to impart to their children middle-class values, high self-esteem, and racial pride. The counselors and the mothers of the girls in this study, likewise, wanted to transmit the traditional values that were strongly held within the community and taught through the African American church.[8] Teen pregnancy, every mother's nightmare, was widely acknowledged as a tremendous problem, so that perhaps even more than in some other communities, the parents, counselors, and program director strongly encouraged talk about self-control and responsibility. The Brighter Horizons girls, when speaking as panelists, were very conscious of the social approval they could evoke from the attentive mothers, who nodded in agreement over statements such as "your parents aren't gonna tell you anything wrong." Even though many of the mothers in the audience had themselves been teen mothers, it was important for them to hear these girls affirm these traditional values. The panelists, although speaking African American Vernacular English, used a Discourse (Gee 1990) embodying "ways of using language, of thinking, feeling, believing, valuing, and of acting" more characteristic of middle-class speech. Their narratives were, at least in part, morality tales that embodied traditional, middle-class values centering around adolescent sexuality: practice abstinence, communicate with your parents, finish school, and get a good job before deciding to have children. If all sociolinguistic markers were stripped from these texts (e.g., "he be"), readers would have a difficult time recognizing the talk as coming from a group of low-income, African American girls.

Mastery of different discourses can have an empowering effect on adolescent girls' perception of themselves. When I first observed the girls interacting in their small groups, many of them used what the counselors characterized as "field hand talk," typical of poor, rural, southern African Americans. Although they were undoubtedly fluent speakers within their community, they lacked the requisite knowledge to transcend the boundaries of this community and function successfully in other contexts. They were unable to employ a Discourse that marked them as members of a *perceived* socially responsible class,[9] an inability that would probably keep them trapped within a cycle of poverty, unable to obtain jobs that required a Discourse more oriented to middle-class concerns. When they first entered the program, none of the Brighter Horizons girls could have managed the panel discussion that took place eighteen months after the groups began meeting.

To fully understand the richness and complexity of older children's language practices, we need to have more data drawn from contexts that have not been well-studied. As Henry (1995:16) says, the social science literature needs more "ethnographic inquiries that focus on how black girls (especially preadolescent girls) come to know and understand their world and how they live within its contradictions." Through discourse, people empower themselves; acquiring a new kind of language can evoke a new kind of social reality (Sapir 1956). Programs designed to increase the well-being of adolescent girls who are considered at risk for early pregnancy provide them with an emotional support structure; in addition, the discourse practices encouraged in such settings can help them redefine their social reality. By interrogating the discourses of sexuality among adolescent African American girls from a sociolinguistic perspective that views language use as contributing to a transformation of one's social identity, we increase our understanding of how older children can become successful participants in more than one cultural context.

NOTES

Although the final interpretations drawn in this chapter are mine, I would like to thank Carolyn Adger and Susan Hoyle for taking the time to provide extensive and thoughtful comments on earlier drafts of this chapter, as well as Ron Gentile, Annette Henry, Monique Keith, Mwalimu Shujaa, and Lois Weis for their assistance. I would also like to thank Sylvia Byrd and Nancy Gee-Williams for giving me the opportunity to work closely with these girls and for correcting any misperceptions I may have held about the community.

1. The names of all organizations and persons used in this chapter are pseudonyms.

2. Although I did not have permission to tape the meetings, the counselors and the girls knew that I would use information from my observations of the meetings and the videotape of the public presentation to prepare professional papers. They were comfortable with this arrangement as long as I concealed their identities.

3. The counselors' dilemma reflected an issue hotly debated in the teen pregnancy literature: whether providing information on birth control implicitly sanctions sexual behavior.

4. This also reflected a developmental difference between the two groups: at no time did I ever observe the younger girls use language to express social commentary.

5. A follow-up evaluation of the girls' lives one year later revealed that Rana had achieved several of her goals. She had graduated from high school, obtained a well-paying job, and had married and was living in "her own house." She also indicated that she was saving money to attend college in the future and still planned to go to law school.

6. Norplant is a contraceptive device implanted under the skin by a physician, usually in the woman's upper arm. It releases hormones that prevent pregnancy on a timed basis, and it is effective for up to five years.

7. The fact that these discourses occurred in a community-based organization controlled by African American women and not in a school-based program was significant, as schools by their political nature are unable to assume the task of allowing adolescent females to articulate viewpoints that violate conventional standards (Fine 1992:49). The counselors urged the girls to break their silence and freely discuss the sexual problems they experienced in their daily lives, a task whose importance for Black women in particular is emphasized by the Black feminist Kesho Yvonne Scott (1991:228).

8. The close connection between the activities of these groups and the churches meant that many groups met in rooms provided by the churches. From reviewing the literature on teen pregnancy prevention programs, I was aware that this alliance was highly unusual in other communities.

9. I qualify this term because, although I felt the girls were already socially responsible in many respects, I believe that differences in language use play a powerful role in determining one's social status. This belief was also shared by the counselors, who were concerned about providing the girls with a different kind of Discourse that would enable them to seek better-paying jobs in state agencies.

7

Of Ritual Matters to Master

Structure and Improvisation in Language Development at Primary School

MARILYN MERRITT

Consider the following interchange between two boys playing with modeling clay:

> Jack: Should we clean up?
> Jason: What time is it?
> Jack: Eleven fifteen.
> Jason: No. We don't have to yet.

We are not surprised to learn that the interlocutors are not three-year-olds, or even five-year-olds, but rather nine- and ten-year-olds in the fourth grade of an American-system school. What makes this interchange fairly sophisticated? The grammatical pre-positioning of question markers and the use of elliptical answers display mature syntactic competence. The telling of time at the level of reckoning quarter hours displays organizational knowledge of the abstract world typically outside the competence of a preschool child. The casual proposal by Jason and acceptance by Jack of the relevance of a question in response to a question display an advanced level of pragmatic development, a facility with indirectness that assumes the answer to the second question bears on the forthcoming answer to the first (Merritt 1976a). The confluence of syntactic, semantic, and pragmatic competencies is nicely displayed when the relevance of the second question and second answer is elliptically confirmed with the word "yet" in Jason's final utterance. Perhaps most impressive, though, is the boys' display of orientation to social constraints on their actions. Orientation to authority is displayed through choice of verbs in the first and last utterances ("Should . . . ?"; ". . . don't have to"). Words also cue orientation to an activity structure ("clean up") and the joint nature of their participation ("Should *we* . . . ?"; "No. *We* . . . .").

In this chapter I discuss an important aspect of language development: the increasing ability to use language in the ritual work that lies at the core of managing social experience, such as Jack and Jason do here. I weave together several threads of my previous work on language in and as social interaction (e.g., Merritt 1976a, b, 1979, 1994b) and my continuing interest in the nature of human creativity and adaptation to social change. I also highlight creative or improvisational acts of communication as they intersect with elements of social experience in the primary[1] classroom. The remainder of this chapter connects with the foregoing example in four ways. I suggest that improvisation upon perceived structures in new contexts is a crucial means by which children expand their competences in both language and management of social experience. I contend that characterizing the management of social experience—an ability whose correlates are still very much at issue (Cazden 1996)—is an important part of constructing an adequate picture of language development, especially among older children and in changing societies. I argue for the special relevance of primary school as a setting for the study of both social experience and language practice. I then analyze, as social experience, several examples and observations from primary school.

Language Development Revisited

One strand of inquiry into children's language development has focused on debate as to whether innate or experiential factors are more important (Chomsky 1972, R. Rymer 1993). Pinker's (1994) recent reformulation of the innatist position lays the groundwork for a bridge between innatist and experientialist views. He adopts the concept of "similarity space," a key property of the language instinct that allows the language learner to go beyond imitation to produce grammatical variations and to interpret, by computing relevance (cf. Blass 1990), newly encountered variations from other models and producers of language. In this view, an instinct for language learning is triggered by and interacts with experiential stimulation, especially that involving other persons.[2] Such a view can be extended beyond the earliest stages of language learning: just as the acquisition of language structure requires more than direct imitation, the management of social experience requires mastery of more than overt, explicitly taught ritual and more than imitation of previously encountered interaction. Active improvisation in managing social experience is both evidence and instrument of a child's language development (Bateson 1994, Merritt 1994b, Olivier de Sardan 1995, Rosaldo 1989).

A Note on Ritual

One sense of the term *ritual* refers to a set of behaviors that are routine formats for accomplishing something in a culturally defined setting. Thus, some researchers of classroom settings have referred to classroom routines as classroom rituals (e.g., Corsaro 1979, Griffin & Mehan 1979). This "routine" sense of the word, though, sometimes overshadows the sense of ritual as a ceremonial rite that pays homage to something sacred. Ceremonial rituals marking major life transitions, such as marriage and death, often consist of highly specified behaviors; we might refer to these as *overt rituals*. But smaller universal rituals, such as greetings, daily affirm the essential sacred worthiness of human beings. Everyday ritual work tends to be conflated with other communicative work, consisting as it does in—often unnoticed—improvised and nuanced adjustments to complex agendas and multiple parties. It is, thus, often *covert*, its presence masked by variable form. The covertness of much modern everyday ritual work (Goffman 1956, 1963, 1971; Merritt 1976a, b) suggests that it is more informally learned than explicitly taught. But this is no indication of lesser importance, for covert ritual is pervasive. Almost any behavior can be read for its impact on *ritual equilibrium*, a general state of mutually held respect between interactants, dependent at least partly on situational expectedness. Indeed, the mastery of linguistically displayed covert ritual is surely part of the fluency that we associate with native speakers in their home communities and a communicative goal for those learning to manage a new social experience.

Ritual Equilibrium in the Primary Classroom

The fact that children throughout the world spend a large proportion of their waking and speaking hours in primary school makes the close investigation of this institutional setting highly relevant to an understanding of their overall linguistic and social development. Although the limitations of mass primary education as a societal mechanism for enhancing individual creativity have been exposed (Caine & Caine 1991, Gardner 1983, Henry 1963, John-Steiner 1985, Ong 1982, Stafford 1994), classroom interaction is nonetheless a rich repository of the improvisational responses that children make to small and large stimuli in their everyday environments (Cazden, John, & Hymes 1972; Rubagumya 1993; Shuy & Griffin 1981; Wilkinson 1982)—a form of creativity often overlooked.

Classrooms are explicitly designed as learning environments, but much of the competence acquired there comes about informally, aligned as it is to structures covertly displayed in the social interaction of students and teachers. As many researchers have noted, the socialization process through which children learn to belong comfortably and effectively in primary school interacts uniquely with the repertoire of social experiences for each primary student in other milieus (Cazden 1988; Heath 1983; Jacob & Jordan 1992; Merritt, Cleghorn, & Abagi 1988; Merritt, Cleghorn, Abagi, & Bunyi 1992; Philips 1993; Scollon & Scollon 1981). Where there are great disparities between the nature of the home and the school environments—such as the basis for child compliance with adult directives, an orientation to language use as predominantly oral or literate, or the affective and authoritative status of various languages or varieties—the social experience of primary school is likely to be associated with social change.

For a number of years I have been observing and researching primary classrooms in the United States and developing countries, notably in Africa. I have been part of two classroom research studies[3]—the first carried out in the eastern United States at a private school catering to middle-class and professional families, the second in Kenya at three different schools representing different language of instruction policies. In addition, through international development work I have observed other schools and, in some cases, community conditions as well as attitudes of teachers and parents. Classroom examples have also been collected from English-speaking students in schools in India, Kenya, and Niger that use American-system pedagogy. In this chapter I focus on children from seven to ten years old, in the second through the fourth grades, although reports and observations of younger children have also informed my thinking. Here I de-emphasize issues of educational outcome and cognitive load; rather, I consider primary classroom interaction as an important social experience for older children in which language practices are key.

Co-management of Ritual Equilibrium and Instrumental Goals

The co-management of two important classroom goals—maintaining ritual equilibrium among all interactants and achieving the instrumental goal of student learning—calls upon the improvisational resources of all participants. The teacher's challenge is to invoke affect and authority in ways that promote children's sense of social belonging while promoting individual learner achievements. But it is the children's creative resources that are most challenged by the need to fulfill several simultaneous demands: to create affective ties, accede to authority, gain ratified access to classroom resources, and align to classmates and teacher.

Affect and Authority

The sense of belonging that comes with socialization to school is important for maintaining social cohesion and classroom order. For a child whose primary social sphere is the home, a natural way to achieve a sense of belonging is to stay close to the teacher, who is the focal point in the classroom. In observations from the U.S. study (which have held up elsewhere as well), children as old as second and third graders seemed to value simple proximity: they would ask to sit at the same table with the teacher, although he or she was working with other students on a different activity. Although when teachers and students come from different social backgrounds, situational authority and affective attraction may be lacking at the outset, affective bonds offer an important resource for both classroom management and motivation (e.g., in this volume, chapter 8, Adger points out one teacher's affective "mother bear" role).

Since most children enter school with a positive attitude toward adults—who heretofore have been seen as caretakers as well as figures of authority—they are usually positively disposed toward their teacher and want to do the right thing, both socially and educationally. The sociologist Fatima Mernissi, in recalling her earliest days of Koranic schooling in Morocco some fifty years ago, gives us a child's perspective on the nature of school authority that remains applicable to much of Islamic West Africa today. The passage gives voice to a young child's desire to please and to the anxiety often caused by the uncertainty of expectations.

Education is to know the *hudad*, the sacred frontiers, said Lalla Tam, the headmistress at the Koranic school where I was sent at age three to join my ten cousins. My teacher had a long, menacing whip, and I totally agreed with her about everything; the frontier, the Christians, education. To be a Muslim was to respect the *hudad*. And for a child, to respect the *hudad* was to obey. *I wanted badly to please* Lalla Tam, but once out of her earshot, I asked Cousin Malika, who was two years older than I, if she could show me where the *hudad* actually was located. She answered that all she knew for sure was that everything would work out fine if I obeyed the teacher. The *hudad* was whatever the teacher forbade. My cousin's words helped me relax and start enjoying school. (Mernissi 1994:3, emphasis added)

Such observations suggest that periods during which students are expected to work alone, rather than in whole-class or small-group sessions, may strain their sense of comfort and competence. Yet the primary instrumental goal of schooling in many locales is that of individual achievement in reading and writing, to be accomplished for the most part while working alone.[4] As time goes on, though, children often come to value task accomplishment as a major part of social belonging, and at the same time they seem to increasingly recognize that positive evaluation by the teacher depends upon adhering to classroom rules. There is, then, a shift from a purely affiliative sense of social belonging to a sense of being a "member" (Sacks 1992b) by virtue of demonstrated competence in both social and academic domains.

Students and teachers, of course, are bound not only by affective ties but by lines of authority. Institutionally structured interaction such as that of primary classrooms is typically asymmetrical. Societal conventions, however, vary considerably with respect to figures of authority, the nature of their legitimacy, and the extent of their power. In many West African rural schools, where there has often been a history of colonial and administrative coercion and where parents have not been well enough informed or involved to become advocates for schooling, teachers have wielded sometimes unrestrained authority. In one school a teacher told of an incident in which a first-grade child who had balked at following his order was punished: the child refused to take his turn sweeping the floor of the classroom and was therefore forced to get down on his hands and knees and was switched with a branch. The terrified child ran home crying, precipitating an unscheduled meeting of the village parent association and fueling mounting tension between the school and the community. The highly punitive form of authority righteously reported by this teacher is only beginning to be challenged in some communities.

Access and Alignment

A classroom contains many students—whose major locus of activity may have heretofore been in the home with only a few, if any, other children—who are now expected to use materials and space in a highly regulated manner. One manifestation of the teacher's authority is the asymmetrical prerogatives of access: the teacher has access to the attention of any student at any time. Students, on the other hand, compete with each other for teacher attention and other resources: learning materials, space, and, especially, conversational partners. Their access is limited and tightly regulated.

Access to resources is invoked through several overlapping and intersecting structures: *participation structures* (e.g., teacher addressing the whole class, teacher working with a small group, students working individually); *activity structures* (e.g., a reading lesson, a science experiment); and the *structure of modalities* (e.g., face-to-face, spoken voice only, spoken voice in language A, spoken voice in language B, nonverbal moves only). Each move strikes a chord, as it were, in the polyvalent display of the social self, in the harmonic construction and reconstruction of ritual equilibrium among classroom participants in various vectors of activity.[5] Any shift in participation structure, activity structure, or modality may constitute a shift in footing on the part of an individual and a shift in the frame of the jointly constructed interaction (Goffman 1981). In the primary classroom situation a frame is often coterminous with a particular vector of activity.

I suggest that the more clearly a move is associated with the invocation of either affect or authority, the more clearly any shift in footing attributable to that move is perceived. Adger (chapter 8, this volume), for example, shows how a shift in register (modality) is associated with classroom authority. Often such moves seem to assert or propose situational prerogative, a major way of negotiating social presence.

In studying the dynamics of particular school environments, this is no small consideration, as the two factors of affect (connoting solidarity and reciprocal displays of deference) and authority (connoting hierarchy and asymmetrical displays of deference) vary significantly across school cultures (e.g., American system, French system, Kenyan system, each with many subsystems) and interact dynamically with the home cultures of the communities sending children to school. In Kenya teachers in rural areas would sometimes address students as "son of (Odhiambo)," thereby invoking not only their classroom authority to summon but also the affect (and adult authority) associated with community membership.

Let us turn now to some of the particulars of access. In the study of U.S. children, a major focus was the way in which those working on individual tasks might gain access to the teacher. An example from a third-grade class illustrates the teacher's formal displeasure with a student's interruption, as well as another student's monitoring of the interchange. [6]

		[Teacher Mrs. I is sitting at a table with a group of children, working with one girl, Vivian, who is reading aloud.]
I →	Chuck:	[while walking up to the table with a book in hand] How many books are we allowed to take out, Mrs. I?
	Mrs. I:	[no response]
I →	Chuck:	[as he reaches table and stops by Mrs. I., who is still engaged with Vivian] Mrs. I, how many books are we allowed to take out?
←	Mrs. I:	[looking at Chuck and putting her finger on his belt] What do you do if I'm talking to somebody else?
	Chuck:	[grimaces and puts book down on nearby shelf]
←	Mrs. I:	[waving finger] You just stand there and I'm gonna see you.
S →	Vivian:	[to Teacher] You can help him.
←	Mrs. I:	[to Vivian] No, I want him to learn and it's hard. [shift in voice quality] Go ahead.
	Vivian:	[continues to read aloud briefly]
RB →	Mrs. I:	[to Vivian]: All right. Excuse me.
		[to Chuck]: M'one. this week.

This example demonstrates the interplay of demands and resources in natural interaction. Chuck intrusively seeks the teacher's attention for his activity, and, when there is no uptake, replays his question. When the teacher ultimately responds, she combines scolding Chuck with a sequence that does not derail (although it delays) Chuck's individual vector of activity (apparently working with a library book); she ritually acknowledges the interruption of the reading vector of activity with Vivian before finally answering Chuck's query.

Vivian's action shows that she is alive to more than the possibility of being interrupted. As a fellow student of Chuck's, and perhaps having found herself in similar circumstances, she offers, "You can help him." However, even though Vivian is the student who currently has ratified access to the teacher's attention, she does not have authority to grant a transfer of access to that attention, especially when the authority of general classroom rules is at issue. Nevertheless, the affect displayed in her offer, as well as the teacher's effort to respond to Chuck's request within a relatively short period of time, are probably important elements in keeping Chuck engaged in the classroom situation, in terms of both social membership (ritual equilibrium) and task accomplishment (instrumental goal).

Participation Structures   In my experience most children in primary school seem to have difficulty learning that membership does not give them full participation rights in the classroom: they are not at liberty to engage the teacher at any moment, nor are they always allowed to speak to other students or to do the same things that other students are doing at the same time. In the U.S. study even third-grade students often found themselves being sanctioned for presuming participation rights that were not approved by the teacher, as shown in the example with Chuck. Ratified social presence requires ritual work.

Many teachers, seeking to minimize misunderstanding, confrontation, and punishment, verbalize classroom rules and try to structure children's expectations about what counts as good and bad behavior. In one Kenyan third-grade classroom a teacher instructed the students to write in their notebooks and finished by saying, "And then I will come to see who has been scratching like a hen." Explicitly taught routines and overt ritual are effective ways for teachers to structure behavioral expectations and to signal major shifts in what is going on. In Kenya, for example, the formal beginning of a class session usually takes place when the assembled children stand up at attention behind their desks or tables and call out in unison, "Good morning (afternoon), teacher."

So long as the participation structure is one of whole group, behavioral expectations may be conveyed directly by the teacher, who may expect to wield absolute authority and receive undivided attention. During whole-class lessons, teachers often structure access to turn-taking opportunities by soliciting bids to answer questions; often students bid on a verbal turn with a nonverbal signal such as raising the hand. In Kenya, enthusiastic students sometimes make an extra effort to draw attention to themselves by noisily snapping their fingers as they stretch out their arms, sometimes shouting out, "Me, me." In addition to group routines, teachers often spontaneously employ unusual moves to target student attention. For example, the science teacher in Jack and Jason's class, while giving instructions for the lab procedures and the materials needed by each team, manages to adroitly address a single student whose behavior is becoming disruptive:

Mrs. P: You'll need a cup. You'll need a bobby pin. You'll need a cork. And
NV →   [turning with raised eyebrows to one squirming student who seems not to be pay-
             ing attention, but not changing her tone of voice or rhythm in the list of "you'll
             need"s]
V →   you'll need to go last if you can't sit in your chair until we're ready.

The teacher's gesture splits her whole-person modality and directs attention to a particular student, thus enabling the verbal modality format ("you'll need") for the whole class to be shared by two vectors of activity and used to sanction one student while continuing to address the whole class.

Activity Structures   Most primary schools now allocate at least a part of the day to small-group activities, which have their own behavioral norms. Some of these, such as the science laboratory experiment of the initial Jack and Jason inter-change, are structured into a number of fairly distinct segments, each of which provides opportunities for teacher monitoring or assistance. In such activity struc-tures, where children work on their own while the teacher walks about and moni-tors the entire class, student requests for teacher attention may be solicited through a nonverbal signal or, in some classrooms, may simply be called out:

                 [The students have been instructed to make predictions as to the results of
                 the experiment in their notebooks. This was to be done before actually car-
                 rying out the measurement part of the experiment.]
Q1 Francois: (to teacher) What do we do after we've filled up with water?
Q2 Teacher: Did you make your predictions yet?
A2 Francois: No.
A1 Teacher: Do that first.

In the next example, drawn from the same classroom activity, Neil poses a question about whether one segment of the activity, calibration, is to be done individually or jointly. The formulation of his query makes it clear that he believes that he and his lab partner are to work together and that he seeks confirmation from the teacher.

Neil: Mrs. P, aren't we supposed to work together to calibrate?
Mrs. P: Well, usually one person will help the other one hold the vial.

In another move called out to the same teacher, Tony does not pose a direct ques-tion but instead makes a comment that displays his understanding that he and his lab partner should make the same prediction. The teacher responds by clarifying that their predictions may be different (may be made individually), that only their results must be the same (achieved jointly).

Tony: [referring to his lab partner] Mrs. P, she didn't make the same prediction as me.
Mrs. P: That's okay. You don't have to make the same predictions. But the results should
          be the same.

Despite the fact that teachers typically give explicit instructions before an ac-tivity starts, it is often difficult to anticipate everything that students will want to know. These three examples show a range of ways (including direct and indirect questions) in which teachers and their students handle emergent concerns about activity structure.

Modalities   Another resource for managing ritual equilibrium is the allocation of different modalities for different vectors of activity. In Kenya, modality shifts often involved code-switching from English to another language for instructional as well as classroom management functions. Some teachers, especially in the early grades, were more explicit in pointing out that they were making a shift from one variety to another, whereas others expected students to make this adjustment themselves. Teachers sometimes shifted from the official language of instruction, English, to the national language, Swahili, or a local language such as Kikuyu, to signal a shift in affect, addressee, vector of activity, or segment of an activity (Merritt et al. 1992).

In American-system schools, different modalities seem to be used to separate primary and secondary vectors of activity, especially when the participation structure is one in which the teacher is working with only a subset of the students. For example, when Mrs. I's primary vector of activity is tutorial work with an individual student, she can simultaneously communicate with a student outside that vector of activity as long as she does not have to use the verbal modality to do so. But requests for attention that use the verbal modality (such as Chuck's request about the library book) cannot be attended to without disrupting the primary vector of activity and are usually negatively sanctioned. Teachers often stated categorically that they were not to be interrupted while working with somebody, but the fact that nonverbal requests for teacher attention were, in practice, far less likely to be negatively sanctioned than verbal requests is something that many students seemed to have learned informally, as covert ritual.

An unspoken rule appears to reserve the full-voice verbal modality for vectors of activity involving the teacher. This rule dictates a kind of deferential ritual behavior in which children, even while seeking to satisfy their own desires, refrain from disrupting the task engagement of others. In the following example, again with teacher Mrs. I. and her third-grade students, we see acknowledgment of the almost-transgressed rule.

> [Teacher Mrs. I is sitting at a table with a single student working on his math.]
>
> → Rob: [approaches the teacher, does not say anything. After a few seconds, during which Mrs. I does not turn to him or otherwise acknowledge him, Rob begins to tap on Mrs. I's shoulder.]
>
> ← Mrs. I: [turns to Rob, saying nothing]
>
> → Rob: Oh, you're busy aren't you?
>
> ← Mrs. I: Yes. Thanks for remembering. [turns back to her work at the table]
>
> Rob: [walks away]

Note in the first arrowed interchange, in which Mrs. I acknowledges Rob's presence but does not speak to him, that Mrs. I is, apparently, protecting the integrity of her primary vector of activity (a math tutorial) by *not* using the verbal modality (which she is reserving for that vector of activity). In the second arrowed interchange Rob does use the verbal modality to officially withdraw his request, and the teacher herself also slips briefly into a verbal reply. But even though the teacher's attention has in fact been pulled away from her primary vector of activity, she seems to succeed in not disrupting the math student's engagement with the math vector of activity (unlike the last example with Chuck interrupting a reading lesson). She thanks Rob for recognizing the rule of not interrupting when she is busy with someone else.

In the next example, with another teacher from the same school, a female student, Lynn, uses a nonverbal approach that clearly displays positive affect, draping her arm around the teacher's shoulder. Though the teacher still refuses to grant access to her attention at that moment (refuses to join Lynn's vector of activity), her manner is friendly and her refusal takes the form of offering an alternative for more quickly advancing Lynn's task vector of activity. In general, as suggested earlier, we note that certain modalities make actions or moves more official or ritually salient.[7] Usually, explicitly verbal moves are more "official" than nonverbal moves and ritually require a response (in order to maintain ritual equilibrium), thereby making their unwelcome use more intrusive, as when Chuck interrupted the reading lesson. However, aggressive nonverbal moves, such as vigorously tapping on the teacher's shoulder, are also difficult to ignore and may similarly require a response.

		[Second grade. Mrs. H is sitting alone with Adam, helping him come up with lists of things he likes and doesn't like about the Christmas holiday.]
→	Lynn:	[approaches the teacher, drapes her arm across the teacher's back and waits for about half a minute]
	Mrs. H:	[to Adam] Presents? All right. What would be another category?
→	Lynn:	[starts rubbing her fist across the teacher's back]
←	Mrs. H:	[pushing Lynn away with one hand] Umm, if you would get your math checked with Connie you'd get out faster. [Connie is a student teacher.]
	Lynn:	[walks away]

In the next example, a third-grade teacher is working with two readers, Billy and Katie, who are taking turns reading aloud. Billy seems temporarily confused by what happens:

	Billy:	[reading] "but they did not use this fine thread" [Peter and Charlie's voices can be heard in the background]
	Mrs. I:	[looks up and scans room]
→		[looking toward Peter and Charlie, shaking head vigorously and using loud voice] Hunh-unh. .
	Billy:	[continues to read aloud briefly]
	Mrs. I:	[toward Peter and Charlie] Hunh-unh, [The group sitting on the rug stares at Mrs. I, who shakes her head "no" several times in an exaggerated fashion.]
←	Billy:	[looks up at teacher with quizzical expression; then turns and follows the teacher's gaze back toward Peter and Charlie and others on the rug; nothing said for several seconds]
←	Billy:	[turning back toward the teacher] I thought you were saying I didn't read it (right).
Q →		What was he doing? [Charlie and then Peter stand up and walk over beside the teacher as Billy speaks. Teacher does not acknowledge Billy's remark or question. A brief side conversation is exchanged between Peter, Charlie, and the teacher concerning what they should be doing.]
D →Mrs. I:		[to Peter and Charlie] Get back to something else that's *quieter*.

Billy:	[resumes reading aloud while teacher is still facing Peter and Charlie] "They kept it for . . ."
Mrs. I:	[snaps back to reading group posture as though she had never left that vector of activity]
Billy:	". . . themselves, and then they went, on, pretending to work until, far into the night."
Mrs. I:	[to Billy] Good.

At the teacher's evaluative "Hunh-unh" (in the high-volume verbal modality normally reserved for the reading vector of activity when the teacher is involved), Billy at first seems confused that the remark might be directed toward his reading. But then he seems to realize that it was intended for someone else, and he proceeds to try to join the teacher's secondary vector of activity, scolding Peter and Charlie ("What was he doing?"). The teacher does not acknowledge Billy or otherwise invite him to be a part of the secondary vector; Billy seems to interpret her lack of uptake as a signal to stay uninvolved, and he soon resumes the activity (reading) for which he is a ratified participant, receiving in a few moments the teacher's positive sanction, "Good."

Wherever there are competing demands for the teacher's attention, we can note at least three teacher options for attending to the secondary vector of activity: (1) including the current participants in her departure from the primary vector ("Oh, look what John has brought for us"); (2) using a split modality involvement (attending to the secondary vector of activity in the nonverbal modality while at least partially continuing to attend to the primary vector of activity with the verbal modality); (3) totally leaving the primary vector of activity for some notable period of time. When the teacher uses the third option, she may simply return as though she had never been gone, as in the Billy example, or she may use ritual brackets as she leaves ("All right. Excuse me") and/or when she returns ("Okay. Where were we?"). I have noticed that teachers exhibit a stylistic preference regarding ritual bracketing; some are more likely to routinely use ritual brackets to enter and leave vectors of activity, whereas others seem to move in and out of various vectors of activity without formally signaling what they are doing. It also seems that teachers in general are likely to be more explicit with younger children—for whom brackets may be more important to accurately interpret what is going on—and expect older children to be more attuned to fellow students' needs and the teacher's need to be involved elsewhere as well. In the example just given, the teacher's nonuse of ritual brackets almost certainly contributed to temporary student misunderstanding, but the student was also able to quickly and accurately reinterpret the teacher's action.

Co-participation among Students   The example with Billy reading illustrates not only the use of multiple modalities in teacher management of ritual equilibrium but also co-participation among students. Students are constantly judging, based on what others are doing and the teacher's reactions, whether they are expected to work separately or jointly, whether the teacher is directing comments to them or others, and what the classroom rules really are at the moment. For instance, when children are working in pairs or small groups, the teacher may intervene to sanction their behavior, as in the next example:

> [Second grade. Mrs. G is instructing Peter, David, and Adam at a table on a
> math assignment. The rest of the class is broken down into small working
> groups.]

Mrs. G: [to David] Did you get twenty-eight?

David: (   )

> [Several loud voices from elsewhere in the room are heard.]

→   Mrs. G: [looks up and scans the room, finally calling out] Shh::! Teddy? Teddy?
> Teddy? [pause] Theodore. Keep your voice down. We're working over here.

Note that Mrs. G does not instruct Teddy to stop talking altogether, as she might
well do in a whole-group lesson, but to simply lower his voice so as not to interfere
with other students' activities.

In the American-system schools that I have observed, students' negative comments to the teacher regarding other students' behavior tend to be either ignored or
negatively sanctioned. Positive comments are usually handled differently. The interchange below shows Sarah providing a supportive ritual move toward Meredith,
confirming her standing in the group as a well-behaved student. There is an almost
explicit reference to Meredith's social self that Sarah is protecting.

> [Second grade, Mrs. G's class. Teacher has been roaming the classroom
> from table to table, helping individual children with their math and other
> projects.]

Mrs. G: [approaching a table] Uh, Meredith. Meredith? Shh . . .

Mrs. G: [sits down beside Sarah at a table]

→   Sarah: She wasn't being herself.

←   Mrs. G: She wasn't being herself.

Though the teacher has sanctioned Meredith's overloudness, she confirms Sarah's
generous willingness to interpret Meredith's unacceptable behavior as an isolable
occurrence not representative of her true social self.

In the fourth-grade science class with international students (an American-system
school in Niger), a student takes the opposite tack toward a fellow student; observing that his lab partner has not followed the correct sequence of procedures, he asserts that this makes her a "cheater." The teacher swiftly leaps into the breach, minimizing both the partner's omission and Mark's accusation:

→   Mark: [pointing to a column on his female partner's lab notebook] You never did
> make your predictions. *Cheater!*

←   Teacher: [to Mark] Now don't call her "cheater." She forgot that column, that's all.

In schools observed in Kenya, teachers were often much more public and extensive in their authoritative evaluations. Students were sometimes encouraged to join
the teacher in acclaiming substantive evaluations for others. Often, after a student
had answered a question correctly, the teacher would encourage the rest of the class
to "clap for him"; when a student did not answer correctly, a teacher might encourage the rest of the class to chant a negative phrase such as "Shame on you." Teachers in Kenya would also admonish students for writing too big and wasting paper, invoking the cost to parents for school supplies. Negative evaluations did not seem
to be subject to the appeal of outside rules or authoritative sources of information,
as is customary in American-system schools.

In general, teachers zealously guard their authority to make evaluative decisions. Student initiatives that seem to usurp teacher authority or prerogative are not welcome and are sometimes severely sanctioned. In the following example from a second-grade classroom in the United States, the teacher is very displeased:

→   Jonathan: [approaches Mrs. G and waits by her for a minute as she works with Adam in a math tutorial]
←   Mrs. G: [looks up and scans the room without acknowledging Jonathan]
→   Jonathan: [to Mrs. G] Edward's been fooling [(around with the   )
←   Mrs. G: [I don't, excuse me [holds her hands up at Jonathan as though to stop his continued talk]. They're, they're in charge of that. You, are to be working on your math. You are behind. You don't, you have not paid attention to two, instructional periods on what-you're stuck on. I'm not helping you anymore. *Sit down.* I expect it all completed by Monday.
     Jonathan: [seems to wince and walks away]

The teacher's wrath is apparently incited by several things: Jonathan has interrupted her, he has not been properly doing his own work, and his monitoring of fellow students is seen as completely inappropriate. The teacher directs his attention back to his own vector of activity and challenges his authority to make any pronouncements about others ("they're in charge of that").

On other occasions when children are working together, there is no teacher intervention. As we might expect, the dialog between students is noticeably different from that between student and teacher and often demonstrates co-monitoring and negotiation, an orientation to maintaining cooperative ritual equilibrium between themselves while at the same time displaying orientation to classroom rules and authority. The following examples are excerpted from the science lesson previously considered:

Q1   Jack: [to Jason] What'd you put?
A1Q2 Jason: [to Jack] I put fifteen. What'd you put?
A2   Jack: I put thirteen.

Here Jack and Jason, while working as lab partners, engage in a question-answer-question-answer sequence to share information about a part of the assignment they have each done individually, each seeking confirmation of the accuracy of his work and acknowledging the right of the other to act as informant.

The next interchange between another pair of students illustrates their recognition that the lab experiment is a joint vector of activity. It also demonstrates how children use language to negotiate participation roles in an underspecified activity structure (deliberately underspecified in the teacher's introduction). The teams of children have been instructed to use the clay provided to fashion two cylinders of the same sizes as others made of acrylic and wood, one large and one small.

Q1   Honey: Do you want to make the large or the small one?
A1   Michael: The small one.
CP   Honey: Okay. I'll make the large one.

Honey initiates a verbal decision-making interchange by offering a choice to her partner. Although she might have responded to Michael's answer by saying that she, too, would like to make the small one and suggesting that he make the large one (thereby, perhaps, causing a reinterpretation of the original question as infelicitous), she instead agrees and asserts her role as complementary.

In a third group, language is also used to determine who will make which cylinder, but there is less deference in the negotiation; the initiator simply announces his intent:

PD   Neil: I'll do the little one and you do the big one.
C   Mariama: Okay.

Neil's assertion could also be seen as a proposal (which includes a directive to his partner) to negotiate before the tasks are actually under way; to negotiate, however, Mariama would likely have to make a negative move such as a complaint ("I don't want to make the big one" or "Why do you always get to do the one you want to do").[8]

Finally, let us consider an expanded version of the initial interchange between Jack and Jason. The students are attentive to the fact that the science experiment is cast within a routine time frame that lasts until 11:30. At least one of the students, Jack, also displays attention to the procedural rules of the science experiment as well as to the duality of participation structure (student-teacher as well as student-student).

		[Jason and Jack have just completed their experiment. Jason has begun to play with the leftover clay by making it into a long cylinder and twisting it and submerging it in the vial of water for the experiment.]
Q1	Jack:	Should we clean up?
Q2	Jason:	What time is it? [still playing with the clay]
A2	Jack:	Eleven fifteen.
A1	Jason:	[still playing] No, we don't have to yet. [the class ends at eleven thirty, as both boys know.] [Jack begins to join Jason in playing with the clay.]
		. . . . .
Q1	Mrs. P:	[a few moments later] Jack, is that part of the experiment? [doesn't wait for response]
Q2		What should you do after you finish?
A2	Jack:	Clean up.
E2	Teacher:	Right. Clean up your materials and write up your conclusions.

Jack's initial question ("Should we clean up?") demonstrates his involvement with two concerns: his classmate Jason, with whom he is carrying out the experiment, and his good standing as a student member of the classroom, one who orients to the rules set up by the authority of the teacher. His question can easily be judged as an indirect attempt to negotiate with his lab partner to follow the rules. When Jason tacitly defines their use of the clay in terms of activity time slots, Jack accepts this rationale. Unluckily, he is the one to be later scolded, when Mrs. P invokes the rules in the second arrowed interchange, "Jack, is that part of the experiment? What should you do after you finish?"; access to the clay, she implies, is available only for the duration of the experiment and does not extend to recreation.

Note, however, that the teacher skillfully minimizes a larger threat to Jack's social self by invoking his knowledge (and therefore his competence). She does not wait for a response to her first question, whose answer would be negative, but rather seems to reformulate her move to generate a positive answer sequence; both questions instance a questioning mode to indirectly sanction Jack's behavior in playing with the clay. After Jack answers her question, "What should you do after you finish?" with "Clean up," she gives a positive evaluative remark, "Right," and "plays back" his answer with more detail, "Clean up your materials and write up your conclusions," thus guiding Jack back to academic task engagement.

Conclusion

I began this chapter by suggesting that it is part of a continuing effort to explore human creativity and adaptation to social change. I have argued that the mastery of ritual work is a critical aspect of children's learning to manage social experiences and that this is an important element of the language development of older children. I have also suggested that because most ritual work must be adapted to ongoing interactional moments, it is inherently improvisational and draws upon the same kind of learning instinct for improvising new expressions out of known structures as does the learning of language itself.

Primary school is a place in which traditional societal values are inculcated, but it also brings children together and exposes them to ideas and ways of doing things with people outside the immediate household. The nature of the primary school experience—whether in highly modernized nations such as the United States or in more traditional rural countries—is one in which a child confronts an institutionalized setting that is different from the household setting in which he or she has been nurtured up to that time.[9] The instrumental focus on acquiring basic literacy, numeracy, and thinking skills may be new, especially for children in traditional rural societies. For virtually all children, ratified access to situational resources at school, and ratified displays of affect and authority, is different from that at home; accordingly, ritual interpretation of behavior that asserts social belonging and enacts social presence occurs differently in the two environments. Rules for school-appropriate participation and the structure of routine activities must be learned and their implementation constantly negotiated with co-interactants; only part of what the child is expected to learn is explicitly taught.

In either home or school environment, both situational instrumentalities and ritual equilibrium are embedded in a social matrix. As children grow older and experience more of the social world, their language practices change and their communicative resources deepen. Through recurrent similar experiences they master the expectations of particular social situations such as primary school—which typically involve the mastery of activity structures and participant structures, as well as language practices embedded in the richer fabric of communicative modalities (nonverbal resources, identifiably distinct linguistic varieties [language, dialect, register], and modality modifications such as tone of voice and loudness). At the same time, they enrich their repertoire of communicative resources for improvisational and creative responses to novel interactional moments. The child improvises responses and initiatives, using as a reservoir for creative inputs what he or she brings to the new setting from previous experiences, including experiences from primary school.

In the classroom, students must manage participation within appropriate vectors of activity. They learn which messages are intended for them and which are not, what they are expected to respond to and how. They are expected to make cognitively demanding academic tasks their primary vectors of activity, but at the same time they must master engagement with other students as they adapt to the rhythm of interchanges, allocation of resources, and co-monitoring of behavior.

The primary classroom is especially interesting because it universally manifests an intricate context in which linguistic resources develop. Multilingual settings are particularly rich, but multiple modalities are constituted in monolingual settings as well. Community environments where primary schools function vary widely— from highly enthusiastic formally educated households to illiterate and even hostile households who would prefer to keep their children at home—and certainly influence children's school behavior. Yet the same parameters can be used to describe classroom behavior across communities. Even though displays of affect and authority may vary widely in different settings, they always appear with claims and regulation of access to classroom resources. Social presence depends upon what co-interactants will accord but also upon what the principal actor invokes or engages—and how skillfully this is attuned to specific structures of activity, participation, and modality.

That discourse is always embedded in activity and participation structures is known, but the details are still not well understood. In any situation, co-management of ritual equilibrium and instrumental goals is likely to be regulated through elements of participation, activity, and modality. The flexibility of modality resources to engage in complex participation and activity structures is, in a sense, unlimited, for the resources for today's improvisation build upon one's assimilation of yesterday's interactional moments with those of the more distant past. Ritual interpretation powerfully shapes both creative expression of individuals and the adaptation of societies to social change.

NOTES

This chapter is dedicated to the memory of Erving Goffman, whose voice still resonates clearly in our dialog. His seminal work has provided the basis for my understanding of ritual in everyday human interaction and has become closely interwoven with my own thinking and extension of concepts about ritual in the settings that I have researched, namely, service encounters and primary classrooms. Because it was my good fortune to study with him as well as to read his work, his influence has been pervasive and would be impossible to fully unravel.

1. The term *primary school* is more common outside the United States, where *elementary school* is the more usual term.

2. Recent work by Gardner (1993) on creativity and gifted individuals suggests an intriguing distinction. Gardner defines creative acts as *only* those that are ultimately accepted and incorporated into the larger system (whether the system be music, art, language, or whatever). To combine Gardner's proposal with Pinker's (1994) terminology, we might say that true creativity is judged by the acceptance of improvisational efforts into the similarity

space. Though a distinction between improvisation and creativity might be difficult to consistently impose upon material such as I discuss here, it highlights the negotiated, tentative character of the arrangements displayed in each excerpt from classroom talk. Since structure and improvisation—or creativity—operate at many levels, the suggestion that true creativity is judged by the acceptance of improvisational efforts into the similarity space might ultimately be useful as an operational definition of competency or mastery of a certain structure or level.

3. The first study was carried out with a grant from the National Institute of Education to Marilyn Merritt at the Center for Applied Linguistics (1978–80), with research associates Frank Humphrey and Stephen Cahir, and uses videotaped data collected in an earlier study funded by the Carnegie Corporation of New York through an award to Roger Shuy and Peg Griffin, also at the Center for Applied Linguistics. The second study was carried out with a grant from the Social Science and Humanities Research Council of Canada awarded to Ailie Cleghorn at McGill University (1986–88); the study was carried out jointly by Cleghorn and Merritt in collaboration with graduate assistants Jared O. Abagi and Grace Bunyi, using direct classroom observation and audiotaping of classroom interaction. Major publications reporting the results of these studies have been included in the references. The science experiment examples were collected in 1995.

4. A primary focus on individual accomplishment as a mode of learning or task accomplishment is not shared by all cultures (Erickson & Mohatt 1982, Jacob & Jordan 1992, Merritt 1994a). Much of the focus on individual activity is an artifact of the literacy orientation of industrial societies (cf. Ong 1982) and their mass formal educational systems spawned in the nineteenth and twentieth centuries—wherein primary orientation is to achieving literacy, numeracy, and the means for individual uncensored access to new information.

5. By vector of activity I mean communicative interchanges and instrumental activities with forward thrust propelled by persistent intention. Two parties may be mutually or separately engaged in more than one vector of activity, and a vector of activity need not be continuously associated with the same participant(s).

6. Transcription conventions particular to this chapter: forward arrow → to draw attention to a particular move; backward arrow ← to indicate a move that is responsive to a prior move; letter labels to identify move characteristics mentioned in the text: Q question (Q1 first question, Q2 second question, and so on), A answer (A1, A2,), C confirmation, E evaluation, P proposal, D directive, I initiating, S supportive, V verbal, NV nonverbal, RB ritual brackets.

7. Normative ranking or "loading" (Merritt 1979) of modalities usually places the verbal modality "ahead" of the nonverbal modality in terms of what is officially most ritually salient and most reportable in terms of demanding redress (e.g., "He didn't answer my question!"). However, some vectors of activity are loaded with differing ranks of modalities; lumber workers at a noisy saw mill may count the nonverbal modality as more official than the verbal (Robert Johnson, personal communication). Recent work on activity structures such as that on leading and nonleading activities (e.g., Beach 1992) is relevant, as is work on dual processing (e.g., Merritt et al. 1988).

8. As an aside, in the last two examples it is boys who either asserted or were given first preference with respect to their female partners. As it occurred, both of the girls, although attending an American-system school and from an upper-middle-class background, hail from African cultures that traditionally accord more deference to males than females, whereas the two boys come from European backgrounds and have spent much of their childhood in developing countries.

9. In nonindustrialized countries such as Kenya and Niger, where mass education is relatively recent, and, in the case of Niger, is still not well received in rural areas, the impact of primary school as an instrument of social change can hardly be denied.

8

Register Shifting with Dialect Resources in Instructional Discourse

CAROLYN TEMPLE ADGER

A hallmark of sociolinguistic development in school-age children is their in-creasing expertise at constructing linguistic register to match other dimensions of social activity (Martin 1983). Other chapters in this volume explore how register modification accomplishes, signals, and reinforces shifts within the social context. This chapter details children's register shifting through contrasting dialect vari-ants: replacing vernacular English dialect features with standard English dialect features during instructional discourse. This register-shifting pattern suggests that dialect appropriateness at school is tied not just to setting (school, classroom) or genre (teacher talk, academic talk), as is widely assumed, or to addressee (Lucas & Borders 1987, Rickford & McNair-Knox 1994) but also to footing: "the alignment we take up to ourselves and others present" (Goffman 1981:128). In the classroom under study, dialect constitutes a register resource for signaling one's footing in re-lation not only to other group members but also to the immediate academic task. Standard English variants are used in taking an authoritative footing—in speak-ing as one who expects to be believed, by virtue of one's academic knowledge.

Dialect and Schooling: Appropriateness Issues

Attention to social dialects in school settings occurs within a generally politically charged environment of race and social class relations (Collins 1988, Delpit 1995, Fairclough 1992, Milroy & Milroy 1991, Smitherman 1986). Despite linguistic ev-idence of dialect equality in language structure and communicative viability (Labov 1972b, Wolfram & Fasold 1974), "dialect choice" at school is subject to appropri-ateness conditions rooted in the elitist traditions of education. In the popular view, there is no choice of dialect at all in educational settings. In fact, standard English and education imply each other: standard English may be defined as "the kind of English habitually used in education and by most of the educated, English-speaking people in the United States" (Taylor 1989:52). This widely accepted standard-dialect-and-school relationship has led to judgments of cognitive incompetence when vernacular speech occurs in such gatekeeping activities as testing (Wolfram 1983). And it provides the sociopolitical means for high school students to resist mainstream values in the school setting by using vernacular features (Fordham, chapter 11, this volume).

Recent quantitative sociolinguistic inquiry into dialect distribution at school supports the widely held view that vernacular features are inappropriate in instructional discourse. Examining language use during academic and nonacademic events within a kindergarten class, a fourth-grade class, and a sixth-grade class where all students used both African American Vernacular English (AAVE) and standard English variants, Lucas and Borders (1987, 1994) found that older children (grades four and six) consistently avoided the vernacular in teacher-led lessons. Only in small-group work without the teacher did vernacular variants appear. The fact that in teacher-led lessons children spoke far less than teachers, as is often the case (Cazden 1988), and that children's talk was functionally limited to responding may have influenced the dialect patterning by constraining linguistic environments for dialect contrast. However, when interviewed, children and teachers asserted that AAVE is inappropriate for instructional discourse, as the popular view holds. Thus, they endorsed the overt norms of appropriate language use (Labov 1966). But in academic interaction in peer groups, the children's use of vernacular dialect features conformed to contrasting, covert norms.

In a context where instruction uses a standard dialect, warns Fairclough (1992), appropriateness is more than a straightforward matching of linguistic features to a situation. At school, appropriateness is likely to become ideology when idealized "representations of sociolinguistic reality . . . correspond to the perspective and partisan interests of one section of society or one section of a particular social institution—its dominant section" (1992:48). The challenge for the analyst is to identify the sociolinguistic appropriateness norms that underlie classroom talk. Here I show that language appropriateness in a classroom, including dialect choices, is sensitive to micro-interactional considerations, as well as to the traditional cultural conventions about standardness and education expressed by the students and teachers in the Lucas & Borders study.

Issues in Identifying Dialects

Complicating investigation into language variation is the flexible nature of dialect. Standard English and vernacular dialects are idealized linguistic constructs, rather than concrete, discrete language varieties that can be definitively characterized. Dialect standardness[1] and vernacularness are better conceptualized as constituting two poles of a language continuum (Labov 1972b, Wolfram & Fasold 1974), because dialects of a language typically share most of their features, often defined contrastively (e.g., copula absence in vernacular dialects). Items subject to dialectal variation are arrayed along the continuum according to the degree of relative stigmatization or prestige within a speech community (Hymes 1962). The term "standard English" is used here to mean a dialect whose features cluster nearer the prestige pole of the dialect continuum for the speech community in which it is spoken.

Dialect and Register

Despite difficulties in defining dialects, clearly language users orient to the notion that some language features fall along a sociolinguistic continuum. Because their place there is governed by some roughly shared norms (Labov 1972b; Shuy, Wolfram, & Riley 1967), dialect features constitute resources for constructing register[2]—ways of speaking made up of those "conventionalized lexical, syntactic, and prosodic [and other] choices deemed appropriate for the setting and audience" (Tannen & Wallat 1993:63; cf. Ferguson 1985). Register shifting with dialect variants involves speakers' selecting items from along the dialect continuum, based both on their perceptions of their speech community's appropriateness norms and their immediate goals in speaking. Considerations such as the social class of speaker and hearer (Labov 1966), interactional roles of speaker and hearer (Bell 1984), and politeness strategies (Brown & Levinson 1987) are involved.

Unless the speech community is construed very narrowly, dialect selection practices for meeting register demands may vary considerably (Labov 1972b). Speakers may not entirely agree on selection criteria for variable language features because of competing appropriateness norms (Wolfram 1991). Among those who generally use the standard dialect zone of the continuum, for example, stigmatized features may well be avoided for the most part, whereas they may be freely used by other speakers.

How children develop register-shifting skills that incorporate dialect features is not well understood (Introduction, this volume; Rickford & McNair-Knox 1994). But because some language norms are prescribed in schools and because standard English is so widely assumed to be the unchallengeable medium of teaching and learning, examining dialect distribution in instructional discourse becomes relevant as evidence of children's communicative competence in the classroom speech community. Syntactic variation is particularly subject to social evaluation and thus to educational prescription (Wolfram 1970). For that reason, and because syntactic features are more salient in the data under consideration than are phonological features,[3] I focus on this aspect of dialect.

Vernacular Dialect in Instructional Discourse

The data examined here come from a three-year, ethnographically based investigation into AAVE speakers' school language experiences in five Baltimore elementary schools located in lower- and working-class[4] neighborhoods (Adger, Wolfram, Detwyler, & Harry 1993).[5] From the first classroom visits, it became clear that while teachers generally used standard English variants,[6] students generally used vernacular English, without negative sanction. However, as I show here, they regularly shifted toward the standard end of the dialect continuum within literacy events and in presentations where they adopted an authoritative footing about the topic at hand. For both teachers and students, then, speaking standard English meant speaking with academic authority—the usual teacher function but a less usual one for students. These patterns are exemplified here in one language arts lesson from Mrs. Henry's fourth- and fifth-grade special education classroom. The patterns described held generally across the nine classrooms in which I was a frequent guest, except for considerable variation in the nature and frequency of events evoking standard English (Adger & Wolfram 1993).

Literacy Events in Mrs. Henry's Classroom

Mrs. Henry taught a self-contained[7] class of special education students, all classified as fourth and fifth graders with mild disabilities—learning disabilities, language learning disabilities, and mild retardation. Class membership shifted somewhat during the year as students came and went. Still, some students remained in the class for both fourth and fifth grades, and some had been at the school since kindergarten. Mrs. Henry had known several of her students before they came to her class, especially those from the self-contained special education class for younger students—Rita, Tyree, Kevin, and Mary. Like other authoritative African American teachers (Delpit 1995), Mrs. Henry was a caring teacher and a firm one. One day when she was not at school, a student connected the group's unruly conduct to her absence, explaining that "Mrs. Henry make us behave." Mrs. Henry's students respected her and liked being in her class.

Eighteen years of teaching learning-disabled students had convinced Mrs. Henry that intensive reading and writing experience enhanced their academic achievement. Consequently, she devoted the most productive, peaceful morning hours[8] to lessons in which students experienced texts, called "stories," in multiple ways: by reading and rereading aloud and silently from published texts; by listening to Mrs. Henry read; by engaging with her in extemporaneous, dialogic text construction and reconstruction (as in the lesson presented here); in prewriting activities involving plot development and other skill building (here, vocabulary); by writing a story summary or a story related to one they already knew, or some new, personal text connected to a holiday or a special school event, such as a field trip; and through combining reading, writing, listening, and telling. Within activities producing writing or written-like language (Tannen 1982b)—most notably here, analytic statements about story structure for Mrs. Henry to write on the board—children shifted into a very careful speaking style with exaggerated intonational contours and standard English features.

The literacy lesson excerpted below exemplifies multiple modalities of text engagement anchored in "Rumpelstiltskin," a familiar story but one they had not previously read together. Although Mrs. Henry calls the lesson event "Read-Aloud," the term is used metonymously: oral reading of the published text serves as the foundation for other literacy-skill activities that address the lesson objective written on the blackboard, "Recall details and describe character traits." These lesson activities constitute interactive frames (Tannen & Wallat 1993) in which teacher and students demonstrate in multiple ways their shared understanding of what is going on. The following list indicates lesson activities and their duration:

Introduction and character traits	13 minutes, 5 seconds
Read-aloud	13 minutes, 15 seconds
Charts	12 minutes, 10 seconds
Pair-work	12 minutes, 30 seconds
Total Read-Aloud lesson	51 minutes

The first lesson activity, introduction and review of character trait vocabulary, is intended to help the students to "get some of these words"—to recognize them and know their meanings for later use in describing "Rumpelstiltskin" characters. Next, Mrs. Henry reads the story aloud, pausing at page-turning breaks to check comprehension and enhance engagement by eliciting student summaries and comments that begin to transform the written story into an oral class text. In the third lesson activity, "Doing Charts," this oral text is reauthored into a new genre during a sort of literary analysis event in which students dictate entries for story map charts detailing the story's setting, characters, problems, events, and solution. In the final lesson activity, students work in pairs to "come up with some words to describe the 'Rumpelstiltskin' characters."

In each lesson phase, students occasionally use vernacular dialect features (e.g., auxiliary deletion, plural deletion), but neither Mrs. Henry nor the other students comment on this. There is a dramatic register shift, however, in discourse tasks (Gumperz 1982) most closely connected to writing. In the charts section of the lesson, where the students convert the story into its new written form through dictation, they deliberately select standard English alternatives.

The following section presents typical excerpts from instructional discourse in which register shifting with dialect resources reflects the emerging social relational context. I quote at some length in order to show the flavor of the talk and to include contextualization cues at activity boundaries that signal register shifts.

"Rumpelstiltskin" Read-Aloud

Lesson Introduction and Character Traits   As the lesson begins, the students bring their chairs to the front of the classroom and form a semicircle around Mrs. Henry. Once they are settled, she selects speakers to present crucial lesson framing elements, such as reading the lesson objective and the vocabulary items listed on the board. She also solicits open, overlapping participation (e.g., "Our story for today is what?" line 1 below). The lesson is thus interactionally constructed out of Mrs. Henry's presentational talk and brief student responses to her questions and other prompts, such as "I know you know that word" (line 9). Student responses and comments are sometimes evaluated explicitly, sometimes implicitly when other students or the teacher take them up. Throughout, the interactional pace is lively and all of the students participate—boys more than girls, some boys more than others. The fact that students speak in short bursts means that relatively few linguistic environments for dialect contrasts occur in this lesson part, as demonstrated in the first excerpt below.

(In the excerpted sections, **boldface** indicates vernacular features of children's speech, Ø represents a word or morpheme deleted by vernacular rules, and <u>double-underlining</u> indicates dialect contrast environments where vernacular does not occur.)

1	Mrs. Henry:		Okay. Uh. Before I start reading, we have a lot to *talk* about and discuss . . and to get some . . things in our heads so you'll know *what* we going to be *doing* today. [4.5] [soft] Move around, Kevin, so Tyree can get up there. O*kay*. [Holding up the book] Our story for today is what?
2	Mary:	→	Rumpel=
3	Monisha:	→	=Rumpelstiltskin.
4	Mary:	→	stiltskin.
5	Mrs. Henry:		Rumpel . . stiltskin. [soft] What did I do with the book.
6	Monisha:		Right there.
7	Mrs. Henry:		O*kay*. Who would like to read the objective up here. Uh, Julius.
8	Julius:		We . . recall . . story . . . detail<u>s</u> . . and describe . . .
9	Mrs. Henry:		I know you know *that* word.=
10	Akeem:	→	=[Character<u>s</u> .
11	Julius:	→	=[Character<u>s</u> .
12	Mrs. Henry:		Characters, okay. You did really well with that reading . . because I know you're going to do well with that ob:jective because you know what recall is all about, right? What is it all about.
13	Julius:		You read a story, you write question<u>s</u> . . about it.
14	Mrs. Henry:		How- what kind of questions do you write.
15	Mary:	→	Recall question<u>s</u>.
16	Julius:		Well, you write it like <u>sentences</u>, <u>sentences</u> [to the story.
17	Mrs. Henry:		[That you have- hm?
18	Julius:		You write it like <u>sentences</u> to the story.
19	Mrs. Henry:		Okay, you know they are recall because you can look right back in the story and [find . . what.
20	Julius:	→	[You . . find the detail<u>s</u> .
21	Mrs. Henry:		The answer or the details. Very good. [loud] And I *knew* you knew the word CHARACTERS because *all* of our stories have what.
22	Julius:		Character<u>s</u> .
23	Mrs. Henry:		All of our fairy tales that we've been working with have *characters*. But I'm so . . surprised an- an- and so *pleased* that you knew that D word. [soft] And what was that D word.
24	Julius:		Detail.
25	Mrs. Henry:		The other D word.
26	Thomas:		Decide.=
27	Akeem:	→	=Describe?=
28	Julius:		=Describe.=
29	Mrs. Henry:		=Describe. Very good.

Much of the student talk that Mrs. Henry elicits throughout the lesson consists of words and phrases that label the points she wants to emphasize: "Rumpelstiltskin" (lines 2–4), characters (lines 10–11, 20), recall questions (line 15), detail (lines 20–21, 24), describe (lines 27–28). In the short responses from students, only one linguistic environment for dialect contrast presents itself, plural marker, and the marker is present in each case. However, since vernacular plural marker deletion applies only at a rate of about 33% (Wolfram 1974a), identifying dialect choice seems unwarranted when student talk is so limited.

Several minutes into the lesson, as students read aloud from character trait charts, vernacular features appear in lesson-related comments. They are boldface in the following dialog:

1	Mrs. Henry:		And this is what *you* are most of the time. I would describe you as this *all* the time, *most* of the time.
2	Thomas:		What?
3	Tyree:		Clam?
4	Mrs. Henry:		No. Stop Kevin and be still. Calm::=
5	X:		=Calm.
6	Mary:		Calm?=
7	Mrs. Henry:		=If someone's calm . . don't you think that Mary's calm. She's real peaceful?
8	Kevin:	→	She **be**=
9	X:		=No. No.
10	X:		Nuh uh.
11	X:		NO.
12	Kevin:	→	NO. SHE **BE** BANGING ON PEOPLE.
13	Mrs. Henry:		Okay, well that's . . that's outside . . where she's=
14	Julius:		=No in the class too.
15	Mrs. Henry:		supposed to. In the *class*room she's calm.
16	Julius:	→	No, she **ain't**.
17	Mrs. Henry:		Okay, what's the next one?

Mrs. Henry responds to the content but not the form of Kevin's "She be banging on people" (line 12) and ignores Julius's "No, she ain't" (line 16).

Later in the vocabulary review, Mrs. Henry asks students to apply the character trait adjectives to characters from a more familiar story, "Little Red Riding Hood." (They are practicing here for the subsequent task of choosing adjectives for "Rumpelstiltskin" characters.) At first, responses are brief—characters' names and adjectives. Then they adopt a descriptive formula: character name + *was* + adjective. When they expand on this formula, vernacular phenomena may appear:

1	Mrs. Henry:		What wor:d would you use to descri:be the woodcutter? We didn't know much about him, but we could . . perhaps figure out something to describe him.
2	Kevin:		He was ki:nd
3	Mrs. Henry:		He was *ki::nd*=
4	X:		=[( )
5	Mrs. Henry:		=[Yes, he was kind. *Okay.* Now that you [know:
6	Julius:		[And he was=
7	Mrs. Henry:		=Okay, Julius, what do you have in mind.
8	Julius:		( ) Little Red Riding Hood was helpful?
9	Mrs. Henry:		Who was she . . okay, who was she- okay, why was she ( )=
10	Julius:	→	=Because she- she **taken** a basket to . . her grandmother.
11	X:		[( )
12	Mrs. Henry:		[Very good? One *one* more and we've got to stop.

13	Kevin:	The- the hunter was smart.
14	Mrs. Henry:	The hunter [was smart?
15	Akeem:	[Oh I know one.
16	Mrs. Henry:	Okay, you all are coming, now you're getting what we we're going to be doing.
17	X:	( )
18	Mrs. Henry:	Yes. What, [what?
19	Akeem:	[The grandmother.
20	Mrs. Henry:	What about the grandmother.
21	Akeem:	She was=
22	Thomas:	=brave, real bra- real real brave.
23	Mrs. Henry:	What [about ( ).
24	Thomas: →	[And she got **ate**. She got **ate**.

Two vernacular verb forms appear here: *taken* in line 10 (the verb is ambiguous between auxiliary deletion and participle generalized as past) and *ate* in line 24 (past tense is generalized as past participle).

In this first lesson section, then, student utterances are generally short and often syntactically elliptical responses to teacher elicitation or lesson formulae that preclude vernacular ("The hunter was smart"). Because student talk is limited, linguistic environments for dialect contrast are limited. Vernacular features do occur in academic talk with the teacher, however, and when that happens, no repair is requested or offered.

Read-Aloud   This pattern continues in the second lesson section where the story is read aloud and discussed: student responses continue to be short, and the vernacular items that occur are accepted. The following excerpt includes Mrs. Henry's presentation of the literacy task and the first comprehension check:

1	Mrs. Henry:	How many of you already know the story of "Rumpelstiltskin."
2	(Many):	( )
3	Mrs. Henry:	Okay. [loud] Okay, now let's listen . . real . . CLOSEly for *all:* the details. You will know the *setting?* Hopefully, you will know the *problem?* And some of the *events* that happened in the story. And you're going to l- listen for the characters and listen to . . be able to *descri:be* some of these characters, all ri:ght? Listen, and you got to sit still, I'm ready. [reading] Once upon a time, [A king commands a miller's daughter to spin straw into gold. She is helped by a little man (Rumpelstiltskin, as it turns out) who spins straw into gold in return for her necklace.]
4	Mrs. Henry:	[Displaying a picture from the story] What is this?
5	X:	Wheel.=
6	X:	=Wheel.=
7	Thomas:	=The wheel.
8	Mrs. Henry:	Spinning wheel. What is this?
9	X:	Necklace.=
10	X:	=The the um.=
11	X:	=The necklace.
12	Mrs. Henry:	The [necklace.
13	Kevin: →	[That **look** like a mic . . ro . . phone right there.

14	Mrs. Henry:	Oh, okay. Here's the girl right here in this picture. Okay (how's she feeling)- how do you think she's feeling here?
15	Monisha:	Sad.
16	Julius:	Sad.
17	Mrs. Henry:	Okay. What's all this stuff around her, see this?
18	Akeem:	Hay, hay.
19	Mary:	[Gold.
20	(Monisha): →	[No this . . straw,
21	Mary:	Straw.
22	(Monisha): →	**(Ain't** hay?)
23	Mary: →	It **look** like it.
24	Monisha: →	**It ain't** much.

Commenting on the pictures and responding to the comprehension questions, students use some vernacular items: verb agreement in line 13 ("That look like a microphone right there") and existential *it* plus *ain't* in line 24. (Line 20 seems ambiguous with respect to copula deletion because the potential sibilant of *is* is bracketed by the /s/ of *this* and the /s/ of *straw*. Transcription of line 22 is uncertain.)

The absence thus far of teacher repair to language form suggests consensus among community members, students and teacher, as to dialect appropriateness: students use vernacular features in this sort of academic talk. The next segment underscores and refines this point. When Mrs. Henry repeats student utterances that include vernacular forms, by way of accepting (Mehan 1979) or questioning them, she substitutes a standard construction for the vernacular, but without the contrastive stress that would convey censure. Here repetition has the typical conversational force of accepting or questioning what the student has said, rather than critiquing its form. This pattern points to the other half of this group's dialect norm: while students often use vernacular forms, teachers use standard forms.

		[The little man spins straw in exchange for the girl's ring. The students are considering what they would do in a similar situation.]
1	Kevin:	I would just have to die:
2	Tyree: →	I wouldn't do **nothing**.
3	Mrs. Henry:	Okay, what did he
4	Thomas: →	I wouldn't do **nothing**.
5	Mrs. Henry:	You would rather *die*?
6	X: →	You wouldn't do **nothing**?
7	X:	( )
8	Mrs. Henry:	You think
9	Thomas: →	I wouldn't do **nothing**. I wouldn't do
	→	**nothing** for the king.
10	Mrs. Henry: →	You wouldn't do anything for the king? You would be locked up in the *room*?
11	X:	I'd [(just say)
12	Thomas:	[When the man came then I'd run out and **ran** away.
		[The little man extracts the promise of the girl's first born, and she and the king are married.]
13	Mrs. Henry:	How many [times did the man come?
14	X:	[Three.=

15	Mrs. Henry:		=The little man. Okay. And what did . . and what was that third promise that she made, *Monisha*?
16	X:		( )
17	Mrs. Henry:		*Monisha*?
18	Monisha:		The baby.
19	Mrs. Henry:		What baby?
20	Monisha:	→	Her first baby, if she **have** it.
21	Mrs. Henry:	→	Whenever she has her first baby, okay? If she . . marries?
22	Monisha:		The king.
23	Mrs. Henry:		Okay. And here we are. What's happening here, Rita? On this page.
24	Rita:	→	[soft] The king Ø kissing.
25	Mrs. Henry:	→	[soft] Who's kissing who?
26	Rita:		The king.
27	Mrs. Henry:	→	The king is kissing who?
28	Rita:		The girl.
29	Mrs. Henry:		Okay. ( ) Why is he kissing her.
30	Thomas:		That **don't** look like the king.
31	Mrs. Henry:		Why is he kissing her.
32	Rita:		Cause she <u>spun</u> all the straw into gold.
33	Mrs. Henry:		And she wants to do what?=
34	Thomas:		=I don't see **no** gold.
35	Mrs. Henry:		It's just the picture, dear. It's not gold, it's . . gold . . what?
36	X:		Straw.
37	Mrs. Henry:		Straw. It-it's not *gold*: like coins of gold, but . . the=
38	Mary:		=The straw <u>is</u> gold.

At several points in this segment, Mrs. Henry repeats a student's comment, substituting a standard variant for a vernacular one. Mrs. Henry's "You wouldn't do anything for the king?" (line 10) rephrases Thomas's "I wouldn't do nothing" (line 9); "Whenever she has her first baby" (line 21) rephrases "Her first baby, if she have it" (line 20); and "The king is kissing who?" (line 27) rephrases "The king kissing" (line 24). In all cases, the teacher implicitly accepts the student's vernacular utterance by requesting elaboration without comment, contrastive stress, or pause for revision.[9] Elsewhere in this lesson, she does the same with vernacular phonological features. For example, she inserts the glide before the first vowel of *furious*—but, again, without contrastive stress. Her rephrasings highlight the dialect norms operating in this classroom: standard English for the teacher (when she takes her usual authoritative footing) and vernacular English for the students (except where they adopt an authoritative footing).

Doing Charts   After the oral reading is completed and the students have returned to their desks, Mrs. Henry leads them in analyzing "Rumpelstiltskin." As they dictate responses to her questions concerning the story's structure, she writes on a large story grammar chart. "Doing Charts" elicits an abrupt change into a presentational register that does not allow vernacular features. Essentially this is written language. Most of the students' analysis is not actually written, because they supply more contributions than the charts can hold; but the presentational register persists:

1	Mrs. Henry:	[loud] Okay. Uh . . think about the setting of this story. Where did this story take place. Think about the setting of the story. Where did it take place.
2	(Akeem):	In the forest.
3	Mrs. Henry:	Uh, in the forest?
4	Julius:	In a *kingdom*=
5	Kevin:	=In a *castle*.
6	Mrs. Henry: →	In a- a ca- in a kingdom. Okay, you- you're giving me some good things, so let's see if we can get it in some kind of a sentence. You're all- everything that you've given me is good, but see can you give me some kind of a sentence. Uh . . Kevin.
7	Kevin: →	[slow] The . . *story* . . <u>took</u> pla:ce
8	Mrs. Henry: →	Takes.
9	Kevin: →	[slow] Take<u>s</u> .. pla:ce in .. the .. kingdom.
10	(Akeem):	In a kingdom.
11	X: →	In A kingdom.
12	Mrs. Henry:	A kingdom. Okay. [writing on the chart, 16 seconds] [loud] And if you want to add more, in a *palace*? Or a palace in a kingdom, in, or- or you might want to say it takes place in uh- the forest *and* the palace in a kingdom? You can
13	Kevin:	In a village?
14	Mrs. Henry:	Uh . . okay. In a village, in a kingdom. [loud] You can, whatever you want to say . . as long as we can go back and sort of verify it from the story, all right? Uh . . PROBlem. There *was* a problem in this story, right? [18 seconds of classroom management deleted][10]
15	Mrs. Henry:	No, the other one (will stay). Now where, where, uh, what's the problem. Raise your hand if you know. Kevin, what do you think.
16	Kevin: →	The problem . . the *problem* <u>is</u> . . that the king . . want<u>s</u> gold.
17	Mrs. Henry:	Okay [(now this is)
18	Kevin: →	[No, the problem <u>is</u> . . that the king <u>is</u> . . going . . to chop off her head.

The shift into the formal, presentational register is preceded by an explicit register cue: "Okay, you're giving me some good things but let's see can we get it in some kind of a sentence" (line 6). (In other lessons, the shift occurs without prompting). In response, Kevin's lesson contributions are carefully crafted. He speaks slowly and loudly as he dictates, using reading intonation that inserts juncture between words and exaggerates the tone contour. Language form becomes publicly remarkable with this shift to a written language register: both teacher and students offer repairs to rhetorical style (not dialectal contrasts) in Kevin's sentence. Mrs. Henry edits his past tense verb to present tense (line 8), and Akeem corrects the article (i.e., "a," not "the" in initial position, (line 10). (Kevin turns to glare at him. It may be that he finds Akeem's criticism inappropriate since Akeem is an auditor rather than the primary addressee here and thus not privileged to comment [Bell 1984]. Perhaps the fact that Kevin and Akeem are out of sorts on this day provides the immediate social situation for Kevin to project Akeem further along Bell's audience role cline to overhearer status, with no rights to response.) Mrs. Henry and another student ratify the article repair. These repairs appear to index special rhetorical register requirements of this discourse activity that include but are not limited to dialect choice.

Where vernacular variants could occur variably, Kevin carefully produces standard alternatives: the copula, the third-person verb marker, the complementizer, and the auxiliary are all present in his problem statement, "The problem, the problem is that the king wants gold. No, the problem is that the king is going to chop off her head" (lines 16 and 18). (*Going* is realized with /ŋ/ instead of his usual /n/.)

Without writing Kevin's problem statement on the chart, Mrs. Henry invites other students to participate, and several eagerly present other problems. The lesson moves quickly now, and Mrs. Henry does not write all of the problems on the chart; nonetheless, students continue speaking in the written language, presentational register. Eleven more problems are suggested, all full sentences and all without vernacular structures. The following segment immediately follows the previous one:

1	Mrs. Henry:		You're getting- all of those were PROBlems. All of those were *problems. Yes.*
2	Julius:	→	The king was . . the king want<u>ed</u> to marry . . the girl.
3	Mrs. Henry:		The miller's daughter. O:kay. Uh, Monisha.
4	Monisha:		The king want<u>ed</u> her to spin the straw into gold. He <u>said</u> that tomorrow if you don't have the straw into gold he would kill her.
5	Mrs. Henry:		Okay. He told a lie. He told a lie. And that was the problem. [17 seconds of classroom management deleted]
6	Mrs. Henry:		Okay.
7	Kevin:	→	The problem . . <u>IS</u> . . that Rumpelstiltskin want<u>s</u> the baby. <u>Is</u> going to take the baby.=
8	Mrs. Henry:		=This story had uh LOTS of problems, didn't it. This story had a lot of *problems.* Okay?
9	Julius:	→	The king want<u>ed</u> . . the uh- girl to turn straw into gold and he want<u>ed</u> to *marry* her.
10	Mrs. Henry:		[soft] I like the way you sai:d that. Okay? Anybody else. Any more problems.
11	Mary:	→	The problem was . . that Rumpelstiltskin want<u>ed</u>
		→	everything that she own<u>ed</u>.
12	Mrs. Henry:		Uh: . . let me see now. He wanted everything that she own:ed. Now we should be writing *all:* of these down: so we can come up with the best ones. [loud] *Think* about everything that everybody's *sai:d* so we can come *ba:ck* . . think about everything that they've said so we can come back and see which ones=
13	Julius:		=I know one.
14	Mrs. Henry:		Yes.
15	Julius:		The king . . the king was um, he was greedy of gold, and he, and ( ) he was greedy of gold and he wantØ to marry the- the- uh girl cause- so she could make a lots of he could make a lot of gold.

Again, verbs have standard English agreement that vernacular rules could delete: presence of the copula, auxiliary, and third-person marker ("The problem is that Rumpelstiltskin wants the baby, is going to take the baby," line 7). Some phrasings seem infelicitous, such as Monisha's waffling between direct and indirect quoting, "The king wanted her to spin the straw into gold. He said that tomorrow if you don't have the straw into gold he would kill her" (line 4), but they are dialectally nearly uniform. Phonologically, there is also evidence of careful register: the past tense morpheme is fully enunciated on *wanted* in lines 2 and 4 (despite Julius's deletion of the morpheme in line 15); /ŋ/ is used instead of /n/; and the past tense marker is present on *owned* (line 11), where it could have been deleted by vernacular rules.

Soon Mrs. Henry announces that the class will have to finish the story map chart on the next day, but she quickly presents the remaining analytic task—identifying the solution to the story's problem. This discourse activity seems to call for comment, rather than presentation, and vernacular features occur:

1	Mrs. Henry:		Uh, the solution. What do you think . . the solution to the prob- we said the PROBlem was something that happened at the beginning. The problem was . . uh that=
2	X:		=Making straw out of gold?
3	Julius:		The solution . . was th- the girl and the little man.
4	Akeem:		The solution <u>is</u> the thing that came last.
5	Mrs. Henry:		What ha- what came last?
6	Julius:		The name.
7	Akeem:	→	The prince or the queen had to guess RumpelstiltskinØ name.
8	Mary:		No, he want<u>ed</u> to get=
9	Monisha:	→	=No the girl had to guess uh Rump=
10	Julius:	→	=Ohh, th- the girl **want** her baby, she **ain't** want- the queen **want** her baby, she **ain't** want to give it up. So she so she <u>made</u> another deal and **get** and <u>got</u> it right.

Even though the literary analysis activity is not quite complete, the task has shifted away from presentation. Akeem and Julius shift back toward the general lesson register, which permits vernacular. There is possessive marker deletion (line 7), third-person marker deletion (line 10), and *ain't* (line 10). But Julius's repair of *get* ("So she so she made another deal and get and got it right," line 10) suggests awareness of the lingering standard English appropriateness conditions, even as he enthusiastically throws out his suggestion.

Overall, then, the charts activity shows general covariation between presenting analytic contributions to be written and using a formal style that incorporates standard English variants. Student responses in this activity are more elaborated and thus longer than in previous activities, producing more linguistic environments for dialectal contrast. But the students avoid vernacular features until the activity's close, when the task has veered away from writing.[11] When the discourse task entails presenting analytic statements for writing on the chart, whether that language is actually written or not, students use a more formal register associated in this speech community (as elsewhere) with writing. This pattern holds across literacy activities in this and other elementary classrooms.

Pair-Work   In the final activity of the "Rumpelstiltskin" lesson, students work in pairs, selecting words from the character trait charts to describe characters and writing their words on paper strips for use the following day. Turning from the written language style of the charts activity to academic talk with peers brings the expectable shift into vernacular that Lucas and Borders describe (1987, 1994)—and the expectable noise. These utterances emerge from the din:

1 Tyree: Who Ø we doing?
2 Julius: King. (   ) Which word Ø you like?
3 Tyree: Greedy.
4 Julius: Yeah, greedy.
5 Tyree: How Ø you spell it?
6 Julius: G-R-E-E-D-Y.
7 Julius: It Ø got a R.

Summary   Across the four lesson activities, students use a rather wide dialect range, from standard English features in the more formal situation, to vernacular English with such generally stigmatized features as *ain't* and habitual *be* in less formal lesson activities. Although the frequently short, elliptical form of student responses in the first two lesson activities neutralizes dialect choice, it seems clear from repair phenomena and distribution patterns that, for students, standard English is reserved for the most formal register, which is used here for generating written language and displaying expertise at literary analysis. In other literacy talk—commenting on the pictures, discussing the story, doing a follow-up activity with peers—vernacular features are not avoided or repaired.

Speaking with Authority

Register shifting with dialect features, examined here in a literacy lesson, also occurs elsewhere when students speak with authority. In extemporaneous, role-played radio advertisements produced during a "store" math activity, students in another fourth- and fifth-grade special education class used standard English forms. In another class, a student used standard variants in explaining a diorama to his class. What unites selling, public explaining, and composing a story grammar is adopting an authoritative stance toward the audience. In these discourse tasks, students speak as "principals" (Goffman 1981)—transformed for the moment from their usual status as mere lesson participants into domain experts. In the lesson participant role, they build lessons with the teacher by supplying the words and phrases that complete her sentences. They supply the bits of knowledge made relevant by her lesson frame, demonstrate their academic engagement, and participate in focusing the lesson. As lesson principals, however, their contributions are far less constrained. It is up to them to construct an appropriate offering by culling their knowledge and to express it by using the linguistic resources that denote the authoritative footing. In this classroom, as in others, the register that covaries with adopting an authoritative footing generally requires a variety of standard English. Here I expand on the social function and value of this register.

Mrs. Henry employs an authoritative register throughout the instructional exchanges. Her informal standard English (Wolfram, Adger, & Christian in press) includes occasional less stigmatized vernacular features, such as copula and auxiliary deletion (e.g., "You'll know what we gonna be doing today"), as is typical for Southern dialect speakers (Wolfram 1974a).[12] In less public situations, as when she pulls a student aside for cajoling, she changes to a mothering register marked linguistically by endearments, lowered volume, and increased vernacular features, but even there stigmatized features are infrequent. Although her teaching role in the classroom community remains constant across public instructional events and private discourse activities, entitling her to the powerful role in both frame types, the register modulation signals a shift in footing—academic authority in one case, "mother" in the other, or as another teacher put it, "mother bear." Thus, there are different grounds (McCallum-Bayliss 1984) for authority in the instructional and cajoling encounters—different social bases, both of which have a place at school (Noblet 1993).

Authoritative footing is a valuable commodity, socially accorded to the teacher to use and to assign. Occasionally students are explicitly nominated to take this footing and sometimes they self-nominate. When this happens, the classroom social balance is altered. Competition often intensifies. Typically, students vie for turns at talking authoritatively by holding the floor, as Julius does here (repeated):

1	Julius:		You read a story, you write questio<u>ns</u> . . about it.
2	Mrs. Henry:		How- what kind of questions do you write.
3	Mary:	→	Recall question<u>s</u> .
4	Julius:	→	Well, you write it like sentenc<u>es</u>, sentenc<u>es</u> [to the story.
5	Mrs. Henry:		[That you have- hm?
6	Julius:		You write it like sentenc<u>es</u> to . . the story.
7	Mrs. Henry:	→	Okay, you know they are recall because you can look right back in the story and [find . . what?
8	Julius:	→	[You . . find the detai<u>ls</u>.
9	Mrs. Henry:	→	The answer or the details. Very good.

Mary correctly answers a question intended for Julius (line 3), but he holds the floor by also answering Mrs. Henry's question ("sentences to the story"). Mary's response is taken up, not Julius's, when Mrs. Henry says, "Okay, you know they are recall" (line 7). He grabs the next response slot by latching onto Mrs. Henry's sentence even before she can turn it into a question (line 8).

Other strategies for getting authoritative speaking slots are more or less competitive: negotiating the participation structure from a one-student response task into a multiple-speaker task by offering alternative or additional authoritative statements, as with the twelve candidates for the "Rumpelstiltskin" problem; using the auditor role to criticize language form, as with calls for article repair ("a kingdom" for "the kingdom"); and in the next segment, leaping into a troubled response. Such bids to assume authoritative footing seem largely attributable to limited access. Throughout the lesson, Mrs. Henry draws students into the discourse, allowing and encouraging overlapping talk and self-nomination, nominating the less vocal, preserving turns for the confused. But authority and authoritative talk are her prerogative, and students vie for a share of it.

Learning Authoritative Footing

Opportunities for students to speak with authority occurred occasionally in all of the classrooms that I studied, but the nature and frequency of these occasions varied. This variation across classrooms means that students must learn some local rules for authoritative talk. The "Rumpelstiltskin" lesson under consideration here occurred when school had been in session for only five weeks. In the following segment, Tyree, who was new to the class that year, less experienced with story grammar tasks and their concomitant language demands, and younger than the others (except Thomas, a visitor),[13] receives help from Mrs. Henry in the charts section when he has trouble formulating an acceptable statement.

1	Mrs. Henry:	Tyree, what do you think the problem was.
2	Tyree:	That . . um ( )
3	Mrs. Henry:	Think about the first part of the story. What all started it. Now a lot of these things you're telling me are events. Think about when the story first started. And then after that problem a lot of things started happening which would be coming under events.
4	Tyree:	( )
5	Akeem:	( )
6	Mrs. Henry:	What, Tyree, what are you trying to say? Stop, stop, Akeem.
7	Tyree:	( ) um ( ) made the um . . a lot of straw.
8	Mrs. Henry:	Who made a lot of straw? He turned the, he didn't make a lot of straw now, what did he do?
9	Akeem:	Turned the straw into
10	Mrs. Henry:	Let him try to think, please. He did what? Rumpelstiltskin did what?
11	Tyree:	Turned the straw into gold.
12	Mrs. Henry:	Turned, it wasn't gold, what did I tell you it was?
13	Tyree:	Um
14	Mrs. Henry:	Gold what?
15	Tyree:	Gold paper.
16	(Many):	Gold straw, gold thread.
17	Mrs. Henry:	Gold thread.

Even though this excerpt comes after many other problem statements, Tyree fails to fashion a praiseworthy response, even with the teacher's help. His difficulty seems to lie with the analytic task, rather than with sentence formulation: Mrs. Henry explains what the others obviously know—that the problem is something occurring early in the story that, in fact, "started it." When Tyree does not respond authoritatively, others attempt to take the floor. Mrs. Henry protects it for him, supports his response building, and corrects his story understanding. (Tyree does learn eventually to speak authoritatively in literacy events but not for several months.)

If Tyree is the least adept at charts talk, Kevin is perhaps the most polished. This is Kevin's second year in Mrs. Henry's class, and he is under consideration here at the beginning of the year for male star student status to replace the previous year's star. In fact, during the character trait sequence (in an interaction not presented here), Mrs. Henry asks if "we have anybody in here who is bossy." Kevin and Julius point to each other and then identify the previous year's male star as having been bossy. Even though Kevin and Julius engage in side talk off and on through this lesson, Kevin supplies many important lesson contributions. Mrs. Henry can count on him to speak authoritatively because he has been socialized to it.

Conclusion

Constructing lessons out of discourse, text, and other socioeducational resources places significant sociolinguistic demands on children and teachers, including the necessity of modulating linguistic register in the ebb and flow of lesson activities within lesson events. Shifting along the dialect continuum is one possibility for accomplishing the register modulation that this social task demands. This chapter has addressed the range and domain of children's register shifting with variable features (standardness/vernacularness) in instructional discourse and the social interactional purposes for shifting.

In Mrs. Henry's classroom and others in Baltimore elementary schools, students' register construction includes vernacular dialect in instructional discourse with teachers. This pattern contrasts with that reported for other schools, but, in both this and the Lucas and Borders (1987, 1994) studies, children shift in instructional settings toward the standard dialect; they consistently apprehend contextual cues to discourse activity types that have relevance for dialect choices; they match variable features to local code expectations; and they control contrasting variants well enough to function in standard English when it is situationally (rather than ideally) appropriate. Far from being linguistically limited (Bereiter & Engelmann 1966), these AAVE speakers skillfully fulfill the implicit register demands associated with speech event participation in their classrooms.

Much of what is known about African American children's talk at school comes from classrooms where teachers who differ ethnically and linguistically from their students misunderstand and devalue children's language use (e.g., Piestrup 1973). Shared ethnicity among Mrs. Henry and her students probably contributes to maintaining norms for dialect appropriateness that are congruent with those of their communities.[14] In the classroom speech community, children have opportunities to use standard dialect features because they have occasion to adopt an authoritative footing. Does the larger culture's "mania for correctness" (Smitherman 1986:209), which generally excludes vernacular varieties from official discourse, operate in this classroom? If official discourse is taken to mean all teaching and learning discourse, then it does not. If official discourse is defined as that in which speakers maintain authoritative footing, then the general rule does apply. In this classroom, children learn variable feature distribution and register-shifting patterns that are more useful than those prescribed in some classrooms, because their language-learning experiences at school accord with community standards.

NOTES

I thank Alice Greenwood, Susan Hoyle, Lynn McCreedy, and Walt Wolfram for comments on earlier drafts of this paper. The research reported in this paper was supported by cooperative agreement No. HO 23 H0008-92 between the Office of Special Education Programs,

U.S. Department of Education, and the University of Maryland, College Park, Department of Special Education, with the Center for Applied Linguistics. The views expressed here do not necessarily represent the official position of the funding agency. Early versions of portions of this chapter were presented at a pre-session of the 1993 Georgetown University Round Table on Languages and Linguistics and at the 1995 annual meeting of the American Association for Applied Linguistics, Long Beach, California.

1. Whereas standard dialects are standardized in the sense of being codified, all dialects are standardized in the sense of being more or less regular. I use the term *standard English* to index the dialects that generally avoid stigmatized features and thus receive social approbation. I have purposefully not capitalized *standard* in the hope of suggesting that there is no single standard for English. Standard English is taken here to include a range of features specified and evaluated within a locally defined speech community.

2. The terms *register* and *style* have been applied synonymously (e.g., Andersen 1990) to ways of speaking differentiated by formality. However, since the term *style* is often applied to culturally based ways of speaking, I use *register*.

3. The data presented here come from videotaping without benefit of external microphone. At the time of the study, I reasoned that recording equipment ought to be kept to a minimum to reduce its intrusiveness. I now believe that teachers and students adjust to recording of any type, although they may never come to enjoy being recorded. External microphones that increase the fidelity of recording are probably worth the intrusiveness risk.

4. All of the schools were eligible for Title I funds, based on data collected by the schools regarding students' socioeconomic status.

5. Administrators in Baltimore City Public Schools were most gracious in providing access to schools for this research. Teachers and other educators generously shared their classrooms with the two researchers, Adger and Jennifer Detwyler, and they patiently answered questions and offered insights. To them and to their students and the parents who allowed us to watch and listen to their school talk, I am deeply grateful. Their names are changed here to protect their privacy. Mrs. Dorothy Henry (her real name), the teacher in whose classroom the discourse discussed here occurred, welcomed me to her classroom frequently over a period of three years—several times a week during the first year and monthly thereafter. I deeply respect her caring and authoritative way with students. Approximately twenty educators participated in the observational study, but research experience density with individuals varied radically; thus, our understandings of classroom events was richer for some classes than for others. Nonetheless, some observations in classes we visited only once or twice proved to be fertile sources of understanding and question generation concerning other classes. Educators included special education teachers of self-contained classes and of pull-out classes (resource rooms), regular education teachers, and speech-language pathologists working in pull-out settings and in other teachers' classrooms. Observations were concentrated on the multiple activities occurring within classrooms, but we also observed in other school settings: in physical education and music classes, in the library, at assemblies, at community meetings with other classes, in the lunchroom, on field trips, and on the playground.

6. Dialect variation was evident across teachers with respect to such diagnostic phonological features as substitution of alveolar stops for interdental fricatives. Variation within teachers included occasional use of less stigmatized vernacular features, such as final consonant cluster reduction and auxiliary deletion. Although it was whispered by administrators and occasionally by other teachers that some African American teachers (who constituted roughly 70% of Baltimore's faculty) did not speak standard English, my impression was that teachers generally avoided highly stigmatized structures, especially syntactic structures, in

instructional discourse. I did not tabulate vernacular feature occurrences in teachers' talk. Perceptions of teachers' speech as nonstandard suggest that norms are not fully shared.

7. A self-contained special education class includes only students with educational disabilities.

8. Actually, "morning" lasted only two hours, since her class went to lunch at 10:30. Her students usually spent thirty minutes of this two-hour block writing in the computer lab.

9. When vernacular English occurs in a more formal context, Mrs. Henry corrects it. The following segment comes from a pre-writing activity in which students dictated questions about a picture of two men on a horse. As in the "Rumpelstiltskin" lesson, this student talk was later transformed into written text used as story writing prompts. Here, Mrs. Henry uses contrastive stress to call for repair of vernacular verbs, and students edit their sentences.

Rita:		Where <u>are</u> they.
Monisha:	→	Were **is** they.
Mrs. Henry:	→	Where ARE they. We already have that.
Rita:	→	Where **is** they goin.
Mrs. Henry:	→	Where ARE they going.
Tyree:	→	**Is** they
Mrs. Henry:	→	ARE they
Tyree:		<u>Are</u> they in the woods.
Monisha:		<u>Are</u> they coming to town.

The connection between standard English and written language is explicit here.

10. Because the classroom is very cold on this day, instructional discourse is occasionally interrupted as Mrs. Henry tells the children to put their arms in their jacket sleeves or retrieve their coats from their lockers.

11. Modulating from dictating to discussing seems to motivate the shift toward use of vernacular features. But evidence from the lesson's first section, the introduction and character traits review, also shows a tendency to prefer standard features early in an activity and vernacular ones later. The tendency was not remarkable in that section because the teacher generally constrained the students' responses, limiting them to words and phrases. A new lesson activity seems to offer students the opportunity to demonstrate academic expertise in the new domain, and to introduce the register for conveying expertise, that prefers standard English.

12. Many African American teachers and other professionals in Baltimore use southern dialect area features. Mrs. Henry grew up in North Carolina and moved to Baltimore as a college student.

13. Stephen was temporarily assigned to Mrs. Henry's class after causing trouble in several other classes. Her mix of firmness and caring for him, along with other students' tolerance, led to his success there. He is not a full member of the class, however, and his assignments are different from others'. In this lesson, he participates in all but the charts activity, during which he does paper and pencil work at his desk.

14. Since I did not spend time in this community, I rely on Baugh's (1983) and Heath's (1983) descriptions of language use by adults and children in other African American communities.

9

The Effect of Role and Footing on Students' Oral Academic Language

LYNN MCCREEDY

Talk at school on academic topics is at the heart of teaching and learning. Children's facility with academic talk, traditionally of concern to teachers and speech/language pathologists concentrating on remediation of language or learning disabilities, has also begun to attract the attention of scholars exploring the development of linguistic and interactional competence (e.g., Heath 1983). In this chapter, I compare the oral academic language of children in two classrooms, focusing on the interactional matrix within which talk took place and on the changes in the children's skill over the course of a school year. I show that differences between the two classes in the roles and footings that the children are encouraged to assume have a significant effect on their oral academic language.

Children gain proficiency in producing oral academic language—that is, talk on lesson-related topics (Adger, Wolfram, Detwyler, & Harry 1993)—when teachers encourage them to articulate how what they are learning relates to what they already know (Heath 1983). By the upper grades of elementary school, Heath (1983) finds, successful students are those who have learned not only to see connections among facts but also to communicate this knowledge by adapting early storytelling skills to increasingly decontextualized uses. If this capability is to develop, children need opportunities throughout elementary school to practice verbal skills in integrating and summarizing lesson content.

In teacher-centered instruction, children's opportunities to talk on lesson-related topics arise mainly when they are asked to respond to a teacher's question or other directive. Such elicitations and responses proliferate during a verbal review (Simich 1984, Simich-Dudgeon & McCreedy 1988): a series of topically linked initiation-reply-evaluation sequences (cf. Mehan 1979) through which a teacher checks on what students have learned.[1] Verbal reviews often follow the main instructional phase of a lesson, though teachers also commonly use them at the beginning of a lesson to link it with a preceding one and to see how much previous content must be retaught. Of the four data excerpts I consider here, three are verbal reviews or topically bounded segments thereof, and the fourth is a small-group discussion and a segment of the immediately following verbal review.

Children's oral academic language is embedded, of course, in an interactional matrix that encourages or fails to encourage its growth. For instance, whether the discourse is monologic (e.g., an oral book report) or constructed by several participants (e.g., verbal reviews), it is always shaped to some degree by what has gone on in the lesson and the larger curricular unit up to that point. Also key is what the children have learned about their teacher's expectations for participation. How teacher and students see their respective roles in a given instance of oral academic interaction determines the footing (Goffman 1981) they assume, and footing, I will demonstrate, greatly affects both the quantity and quality of children's oral academic language.

Speaker Roles in the Classroom

Goffman (1981) points out that the terms *speaker* and *hearer* are not finely tuned enough for describing the array of alignments that people take toward one another as they talk. Hearers, for instance, include both addressed and unaddressed recipients of talk; addressees may be expected to take a turn at talk or to act as audience. But particularly relevant to my discussion are speaker roles:[2] *animator* (one who actually speaks), *author* (one who selects the words and ideas to express), and *principal* (one who stands behind the ideas). In much talk, of course, a single speaker takes all these roles simultaneously, but in elementary school classrooms this is often *not* the case.

The roles of animator and author, most common in my data, seem to be the usual roles for young children in classrooms. Only rarely do children, particularly primary-level students, speak as principals (e.g., comparing two storybook characters, substantiating a claim, or voicing an opinion on an academic subject). Children are often animators, as when they read aloud from a textbook or a list on the chalkboard, recite something (e.g., a poem) written by someone else, or repeat a key term from a lesson. But a child who is asked to define that term in his or her own words is an author. Student authorship occurs, too, when children are asked to describe, explain, or summarize.

What speaking roles an individual takes is not entirely under his or her control, particularly for a student responding to a teacher's elicitation. In much classroom discourse, participants' rights and responsibilities are decidedly asymmetrical (Cazden 1988). The teacher can control the degree to which students' ideas count in the discourse by choosing discussion topics and tasks, choosing whether to phrase elicitations as factual recall questions or as questions requiring comparison or evaluation, and choosing how to evaluate responses. Thus, although children may decide whether and how to respond to an elicitation, the teacher's choices ultimately carry greater weight in determining students' speaker roles.

In verbal reviews, children are called upon to verbalize facts they have learned (e.g., Gall 1984, Geekie & Raban 1994), but the teacher speaks by far the most of any participant. He or she not only opens the activity (e.g., "Okay, class, now let's talk a little bit about our experiments") and closes it (e.g., "Okay, that's all we have time for today. Would you please put your lab books away, and let's get ready to go to art") but can speak after every student turn as well. The teacher thus acts as both author (selecting topics and phrasing elicitations) and principal (whose ideas and evaluative comments govern the discourse). Students in effect act as audience members with intermittent speaking parts. Whether these parts are those of animator or author depends largely upon how much expansion of the common single-word response the teacher allows or encourages. Teachers vary greatly in how definite a script (Schank & Abelson 1977, Tannen 1993c) they have in mind for verbal reviews and what roles they permit students to assume; students' authorship opportunities vary accordingly. In the data I examine here, although students do occasionally voice an opinion, their opportunities to speak as principals are too limited for discussion. The issue is, rather, the extent to which students are animators of the teacher's script, on the one hand, or co-authors with the teacher, on the other, and what changes occur in children's authorship over a few months.

The Classrooms

The discourse considered here comes from two primary-level classes of special education students in two urban schools. Most of the students in these classes came from working-class families: one class was entirely African American; the other was about two thirds White, one third African American, reflecting the general population of these two schools. The all-Black class happened that year to be all male, the mixed class about equally male and female. Students in both classes ranged from six to ten years old. An assortment of diagnoses—emotional disabilities, learning disorders, language or speech disorders—had led to their placement in special education classes. These classes were not radically different from mainstream classes in terms of the organization of time and space or the behavior of teachers and students. The main difference was in the small class size typical of special education classes. Membership changed slightly over the year, but one class had about eleven students and the other about eight. Ms. Vann[3] taught the class with eleven students, the class of African American boys.[4] The other teacher considered here, Ms. Talley, was a speech/language pathologist who came into Mr. Rivers's special education class once a week.[5]

Ms. Vann and Ms. Talley were participants in a study conducted by a team of linguists and educators. One of its goals was to increase the quantity and quality of students' oral academic language through the use of teaching techniques emphasizing cooperative learning and a higher-thinking-skills framework called "Think Tricks" (Adger, Kalyanpur, Peterson, & Bridger 1995; Lyman 1992).[6] All four discourse excerpts examined below come from lessons that use cooperative learning, and two of the four concern Think Tricks, so a brief discussion of these techniques and their desired effect on children's talk is in order.

Think Tricks is a system of seven thinking types: *Recall, Comparison, Contrast, Cause-and-Effect, Idea-to-Example, Example-to-Idea,* and *Evaluation* (Lyman 1992). These types and corresponding symbols are taught with the aim of stimulating children's metacognition and ability to talk about it. They are a means of categorizing teacher questions, student responses, and other interactive tasks according to the cognitive and organizational skills that students are called on to demonstrate. For instance, in an excerpt from Ms. Vann's class discussed below, the students are asked to summarize a previous lesson about Recall, and they mention "cue words" that "go with" that thinking strategy (e.g., *who, where, when*).

Cooperative learning had been introduced in both classrooms. This instructional approach involves more than just working in groups: students are given specific roles, such as recorder and reporter, and are expected to follow guidelines for engaging in the academic task. Study of cooperative learning shows that working in small groups can give students the benefit of rehearsal, feedback from group members, freedom to voice their views, and time to think about what to say (Cohen 1984; Davidson & Worsham 1992; Johnson, Johnson, & Holubec 1994). Such opportunities are expected to promote oral academic language that is more planned than unplanned (Ochs 1979a) and thus somewhat decontextualized, including, for instance, definite descriptions and elaborative detail. Since cooperative learning involves a participation framework more democratic than traditional lesson formats —all members should be speakers as well as hearers—students can, it is hoped, become comfortable performing various speaker roles before a small audience. The benefits of cooperative learning groups are expected to carry over to the academic language that children exhibit in whole-class discussion, including verbal reviews (Davidson & Worsham 1992); this was an intended outcome in our study.

This anticipated result occurred only in Ms. Vann's class. Her students demonstrated that they could produce increasingly decontextualized talk as the school year progressed. Ms. Talley's students, on the other hand, did not. I argue that the speaker roles Ms. Vann guided her students in taking did much to support their language development, but that those promoted by Ms. Talley did not: only Ms. Vann gave her students regular opportunities for authorship. In comparing the classes, I look at each of them at two points in a school year: first in January, then in the spring. The segments presented are short but typical.

Ms. Vann's Class

Winter

The first excerpt is from the beginning of one of Ms. Vann's lessons in January, in which she was teaching her students about Think Tricks symbols. The first major activity of this lesson was to make a bulletin board on Recall. At the front of the room was a chart with clear plastic pockets containing cards with the Recall symbol and cue words such as *what, when,* and *where.* Later in the lesson, the children will be asked to add "recall sentences," supplying details of a story that they had written the day before on strips of poster board. The teacher begins by asking what the children remember of the previous day's lesson. (In the transcription, children's contributions are boldfaced; explanatory material is in square brackets.)[7]

1	T:	Now. All right. Who can remember what we did in our reading lesson yesterday. Carl, look smart.
2	Carl:	**We, um=**
3	T:	=Wait. Wait a minute, I want you to raise your hand. Who can remember what we did in reading yesterday. Gordon's hand is nice and . . straight.
4	Gordon:	**Recalled details.**
5	T:	Okay, we recalled details. Who can explain that. What do you mean by recalling details. Lennie?
6	Lennie:	**It means you call us, you call us to say the words and then, we find the [card with the cue] word, and then ( ) you, and then, um=**
7	T:	=Louder.
8	Lennie:	**You call us to take the card and then give it to you and then you call us to say (about), um, (sentence).**
9	T:	Mmm! You got some good ideas in there. Uh, Tyrone?
10	Tyrone:	**We picked one of us [from our cooperative learning group] and we went up and got a card and we named it and we, we um hanging some sentences [on posterboard strips] with our words. And we broke up into two groups.**
11	T:	Louder.
12	Tyrone:	**And we broke up in two [or 'into'] groups, and that's when we all got a chance to write a sentence about a [cue word on a] card.**
13	T:	Okay, all right. We wrote sentences about the card. Gordon said we recalled details. What does that mean, "we recalled details." How did we do that.
14	Tyrone:	**We went over the story.**
15	T:	We went over the story together. And what specifically did you look for in that story. Greg?
16	Greg:	**Words!**
17	T:	(Words), yes. What else did you look for.
18	Greg:	**Details!**
19	T:	You looked for details. Good thinking, good thinking. What are details, Greg?
20	Greg:	**( )**
21	T:	Where do we find details . . . What did we have to look at to find details.
22	Greg:	**At the pictures.**
23	T:	All right, we looked at the pictures. And we found details. Then we made sentences about the::
24	Greg:	**Pictures!**
25	T:	About the pictures,
26	S:	**And words.**
27	T:	Hmm?
28	S:	**Words and pictures.**
29	T:	All right. We put our sentences in a what. [Pointing toward book]
30	Ss:	**A book.**
31	T:	In a book. Well, the next day we went over the:: [Pointing toward pocket chart]
32	Ss:	**Words.**

33	T:	Words. What are these words about? What are these words called?
34	S:	**[Recall.**
35	Ss:	**[Recall words**.
36	T:	Recall words! They're recall words. And look at those, that symbol right here. [Pointing] What is this symbol for.
37	Ss:	**Recall.**
38	T:	What does this symbol mean.
39	Ss:	**Recall!**
40	T:	What do the middle . . symbols, the little Rs. [Pointing]
41	Ss:	**Recall, recall.**
42	T:	Very good. [Beginning of new activity] Now. Do you know the sentences that we made yesterday?

Ms. Vann and her students do a reasonable job of co-constructing this discourse. With the exception of the fill-in-the-blank and choral responses at the end, the students' contributions to the discussion are self-authored. Since the teacher's purpose here is to review a shared experience, to "remember what we did in reading yesterday" (turns 1, 3), it can be expected that she will elicit context-bound descriptions of what happened. Gordon's response in turn 4, "Recalled details," though, is fairly decontextualized in that it would be interpretable by someone who had not shared the previous reading class with him. This response, though brief, shows thought beyond the level shown by his classmates. He summarizes the previous day's lesson, thus specifying the general topic of the verbal review, and his authorship[8] is accepted by the teacher. As the excerpt continues, the talk becomes more context-bound: Ms. Vann's request for an explanation of Gordon's response ("Recalled details") receives procedural descriptions first from Lenny (turns 6, 8) and then Tyrone (turns 10, 12) that are quite detailed although they would be difficult for an outsider to interpret. But beginning with turn 13, the teacher guides the students to verbalize the connection between the procedural descriptions and the purpose of those procedures. She accepts Lenny's and Tyrone's descriptions ("Okay, all right. We wrote sentences about the card"), but then she puts Gordon's summary back on the floor and elicits further expansion of it: "Gordon said we recalled details. What does that mean, 'we recalled details.' How did we do that." Tyrone offers a response (turn 14) that highlights a different aspect of the previous lesson's work, "We went over the story." The teacher ratifies this response and asks for more information on the procedure from Greg (turn 15). Though brief, Greg's responses, "Words!" (turn 16), and "Details!" (turn 18), are praised (turn 19), probably because he mentions concepts that the teacher wants to bring into the discussion. Although he contributes only single-word utterances and a prepositional phrase ("At the pictures," turn 22), Ms. Vann scaffolds his responses syntactically in such a way that, topically, he also participates in the co-constructed discussion about procedures followed the previous day.

With turn 23, Ms. Vann shifts into a phase of fill-in-the-blank elicitations, which pick up the pace of the interaction and involve everyone in closing down the lesson segment through choral responses of key procedures and terms. From this point on, although student participation is broadened, student authorship is constrained. With turns 33 to 41, the topic is given both summary and closure, bringing it back to the general level at which Gordon originally introduced it.

The teacher's role in this discourse is essentially to guide and enable the children to make topically appropriate contributions to it. What results (despite the series of choral responses at the end) is a discourse co-authored by the teacher and the students.

Spring

The spring segment from Ms. Vann's class is not typical for this class; it is exemplary. However, it is interesting and exciting and, more important, it shows how skilled children can become at oral academic language if given regular practice at authoring.

The background to the segment is as follows. On this day in April, researcher Jennifer Detwyler (JD) was at Ms. Vann's school to discuss with her which other teacher she might mentor (as part of the oral language project) the following school year. Ms. Vann suggested Ms. Bryce, who taught academically gifted children. After lunch, on the spur of the moment, Ms. Vann invited Ms. Bryce and her students to her room to hear the students explaining the Think Tricks that the gifted class might learn about the next year. Ms. Vann opened the verbal review by asking who in her class could explain the symbols. Gordon volunteered as JD was inserting a tape into her cassette recorder; this transcript thus begins near the beginning of his response:

1	Gordon:	**words to go with 'em, and, and when we hear a sentence, that we'll know that, that would help us.**
2	JD:	What are you talking about.
3	Gordon:	**I mean they have words to go with the symbols.**
4	JD:	What symbols.
5	Gordon:	**The, the like the evaluation symbol and the recall symbol.**
6	JD:	Okay, can you show me those?
7	Gordon:	**These, this one.**
8	JD:	What is that.
9	Gordon:	**Recall.**
10	T:	What does recall mean.
11	Gordon:	**It means that you look back into the story to find the information. And this evaluate, it means to, judge something. To weigh it out, to see if (your) mind's, you know . . um. You, um see the, judge the, make up your final decision.**
12	T:	Anyone else? Those are the only two symbols you know about? Oh, come on! Give me another symbol, Victor!
13	Victor:	**Uh, they have, we have another symbol. Two. It looks like the same thing, but it's, but it's um=**
14	T:	=Go show 'em!
15	Victor:	**Both of 'em 're right there! They're called Idea-to-Example, Example-to-Idea. Both of 'em, one, both of 'em mean big ideas, and the little and the, and the small ideas.**
16	T:	Anything else about 'em?
17	Victor:	**I 'own know. [Some Ss snicker]**
18	JD:	Anyone else want to contribute to Example-to-Idea, Idea-to-Example?
19	T:	Anyone else? Come on, you know! . . Lennie, come on! Think of another symbol. There's another symbol. Talk about main idea. Sh! Lennie?

20	Lennie:	**Huh?**
21	T:	Can't do it? Too shy? Okay, Najeem.
22	Najeem:	**Compare and contrast! One's different and one's . .**
23	S:	**Same=**
24	Najeem:	**=same.**
25	JD:	Which one is different.
26	Najeem:	**Contrast.**
27	T:	So, so how would you complete that um (box).[9] What would you do.
28	Najeem:	**You fill it, you fill it . . ous . . outside . . outside,**
29	T:	Uh huh, and what information do you put in it.
30	Najeem:	**Outside the circle, you p- . .**
31	T:	And what information do you put on the outside.
32	Najeem:	**The different.**
33	T:	Okay. And what would you do with the one that has
34	Najeem:	**[Compare!**
35	T:	[the circles with the openings in the middle.
36	Najeem:	**Put the s-, you put the, the word that got, that has same . . in the (middle).**
37	T:	Yeah, all right, very good. Anyone else? Any more symbols? Is that all of them? . . . Is that all of them? I think that's all.
38	S:	**Huh uh . . . ain't all. Ooh!**
39	JD:	Oh! [What is it?
40	T:	[Oh, I'm sorry!
41	S:	**Cause and [effect.**
42	S:	**[Evaluation**
43	T:	Kenneth! No! [Kenneth?
44	Kenneth:	**[Cause and effect.**
45	T:	Yes. Cause and effect. I'm sorry. Talk about it. Where is the cause and effect one?
46	Kenneth:	**R- right there.**
47	T:	Where. Go show me.
48	Kenneth:	**Right here. Cause and effect means whose, what happened, and why did it happen.**
49	T:	Excellent! 'Cause it was c-
50	JD:	[Wooh!
51	T:	[Very good! [Audio break]
52	JD:	He had something=
53	T:	=Oh, I'm sorry. Carl has [something to say.
54	JD:	[Carl?
55	Carl:	**Because it's the reason.**
56	JD:	What, what is the reason. What are you talking about.
57	S:	**Be[cause**
58	Carl:	**['Cause, 'cause that's why it happened. 'Cause of the reason.**
59	JD:	There's a reason that it happened? And what is that related to. Which symbol.
60	Carl:	**Cause and effect.**
61	JD:	Very good!
62	T:	I wanted someone to explain to Ms., to the GATE class, why we're using these symbols. Why. What's the purpose of us using these symbols. Victor?

63	Victor:	**To find out what's the answer.**
64	T:	To find out the answer. To find out information. Gordon!
65	Gordon:	**Well,** [Ss laughing]
66	T:	Sh! Sh!
67	Gordon:	**Well, it has words to go with it, and you hear that word in a sentence, you'll know what symbol goes with it.**
68	T:	Okay! And it teaches you how to organi::ze
69	Gordon:	**Thinking skills.**
70	T:	Right! Right! Thank you.

What is most striking about this discourse is that it is formulated almost entirely by the children, with minimal structural guidance by the adults. After Ms. Vann opens the verbal review (not audiotaped), Gordon speaks. He also turns out to be the last student to speak and shows sensitivity to the fact that general statements are appropriate at such openings and closings. (This may be a specialty of his. Recall that he was also the first student to respond in the January verbal review and did so with a general summary statement.) Although after his initial response (turn 1) it takes a bit of prompting from JD and Ms. Vann (turns 2, 4, 6, 8, 10), he successfully points out, defines, and explains two symbols, those for Evaluation and Recall (turns 5, 7, 9, 11). Victor and Najeem then discuss two symbols each.[10] Najeem is the only child who has fluency problems in this discourse, and Ms. Vann has to do some follow-up prompting (odd-numbered turns 27–35) to elicit from him a basic description of how one compares and contrasts using Venn diagrams. Still, his utterances (even-numbered turns 22–34), taken together, form an adequate description of these Think Tricks; as we shall see, his description is much more complete than those that Ms. Talley's students are encouraged to give in her lesson on this topic. Ms. Vann does not take over the interaction, and Najeem manages to be a co-author.

Overall, the children produce talk that is nearly decontextualized enough to stand on its own. To illustrate this point, I include here their utterances without the elicitations and other prompts. Occasional information is added in square brackets to make the text readable, as is a title:

[Think Tricks: the Symbols That We Have Been Learning About]
[They have] Words to go with them, and when we hear a sentence that we know, that would help us. I mean they have words to go with the symbols. Like the evaluation symbol and the recall symbol. This one [is] Recall. It means that you look back into the story to find the information. And this evaluate, it means to judge something. To weigh it out, to see if (your) mind's [made up]. You see, judge, make up your final decision.

We have another symbol. Two. It looks like the same thing, but it's [not]. Both of them are right there. They're called Idea-to-Example [and] Example-to-Idea. Both of them mean big ideas and the small ideas. Compare and contrast. One's different and one's [the] same. Contrast [is different]. You fill it [i.e., Venn diagram] outside. Outside the circle you [put] the different [information/things]. [For] Compare, you put the word that has same in the middle.

Cause-and-effect [is the symbol] right there; right here. Cause and effect means what happened and why did it happen. Because it's the reason. Because that's why it happened, because of the reason. [That's related to] Cause and effect.

[The purpose of using these symbols is] to find out what's the answer. It has words to go with it. And you hear that word in a sentence [and] you'll know what symbol goes with it. [It teaches you how to organize] thinking skills.

These six- to ten-year-old special education students are the authors of a discourse exhibiting coherence, cohesion, and decontextualization. I suggest that this is due in large part to the fact that their teacher encouraged them, over the course of the school year, to express academic concepts in their own words—to become authors.

Now I consider the class whose students were less successful in developing their oral academic language abilities, Ms. Talley's speech students.

Ms. Talley's Class

Winter

The first excerpt from Ms. Talley's class comes from a whole-class "sharing" following a lesson on the Think Tricks Comparison and Contrast. The lesson had involved three activities. First, Ms. Talley had Jared and Mr. Rivers (the classroom teacher) stand together at the front of the room and solicited from the students ways in which they were the same and different. The second activity was to compare and contrast a mitten and a glove, then two hats. For the third activity, Ms. Talley put the children into two groups of three (all girls and all boys, as it happened). Each group was to draw a single snowman, with each student adding something to the drawing. During the whole-class sharing that followed, Ms. Talley elicited ways in which the snowmen were alike and different. Mr. Rivers wrote these similarities and differences in the appropriate parts of two Venn diagrams on the blackboard, marked "COMPARE" and "CONTRAST." In the segment below, the teacher has just asked each group to name its snowman and to give its picture to her to display next to the Venn diagrams. (One of the girls has accused the boys of copying their ideas, and Walter is registering his objection as Ms. Talley tries to get the verbal review started.)

1	T:	We're gonna look at it.
2	Walter:	**They're different.**
3	T:	We are gonna look at it. What do you think we are gonna do with this. What've we been talking about.
4	Walter:	**We didn't make, we didn't copy off of 'em, 'cause we got a soda can on his hand.**
5	T:	[Rapidly, low tone] Okay, wait a wait a wait a minute. [Louder, higher tone] What do you think we're gonna do? What've we been doin' today, looking at things that are the::
6	Ss:	**Sa:[me!**
7	T:	[Same, a::nd
8	Ss:	**Different!**
9	T:	So, we're gonna look at the snowmen. And we're gonna see what's the same about Jason and Frosty, and we're gonna see what'[s
10	S:	[Frosty and Jason! **Yeeuch!**
11	T:	different. And so Mr. Rivers is putting them up, so we can look at them . . . Okay. Now, first, we're gonna compare. What's compare mean? Looking at things that are the::

12	Ss:	**Sa:[me!**
13	T:	[Same. O[kay. All right, let's look at 'em. We have Jason,
14	Lisa:	**[And different!**
15	T:	Oh, no. Compare just means looking at the: [same.
16	Ss:	**[Same!**
17	T:	Okay. Melissa, Jason and Frosty are up here, so you (go) look over here. Okay. What's one thing- look at them! What's one thing that's the same about both the snowmen.
18	Walter:	**Oh!**
19	T:	All right. [What.
20	Walter:	**[They('ve) both got round, round bodies, and round heads?**
21	T:	Okay.
22	Rivers:	Round shape.
23	T:	Round shape. Good.
24	Rivers:	(Same) shape. [He writes in the Venn diagram.]
25	S:	**Round.**
26	T:	The shape is the same. They (g'n) have round parts to them. Snowballs. [Ronald.
27	R:	**[They both have round eyes.**
28	T:	Both have eyes? Round eyes? Okay. They both have a- Okay, let's let's, let's say they both have, what. What's that whole thing called. [Eyes
29	Ronald or Walter:	**[Face.**
30	Walter or Ronald:	**Eyes, nose, chin, ears,**
31	T:	So what's that called, a-
32	Ss:	**Face** [not all in unison]
33	T:	A face. So they both have a face?
34	Ss:	**[Yes** **[Yeah**
35	T:	Yes. All right.

A number of things could be said about this excerpt.[11] What I focus on here, though, is how the children's utterances are shaped by the teacher. It is striking how much of the time they are filling in blanks as choral responses at the end of the teacher's elicitations, animating the teacher's words. These filled blanks are, to Ms. Talley, the hallmark of student participation. She expects her students to animate occasional bits of her script in order to show that they are paying attention.

Indeed, elicitations that prompt choral responses can be helpful to teachers and students alike. A choral response gets all (or most) of the children to participate, it allows those who are unsure to blend in with the chorus, and it offers comfort to children who do not like responding individually. Vocalizing (and hearing) key terms in chorus reinforces the students' learning of them. Fill-in-the-blank elicitations allow the teacher to tightly control the pace and length of interactions; because, in a choral response, wrong answers tend to be drowned out by correct ones, the teacher can ignore any response not in her script. Such elicitations are particularly useful at points when repair work would cause the interaction to lose its topical and functional focus or its pace, as in the openings or closings of verbal reviews. As we have seen, Ms. Vann used them to conclude her review. Ms. Talley, however, uses fill-in-the-blank elicitations more extensively—in every lesson opening and closing that I have examined, the opening and closing of all verbal reviews within those lessons, and, it appears, at other times when things threaten departure from her script.

The excerpt above shows another way in which the teacher's script prevails: students' suggestions about the snowmen's similarities get changed so that they conform to the teacher's expectations. At turn 17 Ms. Talley opens the actual task of comparison:

17	T:	Okay. Melissa, Jason and Frosty are up here, so you (go) look over here. Okay. What's one thing- look at them! What's one thing that's the same about both the snowmen.
18	Walter:	Oh!
19	T:	All right. [What.
20	Walter:	[They('ve) both got round, round bodies, and round heads?
21	T:	Okay.
22	Rivers:	Round shape.
23	T:	Round shape. Good.
24	Rivers:	(Same) shape. [He writes in the Venn diagram.]
25	S:	Round.
26	T:	The shape is the same. They (g'n) have round parts to them. Snowballs. . . [Ronald.
27	Ronald:	[They both have round eyes.

First Walter and then Ronald author comparisons. Walter (turn 20) says, "They've both got round, round bodies, and round heads?" and Ronald (turn 27) offers, "They both have round eyes." Both boys have contributed well-formed utterances on topic, with appropriate cohesive links to prior discourse (e.g., pronominal use, "both," "round").

But note what happens to their contributions. If their authorship is permitted, it is still subject to heavy editing by both teachers. Although Ms. Talley first accepts Walter's response about round bodies and round heads (turn 21), Mr. Rivers edits it (turn 22) to "Round shape," and Ms. Talley (turn 23) affirms that with "Round shape. Good." Mr. Rivers edits the phrase further (turn 24) to "Same shape," as he writes that in the Venn diagram. This change edits out all of the lexical choices from Walter's response. With Ms. Talley's summary, "The shape is the same" (turn 26), it is Mr. Rivers's edited form that becomes "official."

Ronald's comparison, "They both have round eyes," undergoes similar editing:

27	Ronald:	They both have round eyes.
28	T:	Both have eyes? Round eyes? Okay. They both have a- Okay, let's let's, let's say they both have, what. What's that whole thing called. [Eyes
29	Ronald or Walter:	[Face.
30	Walter or Ronald:	Eyes, nose, chin, ears,
31	T:	So what's that called, a::
32	Ss:	Face [not all in unison]
33	T:	A face. So they both have a face?
34	Ss:	[Yes [Yeah
35	T:	Yes. All right.

Ms. Talley initially accepts Ronald's response (with "okay") in turn 28 but then apparently decides that his level of comparison is not sufficient. She tries two fill-in-the-blank elicitations, which she immediately realizes will not succeed because her script is not obvious enough: "They both have a- Okay, let's, let's say they both have, what." She tries again, with what at first seems like a "regular" *wh*-question, "What's that whole thing called." However, she does not pause for a response, and she ignores a correct response ("face") at turn 29. Her question, it appears, was intended as a preliminary to a fill-in-the-blank elicitation; she begins a list of what is in "that whole thing," and one of the boys continues it: "eyes, nose, chin, ears." Following up on this list with a further fill-in elicitation ("So what's that called, a::"), she gets the response she wants in turn 32. She closes this interactive task by asking (in turn 33) the children to approve her editing of Ronald's "They both have round eyes" to her "They both have a face."

In this excerpt, which is representative of talk in this class, student authorship is discouraged. The oral academic language skill that these students are being taught is how to follow the teacher's script.

Spring

Let us consider now how things progress for this class across the second semester. The spring excerpt is from a lesson in late May that centered around tasting and describing various foods. The children worked in two groups of four, with one child in each group designated its leader. They were to pretend they were from "Erg," a newly discovered planet whose inhabitants do not eat food and know nothing about how it tastes. The "Ergans" were to taste five items (foods A–E) and discuss each sample, first in their groups and then with the whole class. The researcher's observation notes show that Ms. Talley and Mr. Rivers spent a lot of effort directing the children's "group discussions."

The following excerpt about food B is from the brief discussion in group 1 and the whole-class interaction that followed. Two things are noteworthy. First, the quantity of student speech in the small group is meager; the children seem to see their task as coming up with a one-word descriptor. After tasting the food, they quickly say, "Chocolate, chocolate" (turn 13), and their leader raises his hand to indicate that they consider their discussion complete. Second, Mr. Rivers seems to concur that a single-word answer is appropriate. When he comes over in response to the leader's raised hand, although he indicates that the group's answer is not appropriate, he suggests an alternative one-word term, "sweet" (turn 18). So when class discussion time comes, several students in group 1 call out "sweet" as soon as Ms. Talley calls for their ideas. Although they did choose this term from two that Mr. Rivers offered (turns 18, 20), they are really animators of his term here, not authors. And although Mr. Rivers admonishes the children (turn 20) that "we need description," the two teachers and the students seem to concur that a one-word description suffices.

1	T:	All right, [now we have B.
2	Rivers:	[Sit down. Sit down. [Snapping fingers, gesturing toward S in group 2. Somewhat sotto voce.]

3	T:	B is . . [walks over to group 1, picks up their paper plate] going to be this brown . . thing.
4	Tamisha:	**Okay? I know what it is. Because**
5	T:	No, you don't. 'Cause you're from Erg.
6	Tamisha:	**Oh.**
7	T:	Everybody take a piece. That's B.
8	Barbie:	**Don't eat it now!**
9	Tamisha:	**That's what she-** =
10	T:	=Yeah, you can eat it. [Everybody eat it.
11	Rivers:	[crossing to group 2] [Ronald. You gonna get a piece? Everybody get a piece? Good.
12	T:	And now I want you to talk in your group about what you think it tastes like.
13	Grp 1:	[to Al, group leader] **Chocolate, chocolate.**
14	Rivers:	[still at group 2] What does it taste like. Talk it over.
15	T:	Talk it over, now. [Walter raises hand] That's what we're s'posed to be doin' in the group.
16	Rivers:	[Coming over to Al, leaning over] Now, you're the group leader. What does it taste like.
17	Al:	**Chocolate.**
18	Rivers:	No no no no no. What does it taste like. Is [it sweet?
19	Grp 1:	**[Yeah, sweet, sweet**
20	Rivers:	Is it sour? Okay, I thought we needed, no, we didn't, we need description. You don't know what kind of food that is.
21	T:	Okay? Group one's ready?
22	Ss:	**Sweet, sweet.**
23	T:	Everyone think it tastes sweet?
24	Kristen:	**Yes**
25	T:	Okay. [Writes on board.] What, when something's sweet, Ergans want to know what makes it sweet. What, what does make it sweet. Do you have any idea? What makes something sweet?
26	S:	Sug[ar?
27	Tamisha:	**[Sug[ar!**
28	T:	[Sugar. So we could say it was [sugary, couldn't we.
29	Lacy:	**[Can we, can we say somethin'?**
30	T:	Sugary, right? Okay, group 2. Group 2, what do you think.
31	Ron:	**Good=**
32	Lacy:	**=Good.**
33	T:	Uh, you thought it was good? How did it taste?
34	Lacy:	**Sweet=**
35	Ron:	**=Sweet.**
36	T:	Do you, do you agree that it's sweet?
37	Ss:	**Yes**
38	T:	Do you agree that it's sugary?
39	Ss:	**Yes**
40	T:	Okay. Does everybody, how does everybody feel about it.
41	Ss:	**[Fine**
		[Great.
		[Happy, (it) made me feel happy, 'cause it was good!
42	T:	Okay, so you liked it? Everybody likes it.

In this excerpt students' contributions to academic talk compare unfavorably with those from the January segment. The children now seem to assume that the object of cooperative learning groups is to come up with one-word terms to fill slots in the teacher's script. Ms. Talley's script calls for describing the chocolate as "sugary" rather than "sweet." But she doesn't elicit "sugary" from the students, just the base morpheme "sugar," which she expands to "sugary" (turn 28). Group 2 offers two one-word descriptions: "good" (turns 31, 32) and "sweet" (turns 34, 35, 37), and they affirm the teacher's description of it as "sugary" (turn 39). During the discussion, Ms. Talley is writing one-word descriptions on the board, further emphasizing the appropriateness of the one-word response. She does not respond to the comment offered in the form of a sentence at turn 41, "It made me feel happy, 'cause it was good."

Between January and May, then, the children in Ms. Talley's class showed no development in authoring coherent decontextualized responses. Their opportunities to author academic discourse were too infrequent, and, furthermore, only responses that followed the teacher's script were officially recognized. Texts in this classroom continued to be authored by the teacher, with the children animating key terms on cue.

Conclusion

As Schiffrin (1993:236) says, the roles of animator and author entail "very different notions of selfhood," with different responsibilities and privileges. In this chapter I have shown how these speaker roles may emerge in classrooms and to what effect. In the classrooms considered, the contrast in the teachers' encouragement of student authorship corresponds to the academic language proficiency displayed by their students.

Ms. Vann accorded her students substantial responsibilities and privileges as speakers, both within small-group discussions and in whole-class verbal reviews. She credited cooperative learning with the language development her children showed that school year; she called cooperative learning "my baby" and used it virtually daily, so that the children grew accustomed to assuming various speaker roles and working together to construct a range of propositional and discourse types. In their small groups, they produced descriptions, comparisons, contrasts, and explanations; the groups often had to write sentences that were subsequently integrated into a text produced by the class as a whole. Such experience may help to explain how Ms. Vann's students were able to produce an extemporaneous text of such coherence as the springtime discussion of Think Tricks.[12]

The anticipated benefits of cooperative learning did not materialize in Ms. Talley's class. To her, cooperative learning was something interesting to try, but she had the children work in groups only two or three times a month. (Mr. Rivers felt his students were not well enough behaved to stay on task in groups, so he seldom used cooperative learning.) This sporadic use of group work meant that neither the teachers nor the children ever became truly comfortable with a participation framework that included student authorship. Both Ms. Vann and Ms. Talley used cooperative learning groups as a preliminary to whole-class verbal review. But in Ms. Talley's class, the kind of participation framework that she enforced during verbal review seems to have discouraged student authorship in small-group discussions. Instead, children were merely given new ways to play out the roles that they used in this class generally, those of audience and animator. This pattern disempowered those children who were the most successful at pleasing the teacher by being the most successful at animating her script.

Student authorship of classroom discourse is a key element in the potential of cooperative learning to promote students' oral academic language competence. Cooperative learning can hand children a broader range of roles in classroom communication but only when the teacher's alignment with the students is correspondingly flexible. If the teacher insists on retaining sole authorship of the public discourse in the classroom, he or she will probably also stifle student-to-student talk within groups. But when students engage in group activities and class discussions that encourage their authorship, their academic language repertoire can flourish.

NOTES

This chapter is a substantially revised version of "Promoting the Development of Oral Academic Language Competence: the Value of Cooperative Learning," coauthored with Jennifer Detwyler of the Center for Applied Linguistics, presented at a presession of the Georgetown University Round Table on Languages and Linguistics, March 10, 1993. The data excerpts from Ms. Vann's class were collected by Detwyler and those from Ms. Talley's class by Carolyn Adger. I am indebted to both for their insights into the data, based on their fieldwork. The study of which this work was a part, "Enhancing the Delivery of Services to Black Special Education Students from Non-Standard English Speaking Backgrounds," was funded by Cooperative Agreement HO 23H00008-92 from the Office of Special Education Programs of the U.S. Department of Education to the University of Maryland. I was a discourse analyst for the project. Sincere thanks go to Susan Hoyle and Carolyn Adger for their insightful and helpful comments on this chapter.

1. Not all question-answer interchanges between teachers and students are verbal reviews, only those used to check students' learning.

2. Goffman's work has inspired more detailed schemas for the description of speaker and hearer footings, most notably by Levinson (1988), who aims for a universally applicable set of analytical categories. For classroom data, however, I find Goffman's schema to provide a good analytical fit.

3. All teachers and students have been given pseudonyms.

4. Ms. Vann's class was a "self-contained primary" special education class of students performing at early elementary grade levels. Ms. Talley (the second teacher considered) provided speech/language services by visiting a self-contained primary special education class in another school.

5. Ms. Talley also provided pull-out speech/language services for most of these children once a week outside of Mr. Rivers's class. Thus, she taught these students twice a week, and by January, when the first data sample was taped, she was a familiar and regular part of the routine of Mr. Rivers's students.

6. It is particularly important for children in special education classes to develop oral language proficiency, because many are placed in such programs for language problems or

problems of a cognitive, emotional, or behavioral nature that manifest themselves in speech.

7. No attempt has been made to represent the phonological features of African American Vernacular English, but such features of informal style as *gonna* and contracted forms are transcribed. Spelling has been regularized for evidence of speech problems such as the substitution of [w] for [r] and [l] so as not to distract from the content of the children's speech.

8. It might be argued that Gordon speaks as a principal here, for two reasons: he has chosen to put his own thoughts on the record, and the teacher adopts his notion of the overall topic of the lesson being reviewed. The line between author and principal is not easy to determine in classroom discourse, where all children who volunteer responses could be said to speak in order to put on the record what they know, even when responses are memorized bits of text. This complicated area merits further study.

9. Venn diagrams symbolized both Comparison and Contrast and were used as graphic organizers in teaching these concepts as well. For Comparison, the common area of the overlapping circles would be filled in, and for Contrast, the nonoverlapping areas. To use them as graphic organizers, teachers would draw lines in the appropriate areas for the students to write words or sentences comparing or contrasting two objects, stories, etc.

10. Victor talks about Idea-to-Example and Example-to-Idea (turns 13, 15); Najeem talks about Comparison and Contrast (even numbered turns 22–36). This pairing may be explained by the fact that the teacher taught these symbols in pairs. This is not the case with Recall and Evaluation, however.

11. This excerpt is only one topically bounded segment of the verbal review. The footing and types of elicitations remained essentially the same throughout the (rather lengthy) review, however, and a longer excerpt would not be qualitatively very different. At the end, Ms. Talley recapitulates a summary offered by Mr. Rivers, in which two or three *wh*-questions are interspersed with fill-in-the-blank elicitations. She asks where, in the Venn diagram, things that are "the same" and "different" would "go," which elicits prepositional phrase responses authored by the students ("in the middle," "in the circle") that she corrects to "on the outside."

12. Geekie and Raban (1994:178) point out the importance of routines like this one, which scaffold children's literacy development and which they see as an example of the Formats central to Bruner's (1983) Language Acquisition Support System. Literacy-supporting Formats should be particularly helpful to special education students by "distributing their attention over a series of ordered steps" (Geekie & Raban 1994:160). Certainly all students benefit from familiarity with how academic discourse types should be constructed.

10

Finding Words, Finding Meanings

Collaborative Learning and Distributed Cognition

JENNIFER SCHLEGEL

From playground mediations to classroom recitations, children participate in diverse communicative and sense-making activities: they negotiate rules, they participate in institutionally organized performances, and they engage in problem solving. The latter is an integral part of constructing shared meaning in or out of school, but it is especially central to the activity of classrooms, where it functions as a tool for the acquisition of academic knowledge. Children's work in approaching classroom problems shows that, far from being static receptors of information, they are active co-participants in the creation of meaning.

This chapter explores one problem-solving mechanism devised by some fifth-grade students within a collaborative learning environment. The activity investigated is word searches among small groups working on a classroom lesson. By word searches, I mean the general category of the "tip of the tongue" phenomenon—the activity resulting from being unable to recall a word. In the data that follow, word searches are initiated with utterances such as, "Uh, what are those rolly things, they be rolling on the ground. . . ." Word searches are an intriguing type of problem-solving activity in that they are not bounded by any necessary contextual constraints.

Word searches in this fifth-grade classroom are multi-party activities (sometimes successful and sometimes not) that depend on coordinated talk and action by more than one participant and on socially distributed cognition, occurring "across participants and through time" (Mehan 1984:64). The children use each other's experiences and memories as word search resources, in addition to their textbooks and their teacher. These children thus demonstrate that they are members of a community of practice, "a set of relations among persons, activity, and world, over time and in relation with other tangential and overlapping communities of practice . . . [that] provides the interpretive support necessary for making sense of its heritage" (Lave

& Wenger 1991:98). In conducting their word searches, as in conducting other activities, the children are able to draw on shared experiences as group members, classmates, playground peers, neighborhood friends, participants in a cultural community, members of minority groups. But as individuals with experiences derived from other communities of practice, each offers different pieces to the group's construction of knowledge.

Because collaborative learning environments, unlike traditional teacher-fronted instruction, provide children official access to each other, they offer the analyst the opportunity to explore how the multiple relations within a community of practice contribute to the activity of learning. My analysis foregrounds the abilities of the individual children as they work to solve problems by accessing one another's knowledge and negotiating meaning within moment-to-moment interaction.

The data presented in this chapter show how children collaborate in such an environment to make visible the cognitive process of recovering a word. Searching for a word within face-to-face interaction, as Goodwin and Goodwin (1986) show, is not just an individual cognitive process; it is also a socially organized endeavor. It is, furthermore, one that can involve not only talk but, often crucially, gesture. Word searches, they observe, "provide organization for a wide range of vocal and nonverbal phenomena, including both stereotypic and nonstereotypic gestures," and require that "participants attend to such phenomena because they are part of the currency through which appropriate coparticipation in the activity is displayed and negotiated" (1986:52). Members of a complex work environment (such as this fifth-grade classroom) engage in multi-layered verbal and gestural interaction as they make visible the process of reasoning within a collaborative problem-solving effort (Hutchins & Palen 1993). Here I examine the interactive role of gesture and talk in socially distributed cognition.

The children in this classroom structure their successful word searches as three-part activities. The first part of the search process is the collaborative production of and mutual focus on an "imagistic expression"[1] of the word being sought—that is, a nonverbal representation, such as a gesture or a drawing. The second part of the process involves using that imagistic expression as a tool to actually find the word. Finally, the word, once found, must be ratified by the participants. The first and third examples discussed here are instances of word searches structured in this way. The second search is an example of what may happen when the structure is derailed—when there is no demonstrated agreement regarding the meaning of an imagistic expression.

The Children

The videotaped data presented in this chapter were collected during three months of ethnographic fieldwork conducted by Charles and Marjorie Harness Goodwin in spring 1993 in a fifth-grade multicultural classroom in central Los Angeles (see Goodwin, chapter 1, this volume). The majority of the population of the school is Latino (92.2%) and Asian (5.5%), with small percentages of Blacks, Whites, and Filipinos. Earlier grades are taught in both English and Spanish, but fifth grade is taught primarily in English. The teacher of this class was a young white woman.[2] The physical layout of the classroom was designed to foster collaborative learning: the children were seated in groups of four and five, facing one another in an arrangement that facilitated discussion. The children were permanently assigned to their groups, and relationships were generally harmonious.[3]

While transcribing videotapes of the children in their work groups and conducting preliminary analyses of the interactions among students and between the students and the teacher, I noticed numerous instances of word searches. Not only were they of interest as examples of problem solving, but in addition they were literally engaging—I would participate vicariously through the video, trying to come up with words on my own and talking to the monitor, offering my own suggestions. But because I was unfamiliar with some of the strategies used by the children to find the words, I began to recognize the importance of having shared experiences in order to share meaning.

The three word searches I discuss here occurred in two different groups. The two successful cases, as we shall see, are collaboratively structured; indeed, the fact that they are structured is crucial to their success. Examination of the failed search highlights the importance of collaborative engagement in the successful ones. Analysis of these word searches shows how the children may accomplish collaboration within their community, and how they may fail to do so.

Searching for "Tumbleweed"

The first two word searches occur during an assignment given to each group to come up with words that describe the desert and to record these words on a sheet of paper (along with drawing pictures of desert objects). The teacher had recently taken the class on a trip to the desert, and throughout this lesson the students have been recalling words and images from this shared experience. That word searches occur during this assignment is not surprising—failure to recall is ubiquitous in any population, and these children may not be fully proficient in English. Moreover, some of the words are obscure from their perspective. What is interesting is that while the idea of a word comes from the mind, finding the word is achieved through social interaction of a particular, closely structured sort. The cognitive process of searching for a word becomes a socially constructed event organized through the weaving together of gestural and linguistic actions.

Finding an Image

In the first excerpt, the word being sought (as it turns out) is "tumbleweed." First, two of the children, Bonita and Alvaro, work together to agree upon an imagistic expression that represents the idea that they share. This agreed-on imagistic expression becomes, then, a public artifact that the students use as a tool to find the word: they display the artifact to the teacher, who proposes "tumbleweed." This proposal, though, does not mark the end of the search; it remains to be accepted by the group. Three of the four group members do ratify this suggestion, and the search

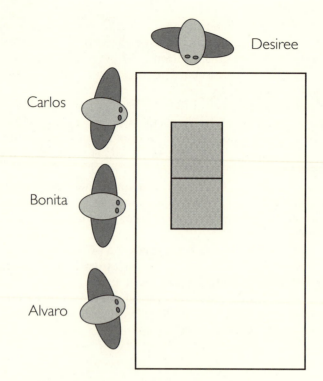

Figure 10.1 "Tumbleweed"—participants

comes to a successful end. The fourth group member does not participate actively in this first word search, and, as we shall see, he is ignored later when he attempts to participate in a second search.

The group members for the first word search, as displayed in Figure 10.1, are Alvaro and Desiree (both of Mexican descent) and Bonita and Carlos (both of Fijian descent). The search begins as follows (in the transcript, // marks the beginning of overlapping speech; all children and the teacher have been given pseudonyms):

1	Bonita:	*((Bonita gazes straight ahead))* uh What are those **rolly** things? *((Bonita, holding a marker, begins twirling her hands as she says "rolly." Alvaro turns his gaze to Bonita as she twirls her hands))*
2		They be **roll**ing on the ground
3		(.3)You know on cartoons or the commercials sometimes?
4		Ib//
5	Alvaro:	//From movies? *((Bonita looks at Alvaro))*
6		(.3) Like the one//with Pee Wee Herman? *((leans back and points index finger as he says "one"))*
7	Bonita:	*((leans back as Alvaro leans back))* //Ye: ah.
8		*((twirls her hands as she speaks))* And then// you start ro: lling
9	Alvaro:	*((twirls his finger, then his hand))* //It goes

10   Bonita: Yeah tho=iye. ((*drops marker*))
       Alvaro: ((*places his hand on his mouth; thought position*))
11   I remember that.

Bonita initiates this word search using four conversational devices: a question as the first pair part of an adjacency pair (Sacks 1992a), a nonverbal embellishment, a verbal embellishment, and a reference to shared knowledge. Her *wh*-question ("what are those rolly things," line 1) overtly requests the participation of another group member in the search; she does not address anyone in particular or look at anyone but gazes straight ahead, inviting any or all of the others to volunteer a response. She embellishes her question through gesture, moving her hands at the wrist in a circular motion. Receiving no immediate answer, she extends her question (line 2) by continuing to gesture and by providing additional information about the unknown term ("they be rolling on the ground") that could increase the chance of another group member's either providing the word immediately or engaging in the search (cf. Goodwin & Goodwin 1986). When there is still no response, she adds still more information, referring, after a slight pause (line 3), to items familiar to her listeners ("cartoons" and "commercials").

The gesture and gaze that play a key role in the search give evidence of the evolving participation framework. Although Bonita's initial question is not addressed to anyone in particular, a collaborative gestural production begins between her and Alvaro as she speaks. As she begins to move her hands in an iconic "rolly" manner, Alvaro lifts his head and brings his gaze to her. At line 5 he speaks, and she turns her gaze to him, ratifying his response and his participation; her silence in response to his utterance implies that she is waiting for more information. Then, as Alvaro extends his turn and embellishes his participation with further information, Bonita interrupts with an affirmation:

6   Alvaro: (.3) Like the one//with Pee Wee Herman? ((*leans back and points index finger*
                  as he says "one"))
7   Bonita: ((*leans back as Alvaro leans back*))
                  //Ye: ah.

Although recipients often overlap speakers in affirmation (Jefferson 1973:57–58), here Bonita interrupts Alvaro *before* sufficient information is given. A premature interruption like this might suggest that she has come up with the answer to the word search, but no such answer follows. Rather, it seems that Bonita has been encouraged to respond not just to Alvaro's utterance but to his gesture. Alvaro leans back and points his index finger toward Bonita as he says "one" in line 6, and Bonita utters her affirmation just after Alvaro makes this gesture but before he says "Pee Wee Herman." She also leans back in her seat in synchrony with him. Through both words and gestures, then, Alvaro communicates his attention to Bonita, and she to him (cf. Kendon 1985:235), and her "Yeah" is not an example of premature timing, but a ratification of the participation framework.

Alvaro's pointing gesture in line 6 also illuminates the intricate organization of the participation framework. The pointing coincides with the word "one" in "Like the one with Pee Wee Herman." Although pointing is generally a deictic gesture, he does not point to any object in the vicinity, but rather to an abstraction. McNeill

(1992:18) points out that such "[a]bstract pointing gestures imply a metaphorical picture of their own in which abstract ideas have a physical locus." In this example, the abstract idea of a movie containing "rolly things" is situated locally in the joint gestural production of the participants. By metaphorically pointing to a movie, Alvaro is connecting the discussion to knowledge presumably shared within a community of peers. The group members can rely on their shared experiences—as students who took a field trip together and as children who participate in and have knowledge of popular culture meaningful to them.

Bonita and Alvaro continue to collaborate verbally and nonverbally:

8   Bonita: ((*twirls her hands as she speaks*))
              and then// you start ro: lling
9   Alvaro: ((*twirls his finger, then his hand*))
              //it goes

Bonita restarts her rolly gesture as she speaks, and Alvaro takes it up too, spinning first his index finger and then his hands in the same motion as Bonita (Figure 10.2). The rolly gestures produced synchronously by the two are iconic: "gestures whose shape links them to lexical components of the talk . . . semantically (i.e., the shape that the gesture describes depicts a/the 'meaning' or referent of a word)" (Schegloff 1984:275). Like the iconic gestures analyzed by Schegloff, these of the children are "pre-positioned relative to their lexical affiliates" and "they are over before their lexical affiliate is produced" (1984:276). However, in the children's search, the lexical affiliate appears to depend on the gestural production. The gestures do not just occur sequentially prior to the lexical affiliate; rather, they serve to stimulate, not just amplify, the term being sought.

The children's gestures reveal the social organization involved in their creation of a shared cognitive perspective. In order to understand the significance of the production of the same rolly gesture by the two participants, we return to Alvaro's deictic gesture in line 6. I have argued that it serves to locate an abstract idea in the local, physical environment. This pointing gesture can also be considered as the preparation phase for the gestural stroke (Kendon 1980) that follows, the rolly gesture that Alvaro produces. The gestural production—both the deictic and the iconic gestures—is not just an external product of Alvaro's thought process but a social phenomenon that produces and is produced by the organization of the interaction.[4] Alvaro's gesture in line 6 accompanies his turn at talk. Bonita interrupts Alvaro with the affirmation (line 7), and Bonita continues with her turn at talk in line 8. Alvaro's gestural display, or turn, has been sustained during Bonita's talk. That sustained deictic gesture becomes the preparation for his iconic gesture produced in synchrony with Bonita in line 9. Although Alvaro's *talk* may be governed by rules of turn-taking that encourage one speaker at a time, his gestures appear to be part of an overarching communicative process whose rules are less obvious.

The role of gestures in this segment, then, is crucial. They do not just accompany or occur with speech; rather, they are part of the essence of the communicative process. Recipients of gestures can acknowledge their understanding of them through either talk or gesture (Streeck 1993); Alvaro uses both. He formulates a meaning

Figure 10.2 "Tumbleweed"—gesture

of Bonita's initial question and rolly gesture and makes his interpretation of this information explicit by establishing a verbal reference ("from movies? Like the one with Pee Wee Herman?") along with a nonverbal, abstract reference (deictic gesture). This example is significant because the participants are presenting a mutual understanding of an utterance ("tumbleweed") that has yet to be made. In this first stage of the word search, they agree referentially and gesturally on an imagistic expression for which they do not yet have a name.

How the two participants mutually achieve an imagistic expression through verbal and nonverbal collaboration is not the only important issue. They also collaborate to make visible the cognitive process of recovering a word.

8   Bonita: *((twirls her hands as she speaks))*
            And then// you start ro: lling
9   Alvaro: *((twirls his finger, then his hand))*
            //It goes

Bonita's "you" in line 8 is very like the proforms (*I* and *you*) used by the physicists in the lab studied by Ochs, Jacoby, and Gonzales (1994); the physicists often use these forms, as they are thinking through problems together, in such a way as to blur the boundaries between the (animate) scientist and an (inanimate) object of scientific inquiry. Like such scientists, the children here are demonstrating that they are deeply engaged in a collaborative meaning-making effort. Bonita, it appears, is referring to Alvaro both as 'you, a student,' and 'you, one who is enacting and representing a nonhuman entity,' and we can see the embodied participation of the children in bringing the image to life. This imagistic expression becomes the ultimate tool allowing them to find the word "tumbleweed."

Finding and Ratifying the Word

Following the synchronous gesturing by Alvaro and Bonita, Alvaro claims to "re-member":

11   Alvaro: *((Alvaro brings his hand to his mouth))* I remember that.
12   let me tell the teacher. *((leaves the group and goes to the teacher))*

As he places his hand to his mouth, displaying a "thinking face" (Goodwin & Goodwin 1986:61), Alvaro remembers "that"—the image being brought from the cognitive to the social realm. By using "tell" (line 12), he indicates that even though he and Bonita do not yet have the answer, they have negotiated a product, if not a finished one. They present it to the teacher for her input. Thus, through ne-gotiation the children have crystallized a notion for which they can now proceed to find a word.

In the second part of the search process, Alvaro's exchange with the teacher oc-curs just out of the camera's reach. The teacher cannot be seen, but it is possible to see Alvaro using the rolly gesture as he speaks to her. What follows is a series of ut-tered "tumbleweed"s.

19   Teacher: →   *((off camera))* Tumbleweed? *((Desiree looks toward Alvaro and the
                                                teacher))*
20   Alvaro: *((off camera))* (.4) (Tumble?)
21   Carlos: (.3) What is that.[5]
22   Bonita: (.7) What.
23   Carlos: (.3) That, *((Carlos points at the picture))*
24   Alvaro: →   Tumblewe//ed *((uttered as he walks back to the table))*
25   Bonita: //It's just be
26   Desiree: →   (1.0) *((to group))* tumble//we:ed.
27   Bonita: *((looks up and out, possibly at the teacher))*
                →   //oh yeah tumblewe: ed.
28   Alvaro: →   (2.4) *((sits))* it's tumblewe: ed.

The teacher offers "tumbleweed" as the solution in line 19, thus ending the second phase of the search.

The third part of the search, a brief but necessary part, consists of ratification of the term. Alvaro says "tumbleweed" in line 24 as he approaches the group. Desiree offers "tumbleweed" to the group at line 26, Bonita repeats it at line 27, and Alvaro utters it a final time at line 28. Note that the fourth member of the group, Carlos, has not demonstrated attention to any part of this word search, nor does he partic-ipate in the ratification of the word.

Searching for "Dried Grass"

A second word search follows immediately, but it is, in contrast to the *tumbleweed* search, unsuccessful. Although "dried grass" is offered by Carlos as a solution, it is never ratified by the other group members. This search lacks the three-part struc-ture seen in the previous one. The most crucial omission is that there is no explicit agreement regarding the image in question: it is difficult to find the appropriate lexeme when one doesn't know what the notion is to begin with. This search also lacks the facilitative gesturing and vocal embellishment indexing a shared experience that characterized the first one. In short, this search does not follow a pattern similar to the first and it fails.

Participation in the prior word search is directly relevant to the way in which the second one proceeds. The assignment, to write down words and draw pictures of things that can be found in the desert, remains the same, and it remains relevant that the group members had recently been on a trip to the desert together. What has changed, however, is the most local level of participation. In the first search, Bonita's initial question was not initially directed to any specific group member, and in fact three of the four group members participated. In this second search, Bonita's initial question ("And what do you call this stuff?") is directed to Alvaro. Immediately a two-party framework is implied and the potential for group collaboration changes. Indeed, Carlos, the member who did not participate in the prior word search, repeatedly offers an answer but is repeatedly ignored.

34	Bonita:	((points to picture and looks at Alvaro as she says "this"))
		and what do you call this stuff
35		(.6) it just sit there on the ground
36	Carlos:	where is the plants.
37	Bonita:	and it's dead?
38	Carlos:	(.3) un (.1) dried grass?
39	Alvaro:	((thinking face))
		(.9) a: : h.
40		(1.0) I really don't know.
41	Bonita:	shhhoot( )//taum
42	Carlos:	//a bunch of dried grass
43		(1.8) a bunch of gri dried grass
44		(1.0) auh lizard. like this?
45	Bonita:	poison ivy?
46	Carlos:	(1.5) a bunch of dried grass.
47		(1.0) a picture by uh
48	Bonita:	(1.3) what elssse.
49	Desiree:	(.6) I draw a lizard,

Here again, an image is produced: Bonita has drawn a series of short lines that are connected at a base. But the meaning of this imagistic expression is not self-evident. Just as meaning was not completely captured by the iconic gesture in the "tumbleweed" example, it is not in the drawn picture here. In order for the search to proceed as a group effort, the meaning of the representation must be negotiated and agreed on—but in this example the search falters during this stage.

Bonita begins by asking "And what do you call this stuff" as she points to her picture. When she gets no immediate answer, she adds verbal embellishment ("It just sit there on the ground," "and it's dead?"), just as she did in the previous excerpt. Nonverbally, however, this sequence is different from the "tumbleweed" one. This time Bonita's gaze does direct the question to a specific individual, Alvaro (line 34). This is a carryover of the participation framework from the tumbleweed example:

Bonita and Alvaro collaborated successfully there, and she recognizes both his competence and his availability by directing her question and her gaze toward him.

Alvaro responds to Bonita's question in lines 39 and 40. Although he does not know the answer, he maintains an active role as the selected next speaker. In line 39, as he says "a: : h" he leans back, puts his index finger to his mouth, and displays a thinking face, which acts as a signal of attention for Bonita, before admitting ignorance.

Carlos suggests an answer to Bonita's question (lines 38, 42, 43, 46). As he speaks, his gaze is continuously directed at the picture he is drawing on the paper. Bonita neither turns her gaze to Carlos nor replies to his suggestions, even though he offers "dried grass" four times. She offers her own answer at line 45 ("poison ivy?"). This is not ratified either, and this word search ends at line 48 as Bonita changes the direction of the discussion with "what elssse."

The lack of collaboration in this search may stem from the dynamics of the group. In this second search, Bonita can be seen as sanctioning Carlos's lack of collaborative effort in the previous one. If this interpretation is correct, Bonita's ignoring of Carlos is evidence of peer socialization: Carlos broke a "rule" by not participating earlier when the floor was open to him, so Bonita "punishes" him.[6]

Comparison of the Two Word Searches

The two searches examined so far differ significantly. The first one, of course, is successful in that a word is not only found but also ratified, whereas the second one fails because no word is agreed on. Several possible reasons for this difference in success suggest themselves. One possibility is that the nature of the words being sought in the two cases differs. In the first search, Bonita and Alvaro use an active gesture that captures the first part ("tumble") of the word that is eventually ratified. In the second example, though, there is little facilitative gesturing (the only gesturing is Bonita's pointing to the picture on the paper), a lack that may be due to the nature of the name being sought: although no term is ratified, the two proposed answers, "dried grass" and "poison ivy," both evoke static images. A second possible explanation for the difference in outcome is that the tumbleweed example is a truly collaborative effort. Its success, as contrasted with the failure of the dried grass example, suggests that for these children, in this setting, collaboration is favored over individual effort. Indeed, the failure of the second search, in which Carlos's contribution is completely ignored, highlights the means by which success is achieved in the first. Related to this explanation is the analysis of the first search that reveals an underlying three-part structure, with the participants orienting to each of the parts. Their awareness (at some level) of the three stages is evidenced in their behavior: in the shared production of a rolly gesture during the first stage, in the product taken to the teacher in the second stage ("Let me tell the teacher"), and finally in the ratification (in the form of repetition) of the suggested solution in the third stage. The second example falters, though. Although there is an image on the paper (Bonita's drawing), there is no display of agreement that such an image will be the foundation for the word search. Although a word is repeatedly suggested by one

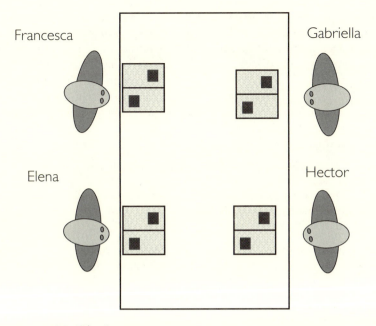

Figure 10.3 "Plow"—participants

member, it cannot be said to be "found," and it is not ratified by anyone else. The second word search fails: the three parts of the search are not achieved and the search is not open to collaboration and participation by all group members.

Searching for "Plow"

The third word search to be discussed provides further evidence that a successful search is a collaborative effort, with a three-part construction, in which both shared references and nonverbal activity are important. This episode occurs at a different table on a different day in the same classroom. Figure 10.3 shows the arrangement of the children (who are all of Mexican descent) in group 2.

Here, again, the nature of the assignment encourages word searches. This assignment differs in that, implicitly, there are no right or wrong answers (as there are when children are asked to remember desert items). The teacher has asked the children to use their imaginations as they look at prints of a surrealist painting by Marc Chagall and to write down anything they see in the painting. Each student in the group is looking at prints in his or her own textbook, and each has his or her own sheet of paper. In this example, then, the imagistic expression is initially located in a painting in the book. Once again, though, an imagistic expression does not exist independently but has to be negotiated by the participants. The word being sought, as it turns out, is "plow."

Most of the talk during this search involves only one student and the teacher. However, when we look at the nonverbal activity, it becomes apparent that the other students are actively involved. They search the surrealistic painting with their gaze during the first stage of the process, attend to each other with glances during the second stage, and finally nod as a form of ratification. The initiator of the search, Hector, uses the textbook, spoken words, and gestures as tools to facilitate the creation of a shared imagistic expression for which he has no name. The imagistic expression, as in the first example, is located in the time and space of nonverbal gestures, but it is also located, as in the second example, in a two-dimensional visual representation on paper.

Hector begins by issuing a directive in line 1 as he looks at his book:

1   Hector: ((*looks at book, looks at group, looks down to book, looks up at teacher*)) Oooo lo: ok.
2   Elena: (1.8) Uhm picture.
3   Hector: (.9) ((*raises right hand*)) Ms. Larson,
4   Teacher: Yeah.

Hector looks up and notices that he is not being attended to by any of the group members. When no one responds either verbally or nonverbally (Elena's utterance is part of the interaction that occurred prior to this sequence), he summons the teacher (line 3)[7] and proceeds to ask a *wh*-question:

5   Hector: ((*Hector points at his book, Gabriella looks at Hector's book, Francesca glances at Hector, then returns her gaze to her book. Elena looks at Hector, glances at the teacher, who is approaching, and returns her gaze to Hector*)) How do you call those things that
6   ((*Hector holds his fisted hands in front of him with palms up*)) you know in the olden days
7   ((*jerks his hands back as he says "pull"*)) they used to pull those the horses?
8   ((*lowers left hand and makes a downward circular motion with his right index finger*)) And they used to make like little holes to plant things? ((*Francesca has been glancing from her book to Hector. Gabriella looks at teacher, who has approached the group. Elena looks from Hector to teacher to Hector.*))

As in the first word search, the speaker refers to something presumably shared, this time knowledge of a past in which horses and plows were used in planting. (In the talk following the search, Hector reveals that he was recalling a photograph of his grandfather as a young farmer working a plow in Mexico.) Hector, like Bonita in the first example, uses gestures to represent the word he is searching for. The lack of others' participation in these embellishments, however, suggests that Hector's imagistic expression is not immediately shared. He uses both deictic and iconic gestures: he points to the picture in the book where he sees the nameless imagistic expression, and he makes a circular motion with his finger in an imitation of digging a hole. In the following transcript, asterisks denote deictic gestures at lines 5, 12, and 18; pound signs denote iconic gestures at lines 6, 7, 8, 13, 19, 21, and 23, where Hector makes motions that represent pushing, pulling, and digging.

5 * Hector: ((*Hector points at his book, Gabriella looks at Hector's book, Francesca glances at Hector, then returns her gaze to her book. Elena looks at Hector, glances at the teacher, who is approaching, and returns her gaze to Hector*)) How do you call those things that

6 #   *((Hector holds his fisted hands in front of him with palms up))* you know in the olden days

7 #   *((jerks his hands back as he says "pull"))*
            they used to pull those the horses?

8 #   *((lowers left hand and makes a downward circular motion with his right index finger.))*
            And they used to make like little holes to plant things?
            ((Francesca has been glancing from her book to Hector. Gabriella looks at teacher, who has approached the group. Elena looks from Hector to teacher to Hector))

9   Teacher: Plant things.

10   Hector: To plant things.

11   Teacher: //Um

12 *   Hector: *((Hector points at the book and thrusts his fisted hands forward as he says "push"))*
            //You know like they hold things

13 #   And the horse are pushing it?

14   Teacher: *((Francesca and Elena look at the teacher as she speaks))*
            Is it a hoe is that what it is called like a=

15   Hector: I think

16   Teacher: *((Gabriella glances at the teacher))*
            =Um (1.3) //a tractor?

17   Elena: *((looking at the teacher with her fisted hands outstretched. She pulls back her right hand as she speaks))*
                  //No cause a hoe is like

18 *   Hector: *((Hector points at the image and slides the book closer to the teacher, who is bending over Gabriella, also looking at Hector's book. Francesca glances at Hector.))*
            No, it's like you know like this kind

19 #   *((Hector lifts his hands as he says "horse." Gabriella looks at her book as the teacher leans over and puts her hand on Hector's book. Gabriella quickly turns back to Hector's book. Elena leans over the desk to see Hector's book))*
            (.4) Like //there's a horse and

20   Teacher: *((the teacher leans over Gabriella's book to glance at Hector's book))*
                  //Let me see

21 # Hector: *((Hector points right index finger down onto desktop. Francesca points to her own book with her pencil. Hector thrusts his hands forward as he says "pushing"))*
            They have like little nee//dle and then they start pushing it like

22   Teacher: //Oh ye: : : ah right (.6) yeah

23 # Hector: That //(.) and they plant things.

24   Gabriella: *((Gabriella looks up from Hector's book and snaps her finger, then looks back down at Hector's book. Elena and Francesca look in their own books, and the teacher looks in Gabriella's book))*
                  //O: : : : : h

Although the other children and the teacher are looking at the same picture in their textbooks, they have not visually located, and thus do not yet share, the imagistic expression that Hector is presenting verbally and nonverbally. After Hector's third attempt at elaboration (beginning at line 18), the other students begin to examine the picture more closely, their focus now on the picture rather than on Hector. At line 20, the teacher looks in Hector's book, and at lines 22 and 24 the

Figure 10.4 "Plow"—sharing an image

teacher and Gabriella both verbalize their recognition of the imagistic expression. Gabriella looks up as she speaks (line 24) and then looks back down at Hector's book. The teacher is looking in Gabriella's book, and Elena and Francesca are looking in their own books (see Figure 10.4).

It is only once the imagistic expression has been seen by the others, and they have confirmed their recognition of it, that the actual word is suggested. The teacher looks up and asks the question (line 25) that serves as the transition to the second part of the word search process: using the imagistic expression as a tool to find the word.

25   Teacher: ((*The teacher and the students look up as the teacher speaks to someone off camera. Then Elena looks up at the teacher, Francesca covers her face with her hands and Gabriella puts her right index finger up to her mouth; thinking face*))
                 What is that what is that called,
26   (.6) You know what that's called

Her question is similar in form to other questions that propose searches ("what are those rolly things," "and what do you call this stuff," "how do you call those things"), although in this case she presumably knows the answer and is trying to elicit it from the students. It is during the utterance of line 25 that the students lift their heads from their books, marking the end of the search for the imagistic expression and the beginning of the second phase, the search for the word itself (see Figure 10.5).

A suggestion is made in lines 28 and 30 and is ratified by Gabriella in line 31:

27   Teacher: ((*The teacher extends her right hand, palm up, and moves it forward as she says "planting." She then extends her right hand further, palm down, and rotates it. Francesca and Elena look at the teacher, Elena taps her pencil on her arm*))
                 The **plant**ing and the the (.) the horses //used to **pu: ll** them
28   X: //Plow.
29   Teacher: Through the //fields?

Figure 10.5 "Plow"—finding the word

30   X: ((*Elena and Francesca turn to the speaker who is off camera*))
                   //Plow?
31   Gabriella: ((*Gabriella looks in direction of the speaker who is off camera*))
                   Uh huh.

The word "plow" is then ratified several more times—by the teacher (lines 32, 35, 37, 38), Hector (lines 33 and 36), and Francesca (who does so by nodding at line 35 in response to the teacher's confirming query):

32   Teacher: ((*right hand, palm up, moves toward person who offered "plow"*))
                   A p//low!
33   Hector: ((*points to off camera speaker, looks at teacher and nods his head*))
                   //Yeah
34   Teacher: ((*nodding slightly, looks at Hector, hand still out*))
                   Was it a plow?
35   ((*slight nod, looks back to off camera person. Francesca nods slightly while looking at the teacher. Elena looks at the teacher*))
                   (.4) Ye//ah
36   Hector: //Yeah.
37   Teacher: (.9) Old fashioned plow.
38   ((*nods head*))
                   Yeah.

This example highlights the importance of achieving a shared imagistic expression in order to continue a word search. Like the tumbleweed example, it reveals the underlying three-part structure of a word search activity among these children. The first part of the process involves collaborating on a shared imagistic expression that represents the word being sought. Although the others do not participate with Hector in producing gestures, they do attend to and follow his deictic and iconic gestures and actively participate in locating the plow in the painting. This imagistic expression is then used as a tool to find the word being sought. The shared perspective of the group is necessary for achieving a common reference in order to continue with the word search activity. Finally, the proposed answer is ratified by the different members of the group.[8]

Conclusion

This chapter has investigated some particulars of group interactions within a classroom. The word search activities provide an opportunity to examine in detail how collaborative learning can be achieved, as the children, members of a community of practice, are "learning to learn" from each other. Analysis of their word searches reveals that meaning is not always situated independently in the mind or gesture of an individual, in a textbook, or in words but is created in the temporal and spatial dimensions of social interactions. Thus, a word can be located through the creation of a shared perspective involving various resources available to the students, including each other as social actors. These data, drawn from a multilingual and multicultural classroom, indicate how the children's varying individual experiences and their shared experiences are resources that guide the construction and negotiation of meaning.

The subtle communicative means employed by the students in their interactions during a problem-solving activity are social processes that can produce and reproduce a framework for collaborative learning in the classroom environment. In attending to each other's talk and nonverbal activity, the children develop patterns of interaction, negotiated independently by each group. The collaboration involves more than the sharing of ideas; it involves the negotiation of the intricacies of communication that in turn reinforce the collaborative atmosphere that the instructional environment provides. Collaborative learning prospers in this classroom because the students make it work; it is an achievement played out in the students' interactions as much as enabled by the teacher's structuring of groups and assignments. Through their group work, the children are taking charge of their own learning.

Two aspects of language socialization (cf. Ochs 1986) are evidenced in these data. First, children invent structure for their learning activities. The three-part sequence is not evident in the word searches among adults discussed by Goodwin and Goodwin (1986). Among these children, though, the process is exposed, with participants' verbal and nonverbal behavior marking the boundaries of each step. It may be that as people are socialized to language use, the steps become less exposed, so that the underlying structure of the word search becomes fully embedded within the activity. Second, the children hold each other to the norms that they create. Such an instance of peer socialization is glimpsed when Bonita ignores Carlos during the second word search; her doing so may act as a sanction against his lack of participation in the first search. In order to understand classroom interaction, we need to know how language is used by students (not only by teachers) as a resource for socialization (O'Connor & Michaels 1993); analysis of word searches offers a glimpse into that process.

Children (like adults) are social actors who bring a lifetime of experience into any interaction. They competently use their experiences, memories, and representations of life to create, negotiate, and share meaning. In the problem-solving activity of searching for a word, they make relevant some aspects of their lived experiences. Word searches present an opportunity for children to actively negotiate meaning and the shared nature of their knowledge in the organization of the process.

NOTES

An earlier version of this paper was presented during a session entitled "Language Categories as Situated, Embodied Practice" at the annual meeting of the American Anthropological Association, November 30–December 5, 1994, in Atlanta. In preparing this paper, I have benefited greatly from discussions with and criticisms and comments from Carolyn Temple Adger, Susan Hoyle, Alessandro Duranti, Adam Kendon, and Paul Kroskrity. I owe special gratitude to Candy and Chuck Goodwin for sharing not only the data but their time, patience, and criticism. Because of their contributions, I feel that this paper is as much a product of collaborative learning as it is about collaborative learning.

1. I am indebted to Adam Kendon (personal communication) for this term. I use the term "imagistic expression" rather than "image" to emphasize that there is no inherent equivalence of meaning between gestures and words.

2. This teacher had enrolled in the Teach for America program following her graduation from Middlebury College with a master's degree in Latin American Studies. Participants in this program, who sign up for two years of service, are sent to a school in need of teachers (and often other necessities such as textbooks and classrooms). At the time of the video-recordings that provide the data for this chapter, this teacher was nearing the end of her second year and had just decided to stay and teach at this school for another year.

3. The students in this classroom, when working in their groups, seem to put aside other individualistic classroom identities, such as "the most popular girl" or "teacher's pet." In the business of learning together, the students are more than able to be academically and socially flexible. Yet because of the range of experiences of children, each group forms its own unique community with its own norms of behavior that operate within the boundaries of the assignment at hand. Ethnographies of classrooms should, ideally, extend beyond the walls of a particular room and into the playgrounds, homes, and communities in which the participants live. Certainly this chapter would benefit from extended ethnographic work.

4. My analysis supports the view that the interworkings of language and gesture are essential to the complex work environment of the classroom, instead of assuming an intrapersonal function of gestures in which they belong "not to the outside world, but to the inside one of memory, thought, and mental images" (McNeill 1992:12).

5. While Alvaro is speaking with the teacher, an interaction occurs between Bonita and Carlos (lines 21, 22, 23, 25) that is more typical of the overall group activity. It highlights the exposed nature of the word search embedded in the overall activity. The relationship between the interactions in these lines is beyond the scope of this chapter.

6. Further review of the videotaped material from the larger corpus of data of which this is a part suggests that Bonita's behavior throughout this assignment can be characterized as more dominant than that of the other group members, thus casting her as a group leader and enforcer.

7. Hector may ask the teacher rather than other group members for help not only be-

cause he gets no response from the other children but also because the assignment is not completely group-oriented; each group member is coming up with his or her own word.

8. The teacher's participation in this search, it may be noted, is different from that in the *tumbleweed* search. In *tumbleweed*, the teacher was one of the resources used by the students to come up with the word tumbleweed; in *plow*, she is a participant in the search. Regardless of whether or not she knows that the search is for the word *plow*, her participation matches that of the students in that she has to locate the surrealistic plow in the painting, use this imagistic expression in the process of finding the word, and then participate in ratification of the word once it is found.

11

Speaking Standard English from Nine to Three

Language as Guerrilla Warfare at Capital High

SIGNITHIA FORDHAM

Black . . . [Americans] gradually developed their own ways of conveying resistance using The Man's language against him as a defense against sub-human categorization. . . . The function of white verbal behavior toward Blacks was to define, force acceptance of, and control the existing level of restraints. Blacks clearly recognized that *to master the language of whites was in effect to consent to be mastered by it through the white definitions of caste built into the semantic/social system.* (Holt 1972:153–54, emphasis added)

Students at Capital High,[1] most of them Black, rent the discourse of power—"standard English"—from nine to three, five days a week. As I use the term here, standard English is more than a structured variety of the language, more than its phonology, syntax, and lexicon. It includes Gee's (1990:xix) notion of Discourses (with a capital D) as

ways of behaving, interacting, valuing, thinking, believing, speaking, and often reading and writing that are accepted as instantiations of particular roles by specific *groups of people*, whether families of a certain sort, lawyers of a certain sort, business people of a certain sort, churches of a certain sort, and so on through a long list. [Discourses] are always and everywhere *social*. Language, as well as literacy, is always and everywhere integrated with and relative to *social practices* constituting particular Discourses. (emphasis in original)

In this expanded sense, standard English incorporates attitudes and styles of speaking and behaving. Of specific interest here, it includes attitudes of hostility and opposition to African American Vernacular English (AAVE) and styles associated with it. Thus, it comes as no surprise that standard English, understood in this broad sense, might be resisted by African Americans, for its "definitions of caste," which stigmatize Black speech, extend easily to Black people as well.

At Capital High, students sense antipathy to Black discourse traditions emanating from the demands of the formal curriculum and from teachers and staff who constantly admonish them to temper their voices, speak in modulated tones, act like "ladies and gentlemen," and generally appropriate not only standard English grammar but also the entire power discourse of the White community. Most Capital students—valuing forms of interaction that emphasize visibility, possession of voice, and a semantic code outside the mainstream culture—reject these adult admonishments, and those who do not are accused by their peers of "acting white." Students at Capital High do use standard English—some more than others—but to most of them it is a socially stigmatized dialect (just as in the wider society AAVE is stigmatized).

I propose a metaphor for the linguistic practices of Capital High students that reflects both their reluctance to be "mastered by . . . the white definitions of caste built into the semantic/social system" (Holt 1972:154) and the strategies they use to appropriate the power discourse that I refer to as standard English. That metaphor is *renting*. Students rent standard English, return it, and rent it again during the next class session. They do not seek to own it. By using it only between nine and three,[2] they display their awareness that it is deemed crucial to academic success, but at the same time they demonstrate their commitment to the Black community, its cultural traditions and practices, and Black "Self production" (Friedman 1992). For some students, renting the discourse of power is a successful, albeit tension-producing, strategy: they manage to retain affective ownership of (a less powerful) Black discourse even while temporarily using the dominant school discourse. Sadly, though, for others, refusal to rent discourse practices that they view as foreign and hostile to their own identity is influential in marking them as academic failures.

The Research Site: The Capital Community

Capital High School is located in a predominantly African American section of Washington, D.C. It is not a typical low-income or inner-city school but a magnet school, attracting students from all socioeconomic segments of the city. Its recruitment efforts are quite successful. More than a fourth of the students are noncommunity residents who travel from various parts of the city to participate in the school's Advanced Placement and Humanities Programs.[3] At the time of my study, the racial composition of the student body was 1,868 Black, sixteen White and two Hispanic students. A large number of the students came from one-parent homes; some lived in public or low-income housing. Almost a fourth of them were eligible for the reduced-price lunch program.

During a multiyear study at the school, conducted in the tradition of sociocultural anthropology, I spent virtually every school day from September to June—and most weekends—in the field, collecting data and trying to understand why, how, and at what cost African American adolescents achieve school success. The first two years of the study were the most intense. During the first one, thirty-three eleventh-grade students whose parents had consented to their participation in the study served as key informants. They were a varied group, representing both high-

and underachieving students, male and female. My interactions with them included classroom observations, home visitations, observations of before- and after-school activities, and formal and informal interviews. I became their altered shadows, watching[4] them as they performed in different social contexts. I also watched and interviewed their parents, teachers, and other school officials.[5] During the second year of the study, an in situ survey was administered to 600 students in grades nine through twelve. For the analysis presented here, data from twelve of the high-achieving students (six males and six females) and twelve of the underachieving students (six males and six females) were examined and interpreted.[6]

Capital's administrative staff consisted of a principal, four assistant principals, five counselors, two librarians,[7] 123 regular classroom teachers, four special education teachers, a transition teacher, and two teachers in the Skills Lab—one for math and one for reading. The support staff consisted of ten cafeteria workers, five clerical aides, two community aides, twelve custodians (including the engineering staff), and a school nurse. The school supported a four-tier curriculum: two special programs (Advanced Placement and Humanities), the regular curriculum in which most of the students were enrolled, and a special education program. Where there were areas of overlap between the regular curriculum and the two special academic programs, students were placed according to performance on standardized examinations.

Like the student body, the teaching staff was predominantly Black. However, virtually every department had at least one White teacher, with the English Department having the largest number, four females. In addition, the teachers of the more advanced classes (e.g., chemistry, government, Advanced Placement English, Advanced Placement physics, Advanced Placement mathematics) were White. They were also the teachers who served as sponsors for the JETS Club, It's Academic, the Chess Club, and so on. Hence, the power and influence of the White teachers in the learning, achievement, and emerging perceptions of Capital's students far exceeded their numbers.

Discourse Style and Rhetorical Resistance

Renting the discourse of power at school is not a simple, dichotomous, full-scale switching between one dialect and another, because standard English and AAVE are distinguished not only by relatively minor grammatical differences but by an overarching rhetorical and stylistic divergence as well. Capital students who choose to pursue academic excellence have to maintain a fine balance between the discourse traditions promulgated by the school and those growing out of their own sociocultural history, which embody the reluctance of African American people to become, symbolically, the Other.[8]

Holt (1972:154) asserts that once African Americans were freed from official enslavement, "language [became] the major vehicle for perpetuating the legitimation of the subsequent stages of oppression." Those who were unwilling or unable to accept and embrace the discourse practices of the larger society were tracked for failure, academic and otherwise. But, in Lorde's (1990:287) words, "the master's [language] will never dismantle the master's house" (cf. Gates 1994); the dominant discourse is ineffective in fighting oppressive social conditions because language propels us to interpret the world through a specific culture and its texts. African Americans resorted to a number of strategies to avoid becoming mired in the larger society's oppressive social structure, including "inversion,"[9] whereby "[w]ords and phrases were given reverse meanings and functions changed . . . , enabling blacks to deceive and manipulate whites without penalty. . . . The purpose of the game was *to appear to but not to*" (Holt 1972:154, emphasis added). Engaging in inversion is just what Capital students do when they rent the standard discourse—when they adopt temporarily, but refuse to claim as their own, the discourse sanctioned by the academy. "Appearing to but not to" be standard English speakers is one way adolescents can negotiate contradictory values centering around academic success and failure.

Inversion, often used for "rhetorical resistance" (Dyson 1995), draws on common African American rhetorical practices that "fuse speech and performance" (Dyson 1995:16). (Such fusion is evident in Martin Luther King, Jr.'s "I Have a Dream" speech: he did not simply say the words; he performed them.) In this regard, Andrews (n.d.:24–25) chronicles the power of "improvisational expression" that embellishes the basic action with decorative flourish. In the predominantly Black high school that he attended in Oakland, California, both talk and athletic events were judged as performance. On the playing field, merely winning was insufficient. How one played (analogous to how one spoke) was even more important. Getting a touchdown, for example, was the easy part; how the player scored was more remarkable—it should be done with the appropriate "attitude" or expressiveness. Here Andrews speaks of running track:

> Valrey started out about two lengths behind. He paced himself, was cool, and didn't panic. His head was level and he looked confident. As he neared the finish line he was breathing down the neck of the [other] trackstar. Valrey passed the grandstand and quickly rocketed ahead of the [other trackstar] toward victory. But this wasn't enough. This wasn't a *signature*. This was merely winning, and sports in East Oakland was not about winning or losing, but how you played the game. Valrey . . . knew what [both schools'] fans wanted: they wanted him to cross the "t" and dot the "i's" of individuality. So in the spirit of customer satisfaction, . . . he flipped his body around and trotted backwards toward the finish line, . . . gazed at the [other trackstar] long enough to tip his shades up to his forehead to politely show his eyes, and then waved goodbye to his opponent . . .—task accomplished—and dashed to the winning 440 finish, arms raised in forever recaptured East Oakland glory (emphasis added).[10]

Sports, then, as well as other forms of entertainment, provide very vivid examples of individuals merging accomplishment and performance to resist some expectations of the dominant culture. Young Black males do not believe they have to become an Other to succeed at sports. Many boys at Capital, viewing the sports world as one in which Black performance style is valued, dreamed of succeeding there, and such dreams—which are only remote possibilities—far outweighed their effort to succeed academically. Many such young men refused to rent standard English in the classroom, and many of them were failing academically.

Acting White

Outside of sports and entertainment, and especially at school, it is a continual challenge, Capital students believe, to avoid "acting white." Black people who act white
are thought to be (perhaps inadvertently) delegitimizing, evading, or repressing the
knowledge attendant to an African American cultural system. They are seen as dis-
solving and reconstructing their identities in order to be perceived as powerful individuals. The danger in acting white is captured in Gramsci's (1971) notion of
hegemony, the tendency of all members of a system to unwittingly uphold its implicit power relations by engaging in those practices sanctioned by the powerful. As
Paul, a high-achieving student, commented, "Blacks judge other Blacks according
to White standards" (interview, February 17, 1983). But Black people who choose
discourses that mimic those of Whites *while in predominantly Black contexts* may well
be marginalized by their community, not just as power seekers but as people who
might use power just as the larger society has historically done, to exploit and de-
humanize African Americans.

The adolescents at Capital have a long list of ways in which it is possible to act
white, including playing golf, going to the country club, going to the Smithsonian,
hiking, dancing to lyrics rather than music, and speaking standard English. An important issue, though, is appropriateness. For example, if one chooses to respond to
a teacher in the discourse of the academy, one is applauded and respected for being
able to display that facility. What many Capital community residents find problematic is the uncritical adoption of the discourse of power when interacting with (or
when inappropriate in the presence of) other Black people.[11]

At Capital, acting white extends to the pursuit of academic excellence: many
students are enormously conflicted by the prevalent assumption that to get good
grades is to act white. On the one hand, acting white may be perceived as unavoid-
able in order to achieve success as defined by the larger society, both in school and
later in the workforce. On the other hand, embracing the cultural principles promulgated by the larger society (including its definition of success) is believed to
constitute uncritical acceptance of the dominant aesthetic and moral system that
oppresses the Black Self. Wendell, one of the high-achieving students, asserted unequivocally that the most important step for school success is to rid oneself of Blackness: "Don't be looked upon as Black [i.e., not being seen as Black] seem like it
change a lot of things sometimes" (interview, May 20, 1983). He explained:
"[White folks] look down on Blacks. . . . They think we ignorant or something.
Something like that. They think we ignorant . . . animals or . . . I don't think no-
body really ignorant—unless their mind gone or something" (interview, March 2,
1983). High-achieving students accused of acting white may be labeled "brainiacs."
Alice defined the term: "'Brainiac' means like, a computer mind—know all the answers. Call me 'computer,' 'computer-head,' and 'brainiac.' I think it's a . . . you
know, I don't—I used to say, 'No, I'm not,' and now I say, 'Sure, I am. Don't you
want to be one?'" (interviews, March 14, May 23, 1983).

On the list of discourse practices that must be shed if one is to be successful in
White society are most forms of improvisational expressiveness. As Kochman

(1972) suggests, the "kinetic element" in Black speech—discourse practices that embrace movement and energy—stigmatizes speakers in the larger society as being devoid of rationality, dispassion, and other logocentric values.[12] Another characteristic that conveys Blackness, and that students like Wendell believe must therefore be jettisoned, is what Williams (1988:47) calls *texture*: "dense, vivid, woven, detailed narratives, relationships, and experiences" with a primary focus on the local and the familiar. Here, too, there is disjuncture between what is valued in the community and what is honored in academic talk. Depersonalization, attention to the universal, argumentation that is sparse and sequential—these attributes typically valued in school speech are at odds with the richly textured discourse of the African American community.

Language in Power Relationships

The accusation of acting white is not the only problem faced by students who seek academic success; another aspect of the web of contestation in which they are tangled comes from experiencing differences in the construction of hierarchical relationships at home and at school. This discontinuity adds to the ways in which the school, as an institution essentially part of the dominant society, tends to define these young people as Other. The discourse practices that are valued by the adolescents, their families, and their community derive from an understanding that, in order to wrest power, a speaker must voice authority. The language of home is direct and powerful, glazed with an icing of bantering, repartée, and deliciously decorated one-liners. Most segments of the African American community assume that power must be conveyed and deference earned through an authoritative use of language; as Delpit (1988, 1995) notes, merely occupying a position of authority (e.g., that of a teacher) does not in and of itself grant power. This assumption is at odds with that of the dominant culture, which practices and values the veiling of power (Delpit 1988, 1995). Many students at Capital complained bitterly that the White (and some of the Black) teachers had no authority in the classroom. Alice, a high-achieving student, said that White teachers were unable to get students' attention. In fact, they did not demand it in ways familiar to the students.

In the community, African American parents enact support for their children largely by setting limits and saying no (Delpit 1988, Fordham 1996). Scott (1991) shows that Black parents highlight the necessity of surviving in the face of violence, both physical and psychic. Thus, the most successful parents (especially mothers) of Capital students nurture but with a twist: preoccupied with safety, they rarely applaud accomplishment. Some mothers explained their lack of praise for their children's academic performance as a leveling agent, a necessary evil designed to keep their children grounded in the norms and values of the Black community and a way of buttressing their children's ability to survive. Norris's mother, for instance, acknowledged that in his presence she suppressed her pride in his academic record in order to model for him the idea that his survival was contingent upon his connectedness to the African American community, not success in academic one-upmanship. Katrina mourned her parents' seeming lack of support for her academic achievement, complaining that they never praised her schoolwork; she said that when she showed her mother a report card on which her (already good) grades had improved, her mother's only comment was, "I see you changed the Bs to As." Furthermore, she reported, her mother was overprotective:

> I remember once, I went to the *library*. And it's not near my house, it's—I can just catch one bus and I'm there. I *could* walk, but it's several blocks. And I went after school, I didn't come home. And I told my sister that I may not be home, I was going to the library. Me, Sakay and I, were in the library, trying to get this thing together. And here comes my sister and my mother, driving up! (Laughter) And out she comes—you know, I guess they were checking up on me—I don't know! And they took me home. I really thought that was unnecessary. (interview, February 8, 1983)

Black adolescents are faced with reconciling the expectations, cultural assumptions, and discourse practices of their homes and community with those of the academy, a task that is especially difficult because at the same time they sense that the demands of the larger society threaten the integrity of the Black Self (Friedman 1992, Holt 1972, Lorde 1990, Williams 1988). Some of them reach a compromise, doing what they label "talking proper" but, as I discuss next, doing so only temporarily and perhaps layering on Black performance style.

Renting a Dialect: Managing Standard English

School presents students caught between colliding cultural systems with inescapable contradictions. Academic success demands that they adopt the very discourse practices that they perceive as ineffectual and oppressive. In their passage into adult status, though, they realize the political reality in which they participate. Some students refuse to display a critical symbol of the pursuit of power in the school context—speaking standard English—and therefore experience the implications of marginal to low academic performance. Many others settle for renting standard English from nine to three while retaining ownership of the discourse practices generally used in the African American community. They do not do so easily, but those who manage it participate in a type of inversion that resonates with the discourse practices of their ancestors, who had various ways of "appearing to but not to." It is both a resistance that preserves the essential Black Self and a means of social mobility. Here I present two typical approaches to the contradictions imposed on Capital students.

Maggie, a high achiever, was well aware of the dialect contrasts in her speech community. In discussing her mother's speech practices, Maggie suggests that she herself rejects bidialectalism, refusing to be seen as both "Us" and "Them," primarily because, as she sees it, such "passing"[13] behaviors are disinguous at best. She asserts that her mother "talks white" on the phone or in contexts outside their home:

> She just talks like that on the telephone, I'll put it like that. When she talks, she puts on airs, you know, sounds White, so you can't tell whether she's White or Black. But when she's around the house, she talks, you know, regular, but when she's out around other people, anywhere out besides the house, she talks in a proper manner. . . .

When my mother [speaks standard English], it appears that she's trying to be some-one she's not. (interview, February 25, 1983)

Maggie views her mother's speech practices as fraudulent—"She's trying to be someone she's not"—and deceptive—"You can't tell whether she's White or Black." Rather than viewing her mother's linguistic practices as evidence of appropriate code-switching within a bidialectal society, she sees them as acting white and there-fore inappropriate. In contrast, Maggie declares that she rarely participates in such linguistic fraud. Indeed, she insists that "I talk the same way all the time" (inter-view, February 25, 1983), in all contexts. More important, she categorizes her consistent linguistic behavior as a more appropriate, more correct—or more stan-dard—way to structure a Black identity. To a large extent, Maggie's characteriza-tion of her own linguistic practices was accurate. In some instances, however, she was forced to rent the school-sanctioned standard English dialect in interactions with teachers and other school officials, and she could be heard switching just as her mother did.

Norris, a brilliant student, had learned to camouflage his academic achievement by renting standard English from nine to three so that his peers did not feel threat-ened by him. He used Black "street speech" (Baugh 1983) as a standard and stan-dard English as a vernacular, and neither his cohorts who were underachieving nor those who were performing as well as he obstructed his academic efforts. He was therefore able to pursue his goals virtually unmolested by his peers.

At Berkeley Elementary, which was, in Norris's terms, filled with "hoodlums, thugs, and the dregs of society," he had been academically ahead of most of the stu-dents in his class and in the school. At the same time, however, realizing that he had to live with those students, he planned a course of action that would minimize any obstacles to his academic future. Norris deliberately chose for friends those in-dividuals whose resistance to standard English discourse practices was greater than his. These peers, he reasoned, would act as camouflage, in exchange for his help on homework assignments and tests. He was not picky about who they were. He simply wanted them to keep the other kids from beating him up or verbally harassing him so that he would be free to pursue his dream of academic excellence:

I didn't want to—you know—be with anybody that was like me [academically] 'cause I didn't want to get beat up. The school I went to, Berkeley, was really rough, see? It was really rough. So I had to hang with people that were tough, you know? Lived in the projects and everything, and known tough and everything. So I used to hang with them. If anybody ever came in my face and wanted to pick on me, they'd always be there to help me. So I always made sure I had at least two or three bullies to be my friends. Even though if it does mean I have to give up answers in class. . . I was willing to give up a little to get a lot. So I did that for elementary school. (inter-view, January 11, 1983)

Norris's alliance with the bullies and hoodlums in elementary school was a success-ful strategy. His close association with peers whose behavior clearly indicated they were not committed to the school-sanctioned discourse empowered him by remov-ing any question about his loyalty to the Black community.

In junior high school he chose to embellish this strategy. Besides making alliances with bullies, he adopted a clown or comedic persona (one component of which was the use of Black street speech), which suggested that he was not very skilled academically. Wearing this mask protected him from the scorn of those who held academic prowess in contempt. The merging of these strategies was still a part of his school persona:

> I had to act crazy then . . . you know, nutty, kind of loony. They say . . . "He's crazy"—not a *class* clown to get on the teachers' nerves, I never did that to the . . . around *them*. I'd be crazy. But as soon as I hit the classroom door, it was serious business. . . . Only the people who knew me knew my crazy side; when they found out I was smart, they wouldn't believe it. And the people that knew that I was smart, they wouldn't believe it if they were told that I was crazy. So I went through [school] like that. I'm still like that *now*, though. (interview, January 11, 1983)

In acting a role, Norris became a discourse chameleon merging with the surrounding context. Among friends, he behaved as if school meant nothing to him; among classmates who were not close friends but who were seeking the same academic goals as he, he conveyed an image of a standard English speaker and an academic competitor. He moved from one discourse style to another in order to alternately mask and display his academic abilities. He realized that he must "fake it in order to make it" (Granfield 1991), and he recognized the drastic differences between the speech practices of Black Americans and those of the dominant population:

> Black people [talk to] each other like—as if they were enemies. And you know, you can be good friends [with another Black person], but you [talk to] them like an enemy. Well, another person [a non-Black person] would consider it as treating them as an enemy, but we call it friendship. Like we tease each other and hit on each other and talk about each other all the time, that's considered friendship. And that's what [the dominant society] call[s] abnormal. But that's the way most Black people I know who are friends *are*. They say, if you can talk about their mother and get away with it, you *must* be their friend. (interview, February 18, 1983:61)

At seventeen, then, Norris made a profound observation about contrasting cultural norms—an observation that, if emphasized by teachers and school officials, could allow them to be more successful at helping their students achieve academically.

Like most other students at the school, both Norris and Maggie spoke standard English at least intermittently between nine and three. Both recognized the discontinuity between the two discourses. Maggie strongly criticized her mother's shifting speech practices and declared that she, unlike her mother, was a greater warrior in the linguistic guerrilla war because she "talks the same way all the time." Norris fully acknowledged his efforts to rent the standard discourse for school purposes. This is extremely telling. Unlike many of his peers, Norris's future was fairly well charted. He was performing well in school, and he realized that he had to continue to do so in order to go to college, especially since his mother was not financially able to send him to school. Even though Maggie's and Norris's perceptions differ, they share the common element of renting the standard discourse style—Norris more willingly than Maggie—and using it almost exclusively for instrumental purposes.

Maggie's and Norris's strategies for renting standard English minimize the appearance of social distance between them and other academic strivers and also demonstrate their continuous allegiance to the Black community in spite of their school success. Their use of Black street speech as a standard allows them to avoid the predictable cacophony—or worse, silence—that accrues to Black adolescents who opt to use the standard English vernacular in inappropriate contexts.

Conclusion

Capital High students who desire to achieve academic success must find ways to confront the fact that a people's "[l]iberation begins with language" (Holt 1972: 156). They do so, largely, by inverting the language norms of the wider society: by treating as a vernacular the Discourse that is elsewhere considered standard. Stigmatized as one way of acting white, this Discourse cannot be owned; it can only be rented for specific instrumental purposes.

The fact that these African American adolescents are engaged in an ongoing war through language does not mean that they are conscious of it—or, if they are aware of it, that they feel free to discuss it publicly. On the contrary, at Capital High, the students' language use fits Scott's (1985) description of a "weapon of the weak." Their resistance to adopting the standard version of English discourse as their standard is not generally understood either by school officials—most of whom, ironically, are Black—or by the larger Black and White populations in Washington. Neither of these populations appears to see African American adolescents' use of the Black discourse style as a deliberate, self-conscious linguistic practice. Rather, the students' failure to embrace the standard is generally understood as group incompetence, an inability to perform a culturally sanctioned task (Inkeles 1968, Ogbu 1981). In contrast to this prevalent view, Lee (1994) has suggested that Black discourse style increases rather than diminishes the longer Black students are in school. Paradoxically, African American adults—parents, teachers, and other school officials—contribute to the continuation of this below-the-surface warfare. These adults seek to teach their children to make the power discourse their standard. A more viable approach, however, might be to recognize and actively promote a strategy that some students already have adopted: to use standard English for purely instrumental purposes. This limited utilitarian use would validate its vernacular status.

What can we do to end the larger guerrilla warfare encoded in these discourse practices? How might we alter social policies and practices in such a way that African American adolescents' daily stigmatization of the standardized version of English is discontinued? What can we do to maximize African American adolescents' academic effort, thereby diminishing academic failure? I do not have complete answers. Nevertheless, it seems to me that we must first understand the *meaning* of the linguistic practices of African American adolescents. I have offered a first step here. While understanding this meaning does not necessarily mean acceptance, it does suggest, at the very least, a questioning of the conventional explanation, linguistic deficiencies of AAVE speakers. What I have suggested here is that conventional explanations miss the mark because they minimize the functioning of Black people's discourse practices as instruments of rhetorical resistance, which nurtures the liberation of a people and reinforces their identity. Given the centrality of Black resistance in the situation presented here, successful policymakers must discontinue the ineffective practice of disregarding cultural and identity issues. Indeed, instead of trying to repair the linguistic practices of African American adolescents, successful policymakers will redirect their energies toward minimizing the linguistic warfare inherent in the ongoing convention of marginalizing and stigmatizing the Black Self.

NOTES

The research on which this analysis is based was initially funded by grants from the National Institute of Education, the Spencer Foundation, and a dissertation fellowship from the American University in Washington, DC. Later, a Spencer Postdoctoral Fellowship and a National Science Foundation Minority Research Grant enabled me to continue the work I had begun. I wish to thank the faculty, staff, and students at Capital High (who cannot be individually identified because of an explicit contract with the District of Columbia Public School System), as well as parents and other adults in the Capital community for allowing me to represent their lives. I am grateful to all of them. In addition, I wish to thank Carolyn Adger, Iris Carter Ford, Les Greenblatt, Susan Hoyle, Renee Larrier, William Leap, and Brett Williams for helpful comments and suggestions on successive drafts of this manuscript.

1. All proper nouns designating either people or places connected to the research site are pseudonyms.

2. Speaking standard English is much more widely practiced in the classroom context than in the larger school setting. This difference is due—at least in part—to the lack of a constant physical presence of school authorities.

3. The Advanced Placement Program is a fictitious name for the rigorous academic program at the school, the magnet program intended to attract students who would not have otherwise attended Capital High School.

4. Elsewhere (Fordham 1996), I assert that it is imperative that the language we use accurately reflect what we do. I go on to point out that ethnographies' representations are constructed on a fault line of violence. This representation—this imaging—is based primarily on written or visual portraits, on watching as a kind of violence imposed on the watched. I am, therefore, self-consciously using the word *watch* rather than *observe* in talking about ethnographic observations, because *watch* is a stronger verb, suggesting scrutiny or surveillance rather than merely noticing.

5. For a more detailed description of the methodology utilized in this study, see Fordham (1996).

6. I was engaged in a multiyear study of academic success at Capital High School during the 1980s. The analysis presented here is based almost exclusively on the findings emerging from the ethnographic component of the study. Only a small segment of the survey data and a select number of the questions in the survey have been analyzed. A recently awarded training grant from the National Science Foundation will enable me to analyze a larger portion of the quantitative data.

7. The school was without a certified librarian until after the spring break in 1983.

8. Elsewhere (Fordham 1996), I use the term *Other* in two radically different ways. First, I use it to refer to the historical or traditional construction of those peoples who are not Euro-American in origin and who are, regardless of their accomplishments, "inevitably . . .

perceived unidimensionally" (Madrid 1992:8). Second, I also use it to refer to those peoples who were initially responsible for creating cultural boundaries by labeling and defining peoples who were seen as culturally or visibly different as *Other*. Hence, I offer the reader the opportunity to understand the othering process from two different perspectives: a social group that has always been othered and the way the traditional Other perceives those who have consistently "othered" them.

9. As Babcock (1978) notes, *inversion* is a widely used concept in anthropology: "I cannot say with certainty exactly when or how the term inversion began to be used in anthropological studies. [It] can be traced back to the *Annee sociologigue* school and the writings of Durkheim, Mauss and Hertz on classification and of van Gennep on rites of passage. Perhaps its earliest use in English is to be found in A. M. Hocart's *Social Origins*, where he remarks: 'Fasting thus seems to be merely a case of *inversion*, that is, a form of ritual specially associated with death, in which everything is done with wrong way round' (1954:120). . . . An important form of symbolic inversion is 'that used to mark a boundary, between peoples, between categories of persons, between life and death. . . . ' [G]roup membership is [thus] determined not only by what members share, but by what the members recognize that 'significant others' do not share. Thus develop the notions of stereotyping and deviance: the definition of those outsiders 'on the periphery' in terms of how they depart from insiders in the direction of nature or chaos (i.e., violation of the social order)" (21–28). My point is that inversion has a long history of usage in anthropological analyses. Holt (1972) uses this concept to talk about the discourse practices of African Americans.

10. Andrews, asserting that professional football involves an inherent "contestation over bodies . . . expressive behavior . . . what is right and wrong . . . good and bad . . . normative and non-normative . . . black and white, the powerful and the powerless" (23), argues that the NFL marginalizes the visibility of Black bodies by trying to deny players the right to invert dominant discourse practices by conflating athletic performance and expressiveness. Athletic accomplishment—running, catching, hitting and sacking the quarterback (and other players)—is what (Black) bodies are paid to do. But dancing in the end zone (like Deion Sanders) is a kind of expressive signature, which enables Black bodies to be clearly identified, distinguishing themselves from White bodies, inverting athletic accomplishment and merging what is central in Black discourse practices: accomplishment and signature.

11. For example, a practicing professional (e.g., lawyer, teacher, doctor, government bureaucrat) is expected to rent the discourse practices of the powerful in institutional contexts. On the other hand, to use these same practices when interacting with other African Americans outside the institutional setting marks one as acting white.

12. In the O. J. Simpson trial, the kinetic speech practices of Johnnie Cochran, the lead defense attorney, provoked the threat of a strike by the court reporters who repeatedly accused him of talking too fast.

13. "Passing" is the term I use (see Fordham 1993) to operationalize the gender-specific process large numbers of women experience as they seek acceptance in the academy, broadly defined, and other professional arenas. In my earlier definition, I noted how important it is for the female body to appear serious, especially in the academy, and how appearing serious is most often associated with males and a male voice. Using that as a backdrop, I argued that "gender 'passing'" is a concerted effort to avoid the appearance of being female, of minimizing essentialized images of femaleness.

12

Working through Language

SHIRLEY BRICE HEATH

How is it I find you in difference, see you there
In a moving contour, a change not quite completed?
You are familiar yet an aberration.
> Wallace Stevens, "Notes toward
> a Supreme Fiction"

Poetry speaks rarely of older children. In contrast to their younger counterparts, youth attract little attention except when adults express frustration when they fail to understand the differences they see between the child that was and the preteen or teen that now is. The older child's gyrations between likes and dislikes, inaction and constant motion, noise and silence, silliness and wisdom strike adults as inexplicable. Overheard language and attempted conversations with youth leave adults at a loss as to how much of a mutual communication system they actually share with young people.

This chapter presents older children at voluntary work in collaborative tasks with adults in youth-based organizations (e.g., Boys and Girls Clubs, youth arts groups, and community sports leagues) and illustrates the extent to which their language use on these occasions depends intensely on active planning, doing, and evaluating with both their elders and peers. Such circumstances—those in which adults work side-by-side with youth to accomplish a joint task over time—have greatly diminished recently. Currently, aside from agricultural households, relatively few families spend time in cross-age tasks that require planning, practice, and productive work across a period of several weeks or months. Yet these are the very situations in which children are most likely to engage in work on tasks beneficial to them and others and to receive extensive authentic practice of linguistic structures that reflect planning ahead, linking current actions to future outcomes, and self-assessing and self-correcting their own behaviors and attitudes.

Just as nurturing, playing, and book reading shape in large part the talk of young children and adults, so joint work tasks shape the language of older children as they collaborate with adults. If young children lack opportunities for nurturing, playing, and imaginative talking with adults, their language development suffers; similarly, if older children have few if any opportunities to engage in joint work tasks with adults, their language development and uses will be affected.

This chapter argues that joint adult-youth work brings about particular kinds of language growth vital for young people to develop habits critical to their learning how to shape ideas and to hypothesize, critique, and plan activities that, in turn, generate more learning opportunities. Data used here are drawn from a decade of close study and participant observation within youth-based organizations—those that place youth at the center of their philosophy and involve youth in decision-making roles throughout the organization. A large portion of data collected in this study consists of audiotapes of young people and their adult leaders jointly carrying out the work of the organization—whether budget and publicity planning, improving practice of bunting and catching fly balls, perfecting performance of a scene for a community play, or preparing to host a Special Olympics for children with disabilities. First, I delineate the challenge that older children present to scholars who wish to study their daily interactions. The importance of *work* for talk is addressed in both current and historical terms, with consideration of what can be learned by attending to how older children talk when they are engaged in collaborative tasks of their own choosing.

Three assertions lie behind the language development claims of this chapter:

1. Changed parenting and household arrangements in the late twentieth century greatly increase the importance of youth organizations for the linguistic and sociocognitive development of older children.
2. Work that extends over time and receives evaluation by authentic outside assessors engages young people in fluid stances and asymmetric roles through which they practice planful behavior and ongoing appraisal of process and product relationships.
3. Young people extend their language development as they accomplish work tasks, play a range of roles, and learn different relations in the multiple voices they assume to maintain social balance among their peers while they also help the collective network achieve group goals.

The parenting and household structural arrangements that predominate in the late twentieth century mean that young people increasingly are left among only their peers, without incentive or direction to take up specific productive tasks that engage them over time. Hence, opportunities to use language structures and planful behavior with steps toward a culminating end or product occur relatively rarely. Except for the fortunate youngster with local grandparents or caring adults not engaged in full-time work outside the household, most of America's youth have only a few hours each month of committed time from adults who join with them in collaborative work.

This void has meant that an additional institution—beyond school and family —is needed in the socialization of young people: youth organizations and their adult leaders. Within some, though certainly not all, communities, organizations committed to youth as resources for their families, communities, and the society at large make it possible for adults to engage with young people in complex ongoing tasks and projects that help advance the linguistic and sociocognitive development of older children.

Work achieved together within such a group requires certain communicative patterns tightly related to the range of roles played out at different points in time by members of the group. For example, at any moment in the work task, any individual may choose to step back from active participation to become a bystander who observes and listens for a while before stepping back in as critic, problem solver, assistant, cheerleader, or troubleshooter. Individuals may in any single session opt for silent or verbal roles and shift stance or perspective almost from minute to minute, with respect to both the task at hand and their involvement in that task. They may choose to take charge or observe, alter or deflect the course of the work, or reveal or keep silent about a crucial tool or resource. The resulting network of roles and stances embraces not only the group but also each member, who is always a potential model or apprentice, instructor or learner. Though by no means a stable "community of learners," the collective groups and networks within them merge to singly engage toward an outcome. This common engagement provides the crucial platform for both witnessing and taking up multiple ways to accomplish work.[1] Each role and stance chosen at any time within the learning network calls on distinct as well as overlapping language resources; the critic must shape utterances so as not to offend the workers but to improve the work; the problem solver must set up possible scenarios in order to convince others that a particular solution is likely to work. Speakers must thus know—or learn—how to reshape, redirect, and correct the work while they also persuade, humor, praise, and argue with the workers.

Older Children and Language Development Studies

Although psycholinguists have given considerable attention to the language development of younger children in play or simple tasks with adults, they have provided very little research on the language of older children. The bits of research we have come primarily from studies in school settings that center on testing the grammatical development of children and their understanding of certain complex syntactic structures. For example, Chomsky (1969) considers the understanding of children five to ten years old of verbs such as *promise*, on the one hand, and *tell, order, want,* and *expect,* on the other. A surprising development in this study was the late and individual patterns of acquisition among some children of the syntactic structures necessary to understand concepts such as the subject of *go* in sentences like this: "John promised Bill to go." Contrary to the general view that children have mastered their native tongue by the time they go to school, Chomsky found that structures commonly associated with the above verbs were still being acquired by children at nine years of age; in essence, older children are still acquiring what may be regarded as the "adult linguistic system" much later than educators and linguists have thought.

A second study (Loban 1963, 1976) includes a cross section of children between the ages of five and eighteen and lays out both the stages and velocity of language development over these years. This work again shows the amount of individual variation among children in the acquisition of longer communication units and elaboration of subject and predicate, adjectival dependent clauses, variety and depth of vocabulary, and clause-embedding techniques. Particularly notable is the variability in expressions of conditionality and tentativeness; statements of supposition, hypothetical reasoning, and conjecture follow much later than the language of labeling and categorizing. Comparing, contrasting, and conjecturing, as well as clarifying and communicating feelings and emotions, come with considerable variability in depth of understanding and facility in production with no consistent relation to social class and occupation or educational level of parents.

By the 1970s, studies of the language of young people take slices of speech from particular settings and center on styles of speaking or the "logic" and "system" of their talk (e.g., Labov 1972a; Smitherman 1986). Summaries of studies of the language development of older children (Romaine 1984) indicate that psycholinguists and linguists have generally focused on one or more grammatical features, usually as acquired by their own children, and leave few answers to the many puzzles surrounding how the language of older children develops in a wide range of settings and circumstances of usage.

Only in the 1980s did researchers begin to locate their work in the day-to-day events of young people's lives across contexts (e.g., Shuman 1986, Goodwin 1990a; see Introduction, this volume). But what of situations in which the young use play and language centrally to forward specific *work* projects? Rarely do adults think of older children as working rather than playing, hanging out, or fooling around. Although adults often try to create playful work opportunities for their older children—through athletics, social clubs, and extracurricular activities—they rarely consider just how young people carry out long-term work in these situations. Parents and coaches frequently declare the numerous benefits for instilling character, discipline, and work habits offered by sports and other extracurricular activities (e.g., Thompson 1993). But just what happens over a baseball season with team members intent on a winning season or with a mural project or dramatic production planned and executed by a group of young people within a community youth organization? This chapter provides answers to this question and considers how language moves tasks along within the work of youth organizations and how that work provides language development opportunities.

Researching Youth: Problems with Ordinary Field Methods

At the outset, it is important to remind ourselves just why studying the language of older children is difficult. Beyond the age of five, children cannot be the captive audience of adults wishing to record their every utterance. Understandably, almost all psycholinguistic studies of language development of infants and toddlers have been based on either the children of psycholinguists or the offspring of mothers who do not work outside the home and can bring their children to laboratories for tests and tasks administered by researchers.

Beyond adult-controlled institutions, such as schools and laboratories, full participant observation of young people's peer groups by adult researchers becomes impossible. Watching, listening, and occasionally asking questions provide the most reasonable ways for adults to collect naturalistic data from peer interactions of older children (Goodwin 1990a), but it is not possible to capture every bit of language such children hear or produce. Thus, standard techniques, such as considering relation of input to output, as studies of younger speakers have tended to do, have to be abandoned in favor of linking language uses to particular social and instrumental (or task-focused) goals of the peer group.

So as children mature, the research enterprise becomes more difficult. Children's growth in vocabulary and adeptness with certain phrases they "pick up" from others may be obvious, but common sense tells us that they also simultaneously hear and produce anew creative utterances of syntactic complexity. Yet these pass without adult notice or respect because the grammar of young people, certainly after the age of nine, may not immediately seem markedly different from the adult version (Chomsky 1969). Asking older children about their understanding of complex grammatical structures brings with it the same difficulties any researcher faces in asking adults such questions: these understandings may be well beyond awareness. Moreover, young people sometimes seem to specialize in either sidestepping adult questioning or providing answers they believe adults want to hear, particularly about such matters as language and behavior.

Furthermore, as children grow older, separating their understanding of concept from their control of constructions for expressing the concept becomes almost impossible. They may, for example, understand that certain objects fall and that some force is "behind" that fall, but they may not have the constructions or vocabulary necessary to express the law of gravity. Thus, although they may well be able to respond correctly to interview queries (or short-answer questions on a science test about gravity), they may not grasp the concept sufficiently to explain, illustrate, or compare that law to any other related to the motion of physical objects. In essence, they sometimes "know" more than they can say. They may have the lexicon but not the syntax to express complex relationships or sequences among events, abstract notions, and causal or coincidental connections. Similarly, they may be adept at "mouthing" what they have heard or read but unable to translate this information into specific cases or "in other words" expressions. Distinguishing then between what children say and what they know continues to present pedagogical and developmental research dilemmas for work with older (as well as younger) children.

As children leave middle childhood (generally understood as ages five through twelve), they enter adolescence, a period almost universally viewed in terms of "storm and stress" because of biological impulses and hormonal turmoil. Marking this period, especially for young people in the United States, are expectations of breakdowns in parent-child discourse and heightened importance of peer-only talk (and secrecy surrounding such talk). In adult-child interactions, young people often adopt language that at best puzzles and at worst offends adults; obscene words and gestures, pretension of ignorance through shrugged shoulders and avoidance of eye contact, and "acting out" can effectively cut adults off from communication with teenagers.

Thus, to study the language of the young, particularly those beyond the age of twelve, scholars must find some way to enter their peer networks through mediated tools or by building trust with a group of teens (who may well be marginal to other youth groups and thus more available to researchers) in order to ask questions and test conjectures. Several studies (none focused on language) have managed to capture valuable information about youth communication through journals or time logs (Csikszentimihalyi & Larson 1984), youth-to-youth interviews (Goodwillie 1993), and adult-guided walks with minimal adult interference (Bryant 1985). Such information is highly valuable, for these studies amply illustrate that older children keenly observe their environments and spend considerable time thinking about the world about them. Writings by youth carried out independently or with minimal adult direction, as well as theater based on scripts that youth themselves create, indicate the extent to which their forms of expression move to the poetic, incisive, and reflective (cf. Shuman 1986). Youth writing about topics they themselves choose, as distinct from topics adults (generally teachers) assign them, remains neglected. The classic work by Anne Frank, *The Diary of a Young Girl* (1958), cannot be an altogether unique representation of the powers of adolescents to see through the world about them and to express their views in highly sophisticated ways without immediate adult direction.

The Work of Youth Organizations

Youth organizations that place young people at the center of activities and give them wide-ranging adult-like responsibilities offer ideal settings for studying just how young people perform self-selected work. Because many members may not know one another before they enter the organization, language becomes central to moving both tasks and social order along. For this study, data were collected in two primary ways. Interactions between the young members and the adults leading the organization were audio-recorded by a field-worker trained in anthropology and linguistics who was young enough to participate in social activities of the youth organization yet clearly an unlikely participant in the group's work. Additional linguistic data were collected by youth organization members who acted as "junior ethnographers" and audiotaped language during activities of members that took place when no adults were present (walks to and from the organization, team travel, and unsupervised adult-assigned tasks).[2] Junior ethnographers transcribed their own tapes, compared them to transcriptions made by a professional transcriber, and provided contextual information to supplement transcriptions as well as metalinguistic interpretations. These ethnographers also reviewed their own theories and beliefs about how and when they talked as they did, when they turned to written communication, and how they perceived settings and audience as critical to their choices. Adults and young people within the youth organizations periodically attended debriefings in which they responded to data samples and analyses with their perceptions of how language worked in the particular situations under discussion.

The youth organizations of this research value young people's potential contributions to their families, communities, and society. Moreover, because most groups operate with minimal budgets, they seek to maximize every possible resource within the organization. Therefore, young people play a wide variety of roles, serving as everything from receptionist to travel planner to junior coach. Remaining within the organization for as long as one year ensures increasing responsibilities for any youth, and almost all such roles include high communication demands for explaining, comparing, persuading, and arguing before a variety of audiences, from local peers and organization members to publicists, funders, visiting consultants, and educators. Young people serve on the boards of their organizations, prepare publicity brochures for their group and community, and write news releases for local newspapers, as well as invitations to special events, such as fundraisers and end-of-year celebrations. An organization may call itself a *family* or *a place to be*, its members' lives there revolving around *working, being there, practicing*, and *getting better*.

Cycles of life within these organizations often culminate in a performance of some type: play-off games; annual shows performed before a variety of audiences; production of a brochure, newspaper, or video; or summer work within the organization's daycare program. The organizations generally follow a four-step pace: planning and preparation, practice, performance, and evaluation, with overlap and reiteration of some phases. For example, a theatrical team coalesces after auditions at the beginning of the summer, prepares one or more plays around topics of interest to teens and their parents, and takes the show "on the road" to local schools, juvenile detention centers, and parent groups during the full academic year. In such cases, the shows' original script and initial performances evolve throughout the year through further practice and in response to evaluations from both team members and audiences. The young people then have a "downtime" of inactivity before they resume another cycle of performance.

Coaching the Show and the Season

Coaches, both athletic and dramatic, provide much of the adult leadership of youth organizations. They usually take major responsibility for planning the season and scheduling practices and facilitate early deliberations among group members about development of rules and standards of performance. Early in the season or in rehearsals, they usually dominate oral language interactions, and they also determine the written materials the group will use. But as practices begin and team members move into the season, adult leaders step back as directors of talk and action and let young people assume more and more responsibilities.

What characterizes young people who come to youth organizations that require complex strategy building, intense attention to group improvement, and strong communication skills? Those who enter the youth organizations of this study come from typical American families: two working parents or a single parent working at least one job outside the household. Like a substantial proportion of students, many older children in this study perform well only sporadically in school, hold heavy responsibilities within their households, and often carry substantial child care obligations for younger siblings. Their neighborhoods, whether inner-city, rural, or located in housing projects of midsized towns, rarely include well-kept parks, shopping centers, or other gathering places for young people, and few offer a range of employment opportunities, either part- or full-time, for youth older than fourteen.

Most of the youth in the organizations described here participate of their own volition, though some enter through the encouragement of a parent or older friend, guidance counselor, or parole officer. Once inside the organization, the young people enter the seasonal or annual cycle described above. Each phase of the cycle is marked by particular features of language use by the coach or director. Usually both newcomers and seasoned members participate together, and the words of the coach receive supplemental interpretation by experienced members.

During the course of the cycle, new members take up certain ways of talking and strategizing that they have heard from the coach and older members. Therefore, it is possible to track over the season the uses of certain grammatical structures as well as the frequency and content of turns at talking by individual youth and by the youth group as a whole. This language development is particularly marked because, as youngsters begin to use certain forms more frequently, adult leaders move to other forms of language that work primarily as background support for the activities of the group. Talk by youth and adults, then, is somewhat "scripted" by the activity cycle, and respective roles and types of contributions by individual youth and the group as a whole shift over time. Moreover, youth pick up certain language features used by adults during phases of this cycle only in accordance with roles and stances they wish to assume. For example, youth know it is inappropriate for them to act as a "holier than thou" director and to speak to their peers about what the group could accomplish if only they would work harder or how the group as a whole could improve its performance if only a particular individual would stop joking. Youth never take on adult voices they hear from coaches who deliver "philosophical setups" or "pep talks" about how good the season, cast, or show will be this time around, the high hopes they all share, and the important responsibilities that rest on the shoulders of the youth.

Once the team moves into practice, coaches give "eventcasts," forward-looking narratives of what will happen in this phase of practice. During the actual practice, coaching swings between ongoing commentary ("Keep it up," "That's right," "Good job," "Not over there, more to the right," "Don't stop, keep going") and demonstrations of particular segmented skills (such as hitting fly balls, entering stage left). Directions generally take the form of hypotheticals or sociodramatic setups, in which youngsters are asked to hypothesize about what could happen under certain conditions ("If we take that entry after her line, how would that be?") or to imagine a particular situation and set of roles ("Okay, top of the seventh inning, 3–2, man on first, and Rodney, bunts—what's gonna happen?"). As the season moves forward, coaches talk less and less frequently, except in punctuated directives ("Speed it up," "Little higher," "Choke that bat"), and young people themselves are asked to take over direction of pieces of the show or certain groups of youngsters to practice particular skills. During evaluation, coaches again step back and generally ask questions that will prompt the young people to debate among themselves: "How did that work," "How do you think it went," and so on.

As the activity cycle moves forward, young people increase their turns at talk as the adult talk diminishes. Adults signal in multiple ways that the action belongs to the young. For example, adults rarely use the pronoun *we* in its inclusive sense; instead, *we* almost always refers exclusively to the youth. Adults talk less frequently, except to ask questions that promote talk *among the youth and not back to the adult* (e.g., "Have you kids forgotten that stage is only twenty feet deep?"). The young focus repeatedly on creating and hypothesizing action through their talk. As they move deeper into their practice cycles, they throw out more hypothetical queries and sociodramatic bids. In a single practice session of several hours, they may ask hundreds of open-ended questions ("Is this gonna work?" "What do you think about switching this around?"). Key linguistic features marking intense phases of practice include the following:

Hypothetical constructions (*if-then*)
"If Roger is comin', runnin' in from third, then what's gonna happen, man, is that you sure don't wanna be in his way."

Modals (*can, should, could,* etc.)
"Can you speed up that scene? Or what can you guys on left stage be doing while you wait for her to enter right?"

Mental state verbs (*think, believe, wish, feel,* etc.)
"She thinks it's gonna go okay, but I believe she's not doin' what she says, I just, like, feel funny about it, you know."

Abbreviated directives
"Over here," "Higher, higher," "Keep it up," "Hey, not so fast," "Run that back to Elena's line."

Along with *if-then* constructions come sociodramatic bids ("Okay, let's just say that scene could be reversed, turned around in action, Tina, what would you do—think, girl, think!"). Adults and youth consider alternative approaches, outcomes, and relationships among particular courses of action and final results. Hypotheticals represent the most obvious ways by which adults and youth relate one set of conditions to one or more outcomes. Modals operate as auxiliary verbs, suggesting obligation, prediction, or permission. Mental state verbs introduce cognitive and affective reflections about the content of expressions that follow.

As adults' use of hypotheticals, modals, and mental state verbs decreases, youth increase their expressions of these forms. But the patterns of change occur in relation to stages of the season. During the days preceding play-offs or end-of-season performances, hypotheticals, modals, and mental state verbs become inefficient because there is now no time for rethinking and reshaping or for posing possibilities. Adults' abbreviated directives increase as the time of actual performance or play-offs approaches, whereas earlier in the season, during practice, there is sufficient time to consider possible outcomes or alternative routes to action.

All of these ways of using language engender actions through focusing the attention of group members on the co-construction of a common scene, task, or event and a shared meaning from the current moment's activities, always with emphasis on how the here-and-now will affect the desired performance or product. The young people's talk also gives a way to step back and reflect openly about whether the situation at hand meets the shared goals of the group. The question of "what is it that we want" sits at the center of movement toward action as well as evaluations after the performance. This language portrays intense investment in the project or performance, as well as an enhanced sense of "we-ness" in the group, conjoined in their commitment to excellent outcomes and assessments by their outside judges—referees, coaches of other teams, and viewing audiences.

The Matter of Work

No one would suggest that older children between the ages of twelve and eighteen actually *learn* complex syntactic constructions such as the conditional or genres such as sociodramatic bids within these youth organizations. They have both receptive and productive knowledge of modals, mental state verbs, directives, and *if-then* constructions before they enter these groups. At school and at home, they have certainly heard conditionals that operate as directives ("If you open your books to page eleven, we'll look at that problem"), threats ("If you raise your voice to me once more, I'll tell your father"), and promises ("If you clean your room, we'll stop by the shopping center later and look for those boots"). In these settings, as well as among their peers, young people have used conditionals to strategize ("If we get six of those, we'll save three bucks"), plan future events ("If we pick him up by seven, that means we'll get to Evan's house before eight"), and state facts about the world ("If that's the homeroom bell, we're late").

What occurs within activities of the youth organizations, however, is extensive *role* and *stance self-assignment* whereby responsibility for planning, creating, and knowing rests within young people. To accomplish work, they enter roles in which they repeatedly hypothesize to check whether what they and others are doing is, in fact, "working." Their definition of themselves shifts from adolescent, teen, or son or daughter to junior coach, receptionist, board member, publicist. The concordance of the entire language base from which this chapter is drawn indicates that—aside from forms of *to be*, mental state verbs, and modals—various forms of *to do* and *to work* appear as the most frequent verbs within the practice phase of the activity cycle (for further detail, see note 1). In other words, young people talk about events, themselves, situations, and changes as *doing* or *working*—moving toward a goal or end. The future is *in* the present; one can never forget, in one's thinking or acting, consequences for the future. Deadlines are real: the show must go on, the play-offs will come; the group must be ready. Pressures from these inevitabilities that carry high risk keep young people's eyes on both the immediate process and the future product.

Vital in this push toward the future is the need to consider alternatives, to think out possible outcomes ahead of time through hypothetical reasoning. Young people acquire extensive practice manipulating several variables on either side of the *if-then* equation, most often on the *if* side, with the *then* side either acted out or interrupted by suggestion of another variable from someone else in the group. For example, one actor in a drama group will say perhaps, "If we, you know, like, get some place where there is no stage, and like, if we have to work right there flat on the floor in a gym or classroom, then we gotta be able to get those main speakers up higher, so why don't we use those boxes—those gray boxes we built for that last show?" Several *if* conditions occur in the cases the speaker gives, and other actors may well join in to propose similar circumstances in which the two main characters might not be sufficiently visible to the audience. These possible circumstances call for a solution worked out ahead of time, and the handling of the several problematic variables or conditions have to be worked through by all members of the group.

Arts logs kept by the youth at random intervals when they are not working onsite at their youth organizations indicate that they also hypothesize mentally during other times of the day about what they will do later. Once in the actual execution of dramatic or visual arts, they continue this internal hypothesizing and self-correction. For example, for those who work in the visual arts, questions commonly occur in their journals as they write about what goes on in their heads as they work (e.g., "If I lay down this texture here, then will it detract from the intensity of color happening above it?"). Typically, youth organizations committed to the arts require youngsters to keep journals to record all the ways they think through or hypothesize outcomes within their current project—a mural, sculpture, or role within a drama. Especially evident in these logs is the revoicing of words or phrases they have heard from adults who monitor their work.

This internal monitoring that operates when young people work alone is openly voiced when the group is in collaboration. Thus, individuals problematize potentialities if certain variables come into play and question outcomes envisioned by other group members. In the example here, a youth group works together to complete a brochure promoting their neighborhood. Materials for the brochure have come from interviews carried out by the young people, who now sit before a computer trying to move from raw texts to the first draft of the actual brochure. Four young people and an adult leader are gathered around the computer, where one young member has been chosen to type the dictated text. (In transcription, / marks overlapped talk, where for a few seconds both parties continue talking.)

(1) Brochure completion
Ldr: ok. so is there some way we can say that?
        [group talks all at once]
Sara: how do you want to say that?
Ldr: let me see (2.2) since we are/
Sara: /now that doesn't make sense
Ldr: I don't think so either
Sara: since we are teens and we consider ourselves (1.2) and our friends experts in this
        area, comma, why don't we say, we asked them /(2.2) what?
Ldr: /who is them?
Delia: our /friends
Sara: /we've already told, yeah/
Ldr: /but we said ourselves and friends

Here the problem is how to begin the brochure—by telling what it is about or by introducing the process for getting the information in the brochure. But in this opening effort, the youth and their leader collaborate to look ahead to what the reading audience needs to know about both the writers and the process of gathering information for the product.

In some cases, what becomes problematic is the correctness of techniques demonstrated by certain members. Following the lead of adults, those demonstrating often accompany their physical demonstration with a script resembling that of a sports announcer (Ferguson 1983). In the next example, young people in a leadership training program of an urban YMCA prepare to help Special Olympics youngsters who have a variety of handicaps prepare for a field day. The young people will be teaching the participants how to take part in events such as the 100-yard dash and the high jump. They practice their coaching of the newcomer participants within the weeks before they actually take up their coaching jobs; some youngsters "play" coach, others, novice learners.

(2) Track and Field YMCA — Leadership training
Larry: like, my name is Larry, I'm gonna be teaching hurdles
David: hi, Larry
Larry: hi [points to hurdles] these are hurdles
Sonja: yeah?
Larry: like this is just for practice. Just in case, if you don't want to trip over it, you cannot over these because they're not (   ) for jumping, they're too deep, like a set. Who knows, what's their weakest leg, or their strongest? [turning to his peers who are looking on and pretending to be other new young recruits]
David: I do /I do
Jack: /oh, oh, oh [Larry laughs]
Larry: don't get hyper
Jack: [standing up] what are (1.2) you supposed to stretch with (   )?

Here the youth enter into an imaginary world where one of their members is *in* the situation of leading youngsters in training for the Special Olympics. The group must imagine both sides as learners: the young coach is learning how to communicate by words and demonstration; the young participants are learning how to take part in Special Olympics events. While encouraging individuals to enter the whole performance and spirit of the competition, the coach must segment pieces of knowledge that will need attention (such as determining which is one's weakest leg or how to position for the start of a race). In assuming these tasks of the coach, which they have learned by apprenticing to their own coach, these young people take up certain syntactic structures and genres, practice them repeatedly, and hone them while adapting them to their own personalities. Practicing these structures and thought processes *in-role* enables youngsters to transfer these same communicative and critical thinking strategies to other situations, as well as to their own internal monitoring of their planful behavior.

The Language of Alterity

As older children engage in roles of work, they mime and mimic their elders, but they also create a *difference* for themselves. Having a role within work allows this flexibility, for, unlike the case of job assignment ("Do this task in this way"), a work role allows for personality and individual style. The young thus create "stability from this instability . . . engaged in this habitually bracing activity in which the issue is not so much staying the same, but maintaining sameness through alterity" (Taussig 1993:129). The issue for the young is that they are *not* their elders in spite of being able to take on roles like those of adults (coach, receptionist, board member). They must therefore bring to these roles their own perceptions and senses and shape the language of their work according to these differences by exaggerating and infusing humor. They are often helped by adults who sanction the "kids will be kids" reality by stepping into a kid-like role.

The following example is drawn from the Track YMCA Leadership group (referred to in example 2) preparing for their coaching jobs for the Special Olympics.

(3) Track and Field YMCA

Jaime: watch, watch. First you count your steps, ok? [he does the jump in slow motion and one of the pretending youngsters claps; turns to adult who is preparing to jump, since he is pretending also to be a young Special Olympic trainee] wait, wait, don't don't do it yet, don't do it yet, come here.

Ldr: [in role as youngster] do I have to go as slow as you did? [laughter from other onlookers]

Jaime: no, see, I just showed it/

Stuart: /do it in full speed

Jaime: no [laughs] allri/

Ldr: [to Jaime, and now in "ordinary" role as coach]
                    /hey, kids are gonna be doing that/

Jaime: /I'll do it

Jack: go on, full speed

Ldr: [to Jaime, continuing in "ordinary" role as coach] you don't have to—you don't [Jack gets up to explain straddle; Jaime doesn't jump] oh, go ahead

Jaime: [to group and looking at Jack *he's* gonna explain the straddle now [the coach steps back in an exaggerated way while Jack, to whom Jaime has pointed, takes over]

Jack: [standing up] straddle. First you gotta (   ) a straight approach, and, like, you gotta see which leg is stronger, either your right—and if it's the right, you gotta come up with your right, if it's your left, you come up with your left. When you start runnin', you, your strong leg (   ) down and your weakest leg goes up, while your shoulder, um= [stops to think]

Stuart: =goes over

Jaime: goes over, ya

Ldr: that's it?

Jack: [to Jaime] want me to keep going?

Jaime: yeah

Following this sequence in which the boys *act* as coach and *act out* the actions they script verbally, they continue alternating roles, asking each other questions and trying different ways of coordinating the timing of the demonstrated action with the verbal running commentary. But humor and exaggeration occasionally break through their seriousness, even while the apprenticing of the boys to the adult coach is incorporated into the setting. At the same time, the adult coach is apprenticed as a young participant preparing for Special Olympics, yet he cannot resist stepping back into his adult role when he philosophically says to the young men, "hey, kids are gonna be doing that." Jaime soon steps in to announce Jack as the coach and explainer, and the adult takes the rebuff with humorous exaggerated movements as he steps back from the action. Within this back-and-forth, both adult and youth gain the perspectives of insider and outsider, learner and instructor, as they practice for what will be a highly authentic test—the actual coaching of the newcomers.

The young people see themselves within adult roles, yet they carry out these roles in ways that both imitate and deviate from those of their adult models. Beyond omitting the philosophical setup that coaches use, the young take the cue from their coaches of letting the action script the language, but they work out for themselves the pacing and sequencing of action and talk. In example 3 Jaime and Jack, along with the leader, debate when the actual demonstration should come in relation to the talk and what the pace should be. The adult coach steps in to act like a young learner and to ask about the pace: is the slowness of the pace part of what the learner should also adopt? Here is an example of both young coach and young participant recognizing that miming *exactly* will not work and that being similar yet different creates the desired result. Furthermore, the youngsters do not go so far as to mimic the coach or carry their mockery to a humorous extreme. The roles are serious, the tasks challenging, and they must get down to practice for the "real" event.

The young coaches work through what their own coach has taken for granted— that they would absorb the pace and sequence of what it takes to do the high jump or start a race—and re-create this knowledge as they play out the role of coach for the Special Olympics participants. Being an actor in a speaking role within this group of young trainers means combining the skills and techniques of coaching with their own adeptness at the field and track events.

Connecting through Discourse

Youth illustrate their connectedness to one another—and not to adults in the organizations—in numerous linguistic habits. Some of these center around the work they must do together, whereas others allow stepping off task to negotiate and maintain interpersonal relationships. Some patterns of language use accomplish both task work and interpersonal gluing at the same time. Similarly, adults who want to bond with youth will take up certain aspects of the language of youth: particular expressions, pronunciations, and gestures. These adult moves to talk like the young must be marked sufficiently so that everyone knows they indicate a deliberate shift of "footing," a move that realigns participants across a strip of behavior (Goffman 1981).

Repetitions, Cooperative Simultaneous Talk, and Latching

All speakers repeat each other's words often; young people, in casual speech, seem to repeat more frequently than adults. For instance, in example 3 Stuart and Jaime repeat "goes over." Earlier in the transcript, Jaime picks up Stuart's suggestion that he actually move at "full speed," and Jack later repeats the phrase. During practice and evaluation sessions, transcripts show, up to one third of phrases comprising two or more words are repeats from previous speakers, incorporated creatively in utterances with different grammatical structures, as direct quotation, or simply as echoes or background to urging on and agreeing with another speaker.

Speakers also often talk over one another, simultaneously saying the same thing, voicing the same idea in different words, or connecting new information to the basic idea in the air. These utterances cannot count as interruptions because the first speaker does not stop talking when others join in. Furthermore, at the end of the utterance or during simultaneous action, evidence mounts that all agree about what is to be said and done.

When this simultaneous talk reaches a peak of multiple overlapping voices "going in the same direction," the phenomenon resembles *swarming* (Tannock, chapter 13, this volume). Feverish action and what may sound like frantic talk come together as young people connect in rapidly overlapping words that simultaneously focus idea and action. "Yeah, I was thinkin' that too," "Hey, not like that, but like he says," "Over there, pick it up, yeah, like that." During such moments, the increased pace, volume, and overlap make it extremely difficult to sort out speakers on audio-recordings, and video-tapes reveal a high pitch of physical involvement: pointing, taking instruments out of the hands of others, gathering round, and waving arms. Although youth show high engagement and focus on task during such occasions, adults, particularly in institutions of formal learning, tend either to step out of the swarm momentarily or to move in to quiet such "noise." They may insist the young step back out of the swarm, refocus, and attribute individual credit for ideas. Young people, in groups without adults, rarely break up such swarmings. Young onlookers, not involved in a particular simultaneity, merely wait for the noise and feverish action to subside. They may then suggest another idea or accept what has transpired and take part later in another flurry.

Another verbal display of connection among young speakers is their habit of *latching*, connecting—with no perceptible interturn pause and with appropriate grammatical continuation—onto a complete or partial phrase uttered by another speaker. Below, the boys continue to prepare for their jobs as Special Olympics trainers by talking about how to instruct the youngsters to line up.

(4) Track and Field YMCA
David: ya, your hands, your fingers, whatever, have 'em, line 'em up=
Stuart: =to what?
          [later after discussion of another problem in instruction]
David: well, there's a line over there, where they line 'em up on the line=
Stuart: =a starting line

As one coach put it, young people in youth organizations are often "in each other's heads—and mouths" so much that they "all talk alike, you know, finish each other's thoughts, sentences, and sometimes all say—or yell—the same thing." These connections with language illustrate something more than shared knowledge: shared ways of "laying it out" or thinking about the current situation and its consequences. Leaders of youth organizations strive to "get across" the fine line of encouraging high-level individual performance—not for the competitive purpose of pitting one individual against another, but for improved group performance. They see shared connected talk as illustrative of group cohesion and agreement around the need for individuals, while displaying their diverse talents at action, to agree verbally on the what and how of the group endeavor. Thus, within an athletic team or theatrical troupe, numerous techniques and skills, mastered at different levels of competence by various individuals, have to be available to mount a successful play-off or show. But the success of the show depends also on achieving a somewhat unified vision of process, outcome, and standards of performance. The same principle goes into creating a successful group-written product or group-mounted celebration, such as an end-of-season banquet and awards dinner.

Revoicing

Revoicing, sometimes referred to as ventriloquizing (Bahktin 1981), appears in the talk of older children when they take on the role of someone else and speak as that person. Three models appear most frequently for these revoicings: peers, adult authorities, and figures from the entertainment world. Young people revoice when they take on a character's identity within an account or to invite inclusion/exclusion attitudes within a stretch of discourse. For example, if peers recount an incident they observed or in which they took part, they often use direct discourse following expressions such as "like he's all" or "like she goes." Whereas in the 1970s, forms of *to go* came to substitute for forms of *to say*, by the 1990s, in most parts of the United States, older children, especially those in the late teens, use speaker name or pronoun plus contraction of *is* or *was* and *all* to introduce a reenactment and revoicing of someone else (e.g., "You know, she's all 'I'm gonna get me a summer job.' Yeah, well, we all know that's not gonna happen, right?"). Most commonly reserved for peers or adult authority and entertainment figures, these injections of direct discourse within an account resemble verbal caricatures of the original speakers.[3]

Mocking behaviors—including not only shifts in grammatical forms and levels of attention to enunciation but also gestures, body posture, and facial expressions—accompany these revoicings. In example 5, young people within a youth theater have been debating among themselves the skit they wish to practice. Members of the group begin to argue, and Amy, who has given Dennis, an African American male, a ride to practice, refers to him as "a monkey." He retorts that she has used a racial term, and she responds that she has not called him a *black* monkey, "just a monkey." He is clearly irritated and wants to "dog" on her or put her down verbally. A few minutes later, he tells a story about the drive to practice, in which Amy's poor driving skills become the butt of Dennis's story, taken by listeners as a grand joke and as an appropriate put-down of Amy in retaliation for her earlier insult to him.

(5) Youth Drama Group[4]

Ldr: she gave you a ride=
Amy: =yes, I think I did/
Dennis: /it was a uh, it was uh, it was uh ride of my life. First, we almost/
Amy: /DENNIS, you know/
Dennis: /first, first, we almost had a wreck coming off my street. "Get ready to die!"/ [said in an altered voice as a stage directive]
Amy: /I'm a good driver, I knew she was gonna wait=

Dennis: =this car was comin' [(3.0); Dennis looks around at his audience expectantly] down the street and was turnin' on my street. She had to pull out—and stop three or four times before you could, and laughin' the whole time. And then, the window (4.0) on the passenger side (2.0) goes down by itself you know. Now, it did this three or four times. And then, you know, you cannot take off in her car when the air conditioning is on. Once you, you come to a stop sign, have to turn the air conditioning off, take off, and then turn it back on. So I'm sittin'/

Amy: /it had [laughing]

Ldr: it's possessed

Amy: 'cause I'll have it all the way down to the floor like [imitates a struggling car against background of group laughter]

Dennis: so I'm sittin' at this stop light, burnin' up, sweatin'. I see the devil sittin' next to me, it was so hot [stands up and uses wide-sweeping hand gestures]. She's sittin' up there [imitates Amy's laugh] he, he, heeeee. An then, we're comin' on our way to Youth Theatre, by Eddy's Chicken, she almost runs the light right into this other car. Her, her friend tells her "STOP." She wouldn't have stopped=

Amy: =I was about to stop=

Dennis: =then=

Amy: =she always just tells me/

Dennis: /we got to Hemphill [street]. I don't know where she was at, she was gonna get in the turn lane and try to go like that [acts like he is in a car and makes a super wide turn using all the lanes]

Amy: [laughter]

Dennis: She's lyin' and says she wasn't but she had her signal on= [said as an aside to the group in a "we-know-about-her" tone]

Amy: =I was not, I was changin' lanes to the middle lane, thank you/

Dennis: /when you drive, Amy, you do not take a big turn like this [again imitating her turn] to get to the next lane, Okay? it was the ride of my life. we got to the, we got to the stop sign up here at Lipscombe, little kid walk out, and she about run over him/

Amy: /I was not, MAN, you lyin'=

Dennis: =I'M lying? Did you or did you not [2.0] almost hit those little kids? [said slowly and with precise articulation]

Amy: I did not [with careful enunciation of the final t]

Dennis: it was a ride of a lifetime [shaking his head in disbelief] believe me

Amy: we'll see if I ever give you a ride again

The storyteller revoices four times within his account of events, once when he "becomes" a stage director or narrator, telling the audience to "get ready." He does so again when he steps into the role of driving instructor, telling a student how to turn a corner; he steps aside to be "with" the group against Amy when he builds his case that she is lying; finally, he assumes adult authority as a judicial official when he asks "did you or did you not . . . ?" Elsewhere he mocks her gestures and driving behaviors. This retelling and these revoicings of an incident in which they both participated allow him to attach his own enacted and retold interpretation to known information. He is thus *reenacting the known*, a behavior that takes place often among young interlocutors to create humor.

Such mocking—ridiculous and exaggerated imitation of the behaviors of another—differs from a tease or brief mimic in that it marks a threatening invasion of another. Mocking, unlike teasing, can take place in either the presence or absence of the mocked individual. Within youth organizations, though, mocking takes place most often in the presence of the individual who is the subject of the mock. The invasive nature of mocks comes from the fact that their success depends on imitating minute segments of behavior recognizable immediately as belonging to the subject but not generally sufficiently distinctive to have received comment by others.[5]

Such reenactments, as well as revoicings, work as playful and therapeutic humor in that they offer ways of "getting back" at someone else for an aggrievance through words rather than direct physical attack. Youth organizations do not tolerate physical violence, but their leaders have a wide range of acceptance of verbal humor and even encourage and participate in it at times (as the leader in example 5 does when she says of Amy's car, "it's possessed"). Adults explain that they perceive teases, mimics, and "good stories" as reinforcement of group collegiality. In addition, leaders—especially of dramatic groups—strongly encourage close observation of other players and members for the success of the performance; a mimic or mock displays good observational skills, as well as a certain kind of intimacy.

Moreover, stories such as Dennis's illustrate another key feature of youth organizations: members replay for others to indicate information and skills known to all members of the group. During rehearsals, some player will inevitably go through the paces of another actor in accompaniment to queries such as "You know when, in the second act, you go over here . . . ?" Both actors, as well as other members of the company, are familiar with the action enacted, but the speaker establishes the base of old information shared by all before moving on to new information or a different interpretation. Adult coaches or directors tend not to reenact or revoice but instead to offer description that calls to mind the scene about to be discussed: "In that second act, before Wendy exits stage left. . . ."

Reenactments and revoicings can redraw lines of power as well as reassign roles. Example 3 illustrates a combined *reenacting* of the coach's ways of talking and demonstrating and *forecasting* of what the youngsters will themselves do as junior coaches. Jaime moves this power play to another level by stepping in and reminding the coach that in this instance, he is no longer the coach, and Jack is now taking over. Thereby, the young people become adult-like and the coach player-like. In example 5 Dennis, who has none of the power of Amy's family, resources, and car, temporarily becomes dominant and Amy-like, while she has to step back and experience his put-down. In both cases, multiple messages are conveyed, and the power base is temporarily shifted by a swing of roles.

In teasing, speakers' shifts of role, stance, and voice enable them to say what they cannot say directly. Teasing depends on intimacy and often embodies ritualistic behavior. It allows expression of sentiments taken for granted by experienced group members and may therefore be used to initiate novices. Teases are tests of the extent to which members can manage the impression of wide-ranging competence, as they respond *in the role they are assigned in the tease*. Accepting the challenge of a tease, such as that Amy experiences in example 5, indicates one is both *a part* of the group and also able to play *a part*. These parts make up the whole, sustaining the integrity of the group.

Laughter, joking around, creating humor, and "mellowing out" sustain the interactional life of work within youth organizations. Moving from inception to completion in a group task necessarily involves disputes, misunderstandings, and rises and falls in the smoothness of paired or small-group relations within the larger group. Flirtation, serious romantic relationships, distress within small groups, and carryovers of misunderstanding and mistrust engendered in another setting can sometimes derail group action. Because youth organizations operate by rules that emphasize acceptance and equanimity within the group as a whole, rips and tears and small-group or clique competitions have to be mended, or the group as a whole is jeopardized. If, as in example 5, members sense that dissent is brewing between two or more individuals, they will stand by and wait for the tease, story, or joke that will clear the air and restore balance. On these occasions, planning, preparing, or practicing for the "real" play go on hold while playful verbal interactions doing the work of social relationships hold the floor.

No Place to Talk

The open floor for talk and the wide range of types of talk allowed in youth organizations stand in contrast to those in many other spaces where young people spend time. Their frequent complaint about schools, families, and jobs is that there is "no place to talk" or "no way I could say anything." Young people carry the perception that few listen to them and many deprecate and misunderstand their communication. Almost no one acknowledges their need to be "in communication" or to "be connected." Beepers or pagers, for example, offer young people both the image and the reality of being always in, or ready for, talk. Even in rural areas, where actual beepers are not available, some young people carry around beeper look-alikes to give them what they see as an urban image of being "in touch."

When adults attend to the communication of the young, they rarely praise their ways of talking. Even when young people's language forms and uses measure up to those that adults perceive to be "standard" or "academic" norms, the young may experience rejection for "not being themselves" and for showing that they have been well-coached in their ideas and voices by adults. The absence of research on the actual language uses of the young when they are in the midst of accomplishing a task or making plans offers only one indication of the low value of their informal verbal interactions, even for researchers. From the public media to their own families, young people hear adults deprecate the music they listen to and their propensity to "hang out" in groups filled with loud talk, giggles, and easily parodied expressions such as "you know," "like," and "really."

In situations both malicious and benevolent, young people hear themselves spoken for. Just as medical or mental health personnel "speak for" their patients or clients, young people find their actions and very being "given away" into the possession of adults who usurp their voice. School authorities, juvenile justice officials, and family members take over the voice of the young and "give" the story, whether in situations of praise or, on other occasions, in negative terms within confrontational settings. The ownership of one's own intentions, actions, and perceptions is grabbed by those who believe that young people either cannot or will not speak adequately or accurately for themselves.[6]

On occasion, the young avoid the silencing routines or put-downs of others by shifting into language unavailable to adults. Teenagers within the United States have long been noted for their ability to give words special meanings and to reverse the meanings of words or create new ones, so that their fast-paced talk among themselves effectively cuts out their elders. Hand signs, particular ways of wearing clothes, as well as choices of clothes, hair styles, body marking, and ornamentations bear secret, rapidly changing meanings that shift before adults can catch on to their uses. For example, in the 1990s adults fail to understand how young people obsessed with body image can use "phat" (pronounced as "fat" and written as *phat* in tagging and graffiti) as a marker of positive assessment. Ignorance of the meanings of such language, adults often make negative inferences.[7]

Chores, Jobs, and Work

Essayist Donald Hall (1993) has pointed out the vast differences among chores, jobs, and work. *Chores* are redundant bits and pieces critical to completion of any *job*, the larger assignment directly given and often supervised by powers beyond the self—whether institution, specific relationship, or accident. When one goes to work at a fast-food chain or in an office, the *job* is assigned and limited. When an automobile owner takes the family car to the repair shop, the *job* to repair comes through the customer-mechanic relationship. When a child spills a glass of milk on the kitchen floor or a tornado wipes out a trailer park, individuals have the *job* of cleaning and clearing.

In contrast, young people within youth organizations often speak of what they do there as "real jobs"—as "actress," "junior coach," "receptionist," or "board member." These jobs give them *roles* that involve them in *work*. Here, *work* is distinguished from *chores* and *jobs*, for with work comes some kind of planning and decision-making assignment, as well as pleasure, self-direction, creativity, and enthusiasm. Hall tells us that often when we have finished chores and our job, we can "*then*— as a reward—. . . get to work" (1993:4). For the fortunate, this *work* is *life*. Early memories of chores, jobs, and work repeatedly mark autobiographies as individuals remember times they spent in their youth immersed in either a work project with an older person or self-assigned work.[8] Many of today's youth have no counterpart to these occasions, coming from families in which both parents hold jobs outside the household or a single adult who works full-time outside the household maintains a family. Shared tasks and times for adult and older child to work jointly either do not exist or they take place in highly structured settings, such as fee-for-service programs (karate, ballet) and specialized camps devoted to sports or music. In these settings, adult instructors have the goal of improving youngsters' specific skills so that they may return a better player or artist.

Work within a role encompasses planning, preparing, practicing, performing, and assessing. The language used to plan how to play the role, as well as the language spoken within the role, offers vital practice for planning, thinking ahead, seeing the future, and understanding the consequences of current actions and thoughts for the next step and often for a distant end. In all societies, such events include observation, demonstration, trial and error, reflection, and display. Some groups add oral language forms that script the action by laying out ahead of time procedures and alternatives and considering products and performances. Legitimate peripheral participation whereby an individual watches, takes part, and chooses to move into particular phases and roles of the activity pushes learning along. It is the "practice as a whole, with its multiplicity of relations—both within the community and with the world at large" (Lave & Wenger 1991:14) that enables verbal expression of consequences, conditions, and process. Both continuity, carrying on what the adult does and says, and displacement, creatively reshaping the work and its meaning, come about through the work of the adult and young learner. In many societies, the young must learn not only how to *do* the work, but also how to *say* work, or talk through work in the language necessary to display verbally to others what it is about and how it proceeds. Formal education, generally intent on removing learning from work and placing it within chores and jobs through discrete bit-by-bit information and skill buildup as well as assignment of tasks, values highly the *saying* that surrounds chores and jobs. Students are asked individually to solve word problems made up around the imaginary construction of a playhouse; they rarely have the opportunity to plan and build a playhouse with cross-age peers who could serve as models and "voices of the mind" as they scaffold tasks for their younger counterparts (Vygotsky 1978, Wertsch 1991). Educators expect that the practice of doing and saying within chores and jobs will enable performance in work. But because work embodies role assumption and the revoicing of the action through one's role perspective, the skills and habits of mind that come from chores and jobs often do not carry over into work.

Conclusion

A consistent message throughout this chapter is that older children who engage regularly in ongoing work with adults learn how to make things happen and how to sustain social order while developing the language critical for thinking ahead to shape future outcomes. This learning is just the kind of work that youth, more often than not, are accused of *not* being able to achieve: complex group tasks involving planning, preparation, practice, performance, and evaluation. Older children's behaviors and language while engaged in productive tasks—other than those under direct adult supervision—have received almost no attention. This neglect surely derives in part from the general view that older children are not capable of work without adult direction and prefer to spend their time playing, troublemaking, and being with their friends. More serious than this negative public image of youth, however, is young people's actual lack of experience in working under the facilitation of adults toward a group project. Necessary to successful completion of such work are all the communication, planning, and responsibility-building skills that American employers maintain will be needed in the future workforce.

The language of older children in youth organizations that value them as resources develops in coordination with the practice of taking on a range of roles in the seasonal cycle of the group's work. While playing many of the "adult" roles necessary to maintain the organization—fundraiser, receptionist, promoter—young people also maintain social relations with their peers and negotiate verbally the disagreements and tensions that arise from the shifting pace and demands of the group's work.

As families and communities change, older children spend more and more time with their peers. Without the structure of work on a sustained group project, young people can create a limited range of types of "work" for themselves. From highly positive efforts (such as launching cleanup campaigns for city parks) to harmless mischief to high-risk behaviors, older children, left to their own devices, establish rules, hierarchical rankings, and challenges of achievement. Anyone who has observed a group of skateboarding fourteen-year-olds cannot doubt the group work involved in their finely tuned maneuvers, determined practice, and increasingly elevated levels of risk taking. From organizing garage bands who find ways to cut compact discs of their music to coloring one another's hair to planning tagging forays, young people succeed at planning and carrying out work they devise in the absence of other available activities.[9]

In summary, the talk of youth at work carries many features that indicate adeptness in planful and collaborative behaviors. In addition, their playful talk within work occasions helps them negotiate social relations peacefully and with the drama and humor that sustain social order so that the work can go forward. The idea that young people engage in "productive" language centered in work tasks (particularly outside classrooms) rarely enters accounts of the lives of older children or adolescents. It is thus the job of ethnographers and linguists to make as explicit as possible the lives of youth outside adult-dominated institutions, such as schools and families. We need much more knowledge of peer interactions around tasks and young people's grammatical and discourse structures. We need to understand the social organizational processes that sustain a sense of communal commitment to a process of work, which older children need to broaden their range of grammatical structures and uses of language.

Until settings for work projects with adults who view youngsters as legitimate resources greatly expand within U.S. society, youth organizations, as primary institutions that enable the young to work (and play) through language, will grow increasingly critical to the preparation of youth for entry into the world of work as adults. In the study of the language of older children, these sites deserve support and attention comparable to that previously given to families and schools as sites of language learning and socialization into habits and values essential in adult life. Linguists and other social scientists have a responsibility to distribute their attention more equitably to language development across the age span. They must resist the seductiveness of romanticized childhood or first-time utterances and actions to take up the rapid-fire action of seasonal rounds of maturation of children beyond the earliest years. It is this work that will help us turn back to the poet's words and alter them as we find the "familiar" not the "aberrant" in the young, recognizing and understanding them as moving contours of difference.

NOTES

The research on which this chapter is based was funded by the Spencer Foundation in two grants awarded to Heath and Milbrey W. McLaughlin between 1987 and 1997 for the study of youth in their out-of-school lives. The study took place in three major metropolitan areas and more than a dozen midsized towns (population between 25,000 and 100,000) and rural counties. The language corpus collected in situ includes approximately a million and a half words and has been analyzed with the help of a concordance program and several programs that aid in discourse analysis. The organizations chosen for study were only those judged by youth in the local community as effective. Oversubscribed seasons, waiting lists, and established reputations among alumni and community adults further substantiated youth judgments of "effectiveness." For further detail on selection methods and characteristics of the youth organizations, see Heath and McLaughlin (1993) and McLaughlin, Irby, and Langman (1994).

1. Terms such as "community of learners" often take *community* as given and stable without considering that many collectives accomplish work jointly without sharing features usually assigned to residential or institutional communal groups. Ludwig Fleck's (1935) term *denk colectiv* or "thought collective," used to describe a group of professionals working together on a common task (such as a cure for syphilis), more closely reflects what occurs within the youth organizations from which data are drawn for this chapter. Here joint work is directed toward task achievement, and the thinking of those involved reflects the shifting stances, roles, and activity shaping contributed by individual members. The outcome itself, as well as the ongoing representation of the joint achievement, carries the stamp of the thought collective. Other work that also closely relates to concepts such as community of learners draws heavily on the work of scholars, such as Vygotsky (1978), Tharp and Gallimore (1988), Wertsch (1991), and Rogoff (1994), who have contributed theories of learning that stress the social nature of working together within a task and the varieties of platforms for learning (e.g., apprenticeship) that collaborative tasks provide.

2. These young field-workers volunteered to become members of the Stanford University research team. They were paid for submission of audiotapes, transcripts of these, and sessions of analysis of these transcripts with senior field-workers.

3. The most extensive discussion of a major type of revoicing may be found in Rampton (1995), an extended treatment of the ways in which multiracial urban youth in Great Britain take up one another's languages upon occasion in order to cement relationships, display particular arenas of competence, and illustrate their ways of managing to "live with difference."

4. Within this project, it is our practice to avoid using the same piece of data several times. However, the scarcity of narratives within the corpus of over a million and a half words, as well as the infrequency of the kinds of occasions most likely to generate stories—tense disagreement among youth members—has meant that we have used the story of Dennis and Amy for different purposes in several publications. For more detail on the role of stories within youth talk, see Heath (1994). An additional account of the role of narratives, particularly among adolescent males, may be found in Tobin (1996), who argues that certain kinds of narratives may serve particular functions for them.

5. The threatening features of a mock are illustrated by the mock fights that take place in Thailand before boxing matches. Before entering the ring, opponents come out and face each other with mocking behaviors. But they must not include exaggerated gestures of attack and retreat; instead, the success of their mocking of the opponent depends on capturing very small, seemingly insignificant but instantly recognizable features of the other's ges-

tures, movement, or posture. The audience applauds each mocking partner separately, thus giving the loser of the prelude to the "real" fight a substantial psychological blow (Mark Worland, martial arts trainer, Palo Alto, CA, personal communication). For further discussion of the work of certain types of humorous play among older children, see Heath and Soep in progress.

6. Accounts of authorities speaking for those with less power occur frequently in the literature on interaction between medical authority and patient, attorney and client, or job applicant and employment office bureaucrat. Those in power often tell those without power not only when to speak but also what they can say. In addition, they often silence the others and take on their voices. See Sansom (1982) for description of such word theft within an Australian Aborigine group.

7. In societies around the world, ways of separating the language of the young from that of adults appear frequently, but often only as additional or oppositional layers of meaning to the language shared by all members of the society. In some societies, however, the young develop their own language, using local languages of adults as the matrix or base language and mixing in other languages as well as creating new meanings. Both tsotsitaal and iscamtho, spoken primarily among young males in townships of South Africa, have developed as separate and "secret" language varieties (Ntshangase 1995).

8. Hall, who has written extensively about work (1993), provides numerous illustrations of the ways in which work of the old and the young, side by side, has characterized descriptions of America from the time of de Crèvecoeur imagining his American farmer to Hall remembering his own parents with their children working alongside them in gender-segregated tasks divided between the kitchen and the barn. Children's literature and autobiographies still abound in accounts of children and adults working side by side to accomplish a shared goal; see, for example, Rushdie (1990), Mead (1972), and her daughter's account of her own life and that of four other professionals (Bateson 1989). Mead captures ways to instill the work of learning by recounting how her grandmother taught her to observe: "On some days she gave me a set of plants to analyze; on others, she gave me a description and sent me out to the woods and meadows to collect examples, say, of the 'mint family.' . . . I learned to observe the world around me and to note what I saw — to observe flowers and children and baby chicks. She taught me to read for the sense of what I read and to enjoy learning" (1972:47).

9. This extraordinarily detailed work, as well as its dependence on a strict hierarchical organization with division of labor, has been documented well in accounts of gang life. See, for example, Los Solidos Nation (1995).

13

Noisy Talk

Conversation and Collaboration
in a Youth Writing Group

STUART TANNOCK

Collaborative endeavor has frequently been described by educators and philosophers through an analogy with conversation or dialogue. Conversation, particularly through the work of conversation analysts, has been shown to be thoroughly collaborative. But the active role of conversation in furthering collaborative endeavor has been less frequently examined. Although reformers in schools, universities, and workplaces have become increasingly interested in collaborative work, they have paid limited attention to the ways in which conversational interaction structures and supports the successful completion of collaborative tasks.

In this chapter, I examine the significance that a particular kind of conversational interaction—noisy or simultaneous talk—had for a group of youths and adults working together on a collaborative writing project. Over the course of a four-month period, these young people and adults came together in a neighborhood-based organization to plan, write, discuss, argue, and negotiate the production of a brochure that would represent the history and interests of their neighborhood community. Talk and task intersected in the work of this writing group in ways that might be expected of any productive collaboration; through questions, argument, hedging, evaluation, and expressions of disagreement, the shape of the brochure gradually emerged. But talk and task also intersected in messier and noisier ways. "Noisy talk"—banter, laughter, simultaneous and overlapping speech, swells of volume and excitement—came right along with the group's seemingly more task-focused conversation. This noisy talk, far from being just "noise," played a central role in developing a cohesive group identity and in members' negotiating of various stages of the writing task. In other words, noisy talk got things done.

The kinds of conversational interactions I refer to here as noisy talk have been identified by Edelsky (1993) and Coates (1995) through the more theoretized notion of a "collaborative floor," and their work provides a point of departure for analysis of the data presented in this chapter. However, whereas Edelsky and Coates frame their discussions of the collaborative floor largely in terms of conversational structure, I discuss conversation in terms of its place in the structure of an ongoing collaborative project. Different kinds of noisy and informal interaction emerged within the ebb and flow of particular types of subtasks and steps in the production of the neighborhood brochure. Whereas banter, laughter, joking, and overlap appeared as both diversion from and frame for these activities, at times noisy talk also constituted task-focused work. In response sequences to individual criticisms or suggestions, for example, the writing group demonstrated heightened interest and involvement through a phenomenon I term "swarming." And in group composing sessions, noisy talk emerged through the activity of on-line group improvisation—a process in which text and talk, directive and question, recitation and invention mixed in complex ways.

Collaborative Work and Language Use

Collaborative work was the focus of increasing interest and acceptance throughout the late 1980s and early 1990s. In business, reformers pointed to the benefits for both workers and managers of replacing traditional corporate hierarchies with collaborative work teams and with structures of participatory management (e.g., Marshall 1995, Peters 1988).[1] In schools and universities, "new ideas about thinking and learning shifted the focus from classrooms of individual learners to small groups being coached to construct knowledge jointly through collaborative and complex problem-solving in a variety of active learning situations" (Heath & Langman 1994:82). The teaching and practice of writing in particular—both in schools and workplaces—became a central site for the development and discussion of various models of collaboration (Blyler & Thralls 1993, Cross 1994, Forman 1992, Lunsford & Ede 1990).

Discussions of collaborative work regularly invoke images of conversation and dialogue. Bruffee (1984:642), for example, writes that "collaborative learning provides a social context in which students can experience and practice the kinds of conversation valued by college teachers." J. Rymer (1993:181), in a review of the ongoing changes in writing pedagogy, summarizes: "[W]e [writing instructors] are relinquishing our traditional roles as authority figures, performers, and masters guiding apprentices, so that we can collaborate with our students, engaging them in conversation and acknowledging that our talk shapes our reality as a social group, and, in turn, our pedagogy." Despite such rhetoric, reformers interested in promoting collaborative models of instruction and work have rarely paid close attention to specific ways in which language structures, supports, or undermines collaborative endeavor. Which specific forms of conversation should be valued by college teachers? How exactly does talk shape collaborative activity?

Heath and Langman (1994) point out that failure to attend to the differing linguistic practices of traditional and collaborative classrooms and workplaces subtly undermines reform efforts. Language conventions, such as those associated with traditional top-down instruction, "are highly interdependent with a sense of role, title, and responsibility, and are thus not easily dropped" (1994:83). Consequently, close studies of classroom interactions have found that

> situations created with the intention of distributing learning across a small group (such as that composed of teacher and several students in writing conferences) more often than not reflected micromanagement strategies that led participants to reenact major features of traditional classrooms such that a single individual often emerged as the only active participant while others sat by passively. (1994:83)

Heath and Langman's study of the register of coaching is motivated, at least in part, by the need to know more about the kinds of linguistic practices involved in successful collaborative projects (interest in coaching as a model of instruction is part of the more general interest in collaborative work). In this chapter, I analyze a kind of linguistic practice—noisy talk—that, although often thought of as annoying, disruptive, or distracting (particularly in classrooms or small work groups), may be an important part of collaborative endeavor. As I focus on the relationship of conversation and collaboration, I attempt to address the complicated question of how activity structures talk and of how talk, in turn, structures activity.

Conversation and the Collaborative Floor

Edelsky (1993) developed the notion of a collaborative floor to account for phenomena she observed while studying conversational interaction among professional colleagues in a series of university committee meetings. In the "single floor" that predominated for most of the meeting time, participants took turns to speak or "hold the floor." At certain moments, however, a collaborative floor emerged in which several speakers appeared to be speaking simultaneously, giving an "impression of more raucousness and overlapping" (Edelsky 1993:192). Collaborative floors tended to have more simultaneous speech, laughter and joking, overlapping, and shorter turns than single floors. Collaborative floors also had a different "functional feel" compared to single floors:

> [C]ertain functions predominated in single floors but not collaborative ones (reporting, soliciting response, and validating/agreeing) or collaborative floors but not single ones (joking, hitching on/chiming in). Managing the agenda (reporting on items, seeking opinions and information, etc.) was the predominant (but not sole) activity when single floors were occurring. Time-outs from the agenda more often (but not always) coincided with collaborative floors. (Edelsky 1993:217)

Edelsky (1993:196) differentiated two types of collaborative floors: "seeming free-for-alls and, more frequently, cases of several people being on the same wavelength." Coates (1995) picks up the notion of a collaborative floor, but uses it slightly differently. For Coates, the collaborative floor characterizes not just moments within a conversation but entire conversations—in particular, friendly conversations among women. In women's friendly talk, writes Coates, "the construction of talk is a joint effort. . . . [T]he group takes priority over the individual and the women's voices combine to create a shared text" (1995:1). Identifying the same quantitative differences between collaborative and single floors as Edelsky—more co-construction, overlap, joking, and laughing—Coates (1995:11) insists on the qualitative difference of the collaborative floor as well: "[T]he collaborative floor is a shared space, and therefore what is said is construed as being the voice of the group rather than of the individual." Coates (1995:20) sees collaborative floors as central to the "construction and maintenance of good social relations, not the exchange of information." Collaborative floors emerge in "talk-as-play," which is "inevitably structured differently from talk-as-serious-business" (Coates 1995:20).

The notion of the collaborative floor is an important and useful one, at the very least to point to forms of conversational interaction in which the minimization of overlap is not a priority for participants (pace Sacks, Schegloff, & Jefferson 1974). However, the concept does present a number of difficulties for conversation analysts. First, the collaborative floor is defined by Edelsky and Coates largely in terms of conversational structure. But if all conversation is inherently collaborative, and if most conversation regularly contains overlap, co-construction, simultaneous speech, joking, and laughter, then it becomes difficult to determine the point at which a single floor gives way to a collaborative floor. This concept of different conversational structures seems to beg the question of where, when, and why the features referred to by the notion of a collaborative floor occur. Coates's assumption that entire conversations may unfold on a collaborative floor means that she does not link the emergence of the collaborative floor to any specific activities. Edelsky (1993:219), meanwhile, writes that in the university committee meetings she studied, "there seemed to be no pattern" to account for the emergence of a collaborative floor. To answer the open question Edelsky (1993:222) leaves at the end of her paper—"What are the cues and mechanisms which invite a collaboratively developed floor?"—it is necessary to look at the relationship between conversation and the structure of collaborative group activity.

A second concern with the notion of the collaborative floor arises from Edelsky's and Coates's tendency to identify the concept with what other discourse analysts have called the "sociorelational frame," "phatic communication" (Coupland, Robinson, & Coupland 1994); less formally, "small talk," "banter," or "chatter" (Erickson & Shultz 1982); or even simply "ordinary conversation" (Drew & Heritage 1992).[2] Studies of talk in institutional interactions (meetings, classrooms, medical interviews) have generally noted a distinction between purposive talk that deals with the "business at hand" and informal chatter or conversation (e.g., Boden 1994, Coupland et al. 1994, Linde 1988). Casual chatter, which frequently occurs as an opening and closing frame for more institutional talk, is important for participants to construct and negotiate their social identities and relationships. The boundary between task-focused talk and sociorelational talk is not absolute—sociorelational work is inevitably accomplished by task-focused talk, and vice versa—but is derived from distinctions that are salient for conversational participants themselves (Coupland et al. 1994:90). Even though I agree with Coates and Edelsky that noisy talk (the collaborative floor) can be an important part of "time-outs" from the agenda, I argue that noisy talk can equally be a central way for groups to manage and further the agenda.

The analysis presented here thus differs from the work of Edelsky and Coates in several ways. I analyze talk that gives an impression of more raucousness and over-lapping not as a (necessarily) different kind of conversational structure but in terms of its functional and structural relation to an ongoing collaborative endeavor. I identify three different kinds of noisy talk:

1. Noisy talk as part of nontask-focused (or sociorelational) interaction. I analyze, as an example, the emergence of noisy talk in a story-chaining sequence that opened one of the group's meetings.
2. Noisy talk as part of task-focused interaction. As an example, I analyze group response sequences that occurred during the group's planning and negotiating of different segments of its writing project. I use the term "swarming" to refer to such sequences.
3. Noisy talk as part of task-scripted interaction. An example is the noisy talk that emerged as participants improvised text on-line in group composing sessions.

In identifying these various kinds of noisy talk, I suggest that whereas noisy talk can be an important part of talk-as-play, as suggested by Coates, it can also be centrally implicated in talk-as-business.

The Youth Writing Group

The youth writing group studied in this chapter formed as part of a neighborhood literacy program run by an inner-city community center in the eastern United States. Launched with the goal of promoting literacy "as a tool for freedom and empowerment for *all* members of our community," the literacy program sought to provide alternative learning environments for "at-risk" teenagers and to improve teen writing skills "with tasks that have an impact on the neighborhood."[3] The neighborhood brochure project was designed to produce a document that would improve the poor public image of the neighborhood in which the community center was located (I give this neighborhood the pseudonym "Cityside"). Community center leaders and youth members had three explicit goals in designing this project: (1) to improve youth writing, interviewing, planning, and computer skills; (2) to learn about success and the kinds of people who were successful in the neighborhood; (3) to produce "a piece of writing that works . . . that makes a difference to the people who wrote it and the people who read it." Project organizers also hoped to provide youths with the experience of working collaboratively in a group and with the opportunity of being involved in work that had value, that they could care about.

Six teens—five female and one male—joined the group: Lisa, Sara, Mary, Delia, Andrea, and Tony (all pseudonyms). Some had learned about the project from teachers at school; others had been previously involved with activities at the community center. All were juniors and seniors at local high schools. The group was headed by two adult leaders (one female, one male) and by a researcher/observer (female), who took an active participatory role in the group's work: in the transcripts below, I refer to the female leader as "Leader 1," the male leader as "Leader 2," and the researcher/observer as "Observer." Over the course of a four-month period, the group met twice weekly (on average) to plan and develop the brochure. In addition to work at meetings, members were responsible for interviewing neighbor-hood residents and leaders and for some amount of writing at home.

Like any collaborative effort, the group had its share of ups and downs. At times, group members experienced frustration, boredom, interpersonal tension, and disen-gagement from their task—particularly as the project ran about a month overtime. Youths were sometimes late for meetings, and one member regularly missed meet-ings. At the end of the project, some of the leaders expressed disappointment with what had been the pilot project of their literacy program; they had hoped for more and better writing to be produced and for more engagement by the teen partici-pants. They felt that more scaffolding should have been provided to help the group move through its various tasks. But a brochure was successfully produced, and final written evaluations by the youth members of the group were all positive; all men-tioned, in particular, the positive experience of working in and becoming a member of a collaborative writing group.

In this chapter, I focus on some of the more cohesive—and perhaps more suc-cessful—moments of the group's work together. I am interested specifically in oc-casions when noisy talk was the result of focused interaction. Noisy talk, of course, was also frequently the result of unfocused interaction, of youths carrying on mul-tiple conversations at once and simply not attending to one another. Leaders and teens alike complained in their final evaluations of the lack of focus that had hin-dered some of the group's meetings. One leader felt that "we did not cue literate events, we did not make it clear when we're down to work," while another com-plained that there were "lots of official friendships being formed but little focus on task."

Differences, however, between focused and unfocused noisy talk often elude par-ticipants and researchers at the moment. What may appear to be chaotic, dysfunc-tional interaction in situ may reveal itself to be tightly organized, functional, and productive under close linguistic analysis.[4] Although many of the complaints of lack of focus are probably justified, some of the noisiness in group interaction results from group members' intense involvement in task-driven work. Moreover, some of the chatter that surrounded or distracted from task-driven work contributed to de-veloping the group's working relationships. It is to such sociorelational uses of noisy talk that I turn first.

Story Chaining: The Emergence of a Collaborative Floor

In the conversational interactions of the youth writing group, noisy talk often emerged in time-outs from the agenda and in talk-as-play. Casual chatter regularly occurred at the beginning and end of meetings and in moments of transition and tension. Forming a sociorelational frame—which participants recognized as being distinct from a more goal-oriented frame of interaction—this casual chatter served broadly to mediate identities and relationships within the group. Not all casual chat-ter was noisy; much of this talk took place in a very orderly one-at-a-time single floor. But the conversational features of the collaborative floor made it highly appropriate for the creation of a common group identity. Through noisy, simultaneous, "shared time" talk, group members could easily and effectively create the sense of shared group membership, or, as Goffman (1959) puts it, of a "working consensus."

Sociorelational talk served different functions depending on its sequential location within the group's meetings. As part of the opening and closing sequences for meetings, casual chatter enabled individuals to make the transition between their identities as group members and the rest of their lives; given the nature of their task, "real life" identities were highly relevant for the group's activities. Youths and adults would catch each other up on the events in their lives since the last time they had met, anticipate and plan for future events, and talk randomly about fashion, TV, boyfriends and girlfriends, teachers and classes, families, and so forth. Within the middle of meetings, group members would frequently make jokes or take time-outs for chatter in order to smooth over moments of tension or frustration. Transitions between tasks provided a further opportunity for the development of individual and group relationships through the sharing of identities, experiences, attitudes, and ideologies.

Here I analyze a single example of a sociorelational use of noisy talk—the creation of a collaborative floor through a process that Kalcik (1975) has called "story chaining." Story chaining—in which the telling of one narrative triggers the telling of another by a different narrator—may either "result from a competitive desire to 'top' the previous narrator's story or from an urge to support her by sharing a similar experience" (Kalcik 1975:5).[5] For the members of the writing group, this particular occasion of story chaining was clearly seen to be collaborative and supportive. From the start, members participated through questions, comments, and laughter in the telling of one another's stories. As each story was told, the group became more involved and more excited, laughing and talking all at once. The interaction eventually reached a crescendo in which multiple stories were being told simultaneously. Story chaining, in this instance, was not just a serial but a cumulative process; by its end, both topic *and* time were shared as group members participated in the experience of truly "talking together."

The story-chaining sequence discussed here took place at the beginning of a meeting in the second month of the group's work. Seven members of the group were present (the female leader, the adult observer, Sara, Delia, Andrea, Lisa, and Tony). One member (Sara) arrived at the meeting with her leg in a cast. This new development triggered a series of shared accident stories in which every member present recounted an experience (or lack of experience) of an injury. The series had three successive and cumulative stages: the group moved from co-participation in the construction of one another's narratives, to participation in a collaborative floor, to the simultaneous telling of accident stories. Although the entire series was collaboratively constructed, the nature of conversational collaboration changed as each of these successive stages layered upon the others.

This particular story-chaining sequence was initiated by the two adults; first the observer and then the group leader told narratives of personal injuries. During the collaborative floor, the two adults participated only minimally; during the noisy talk of simultaneous telling of stories, the two were again central participants. On other occasions, youth members initiated story chains and topic sequences in the group's nontask-focused interactions—especially after the first few meetings when a sense of group membership had been developed. In other instances of sociorelational noisy talk, adult leaders pitched in comments alongside, underneath, and on top of youth banter.

After the group had been chatting for several minutes, the observer started to tell a story about having hurt her knee as a child and having had her mother tell her to "quit whining." Her mother later felt terrible, the observer explained, when a doctor confirmed that there really was something wrong with her knee. Rather than listening quietly to the observer's narrative, the other group members quickly jumped in to participate in the story's telling (an opening bracket marks the onset of overlapping speech; a closing bracket marks the end of overlap, regardless of alignment):

```
(1)  1  Observer:  And she said, ah, quit whining.
     2  Andrea:    [Hhhh,              [oo::h.]
     3  Leader 1:  [Yeah, that's what  [they do.] Mhm.        ]
     4  Observer:                      [And she] wouldn't take] me to
     5                the do(h)ct(hh)or.
     6  Sara:      Really?
```

Appreciation and response are marked by Andrea's laughter (line 2), by the leader's assessment of the commonality of the experience described by the observer (line 3), and by Sara's question-form expression of interest and empathy (line 6). All of these responses take place within the middle of the observer's narrative.

Group members also co-participated in narrative production by animating or describing characters in the stories of others. In the following example, which took place towards the end of the story chain, Tony twice jumps in to provide comic and dramatic explanations for accidents and injuries being described by others:

```
(2)  1  Observer:  I broke my collarbone when I was a baby.
     2  Tony:      ((Snorts)) Oh [you was one of them] wi::ld babies,=
     3  Andrea:                  [Hhh. Ha ha.]
     4  Tony:      = jumping off the cri::b like you was one of the
     5             Duke boys.
     6  Observer:  I jumped off the counter.
     7  Andrea:    [Hhhh.]
     8  X:         [Hhhh.]
     9  Sara:      [You did?] I did something stupider, I put my hand
    10             in a toaster.
    11  Leader 1:  NO YOU DID NO::T.
    12  Sara:      Yes I did. Right there. You can see it, a scar. I was
    13             three years old. I put my hand in the toaster.
    14  Tony:      She was like, I'm tired of waiting on ma::.
```

Tony's guess at what happened to the observer to cause her to break her collarbone, while wrong, is nonetheless not completely rejected by the observer. In an example of lexical repetition that Goodwin (1990a) calls "format tying," the observer repeats (in line 6) Tony's choice of verb, "jump off" (line 4), thereby managing to incorporate ("tie in") his explanation with her own. Tony, in elaborating upon Sara's opening account of her toaster story, actually constructs, and attributes to Sara, a hypothetical thought that might have motivated her decision to put her hand in the toaster (line 14).

A topic-comment format provided a further way for members to co-participate in narrative production. In the example above, after Sara claims to have put her hand in a toaster (line 9), the leader's formulaic comment/response of mock disbelief ("No you did not," line 11) simultaneously conveys agreement with Sara's assessment that this was a stupid thing to do and calls for Sara to say more. Topic-comment interactions occurred in the transitions between extended narratives, such as in the following transition between the observer's initial accident story and a subsequent story of a childhood ear infection told by the group leader:

```
(3)  1   Observer:   And he goes, how can you wa(hh)lk?
     2   Andrea:     Hm hm hm? =
     3   Observer:   =M(hh)y mother was [li(hh)ke] hhhhhhh.
     4   Leader 1:                      [O::::h go:d.]
     5   Sara:       Mmm.=
     6   Leader 1:   =My mother beat me, my godmother,
     7               my sweetheart, beat me one time.=
     8   Lisa:       =I'd beat her back, my mother [try to beat me.]
     9   Leader 1:                                 [Cause I told her]
     10              that my ear hurt. But what it wa::s,
     11  Observer:   [An ear infection.]
     12  Leader 1:   [I had lied] so darn much, I guess, I guess I was
     13              about eight or nine years old . . .
```

In making comments on opening topic statements of other speakers, group members retrospectively constitute such topic statements as calls to which they then respond. The leader's story preface ("My mother beat me," line 6)—itself a response tied lexically and syntactically to the final sentence of the observer's story ("My mother was . . . ," line 3)—is treated by Lisa as a call; Lisa consequently offers as a personal response, "I'd beat her back, my mother try to beat me" (line 8). Likewise, the leader's topic preface ("But what it was," line 10) becomes a call for the observer, who guesses "an ear infection" in response (line 11).

In these examples of group participation in storytelling, there is some overlapping, but nothing excessive for ordinary, single-floor conversation. A collaborative floor emerges later, at the end of the third story of the story-chaining sequence—after the observer's initial story, and after two back-to-back stories told by the leader (the first describing how she was wrongfully beaten by her mother when, as a child, she had complained of an ear infection, the second recalling a neighbor in Cleveland who had exploited a leg injury in order to get errands run for her). It is as if a critical mass were reached at this point in the story chain, a point at which group members recognized the occasion as one for the joint construction and articulation of a shared group experience, rather than of a series of individual experiences to which the group would respond:

```
(4)  1   Andrea:   My little brother and I have been extrao:rdinarily
     2             unlucky. We've never broken or strained
     3             [anything.]
     4   Lisa:     [Same here.]  [Never] in my life.
     5   Tony:                   [Who:a man.]
```

```
 6  Andrea:    Neither of us [has ever been] [in the hospital.]
 7  Tony:                    [I BROKE MY FOOT.]
 8  Sara:                                  [You're no:t un]=
 9             =lucky, trust me, it's a [pai::n in the butt.]
10  Tony:                                [I'm telling you.]
11  Observer:  It [is, yeah.]
12  Sara:         [I've broken] a finger, an elb [ow,] and my-=
13  Leader 1:                                    [Mhm].
14  Sara:      = well, I've done this to my le [g.]
15  Lisa:                                     [I] would never
16             br[eak one of my bones.] I never-
17  Tony:        [I've broken a a:rm,]
18  Tony:      a [foo[t,
19  Lisa:        [I  [wouldn't ( ) myself in ( ) like that.]
20  Sara:           [Peter, my brother, you know how s-]
21             [school] nurses are stupid . . .
22  Tony:      [a:::nd-]
```

In this interaction, four of the five youths present (Andrea, Lisa, Sara, and Tony) offer accounts of their injuries (or lack of injuries) almost simultaneously, while the group leader and the observer offer brief, supportive comments. Most of the contributions are relatively short, and most are overlapping. No one stands out as "having the floor," and no speaker appears to cut short his or her utterance so as to avoid overlap; this is the group as a whole talking about its collective experience. Many utterances are tied to one another through lexical and syntactic repetition. Sara echoes Andrea's initial "unlucky" (lines 2 and 8), and Tony, Sara, and Lisa all echo Andrea's initial format of [Noun(person) + Verb(break) + Noun(body part)]:[6]

We've never broken or strained anything.	(Andrea, line 2)
I broke my foot.	(Tony, line 7)
I've broken a finger, an elbow, and . . .	(Sara, line 12)
I would never break one of my bones.	(Lisa, lines 15–16)
I've broken a arm . . .	(Tony, line 17)

Overlapping continues for several more seconds until the narrative launched by Sara in lines 20–21—at a moment when Lisa is still affirming her decision never to break any of her own bones (lines 15–16, 19) and Tony is continuing to list the body parts he has broken (lines 17, 18, 22)—eventually takes sole possession of the floor. Sara's narrative picks up the topic of "things that happened to my brother," introduced by Andrea's statement at the onset of the collaborative floor (lines 1, 20).

Following this excerpt, involvement, noise, and excitement levels continued to rise among the members of the group and reached a crescendo when Lisa told a story that sent the entire group into fits of laughter. Lisa explained to the group how, when she was seven years old and had just learned to ride a bicycle, she wondered what would happen if she put her foot into the spokes of the front wheel. The result: she flipped head over heels and her bike ran her over. In the aftermath of this story there was an almost constant stream of laughter as different members of the group jumped in to tell still other stories of crazy accidents and injuries. These stories were told almost simultaneously; except for the occasional lull, there were always two people speaking at once and sometimes three. The sequence came to a head with the following three stories told by Tony, the group leader, and the observer:

(5) 1 Leader 1:   My daughter said she [( ) someone, ah-]
     2 Observer: [Now I've been interested] in
     3   that question my [self.] I've tried it out too.
     4 Leader 1:   [the freezer.]
     5 Observer: [Well I had a worse] thing=
     6 Leader 1:   [She put her tongue in the fridge.]
     7 Observer: =[with the kickstand on my bicycle that holds it,=
     8 Sara: [That is so:: painful. I've never- Oh, oh, yu::ck.]
     9 Observer: =you know, when you-] when you put it [down. It=
    10 Tony: [It works=
    11 Observer: =sticks out, you know, and then when you pedal it=
    12 Tony: =the same on a *button* on a *coa:t.* You get a button=
    13 Observer: =goes ( ).]
    14 Tony: =real *co::ld.*]
    15 Leader 1:   Hhh.
    16 Sara: [It's like I had that-]
    17 Observer: [So I got in the habit of-] *while* I was *riding,=
    18 Tony: [(   )] the button on my jacket? Well one=
    19 Observer: =taking my leg back, and *kicking* it, but if you=
    20 Tony: =day it was real co::ld, and I put my *lip* on that=
    21 Observer: =kicked too ha::rd (   ).]
    22 Tony: =*but*ton, and it wouldn't come off].
                    ((*laughter*))
    23 Tony: I'm walking around with my *button* on my *lip* like
    24   aaarrrlll.
    25 Lisa: [Oo::h it just (   ) when you're (   ).]
    26 Tony: [It didn't come off so I thawed it out in (   ).]

In this sequence, the group leader tells a story about her daughter sticking her tongue in the freezer and presumably getting it stuck there (lines 1–6). The observer tells a story about kicking her kickstand back on her bicycle while riding and presumably getting into an accident (lines 5–21). Following the leader's story and overlapping with that of the observer, Tony tells of how he once got his lip stuck to a cold button on his jacket (lines 10–26).

The movement of the story-chaining sequence, as revealed in examples 1–5, from narrative co-construction (on a single floor) to a collaborative floor to simultaneous storytelling illustrates the difficulties inherent in describing phenomena such as overlapping and simultaneous speech in terms of different conversational structures. The last interaction in example 5 would probably not be considered a collaborative floor; structurally, it looks as if the group has moved to two separate (if related) conversations, each having essentially single floors. One conversation focuses on the topic of tongues and lips sticking to freezing metal and ice, while the other continues with the topic of bicycle accidents.

The emergence of a collaborative floor, then, seems fleeting, and it becomes exceedingly difficult to determine its boundaries. Overlapping and simultaneous talk can be discussed far more coherently in terms of the group's ongoing activities. It is the story-chaining sequence that provides for the functional continuity and significance of the different kinds of talk and interaction discussed in this section. Rather than describing a series of shifts between types of floors, we can more usefully point to the gradual and continual increase in noise, laughter, excitement, and simultaneous and overlapping speech. Overlap and simultaneity, far from being accidental or incidental, provide a crucial resource for creating a sense of "coming together." In other words, the experience for both speakers and listeners of the alternative possibility of a flat and serial chain of stories told end to end is far different from the experience of a group of stories told first one by one and then increasingly simultaneously. If the activity of story chaining shapes the emergent nature of talk and interaction, talk and interaction—in particular, overlap and simultaneous speech—may also be said to shape the nature of the group's construction of a shared narrative of experience.

There are several reasons for considering the simultaneous stories told by Tony, the group leader, and the observer to be a shared group activity rather than separate conversations. All three are clearly linked by a single group-defined topic of conversation (accident stories). The narratives told by Tony and the observer also seem to be closely aligned in timing: simultaneous pauses in these narratives occur at both lines 13–14 and 21–22. But most importantly, the group members themselves saw these narratives as constituting a shared conversation. By the end of Tony's narrative about his lip sticking to a frozen button, only one member of the group (Delia) had not yet told a story about her experience. Thus, out of the noisy melee of simultaneous talk, Sara and Tony called to Delia to join them:

(6) 25 Lisa: [Oo::h it just (   ) when you're (   )]
     26 Tony: [It didn't come off so I thawed it out in [(   ).]
     27 Sara: [HEY]
     28   DELIA, what have you done.
     29 Tony: YEAH YEAH YOU SITTING OVER THERE LAUGHING AT US,
     30   come on, I wanna hear the incredibly stupid
     31   things you've done.
     32 Delia: Wanna know what I di:d, when I was little?
     33 Leader 1: I don't know what I did.
     34 Delia: I didn't know how to ride a bike at a:ll, [and-]
     35 Leader 1:   [And you
     36   got on.]
     37 Delia: Yea:h, I got o:n, because, everybody had a bike in
     38   my family . . .

In turning to Delia, Sara and Tony construct the previous noisy talk as a shared group activity. "You sitting over there laughing at us," says Tony. As a group activity, the group seemed to recognize the importance of having all of its members participate. As soon as the "summons" was offered to Delia, everyone who had previously been talking over one another fell silent and focused their attention on Delia's narrative.

Delia told the group a story about getting on a bike as a young child without being able to reach the pedals and rolling straight down a hill into cross traffic—miraculously, without getting seriously injured. When she had finished, and other members had expressed their collective amazement, the group then made a swift and abrupt transition to task-focused talk:

(7) 1 Delia: [My mom was like-]
     2 Leader 1:   [The Lord was taking care] of *this* baby, cause he
     3   takes care of babies and foo::ls, and I don't know
     4   which one you were, but he took care of you.
                    ((*laughter*))
     5 Delia: I was bo(hh)th.
     6 Lisa: Alright *focus*, let's get it on.=
     7 Observer: =Alright, so To [ny], why don't you- =
     8 Tony: [Focus.]
     9 Lisa: =Get it on?
    10 Observer: Give your plan.

Through the story-chaining sequence, the group had drawn on both shared life experiences and shared talking time to create a common sense of the time to move to
focus (lines 6, 7, and 8). When all the members of the group had constituted themselves as a group—through participation in the story chain—they seemed ready to
start on their writing work.[7]

Although opening chatter among group members was rarely as inclusive and integrated as it was in this meeting, the story-chaining sequence is an exemplar of the
possible sociorelational functions of noise. Perhaps coincidentally, the meeting that
followed was one of the group's most productive; group members came up with and
negotiated several new ideas, substantially rethought sections of the brochure, and,
quite unusually, were willing to work late.

Swarming: Group Response Sequences

The youth writing group occasionally had guest lecturers come to meetings to ad-
vise them on various aspects of their work. One lecturer—who helped the group on
several occasions develop their writing and planning skills—wanted to tell other
high school students about the group's project and asked the members to help her
develop an effective plan for presenting what they were doing to other teenagers.
The planning session required group members to think reflexively about their own
experience of working together to produce the neighborhood brochure. One of the
most important and distinctive features of this experience, they decided, was the
nature of their group talk and interaction:

(8) 1 Lisa: I think it's important to u:m- not to make this sound
     2   like=
     3 Andrea: =like-=
     4 Lisa: =a classroom event, or anything like that. [We're]=
     5 Lecturer: [Okay.]
     6 Lisa: =kind of casual.
     7 Andrea: Yeah, this [is real *informal*, we're all sit=
     8 Sara: [*Ki*(hh)nd of. They use words=
     9 Andrea: =[ting here] talking at [the same time.]
    10 Sara: =[like-] dwee::b,   [neo-maxi,] *daggy,*=
    11 Leader 2: [Kind of slaggy.]

12 Tony: [This is slang.]
13 Sara: =and sla::g.

Simultaneous and overlapping talk, as described in Andrea's comments (lines 7 and 9), were thus salient, valued, and articulated by one of the group's members. Simultaneous and overlapping talk, as present in the structure of this particular interaction, played a part in the group's task-focused work and in the exchange of information. Group members simultaneously jump in to elaborate upon Lisa's suggestion that the group's interactional styles contrasted with traditional classroom events. "We're all sitting here talking at the same time," says Andrea, talking at the same time as Sara, Tony, and the group's second leader. "We can use our own vocabulary here," is the central message of Sara's and Tony's contributions. In a wave of laughter and excitement—and of more overlapping speech—group members went on to offer still other examples of favorite slang words.

These kinds of interactions I call swarming—for the impression one has in listening to them is of a sudden buzz of excitement, as group members talk all at once in response to something someone has said or done. Swarming is a group response sequence in which members demonstrate heightened involvement or interest following the introduction of an idea or criticism. Characterized by many of the features identified with the notion of a collaborative floor, swarming can involve increased overlapping, simultaneous talk, co-construction, shorter turns, a large number of speakers talking in close proximity to one another, and frequent laughing and joking. In example 8, the male leader jumps into the discussion of how casual the group's meetings are by parodically using one of the teens' slang words he has just learned ("Kind of slaggy," line 11). Joking in these episodes seems to mark excitement about ideas rather than distraction from task.

Edelsky (1993:219), in her discussion of collaborative floors in the university meetings she studied, suggests (but without elaboration) that collaborative floors may frequently be response sequences: "[S]econd pair parts of adjacency pairs (primarily, answers in question/answer sequences) were . . . often the openers of collaborative episodes. Apparently a question . . . often appeared legitimately answerable by many at once." Swarming episodes in the meetings of the youth writing group, although never appearing in response to questions, had the distinct feel of being such "second pair parts of adjacency pairs." The significance of swarming episodes for the group's task-driven work was to indicate (and perhaps create) a close alignment among group members (or at least some subset of group members) and thereby to construct the first pair part of the adjacency pair—the newly introduced idea or criticism—as being highly salient or central to the group's work.

Swarming occurred during the group's planning and negotiating of various segments of its project. Whereas with sociorelational noisy talk (such as the story-chaining sequence) group members built off of one another's experiences to construct a shared group experience, in swarming group members built off of one another's ideas and arguments to construct a collective argument. And whereas the adult leaders seemed to participate fully in the group's sociorelational noisy talk, the leaders tended to drop out of or stand back from swarming interactions. In the meetings of this particular writing group, adults never initiated swarming episodes;

they did occasionally make comments during such episodes, but these tended to be fairly brief, fairly minimal.

In example 8, swarming is supportive: group members jump in to elaborate Lisa's initial idea. Swarming can also be confrontational, a leaping on a criticism made of someone's comment or activity. One such example occurred in the planning session in which group members helped the visiting lecturer prepare a presentation about their project:

```
(9)   1   Lecturer:    I could do a little straight info. Then I could say,
      2                well, let me tell you about a project tha:t, um, some
      3                people, on the City[side are doing-]
      4   Sara:                          [People, you can't] say people.
      5   Lisa:        No, that's what [we're telling you.] Yes, if you say=
      6   Sara:                        [We're teenagers.]
      7   Lisa:        =teenagers [it's like a] direct assoc=
      8   Lecturer:               [Aren't you peo(h)ple t(hh)oo?]
      9   X:                      [( ) school ( ).]
     10   Lisa:        [=iation [there.]
     11   Tony:        [=We're [people.]
     12   Sara:                [But if] you say people, they'll think
     13                people, they'll [think] adu:lts.
     14   Lisa:                        [People.]
     15   Tony:        [Yeah.]
     16   Lisa:        [Yeah.]
```

First, Sara jumps in, criticizing the lecturer's choice of words (line 4). Lisa immediately picks up on Sara's criticism and reconstructs it as the collective voice of the group ("that's what we're telling you," line 5). Indeed, the rapid-fire, overlapping argument put together by Lisa and Sara creates the impression that this is a single collectivity rather than two separate individuals speaking. Tony joins the duo as well; when the lecturer laughs, asking whether the group members aren't people too, he jumps in to rebuff her ("We're people," line 11). The affirmations of one another's contributions ("Yeah," lines 15, 16), typical of swarming episodes, add to the impression of a united front. The lecturer, who had by this point in the session established a productive working relationship with the group, goes on to accept the comments made by Sara, Lisa, and Tony as useful and constructive criticisms; the three had pointed out quite effectively the rhetorical and political implications of her word choice.[8]

The joint construction of a collective argument, as in the above example, was a central factor in the significance of swarming for moving the group's task-related discussions along. In the following example, the group has been talking about whether to include a separate section in their brochure on the history of their neighborhood or whether to incorporate the history into the senior citizen section. Lisa points out that one of the purposes of the brochure is to get people to move to the Cityside neighborhood and argues that for such a purpose history is irrelevant:

```
(10)  1   Lisa:    Realistically, why would you come to the Cityside
      2            for what happened here, a whole-=
      3   Tony:    =Two hundred [years ago?]
```

4	Lisa:	[Man::y years] ago. [Okay?]
5	Sara:	[When] they get
6		here they can find out about the [history.]
7	Tony:	[Yeah.]
8	Lisa:	[Right.]
9	Sara:	But before, the-=
10	Leader 1:	=O:::h.=
11	Tony:	=They can call me.

Tony and Sara, in complete agreement, quickly jump in to help Lisa construct her argument. When Lisa momentarily falters, presumably searching for the right words to complete her utterance (line 2), Tony completes her utterance for her (line 3). Sara then spells out the implications of Lisa's argument in lines 5–6. While overlap is minimal in this example, other features typical of swarming episodes are present: the affirmations of each other's contributions ("Yeah" and "Right" in lines 7 and 8) and Tony's joke (made in this moment of increased excitement and energy surrounding the collective construction of a focused argument) that newcomers to the neighborhood can always ask him about history anyway (line 11).

In swarming episodes, group members frequently jump in or pile on to elaborate on an initial comment before it is even completed. In another meeting, Lisa proposed that the group give a draft version of their brochure to high school students to receive preliminary feedback; she argued that it did not matter whether or not these students knew anything about Cityside, because they would be called on only to evaluate the writing itself. Before she is finished outlining her idea, her suggestion is quickly taken up by other group members:

(11)	1	Lisa:	I don't think it's relevant whether or not they know
	2		about the City[side, because] some people who=
	3	Mary:	[To make it like-]
	4	Lisa:	=even *live* here might not know about it. But just to
	5		tell us, you know, that sounds [*quee::r.*]
	6	Andrea:	[What they] *think*
	7		about it, like an expe:rim[ent, Citysiders=
	8	Mary:	[Like an objective=
	9	Andrea:	=reading] the brochure, [a con]*trol.*
	10	Mary:	=criticism.]
	11	Tony:	[That's *daggy.*]

Mary and Andrea, in enthusiastic support, simultaneously and independently draw the same analogy from Lisa's comments. Mary initiates her response ("To make it like" in line 3) prior to Andrea's response, but completes it ("Like an objective criticism" in line 8) only after Andrea has herself made a parallel connection ("like an experiment" in lines 6–7). Andrea then elaborates, making her own analogy more precise ("a control" in line 9), as Tony pitches in what was one of the group's ultimate marks of acceptance: "That's daggy" (line 10). This collective response, so tightly woven in time, linguistic form, and interpretive agreement, both indicates that the group is operating together "on the same wavelength" and marks the idea as one immediately acceptable to their ongoing project.

Heightened and simultaneous evaluations constituted another characteristic feature of swarming. Usually, when ideas were introduced by individual members, the group was restrained, withholding evaluative comments; often it fell to the group's leaders to respond to ideas or to solicit discussion from other members. Occasionally, however, as with the following idea, introduced by Sara, about using a flower motif to structure the brochure, the group immediately became animated:

```
(12)  1  Sara:        No, it's not that, I- it just- it was a thought. Okay, on
      2               the front page, you have a bu:d. [And then like you=
      3  Delia:                                     [Yeah, that's what I=
      4  Sara:        [=go through] all the bottom of the pages, and=
      5  Delia:       [=was thinking.]
      6  Observer:    [=Oh, that's neat.]
      7  Sara:        =instead of doing a film strip, you do lea:ves, but you
      8               could put [pictures in the leaves] and words and=
      9  Lisa:                  [Right, and that's good.]
     10  Sara:        =the last page it turns [into a flower,]
     11  Delia:                               [That's what I] was
     12               thinking [about.]
     13  Lisa:                 [and it] [says the Cityside.]
     14  Tony:                          [Alri:::ght].
     15  Observer:    That's [grea::::t.]
     16  Leader 1:           [There you] go, love it, write it down.
     17  Delia:       [That's just what I was thinking about.]
     18  Mary:        [That sounds pretty [good.]
     19  Leader 1:                        [That's another idea.]
     20  Andrea:                          [Hhh]hhh I lo:ve it, I'm thinking
     21               hhhhh.
```

Delia's repeated claims (and possible attempts to compete for the floor) that she too was thinking of Sara's idea (lines 3–5, 11–12, 17), whether or not they are true, have the effect of marking the concept as a valuable one and as one that is more than a single individual's suggestion. Five members of the group—the observer, the group leader, Tony, Lisa, and Mary—jump in with overlapping expressions of enthusiasm for Sara's idea. Lisa quickly starts to elaborate possibilities for the design suggested by Sara (line 13). Andrea, participating in the excitement with her laughter, makes fun of and imitates (lines 20–21) both the leader's "love it" (line 16) and Delia's multiple claims to co-authorship ("I'm thinking").

Swarming responses were followed either with the immediate acceptance of an idea, as in the above episode, or with protracted efforts to work out the initial critique or suggestion. In either case, swarming marked the centrality of the topic for the group's work. As in the story-chaining sequence discussed previously, I suggest that the simultaneity of responses had a radically different effect for participants than the possible alternative of a flat, linear series of nonoverlapping responses. Simultaneity, overlap, laughter, and joking, in other words, were neither accidental nor incidental; rather, the quick fire of supporting or colluding comments sealed these responses as group responses. Through this construction of group response, swarming played an important role in shaping the direction and pace of the group's task-focused interactions, as well as the involvement levels of its members.

Jam Sessions: Composing in Group

To this point, I have discussed noisy talk that is shaped by (or constituted as) what are essentially conversational activities—story-chaining and response sequences. Noisy talk (of a focused kind) also shaped, and was shaped by, the writing group's nonconversational activity. Some of the group's meetings were conducted as writing sessions. The group would gather around a computer terminal, and, as one member sat at the keyboard and typed, the group members would compose text word by word and line by line. In these "jam sessions," noisy talk that had features similar to those identified with the notion of the collaborative floor occurred regularly. Jam sessions involved considerable amounts of overlapping, simultaneous speech, co-constructions, relatively short turns, joking, and laughter.[9] As with sociorelational noisy talk, the group's adult leaders participated fully in the noisy talk that emerged during group composing. However, the adults' role in directing the group's work and in calling attention to specific writing problems was greater during the more orderly interaction that surrounded noisy talk in these composing sessions. In other words, noisy talk occurred at moments when the teen members were fully engaged in the task at hand and did not need any external adult-supplied direction or motivation.

Noisy talk in jam sessions was task-scripted talk: it was shaped by the process of dictating, editing, and inventing text, by the interactions between conversation and the print appearing on the computer monitor. Group members focused not so much on one another's talk, as they did in swarming episodes, but on the emergent text itself. Overlapping contributions were thus linked through the common focus and material of the group's editing attention, rather than through the joint construction of any single, collective argument. As the group read the writing on the screen, members would simultaneously throw out a variety of different suggestions and criticisms:

(13) 1 Sara: In our estimation, your choice is *pretty* limited. The
      2   majority of tee:ns have their ideas abou::t-
      3 Mary: Different community [centers.]
      4 Delia: [You can say] *many* of us
      5   ha[ve-]
      6 Sara: [*Wai*::t.] Now does *that*- that's phrased weird.
      7   The majority [(   ) of teens,]
      8 Lisa: [Community centers] should be-
      9   should come *after* [(   ) the dance clubs.]
     10 Sara: [have *their* ideas?]

In lines 1–3, Sara and Mary are reading a section of the brochure devoted to teen interests and activities off of the computer monitor. The group has previously decided that in order to reach and inspire potential teen readers of its brochure, it should emphasize in its writing that the brochure has been produced by teens; thus, Delia suggests changing "the majority of teens" to "many of us" (line 4). Sara meanwhile picks up on the peculiar phrasing of "The majority of teens have their ideas" (lines 6–7,10) and later suggests replacing this with "teens have ideas." Overlapping with Sara, Lisa proposes mentioning dance clubs before community centers (lines 8–9), because (as she goes on to explain) dance clubs are more likely to attract the attention of teen readers. Having quickly produced this succession of ideas, the group continued to discuss, for the next several seconds, the merits of each suggestion.

Text and talk, directive and question, recitation and invention were mixed in rapid and complex manner by group members as they participated in jam sessions. Sometimes individuals would read out the written beginnings of sentences and then attempt to improvise new endings orally, or they would latch onto the spoken utterances of others (recited or improvised) and attempt to extend these into complete and effective sentences. At other times, individuals would link not written text with talk, but talk with talk, as they combined the improvisations of other members. Alternatively, members could individually write out new versions and then read these to the rest of the group.

Several of these different strategies may be seen in the following example, in which the group works on another sentence in the teen section of its brochure:

(14) 1 Tony: Oh, all right. So:, all right, next sentence i:s-=
      2 Mary: =Okay, just like a bud awaits to burst into full bloom,
      3   so do our teens.
      4 Tony: I don't like it.
      5 Observer: So do [our teens what.]
      6 Andrea: [So do our teens] what.
      7 Delia: So do our teens await [to burst into full blossom.]
      8 Lisa: [So do our teens in the]
      9   process of maturing.
     10 Mary: Hhhhhh.
     11 Andrea: Yea::h, so do our teens await- maturing.
     12 Mary: But does a bud *wait*, [or does a bud (   ).]
     13 Observer: [Yeah, you don't want] await,
     14   right?
     15 X: Right?
     16 Mary: [So, what *do* we want?]
     17 Andrea: [So do our] teens [mature.]
     18 Mary: [So, you say just] like a bu::d,
     19   *burst* into full bloo:m,
     20 Andrea: So [do our teens] mature.
     21 Mary: [so do our teens.]
     22 X: Yea:h. . .
     23 Mary: Cause they're not waitin. Cause I know I'm not
     24   waiting. So get rid of await.

In line 2, Mary reads the sentence from the text on the computer screen. Following Tony's negative evaluation ("I don't like it," line 4), Andrea and the observer almost simultaneously highlight what they see as the main problem with the sentence—the ellipsis in the final clause (lines 5 and 6). Delia and Lisa offer overlapping and alternative elaborations of the problematic clause ("So do our teens await to burst" in line 7 and "So do our teens in the process of maturing" in lines 8–9); Andrea then combines both Delia's and Lisa's suggestions ("so do our teens await maturing" in line 11). Through this process, the problematic text ("so do our teens") is recited by five different group members.

The group then turns its attention to the problematic word choice in the text of "await" (or "wait"). Negotiation here takes a variety of forms: Mary asks a general question of whether the verb "wait" is appropriate for the subject "bud" (line 12); the observer affirms Mary's question as a valid one and issues an indirect directive to Tony sitting at the keyboard ("you don't want await, right?" in line 13); Andrea and Mary offer a couple of possible alternatives (lines 17, 18–19); and finally Mary makes a joke about the inappropriateness of "wait" and tells Tony directly to "get rid of" the offending word (lines 23–24). If talk works with and shapes text in this interaction, text can also be seen to be subtly shaping talk; in lines 16 and 18, Mary picks up the adverbial "so" from the text and uses it as a discourse marker in her interactions with the rest of the group—"So, what do we want?" and "So, you say just like a bud burst into full bloom."

Text produced in jam sessions was frequently collaborative down to the last word. In order to illustrate the way in which the group collectively worked through the initial suggestion of an individual member, I examine here the full course of developing a single sentence of text in the brochure. In the interaction in example 14 above, the group decided to incorporate the adverbial phrase "while in the process of maturing," first suggested by Lisa (lines 8–9). After doing some more rewriting, the group again paused to read and evaluate their work as it appeared on the computer monitor:

(15) 1   Mary: While in the process of maturing, teens realize that
      2   there are very little activities for them to- get
      3   actively involved in.
      4   Observer: How bout- [I don't like *teens*] realize, but, you=
      5   Leader 1:   [How bout very few.]
      6   Observer: = know, [*we*.]
      7   Delia: [We.]

In lines 1–3, Mary is reading the already written text. As was typical with jam sessions, the reading generated simultaneous and different responses from the group. The observer and Delia suggest changing "teens" to "we" (lines 4–6 and 7), again for the purpose of highlighting the shared identity of the brochure's authors and their intended readers. At the same time, the group leader suggests changing "very little" to "very few" (line 5).

The group tried to incorporate the change suggested by Delia and the observer, orally working through how the text should be rewritten:

(16) 1   Leader 1:   While in the process of maturing,
      2   Andrea: Wait a- [wait a minute.]
      3   Mary: [While in the process] of [maturing.]
      4   Leader 1:   [we realize] tha:t-
      5   [there a:re,]
      6   Delia: [While *in*] the pro:cess [of] maturing-
      7   Andrea: [Speak.]
      8   Leader 1:   that [there are-]
      9   Sara: [That] we need more.

In a chorus of overlapping recitations, first the leader (line 1), then Mary (line 3), and then Delia (line 6) read out the opening adverbial phrase of the written text.

To these recitals, the leader adds the first alteration, changing "teens realize" to "we realize" (line 4). Sara and the leader then offer overlapping and alternative possibilities for changing the next part of the sentence: the leader suggests "that there are" (line 8) while Sara proposes "That we need more" (line 9).

Lisa had pointed out shortly after Delia and the observer's initial suggestion that it sounded repetitive to keep saying "we" in the text. As the group started to generate an excess of "we's" in its revisions, Tony reminded them of this critique by playfully producing a rising string of "we" sound effects (line 1 in the example below). The group then turned its attention to the problem of reducing the number of "we's":

(17) 1   Tony: We, we, we, we, [we::, WE:::, WE:::::.]
      2   Lisa: [(   ).]
      3   Leader 1:   Or, or we are in the process of maturing and
      4   realize-
      5   Observer: Yeah.
      6   Leader 1:   Rather [than] an- and take that we out=
      7   Observer: [And realize.]
      8   Leader 1:   [=cause we're gonna-]
      9   Tony: [That's right.]
      10 Mary: We are in the process of maturing and realize that
      11   there are very little activities for *us* to get actively
      12   involved in.

The leader uses ellipsis to get rid of one "we" before the verb "realize" (line 3), and her suggestion is supported by both the observer (lines 5, 7) and Tony (line 9). Mary then produces a final version of the sentence that has a single "we" in it (which she manages to do by introducing the accented accusative "us," lines 10–12). This single sentence is thoroughly collaborative: seven of eight group members present at this particular meeting (Delia, the observer, the group leader, Lisa, Mary, Sara, and Tony) participated directly in its production.[10]

The youth writing group used a variety of authorial arrangements for actually writing text. Members would write individually, both at home and during meeting time; at meetings, the group would sometimes split up into pairs to compose; and, as was the case at the meeting examined here, the group would write together in jam sessions. (Text was also constantly shaped, of course, by general negotiations and discussions.) What was the significance, then, of jam sessions for the group's writing process when compared with these other arrangements? The efficiency and productivity of jam sessions are difficult to judge. In the meeting examined here, the group covered a lot of ground, considering several different versions of the teen section of the brochure and dealing with problems in wording, in tone, in choice of metaphors, in realism of assumptions, and in the practicality of their written suggestions. But the process was also tedious; members and leaders grew frustrated at times, as arguments went around in circles and as what seemed like hours were spent tinkering with a single sentence. The intensity of group concentration in jam sessions was difficult to sustain, and the focus of some group members frequently had to be called up by others.

The real significance of jam sessions came through in the group members' final evaluations of the project. Members were asked in these final evaluations whether they felt a sense of ownership for the brochure, whether this sense of ownership was felt individually or as a group, and, if they didn't feel a sense of ownership, who they felt owned the brochure. The following are the responses of the four members who filled out the evaluations:

"We did, no page was just one person."	(Mary)
"Everybody had a little piece of each section."	(Tony)
"As a group."	(Delia)
"Whoever did page mostly, but others' ideas intertwined."	(Lisa)

Many factors in the group's work, of course, contributed to such evaluations. But jam sessions were just those occasions that produced a collaborative group voice directly engaged with the production of text. As seen here, even the creation of a single sentence emerged as a collective group effort. The conversational features of latching, co-construction, overlap, and simultaneous speech became central resources in producing a thoroughly collaborative piece of writing.

Conclusion

In isolating these three different types of noisy talk, I have pointed to the varying functions of such talk and to the different frames and activity-sequences within which such talk may be found. The nature of the group's collaboration in producing noisy talk varied across activity-sequences. Group members built off one another's experiences in sociorelational banter; they seized on one another's arguments and ideas in swarming; and their talk in composing sessions helped them co-construct group textual inventions (surface language). As a conversational resource, noisy talk had a number of different (if overlapping) roles to play. Sharing both topic and time in talk helped the group construct a sense of shared experience; the increased excitement and energy of overlapping and simultaneous speech helped provide immediate and clear indications of close group alignment and of the centrality of certain ideas to their collective work; and co-construction, latching, overlap, and simultaneous speech became group resources for producing thoroughly collaborative text.

Story chains, group responses, and group composing are examples of activity-sequences that motivate noisy talk and are themselves constructed out of noisy talk. Noisy talk is motivated by other activity-sequences as well: in the youth writing group, for example, stretches of overlap and simultaneous talk (marked by the absence of increased levels of excitement) also occurred when the group collaboratively constructed lists of restaurants in the Cityside neighborhood, Cityside sights and attractions, and possible interviewees. Listing, in fact, occurs in several of the interactions discussed previously: in the story-chaining sequence where the teens rhyme off the various parts of their bodies they have broken (example 4) and in the swarming episode where the teens begin to list their favorite slang words (example 8). The collaborative floor may, at least on some occasions, be a "listing floor."

In discussing the interaction of collaborative endeavor and conversational structure, I have implied that noisy talk in the meetings of the youth writing group was associated with speakers' identities as teenagers. But overlap, simultaneous speech, co-construction, and the whole collaborative floor concept have been widely associated with women's ways of speaking (Coates 1995, Edelsky 1993, Kalcik 1975). Thus, it is quite possible that data analyzed here in effect reveal the gendered nature of noisy talk (seven of the group's nine members were female). If, however, the noisy talk discussed here is associated with speakers' gender identities, it also characterizes a site constituted as the meeting place of a *youth* writing group, in which members were explicitly oriented to their identities (or nonidentities) as youths.

Along with the teen members, the adult leaders of this group participated in the noisy talk—more so during group composing sessions and sociorelational banter than in swarming episodes. The neighborhood-based organization had, however, come into being with a strongly held conviction by leaders that the writing group was a youth-based, youth-oriented site—in deliberate contrast to other institutional sites (such as schools) in which youths were typically expected to orient to the ways of their institutional leaders. These adults had, in other words, attempted to create what Heath and McLaughlin (1994:475) call a "border zone"—"a place for inner-city young people not only to be but to take an active role in a variety of situations within the institutions while they look both ways, to their own streets of the inner city and to the mainstream institutions of employment and education." Talk, as Heath and McLaughlin note, is central to the successful creation of such border zones. In their effort, adult leaders had to provide space for youths to pace and shape conversational interactions, even as they attempted to guide youths into knowing and being able to participate in mainstream institutional roles, rights, and responsibilities.

The importance of conversational interaction to the successful constitution of the writing group as a youth-oriented site can perhaps best be seen in the final project evaluations written by the youth members themselves. Teens were asked whether they felt their experience with the writing group differed from their experience of school and, if so, how. They were also asked how they felt the adult leaders had treated them. Everyone agreed the group experience was different from school experience, and everyone agreed they had been treated as equals: Mary said the group was "more relaxed"; Delia said that "talking to everybody" was fun; Tony wrote that he felt the teens "could say everything" they wanted; Lisa liked that "we got to bullcrap for a while" and appreciated the fact that the group got to "sit in a circle and see everyone's expressions." Recalling Andrea's comment, quoted before, in which she explained what she liked about the group—"Yeah, this is real informal, we're all sitting here talking at the same time"—I suggest that noisy talk was at least one factor that led Tony to say of the youth writing group at the very end: "It was like nine people smooth all the way through." Noisy talk, then, helped the Cityside youth group get its writing done, but it also helped make the Cityside writing group a place for youths.

NOTES

The data analyzed here come from Shirley Brice Heath and Milbrey W. McLaughlin's multiyear research project, "Language, Socialization, and Neighborhood-Based Organizations," funded by the Spencer Foundation. I would like to thank Shirley Brice Heath for giving me access to the language data from that project and for help in conceptualizing the frame for this chapter. I would also like to thank Carolyn Adger, Susan Hoyle, Elizabeth Traugott, and Keli Yerian for their comments on earlier versions of this chapter.

1. The rhetoric of worker empowerment with which American managers have introduced collaborative work teams has been shown to be of questionable merit (see Grenier 1988, Mumby & Stohl 1991, Parker & Slaughter 1988). For the purposes of this chapter, however, it is enough to note that critiques of collaborative work teams and participatory management structures as they currently exist in American workplaces are usually made in the name of the ideal of collaborative work.

2. This statement is more true of Coates's analysis than of Edelsky's. Edelsky, as may be seen from the quotation above, recognizes that collaborative floors are sometimes involved with "talk as serious business." In fact, Edelsky (1993:217) states explicitly that the difference between single and collaborative floors "is not simply the difference between meeting talk and conversations." However, this statement is made as a caveat to her main argument; Edelsky provides little indication of how and where collaborative floors participate in task-driven talk.

3. Quotations in this section of the chapter are taken from community center documents describing the literacy program.

4. Focused noisy talk can certainly have negative aspects, as will be discussed below; for example, swarming has the potential to be a threatening experience for some, and the cacophony of voices in group composing sessions can be overwhelming.

5. Tannen (1984:100) uses the term "story round" to refer to the same phenomenon: "a particular kind of story cluster, in which speakers exchange stories of personal experiences that illustrate similar points."

6. Tannen's (1989:96) observation that, through repetition, "the individual speaks through the group, and the group speaks through the individual" seems particularly apt here. Repetition, as she points out, "not only ties parts of discourse to other parts, but it bonds participants to the discourse and to each other, linking individual speakers in a conversation and in relationships" (1989:51–52).

7. Such abrupt and explicit topic shifts were regularly used by the group to shift (back) into task-focused work. Both youth members and adult leaders would call for the group to "focus." While such calls were generally successful, the boundaries between talk-as-play and talk-as-business were not rigidly defined for the group. Thus, in this case, Lisa, after initiating the shift in frame (line 6), parodies herself as she playfully suggests her own casual phrasing for the observer to use (line 9). Group members would often stand back to joke about their ongoing work; they would also draw on stray conversation in constructing arguments (see note 10).

8. Swarming episodes such as this one, however, have the potential to be quite threatening. Such confrontational swarmings occurred three times in this meeting with the visiting lecturer. These episodes did not seem to reflect any real hostility or conflict—the teens later all gave very positive evaluations of their interactions with this lecturer—but rather were the interactions of a collection of individuals who had formed themselves into a group with an outsider. Even when not confrontational, swarming can have the effect of eliminating the possibility of dissent or disagreement.

9. I borrow the term "jam session" from Coates (1995).

10. The gradual emergence of this single sentence of text evokes Bakhtin's (1984, 1986) discussions of "multivoicedness" and "dialogicity." Bakhtin draws a distinction between the notion of "utterance"—the concrete turns at speech (or writing) of specific individuals—

and that of "voice," which he describes as a socioideological viewpoint that may represent a collectivity, an epoch, a speech genre, or an individual (e.g., see Bakhtin 1984:184). Utterances, writes Bakhtin, (1986:124), may contain "voices that are sometimes infinitely distant, unnamed, almost impersonal," as well as voices "resounding nearby and simultaneously"—voices, in the latter case, that may be the repeated or constructed utterances of other speakers. Bakhtin was interested, for the most part, in literary texts in which a single author orchestrates a number of different "voices." The neighborhood brochure produced by the youth writing group, on the other hand, was composed not only of multiple voices, but of multiple utterances (multiple authors) as well. The orchestration of voices (in Bakhtin's sense) may be seen more clearly elsewhere in the writing group's work. At one point (following the interaction shown in example 14), the group combined the suggestions of two of its members to produce the following introduction to the teen section: "Hey teens, what's up! We are like buds ready to burst into full bloom." Lisa pointed out that this text was made strange by the contradictory voices it contained. Referring to a story the observer had told during the opening moments of the meeting (a story about the absurdity of a dance performance in which teens with very modern feathered haircuts had been dressed up in traditional Hungarian costumes), Lisa explained her reasoning:

1	Lisa:	You know what that sounds goofy, not the: sentence
2		itself, but if you say, hi:: teens, what's up, we as buds are-
		((laughter and general agreement from group members))
3	Lisa:	We're gonna have to cut that out, because you know what,
4		that's like what (the observer) was just saying. How there
5		was these dancers, and they were wearing these OLD-
6		FASHIONED costumes with their hair sticking up. And
7		that's like mo:dern, and we can't be saying that with
8		bu::ds, you know what I'm saying?

Agreeing with Lisa, the group decided to eliminate the "modern" voice and continue with the "old-fashioned" voice; by the interaction shown in example 15, "Hey teens what's up! We are like buds ready to burst into full bloom" had become "We are like buds waiting to burst into full bloom. While in the process of maturing, teens realize that there are very little activities for them to get actively involved in." The struggle to incorporate both a modern (young, fun, colloquial) voice and an old-fashioned (poetic, journalistic, serious) voice re-occurred throughout the group's work on the teen section. But in this particular instance, the combining of multiple utterances (authors) led to the elimination of multiple voices. The fundamental nonequivalency of utterance and voice should, therefore, be central to our interpretations and evaluations of collaboratively (and singly) produced work and should stand as a reminder of the ever-present reality of committee prose.

References

Adger, Carolyn Temple. 1984. Communicative competence in the culturally diverse class-room. Ph.D. dissertation, Georgetown University.

———. 1986. When difference does not conflict: Successful arguments between Black and Vietnamese classmates. *Text* 6:223–37.

———. 1987. Accommodating cultural differences in conversational style: A case study. In *Research in second language learning: Focus on the classroom*, ed. James P. Lantolf and Angela Lobarca, 159–72. Norwood, NJ: Ablex.

Adger, Carolyn Temple, Maya Kalyanpur, Dana Blount Peterson, and Teresa L. Bridger. 1995. *Engaging students*. Thousand Oaks, CA: Couvier.

Adger, Carolyn Temple, and Walt Wolfram. 1993. Demythologizing the home/school language dichotomy: Sociolinguistic reality and instructional practice. Paper presented at the Annual Meeting, American Educational Research Association, Atlanta.

Adger, Carolyn Temple, Walt Wolfram, Jennifer Detwyler, and Beth Harry. 1993. Confronting dialect minority issues in special education: Reactive and proactive perspectives. In *Proceedings of the Third National Research Symposium on Limited English Proficient Student Issues: Focus on middle and high school issues*. Washington, DC: U.S. Department of Education, Office of Bilingual Education and Minority Languages Affairs.

Adler, Patricia A., Steven J. Kless, and Peter Adler. 1992. Socialization to gender roles: Popularity among elementary school boys and girls. *Sociology of Education* 65:169–87.

Andersen, Elaine Slosberg. 1990. *Speaking with style: The sociolinguistic skills of children*. New York: Routledge.

Andrews, Vernon Lee. n.d. Black bodies—white control: The Black male athlete, media discourse and the contested terrain of white sportsmanship. Unpublished paper, Department of Sociology, University of Wisconsin-Madison.

Anzaldúa, Gloria. 1987. *Borderlands/La frontera: The new mestiza*. San Francisco: Spinsters/Aunt Lute.

Au, Katherine Hu-Pei. 1980. Participation structures in a reading lesson with Hawaiian children: Analysis of a culturally appropriate instructional event. *Anthropology and Education Quarterly* 11:91–115.

Auer, Peter. 1984. *Bilingual conversation*. Amsterdam: John Benjamins.

Ayoub, Millicent, and Stephen Barnett. 1961. Ritualized verbal insult in white high school culture. *Journal of American Folklore* 78:337–44.

Babcock, Barbara A. 1978. Introduction. In *The reversible world: Symbolic inversion in art and society*, ed. Barbara A. Babcock, 13–36. Ithaca, NY: Cornell University Press.

Bakhtin, Mikhail. 1981. *The dialogic imagination*, ed. Michael Holquist, trans. Caryl Emerson and Michael Holquist. Austin: University of Texas Press.

———. 1984. *Problems of Dostoevsky's poetics*, ed. and trans. Caryl Emerson. Minneapolis: University of Minnesota Press.

———. 1986. *Speech genres and other late essays*, ed. Caryl Emerson and Michael Holquist, trans. Vern McGee. Austin: University of Texas Press

Barnes, Melanie K., and Anita L. Vangelisti. 1995. Speaking in a double-voice: Role-making as influence in preschoolers' fantasy play situations. *Research on Language and Social Interaction* 28:351–89.

Barth, Fredrik. 1969. Introduction. *Ethnic groups and boundaries*, ed. Fredrik Barth, 9–38. Boston: Little, Brown.

Bateson, Gregory. 1972. *Steps to an ecology of mind*. New York: Ballantine Books.

Bateson, Mary Catherine. 1989. *Composing a life*. New York: Atlantic Monthly Press.

———. 1994. *Peripheral visions: Learning along the way*. New York: Harper Collins.

Baugh, John. 1983. *Black street speech: Its history, structure, and survival*. Austin: University of Texas Press.

Beach, King. 1992. The role of leading and non-leading activities in transforming arithmetic between school and work. Paper presented to the American Educational Research Association, San Francisco.

Beach, Richard, and Susan Hynds, eds. 1990. *Developing discourse practices in adolescence and adulthood*. Norwood, NJ: Ablex.

Bean, Frank, and Marta Tienda. 1987. *The Hispanic population of the United States*. New York: Russell Sage.

Bell, Allan. 1984. Language style as audience design. *Language in Society* 13:145–204.

Bennett, Adrian. 1981. Interruption and the interpretation of conversation. *Discourse Processes* 4:171–88.

Bereiter, Carl, and Siegfried Engelmann. 1966. *Teaching disadvantaged children in the preschool*. Englewood Cliffs, NJ: Prentice-Hall.

Bernstein, Basil. 1971. *Class, codes, and control*. London: Routledge.

———. 1972. A sociolinguistic approach to socialization: With some reference to educability. In *Directions in sociolinguistics: The ethnography of communication*, ed. John J. Gumperz and Dell Hymes, 465–97. New York: Holt, Rinehart & Winston.

Best, Raphaela. 1983. *We've all got scars*. Bloomington: Indiana University Press.

Biber, Douglas, and Edward Finegan, eds. 1994. *Sociolinguistic perspectives on register*. New York: Oxford University Press.

Bing, Janet M., and Victoria L. Bergvall. 1996. The question of questions: Beyond binary thinking. In *Rethinking language and gender research: Theory and practice*, ed. Victoria Bergvall, Janet M. Bing, and Alice F. Freed. New York: Longman.

Blass, Regina. 1990. *Relevance relations in discourse: A study with special reference to Sissala*. New York: Cambridge University Press.

Blyler, Nancy, and Charlotte Thralls, eds. 1993. *Professional communication: The social perspective*. Newbury Park, CA: Sage.

Boden, Deirdre. 1994. *The business of talk: Organizations in action*. Cambridge, MA: Polity Press.

Boggs, Stephen T. 1985. *Speaking, relating, and learning: A study of Hawaiian children at home and at school*. Norwood, NJ: Ablex.

———. 1990. The role of routines in the evolution of children's peer talk. *Conversational organization and its development*, ed. Bruce Dorval, 101–30. Norwood, NJ: Ablex.

Bouvier, Leon, and Vernon Briggs. 1988. *The population and labor force of New York: 1990–2050*. Washington, DC: Population Reference Bureau.

Bradac, James J., Anthony Mulac, and Sandra A. Thompson. 1995. Men's and women's use of intensifiers and hedges in problem-solving interaction: Molar and molecular analyses. *Research on Language in Social Interaction* 28:93–116.

Brenneis, Donald, and Laura Lein. 1977. "You fruithead": A sociolinguistic approach to children's dispute settlement. In *Child Discourse*, ed. Susan Ervin-Tripp and Claudia Mitchell-Kernan, 49–65. New York: Academic Press.

Brown, Penelope, and Stephen C. Levinson. 1987. *Politeness: Some universals in language usage*. New York: Cambridge University Press.

Bruffee, Kenneth. 1984. Collaborative learning and the "conversation of mankind." *College English* 46:635–52.

Bruner, Jerome S. 1983. *Child's talk: Learning to use language*. New York: Oxford University Press.

Bryant, Brenda K. 1985. The neighborhood walk: Sources of support in middle childhood. *Monographs of the Society for Research in Child Development* 50(3), Serial No. 210.

Burbank, Victoria. 1994. *Fighting women: Anger and aggression in aboriginal Australia*. Berkeley: University of California Press.

Burns, Allan F. 1980. Interactive features in Yucatec Mayan narratives. *Language in Society* 9:307–19.

Caine, Renate Nummela, and Geoffrey Caine. 1991. *Making connections: Teaching and the human brain*. Alexandria, VA: Association for Supervision and Curriculum Development.

Cameron, Deborah. 1992. "Respect, please!": Investigating race, power and language. In *Researching language: Issues of power and method*, ed. Deborah Cameron, Elizabeth Frazer, Penelope Harvey, M. B. H. Rampton, and Kay Richardson, 113–30. New York: Routledge.

Cameron, Deborah, Elizabeth Frazer, Penelope Harvey, M. B. H. Rampton, and Kay Richardson. 1992. *Researching language: Issues of power and method*. New York: Routledge.

Cazden, Courtney B. 1988. *Classroom discourse: The language of teaching and learning*. Portsmouth, NH: Heinemann.

———. 1996. Communicative competence 1966–1996. Paper presented to the American Association for Applied Linguistics, Chicago.

Cazden, Courtney, Vera John, and Dell Hymes, eds. 1972. *Functions of language in the classroom*. New York: Teachers College Press.

Chávez, Linda. 1991. *Out of the barrio: Toward a new politics of Hispanic assimilation*. New York: Basic Books.

Cheshire, Jenny. 1978. Present tense verbs in Reading English. In *Sociolinguistic patterns in British English*, ed. Peter Trudgill, 52–68. London: Edward Arnold.

———. 1982. Linguistic variation and social function. In *Sociolinguistic variation in speech communities*, ed. Suzanne Romaine, 153–66. London: Edward Arnold.

———. 1991. Variation in the use of *ain't* in an urban British English dialect. In *Dialects of English: Studies in grammatical variation*, ed. Peter Chambers and J. K. Trudgill, 54–73. London: Longman.

Chomsky, Carol. 1969. *The acquisition of syntax in children from 5 to 10*. Cambridge, MA: MIT Press.

Chomsky, Noam. 1972. *Language and mind*. New York: Harcourt Brace Jovanovich.

Cicourel, Aaron V. 1970. The acquisition of social structure: Toward a developmental sociology of language and meaning. In *Understanding everyday life*, ed. Jack D. Douglas, 136–68. Chicago: Aldine.

Clark, Herbert H., and Edward F. Schaefer. 1987. Collaborating on contributions to conversations. *Language and Cognitive Processes* 2:19–41.

Clayman, Stephen E. 1992. Footing in the achievement of neutrality: The case of news-interview discourse. In *Talk at work: Interaction in institutional settings*, ed. Paul Drew and John Heritage, 163–98. New York: Cambridge University Press.

Coates, Jennifer. 1989. Gossip revisited: Language in all-female groups. In *Women in their speech communities: New perspectives on language and sex*, ed. Jennifer Coates and Deborah Cameron, 94–122. New York: Longman.

———. 1991.Women's cooperative talk: A new kind of conversational duet? *Anglistentag 1990, Margurg 1991 Conference Proceedings*, 296–311. Tübingen: Max Niemeyer Verlag.

———. 1994. The language of the professions: Discourse and career. In *Women and career: Themes and issues in advanced industrial societies*, ed. Julia Evetts, 72–86. London: Longman.

———. 1995. The construction of a collaborative floor in women's friendly talk. Paper presented at LSA Summer Institute, Albuquerque, New Mexico, July.

———. 1996. *Women talk: Conversation between women friends*. Cambridge, MA: Blackwell.

Cohen, Elizabeth G. 1984. Talking and working together: Status, interaction and learning. In *Instructional groups in the classroom: Organization and process*, ed. Penny Peterson and Louise C. Wilkinson. New York: Academic Press.

Collins, James. 1988. Language and class in minority education. *Anthropology and Education Quarterly* 19:299–326.

Cook-Gumperz, Jenny. 1977. Situated instructions: Language socialization of school-age children. In *Child discourse*, ed. Susan Ervin-Tripp and Claudia Mitchell-Kernan, 103–21. New York: Academic Press.

———. 1986. Keeping it together: Text and context in children's language socialization. In *Languages and linguistics: The interdependence of theory, data, and application*, ed. Deborah Tannen and James E. Alatis, 337–56. Washington, DC: Georgetown University Press.

———. 1995. Reproducing the discourse of mothering. In *Gender articulated: Language and the socially constructed self*, ed. Kira Hall and Mary Bucholtz, 401–19. New York: Routledge.

Corsaro, William. 1977. The clarification request as a feature of adult interactive styles with young children. *Language in Society* 6:183–207.

———. 1979. "We're friends, right?": Children's access rituals in a nursery school. *Language in Society* 8:315–37.

———. 1985. *Friendship and peer culture in the early years*. Norwood, NJ: Ablex.

———. 1994. Discussion, debate, and friendship processes: Peer dispute in U.S. and Italian nursery schools. *Sociology of Education* 67:1–26.

Corsaro, William A., and Thomas A. Rizzo. 1990. Disputes in the peer culture of American and Italian nursery-school children. In *Conflict talk: Sociolinguistic investigations of arguments in conversations*, ed. Allen D. Grimshaw, 21–66. New York: Cambridge University Press.

Coupland, Justine, Jeffrey Robinson, and Nikolas Coupland. 1994. Frame negotiation in doctor-elderly patient consultations. *Discourse and Society* 5:89–124.

Cross, Geoffrey. 1994. *Collaboration and conflict: A contextual exploration of group writing and positive emphasis*. Cresskill, NJ: Hampton Press.

Crystal, David, and Derek Davy. 1969. *Investigating English style*. Bloomington: Indiana University Press.

Csikszentimihalyi, Mihaly, and Reed Larson. 1984. *Being adolescent: Conflict and growth in the teenage years*. New York: Basic Books.

Davidson, Neil, and Tony Worsham, eds. 1992. *Enhancing thinking through cooperative learning*. New York: Teachers College Press.

Delpit, Lisa. 1988. The silenced dialogue: Power and pedagogy in educating other people's children. *Harvard Educational Review* 54:280–98.

———. 1995. *Other people's children: Cultural conflict in the classroom*. New York: New Press.

Deprez, K., and K. Persoons. 1984. On the identity of Flemish high school students in Brussels. *Journal of Language and Social Psychology* 3:273–96.

Dittman, A. T. 1972. Developmental factors in conversational behavior. *Journal of Communication* 22:404–33.

Dorr-Bremme, Donald W. 1990. Contextualization cues in the classroom: Discourse regulation and social control functions. *Language in Society* 19:379–402.

Dorval, Bruce, and Carol O. Eckerman. 1984. Developmental trends in the quality of conversation achieved by small groups of acquainted peers. *Monographs of the Society for Research in Child Development* 49(2), Serial No. 206.

Drew, Paul, and John Heritage, eds. 1992. *Talk at work: Interaction in institutional settings*. New York: Cambridge University Press.

Dumesnil, James, and Bruce Dorval. 1989. The development of talk-activity frames that foster perspective-focused talk among peers. *Discourse Processes* 12:193–225.

Duncan, S. 1972. Some signals and rules for taking speaking turns in conversations. *Journal of Personality and Social Psychology* 23:283–93.

Dundes, Alan, Jerry W. Leach, and Bora Ozkok. 1986. The strategy of Turkish boys' verbal dueling rhymes. In *Directions in sociolinguistics*, ed. John J. Gumperz and Dell Hymes, 130–60. Oxford: Basil Blackwell.

Duran, Richard P., and Margaret H. Szymanski. 1995. Cooperative learning interaction and construction of activity. *Discourse Processes* 19:149–64.

Duranti, Alessandro, and Charles Goodwin, eds. 1992. *Rethinking context: Language as an interactive phenomenon*. New York: Cambridge University Press.

Dyson, Michael Eric. 1995. *Making Malcolm: The myth and meaning of Malcolm X*. New York: Oxford University Press.

Eckert, Penelope. 1988. Adolescent social structure and the spread of linguistic change. *Language in Society* 17:183–207.

———. 1989a. *Jocks and burnouts: Social categories and identity in the high school*. New York: Teachers College Press.

———. 1989b. The whole woman: Sex and gender differences in variation. *Language Variation and Change* 1:245–67.

———. 1993. Cooperative competition in adolescent "girl talk." In *Gender and conversational interaction*, ed. Deborah Tannen, 32–61. New York: Oxford University Press.

Eckert, Penelope, and Sally McConnell-Ginet. 1992. Communities of practice: Where language, gender, and power all live. In *Locating power: Proceedings of the Second Berkeley Women and Language Conference*, ed. Kira Hall, Mary Bucholtz, and Birch Moonwomon, 89–99. Berkeley: Berkeley Women and Language Group, University of California.

———. 1995. Constructing meaning, constructing selves: Snapshots of language, gender, and class from Belten High. In *Gender articulated: Language and the socially constructed self*, ed. Kira Hall and Mary Bucholtz, 469–507. New York: Routledge.

Edelsky, Carole. 1977. Acquisition of an aspect of communicative competence: Learning what it means to talk like a lady. In *Child discourse*, ed. Susan Ervin-Tripp and Claudia Mitchell-Kernan, 225–43. New York: Academic Press.

———. 1993. Who's got the floor?" In *Gender and conversational interaction*, ed. Deborah Tannen, 189–227. New York: Oxford University Press.

Eder, Donna. 1985. The cycle of popularity: Interpersonal relations among female adolescents. *Sociology of Education* 58:154–65.

———. 1988. Building cohesion through collaborative narration. *Social Psychology Quarterly* 51:225–35.

———. 1990. Serious and playful disputes: Variation in conflict talk among female adolescents. In *Conflict talk: Sociolinguistic investigations of arguments in conversations*, ed. Allen D. Grimshaw, 67–84. New York: Cambridge University Press.

———. 1991. The role of teasing in adolescent peer culture. In *Sociological studies of child development, Vol. 4*, ed. S. Cahill, 181–97. Greenwich, CT: JAI Press.

———. 1992. Girls' talk about romance and sexuality. Paper presented at Alice in Wonderland: The First International Conference on Girls and Girlhood, Amsterdam.

———. 1993. "Go get ya a French!": Romantic and sexual teasing among adolescent girls. In *Gender and conversational interaction*, ed. Deborah Tannen, 17–31. New York: Oxford University Press.

———. 1995. *School talk: Gender and adolescent culture.* New Brunswick, NJ: Rutgers University Press.

Eder, Donna, and Janet Lynne Enke. 1991. The structure of gossip: Opportunities and constraints on collective expression among adolescents. *American Sociological Review* 56:495–508.

Edwards, Jane A., and Martin D. Lampert, eds. 1993. *Talking data: Transcription and coding in discourse research.* Hillsdale, NJ: Erlbaum.

Eisenberg, Ann, and Catherine Garvey. 1981. Children's use of verbal strategies in resolving conflict. *Discourse Processes* 4:149–70.

Eisikovits, Edina. 1991a. Variation in subject-verb agreement in Inner Sydney English. In *English around the world: Sociolinguistic perspectives*, ed. Jenny Cheshire, 235–55. New York: Cambridge University Press.

———. 1991b. Variation in the lexical verb in Inner Sydney English. In *Dialects of English: Studies in grammatical variation*, ed. Peter Trudgill and J. K. Chambers, 120–42. London and New York: Longman.

Emihovich, Catherine. 1986. Argument as status assertion: Contextual variations in children's disputes. *Language in Society* 15:485–500.

Erickson, Frederick. 1984. Rhetoric, anecdote, and rhapsody: Coherence strategies in a conversation among black American adolescents. In *Coherence in spoken and written discourse*, ed. Deborah Tannen, 81–154. Norwood, NJ: Ablex.

Erickson, Frederick, and Gerald Mohatt. 1982. Cultural organization of participation structures in two classrooms of Indian students. In *Doing the ethnography of schooling*, ed. George D. Spindler. New York: Holt, Rinehart, and Winston.

Erickson, Frederick, and Jeffrey Shultz. 1982. *The counselor as gatekeeper: Social interaction in interviews.* New York: Academic Press.

Ervin-Tripp, Susan. 1977. Wait for me, roller skate! In *Child discourse*, ed. Susan Ervin-Tripp and Claudia Mitchell-Kernan, 165–88. New York: Academic Press.

Esteves, Sandra María. 1984. *A bilingual tropical downpour.* Bronx, NY: African Caribbean Poetry Theater.

Evaldsson, Ann-Carita. 1993. *Play, disputes and social order.* Linköping: Department of Communication Studies, Linköping University, Linköping Studies in Arts and Sciences, No. 93.

Fairclough, Norman. 1992. *Critical language awareness*. London: Longman.

Falk, Jane. 1980. The conversational duet. *Proceedings of the Sixth Annual Meeting of the Berkeley Linguistics Society* 6:507–14.

Ferguson, Charles. 1983. Sports announcer talk: Syntactic aspects of register variation. *Language in Society* 12:153–72.

———. 1985. Editor's introduction. *Discourse Processes* (Special issue: Special Language Registers) 8:391–94.

Fernández, Micho. 1972. A glossary of Spanglish terms. *New York Magazine* August, 7:46.

Fine, Gary Alan. 1981. Friends, impression management, and preadolescent behavior. In *The development of children's friendships*, ed. Steven R. Asher and John M. Gottman, 29–52. Cambridge University Press.

Fine, Michelle. 1992. Sexuality, schooling, and the adolescent female: The missing discourse of desire. *Harvard Educational Review* 58:29–53.

Flax, Jane. 1990. *Thinking fragments: Psychoanalysis, feminism, and postmodernism in the contemporary West*. Berkeley: University of California Press.

Fleck, Ludwik. 1935/1979. *Genesis and development of a scientific fact*. Chicago: University of Chicago Press.

Flores, Juan, and George Yudice. 1990. Living borders/Buscando America: Languages of Latino self-formation. *Social Text* 24;8(2):57–84.

Florida Center for Children and Youth. 1990. *Report on conditions of children in Florida*. Tallahassee, FL.

Foley, Douglas. 1990. *Learning capitalist culture: Deep in the heart of Tejas*. Philadelphia: University of Pennsylvania Press.

Fordham, Signithia. 1993. "Those loud Black girls": (Black) women, silence, and gender "passing" in the academy. *Anthropology and Education Quarterly* 24:3–32.

———. 1996. *Blacked out: Dilemmas of race, identity and success at Capital High*. Chicago: University of Chicago Press.

Forman, Janis, ed. 1992. *New visions of collaborative writing*. Portsmouth, NH: Heinemann.

Foucault, Michel. 1980. *Power/knowledge: Selected interviews and other writings 1972–77*, ed. Colin Gordon. Brighton, England: Harvester.

Frake, Charles O. 1977. Plying frames can be dangerous: Some reflections on methodology in cognitive anthropology. *Quarterly Newsletter of the Institute for Comparative Human Development* 1:1–7.

Frank, Anne. 1958. *The diary of a young girl*. New York: Modern Library Editions.

Freed, Alice F. 1995. Language and gender: Review essay. In *Annual Review of Applied Linguistics*, ed. William Grabe, 3–22. New York: Cambridge University Press.

Friedman, Jonathan. 1992. The past in the future: History and the politics of identity. *American Anthropologist* 94:837–59.

Gal, Susan. 1988. The political economy of code choice. In *Codeswitching: Anthropological and sociolinguistic perspectives*, ed. Monica Heller, 245–64. New York: Mouton de Gruyter.

Gall, Meredith. 1984. Synthesis of research on teachers' questioning. *Educational Leadership* 42:40–49.

Gallagher, T., and H. Craig. 1987. An investigation of pragmatic connectives within preschool peer interaction. *Journal of Pragmatics* 11:27–37.

Gardner, Howard. 1983. *Frames of mind: The theory of multiple intelligences*. New York: Basic Books.

————. 1993. *Creating minds: An anatomy of creativity seen through the lives of Freud, Einstein, Picasso, Stravinsky, Eliot, Graham, and Gandhi*. New York: Basic Books.

Garvey, Catherine. 1975. Requests and responses in children's speech. *Journal of Child Language* 2:41–63.

————. 1984. *Children's talk*. Cambridge, MA: Harvard University Press.

Gates, Henry Louis, Jr. 1994. *Colored people: A memoir*. New York: Alfred A. Knopf.

Gee, James Paul. 1989. Two styles of narrative construction and their linguistic and educational implications. *Discourse Processes* 12:287–307.

————. 1990. *Social linguistics and literacies*. New York: Falmer Press.

Gee, James, P., Sarah Michaels, and Mary Catherine O'Connor. 1994. Discourse analysis. In *Handbook of qualitative research in education*, ed. Margaret LeCompte and Judith Priessle, 227–91. New York: Academic Press.

Geekie, Peter, and Bridie Raban. 1994. Language learning at home and school. In *Input and interaction in language acquisition*, ed. Clare Galloway and Brian J. Richards, 153–80. New York: Cambridge University Press.

Giles, Howard, Justine Coupland, and Nikolas Coupland. 1991. Accommodation theory: Communication, context, and consequence. In *Contexts of accommodation*, ed. Howard Giles, Justine Coupland, and Nikolas Coupland, 1–68. New York: Cambridge University Press.

Giles, Howard, and Peter M. Smith. 1979. Accommodation theory: Optimal levels of convergence. In *Language and social psychology*, ed. Howard Giles and Robert N. St. Clair, 45–64. Oxford: Basil Blackwell.

Gilligan, Carol. 1982. *In a different voice: Psychological theory and women's development*. Cambridge, MA: Harvard University Press.

Gilmore, Perry, and Allan A. Glatthorn, eds. 1982. *Children in and out of school: Ethnography and education*. Washington, DC: Center for Applied Linguistics.

Goffman, Erving. 1956. The nature of deference and demeanor. *American Anthropologist* 58:473–502.

————. 1959. *The presentation of self in everyday life*. New York: Doubleday.

————. 1961. *Encounters: Two studies in the sociology of interaction*. Indianapolis: Bobbs-Merrill.

————. 1963. *Behavior in public places: Notes on the social organization of gatherings*. New York: Free Press of Glencoe.

————. 1971. *Relations in public: Microstudies of the public order*. New York: Basic Books.

————. 1974. *Frame analysis*. New York: Harper and Row.

————. 1978. Response cries. *Language* 54:787–815.

————. 1981. Footing. *Forms of talk*, 124–59. Philadelphia: University of Pennsylvania Press.

Goldstein, K. S. 1971. Strategy in counting out: An ethnographic folklore field study. In *The study of games*, ed. Elliott M. Avedon and Brian Sutton-Smith, 167–78. New York: John Wiley and Sons.

Goodwillie, Susan. 1993. *Voices from the future*. New York: Crown Publishers.

Goodwin, Charles. 1987. Forgetfulness as an interactive resource. *Social Psychology Quarterly* 50:115–30.

————. 1994. Professional vision. *American Anthropologist* 96:606–33.

Goodwin, Charles, and Marjorie Harness Goodwin. 1990. Interstitial argument. In *Conflict talk: Sociolinguistic investigations of arguments in conversations*, ed. Allen D. Grimshaw, 85–117. New York: Cambridge University Press.

Goodwin, Marjorie Harness. 1982. Processes of dispute management among urban black children. *American Ethnologist* 9:76–96.

————. 1983. Aggravated correction and disagreement in children's conversations. *Journal of Pragmatics* 7:657–77.

————. 1985. The serious side of jump rope: Conversational practices and social organization in the frame of play. *Journal of American Folklore* 98:315–30.

————. 1988. Cooperation and competition across girls' play activities. In *Gender and discourse: The power of talk*, ed. Alexandra Dundas Todd and Sue Fisher, 55–94. Norwood, NJ: Ablex.

————. 1990a. *He-said-she-said: Talk as social organization among black children.* Bloomington: Indiana University Press.

————. 1990b. Tactical uses of stories: Participation frameworks within girls' and boys' disputes. *Discourse Processes* 13:33–71.

Goodwin, Marjorie Harness, and Charles Goodwin. 1986. Gesture and coparticipation in the activity of searching for a word. *Semiotica* 62:51–75.

————. 1987. Children's arguing. In *Language, gender and sex in comparative perspective*, ed. Susan U. Philips, Susan Steele, and Christine Tanz, 200–48. New York: Cambridge University Press.

Gramsci, Antonio. 1971. *On intellectuals: Selections from the prison notebooks*, ed. Quintin Hoare and Geoffrey N. Smith. New York: International.

Granfield, Robert. 1991. Making it by faking it: Working-class students in an elite academic environment. *Journal of Contemporary Ethnography*. 20:331–51.

Greatbatch, David. 1988. A turn-taking system for British news interviews. *Language in Society* 17:401–30.

————. 1992. On the management of disagreement between news interviewees. In *Talk at work: Interaction in institutional settings*, ed. Paul Drew and John Heritage, 268–301. New York: Cambridge University Press.

Green, Georgia. 1982. Colloquial and literary uses of inversions. In *Spoken and written language: Exploring orality and literacy*, ed. Deborah Tannen, 119–53. Norwood, NJ: Ablex.

Greenwood, Alice. 1989. Discourse variation and social comfort: a study of topic initiation and and interruption patterns in the dinner conversation of preadolescent children. Ph.D. dissertation, City University of New York.

————. 1996. Floor management and power strategies in adolescent conversation. In *Rethinking language and gender research: Theory and practice*, ed. Victoria Bergvall, Janet M. Bing, and Alice F. Freed, 77–97. New York: Longman.

Grenier, Guillermo. 1988. *Inhuman relations: Quality circles and anti-unionism in American industry.* Philadelphia: Temple University Press.

Griffin, Peg, and Hugh Mehan. 1979. Sense and ritual in classroom discourse. In *Conversational routine: Explorations in standardized communication situations and prepatterned speech*, ed. Florian Coulmas. The Hague: Mouton.

Gumperz, John J. 1982. *Discourse strategies.* New York: Cambridge University Press.

Gumperz, John J., and Jenny Cook-Gumperz. 1982. Introduction: Language and the communication of social identity. In *Language and social identity*, ed. John J. Gumperz, 1–21. New York: Cambridge University Press.

Gumperz, John J., and Margaret Field. 1995. Children's discourse and inferential practices in cooperative learning. *Discourse Processes* 19:133–47.

Gutierrez, Kris D. 1995. Unpackaging academic discourse. *Discourse Processes* 19:21–37.

Hall, Donald. 1993. *Life work.* Boston: Beacon Press.

Halliday, M. A. K., and Ruqaiya Hasan. 1976. *Cohesion in English.* London: Longman.

Halmari, Helena, and Wendy Smith. 1994. Code-switching and register shift: Evidence from Finnish-English child bilingual conversation. *Journal of Pragmatics* 21:427–45.

Harding, Sandra. 1982. Is gender a variable in conceptions of rationality? A survey of issues. *Dialectica* 36:225–42.

Hare-Mustin, Rachel T., and Jeanne Maracek. 1988. The meaning of difference: Gender theory, postmodernism, and psychology. *American Psychologist* 43:455–64.

Hart, H. L. A. 1951. The ascription of responsibility and rights. *Essays on logic and language*, ed. A. Flew, 145–66. New York: Philosophical Library.

Heath, Shirley Brice. 1982. What no bedtime story means: Narrative skills at home and school. *Language in Society* 11:49–76.

———. 1983. *Ways with words: Language, life, and work in communities and classrooms.* New York: Cambridge University Press.

———. 1994. Stories as ways of acting together. In *The need for story: Cultural diversity in classroom and community,* ed. Anne Haas Dyson and Celia Genishi, 206–20. Champaign, IL: National Council of Teachers of English.

Heath, Shirley Brice, and Juliet Langman. 1994. Shared thinking and the register of coaching. In *Sociolinguistic perspectives on register,* ed. Douglas Biber and Edward Finegan, 82–105. New York: Oxford University Press.

Heath, Shirley Brice, and Milbrey W. McLaughlin, eds. 1993. *Identity and inner-city youth: Beyond ethnicity and gender.* New York: Teachers College Press.

———. 1994. Learning for anything everyday. *Journal of Curriculum Studies* 26:471–89.

Heath, Shirley Brice, and E. Soep. In progress. Art as playful work or working play?

Hemphill, Lowry. 1989. Topic development, syntax, and social class. *Discourse Processes* 12:267–86.

Henley, Nancy M. 1995. Ethnicity and gender issues in language. In *Bringing cultural diversity to feminist psychology: Theory, research, and practice,* ed. Hope Landrine, 361–95. Washington, DC: American Psychological Association.

Henry, Annette. 1995. Growing up black, female and working class: A teacher's narrative. *Anthropology and Education Quarterly* 26:251–78.

Henry, Jules. 1963. *Culture against man.* New York: Random House, Vintage.

Heritage, John. 1985. Analyzing news interviews: Aspects of the production of talk for an overhearing audience. In *Handbook of discourse analysis, Vol. 3,* ed. Teun van Dijk, 95–117. New York: Academic Press.

Heritage, John, and Andrew L. Roth. 1995. Grammar and institution: Questions and questioning in the broadcast news interview. *Research on Language and Social Interaction* 28:1–60.

Hess, Lucille J., and Judith R. Johnston. 1988. Acquisition of back channel listener responses to adequate messages. *Discourse Processes* 11:319–35.

Hewitt, Roger. 1986. *White talk, black talk: Interracial friendship and communication amongst adolescents.* New York: Cambridge University Press.

Holt, Grace Sims. 1972. "Inversion" in black communication. In *Rappin' and stylin' out: Communication in urban black America,* ed. Thomas Kochman, 152–59. Urbana: University of Illinois Press.

hooks, bell (Gloria Watkins). 1989. *Talking back: Thinking feminist, thinking Black.* Boston: South End Press.

Houston, Marsha. 1990. Difficult dialogues: Report on the 1990 conference on research in gender and communication. *Women and Language* 13:30–32.

Houston, M., and C. Kramarae. 1991. Speaking from silence: Methods of silencing and of resistance. *Discourse and Society* 2:387–99.

Hoyle, Susan M. 1989. Forms and footings in boys' sportscasting. *Text* 9:153–73.

———. 1991. Children's competence in the specialized register of sportscasting. *Journal of Child Language* 18:435–50.

————. 1993. Participation frameworks in sportscasting play: Imaginary and literal footings. In *Framing in discourse*, ed. Deborah Tannen, 114–45. New York: Oxford University Press.

————. 1994. Children's use of discourse markers in the creation of imaginary participation frameworks. *Discourse Processes* 17:447–64.

Hudson, Barbara. 1984. Femininity and adolescence. In *Gender and generation*, ed. Angela McRobbie and Mica Nava, 31–53. London: Macmillan.

Hughes, Linda. 1993. "You have to do it with style": Girls' games and girls' gaming. In *Feminist theory and the study of folklore*, ed. S. T. Hollis, L. Pershing, and M. J. Young, 130–48. Urbana: University of Illinois Press.

Hutchins, Edwin, and Leysia Palen. 1993. Constructing meaning from space, gesture, and talk. Paper presented at NATO-sponsored workshop on "Discourse, tools, and reasoning: situated cognition and technological supported environments," Lucca, Italy, November 2–7.

Hymes, Dell. 1962. The ethnography of speaking. In *Anthropology and human behavior*, ed. T. Gladwin and W. Sturtevant, 13–53. Washington, DC: Anthropological Society of Washington.

————. 1974a. *Foundations in sociolinguistics: An ethnographic approach.* Philadelphia: University of Pennsylvania Press.

————. 1974b. Ways of speaking. In *Explorations in the ethnography of speaking*, ed. Richard Bauman and Joel Sherzer, 433–51. New York: Cambridge University Press.

Inkeles, Alex. 1968. Social structure and the socialization of competence. *Harvard Educational Review*, Reprint Series, No. 1:50–68.

Institute for Puerto Rican Policy. 1992. *Puerto Ricans and other Latinos in New York City today: A statistical profile.* New York.

Jacob, Evelyn, and Cathie Jordan, eds. 1992. *Minority education: Anthropological perspectives.* Norwood, NJ: Ablex.

Jefferson, Gail. 1973. A case of precision timing in ordinary conversation: Overlapped tag-positioned address terms in closing sequences. *Semiotica* 9:47–96.

————. 1978. Sequential aspects of storytelling in conversations. In *Studies in the organization of conversational interaction*, ed. Jim Schenkein, 219–48. New York: Academic Press.

Johnson, David, Roger Johnson, and Edyth Holubec. 1994. *The new circles of learning: Cooperation in the classroom and the school.* Alexandria, VA: Association for Supervision and Curriculum Development.

John-Steiner, Vera. 1985. *Notebooks of the mind: Explorations of thinking.* Albuquerque: University of New Mexico Press.

Kalcik, Susan. 1975. ". . . like Ann's gynecologist or the time I was almost raped": Personal narratives in women's rap groups. In *Women and folklore*, ed. Claire Farrer, 3–11. Austin: University of Texas Press.

Katriel, Tamar. 1985. Brogez: Ritual and strategy in Israeli children's conflicts. *Language in Society* 14:467–90.

————. 1987. "Bexibudim!" Ritualized sharing among Israeli children. *Language in Society* 16:305–20.

Kendon, Adam. 1980. Gesticulation and speech: Two aspects of the process of utterance. In *The relation between verbal and nonverbal communication*, ed. Mary Ritchie Key, 207–27. The Hague: Mouton.

————. 1985. Behavioral foundations for the process of frame attunement in face-to-face interaction. In *Discovery strategies in the psychology of action*, ed. G. P. Ginsburg, Marylin Brenner, and M. von Cranach, 229–53. London: Academic Press.

Kernan, Keith T. 1977. Semantic and expressive elaboration in children's narratives. In *Child discourse*, ed. Susan Ervin-Tripp and Claudia Mitchell-Kernan, 91–102. New York: Academic Press.

Klein, Flora. 1980. A quantitative study of syntactic and pragmatic indicators of change in the Spanish of bilinguals in the U.S. In *Locating language in time and space*, ed. William Labov, 69–82. New York: Academic Press.

Kochman, Thomas, ed. 1972. *Rappin' and stylin' out: Communication in urban black America*. Urbana: University of Illinois Press.

———. 1983. The boundary between play and nonplay in black verbal dueling. *Language in Society* 12:329–37.

Kramarae, Cheris. 1990. Changing the complexion of gender in language research. In *Handbook of language and social psychology*, ed. Howard Giles and W. Peter Robinson, 346–61. New York: John Wiley and Sons.

Krauss, Robert M., and S. R. Fussell. 1988. Other-relatedness in language processing: Discussion and comments. *Journal of Language and Social Psychology* 7:263–66.

Labov, William. 1966. *The social stratification of English in New York City*. Washington, DC: Center for Applied Linguistics.

———. 1972a. *Language in the inner city: Studies in the Black English Vernacular*. Philadelphia: University of Pennsylvania Press.

———. 1972b. *Sociolinguistic patterns*. Philadelphia: University of Pennsylvania Press.

———. 1994. *Principles of linguistic change*. Cambridge, MA: Blackwell.

Labov, William, and David Fanshel. 1977. *Therapeutic discourse: Psychotherapy as conversation*. New York: Academic Press.

Lave, Jean, and Etienne Wenger. 1991. *Situated learning: Legitimate peripheral participation*. New York: Cambridge University Press.

Leaper, Campbell. 1991. Influence and involvement in children's discourse: Age, gender and partner effects. *Child Development* 62:797–811.

Lee, Felicia R. 1994. Lingering conflict in the schools: Black dialect vs. standard speech: Grappling with ways to teach young speakers of black dialect. *The New York Times*, January 5:A1, D22.

Leech, Geoffrey. 1971. *Meaning and the English verb*. London: Longman.

Lein, Laura, and Donald Brenneis. 1978. Children's disputes in three speech communities. *Language in Society* 7:299–323.

Lemke, Jay L. 1990. *Talking science: Language, learning, and values*. Norwood, NJ: Ablex.

Lerner, Gene. 1995. Turn design and the organization of participation in instructional activities. *Discourse Processes* 19:111–31.

Lever, Janet Rae. 1978. Sex differences in the complexity of children's play and games. *American Sociological Review* 43:471–83.

Levinson, Stephen. 1988. Putting linguistics on a proper footing: Explorations in Goffman's concepts of participation. In *Erving Goffman: Exploring the interaction order*, ed. Paul Drew and Anthony Wootton, 161–227. Boston: Northeastern University Press.

———. 1992. Activity types and language. In *Talk at work*, ed. Paul Drew and John Heritage, 66–100. New York: Cambridge University Press.

Lewis, Oscar. 1965. *La Vida: A Puerto Rican family in the culture of poverty—San Juan and New York*. New York: Random House.

Linde, Charlotte. 1988. Linguistic consequences of complex social structures: Rank and task in police helicopter discourse. In *Proceedings of the Fourteenth Annual Meeting of the Berkeley Linguistic Society*, ed. Shelley Axmaker, Annie Jaisser, and Helen Singmaster, 142–52.

Loban, Walter. 1963. *The language of elementary school children*. Champaign, IL: National Council of Teachers of English.

————. 1976. *Language development: Kindergarten through grade twelve*. Urbana, IL: National Council of Teachers of English.

Longino, Helen E. 1987. The ideology of competition. In *Competition: A feminist taboo?*, ed. V. Miner and H. E. Longino, 248–58. New York: Feminist Press at the City University of New York.

Lorde, Audrey. 1990. Age, race, class, and sex: Women redefining difference. In *Out there: Marginalization and contemporary cultures*, ed. Russell Ferguson, Martha Gever, Trinh T. Minh-Ha, and Cornel West, 281–88. Cambridge, MA: MIT Press.

Los Solidos Nation. 1995. Rulebook. *Harper's Magazine* 290(1739):18–20.

Lucas, Ceil, and Denise Borders. 1987. Language diversity in classroom discourse. *American Education Research Journal* 24:119–41.

————. 1994. *Language diversity and classroom discourse*. Norwood, NJ: Ablex.

Lunsford, Andrea, and Lisa Ede. 1990. *Singular texts/plural authors: Perspectives on collaborative writing*. Carbondale: Southern Illinois University Press.

Lyman, Frank T., Jr. 1992. Think-pair-share, thinktrix, thinklinks, and weird facts: An interactive system for cooperative thinking. In *Enhancing thinking through cooperative learning*, ed. Neil Davidson and Tony Worsham, 169–81. New York: Teachers College Press.

Maccoby, Eleanor E. 1990. Gender and relationships: A developmental account. *American Psychologist* 45:513–20.

Madrid, Arturo. 1992. Missing people and others: Joining together to expand the circle. In *Race, class, and gender: An anthology*, ed. Margaret L. Andersen and Patricia Hill Collins, 6–11. Belmont, CA: Wadsworth.

Maltz, Daniel N., and Ruth A. Borker. 1982. A cultural approach to male-female miscommunication. In *Communication, language and social identity*, ed. John J. Gumperz, 196–216. New York: Cambridge University Press.

Mann, Evelyn, and Joseph Salvo. 1984. Characteristics of new Hispanic immigrants to New York City: A comparison of Puerto Rican and non-Puerto Rican Hispanics. New York: Department of City Planning.

Marshall, Edward. 1995. *Transforming the way we work: The power of the collaborative workplace*. New York: American Management Association.

Martin, J. R. 1983. The development of register. In *Developmental issues in discourse*, ed. Jonathan Fine and Roy O. Freedle, 1–39. Norwood, NJ: Ablex.

Maynard, Douglas W. 1985a. How children start arguments. *Language in Society* 14:1–29.

————. 1985b. On the functions of social conflict among children. *American Sociological Review* 50:207–23.

McCallum-Bayliss, Heather. 1984. *The modal verbs of English*. Bloomington, IN: Indiana Linguistics Club.

McHoul, A. W. 1990. The organization of repair in classroom talk. *Language in Society* 19:349–77.

McLaughlin, Milbrey Wallin, Merita A. Irby, and Juliet Langman. 1994. *Urban sanctuaries: Neighborhood organizations in the lives and futures of inter-city youth*. San Francisco: Jossey-Bass.

McNeill, David. 1992. *Hand and mind: What gestures reveal about thought*. Chicago: University of Chicago Press.

McTear, Michael. 1985. *Children's conversation*. New York: Basil Blackwell.

Mead, Margaret. 1972. *Blackberry winter: My earlier years*. New York: William Morrow.

Mehan, Hugh. 1979. *Learning lessons: Social organization in the classroom*. Cambridge, MA: Harvard University Press.

————. 1982. The structure of classroom events and their consequences for student performance. In *Children in and out of school*, ed. Perry Gilmore and Allan A. Glatthorn, 59–87. Washington, DC: Center for Applied Linguistics.

———. 1984. Institutional decision making. In *Everyday cognition*, ed. Barbara Rogoff and Jean Lave, 41–66. Cambridge, MA: Harvard University Press.

Mendoza-Denton, Norma. 1995. Opposition, collaboration, and stance in conversation. Paper presented at the Linguistic Society of American Summer Institute, Conversation Analysis class.

Mernissi, Fatima. 1994. *Dreams of trespass: Tales of a harem girlhood*. Reading, MA: Addison-Wesley.

Merritt, Marilyn. 1976a. On questions following questions in service encounters. *Language in Society* 5:315–57.

———. 1976b. Resources for saying in service encounters. Ph.D. dissertation, University of Pennsylvania.

———. 1979. "Communicative loading" and intertwining of verbal and non-verbal modalities in service events. *Papers in Linguistics* 12:365–92.

———. 1994a. Advancing education and literacy in Niger: Observations, reflections, and recommendations. Consultant report. Niamey, Niger: UNICEF.

———. 1994b. Repetition in situated discourse—Exploring its forms and functions. In *Repetition in Discourse, Vol. 1*, ed. Barbara Johnstone, 23–35. Norwood, NJ: Ablex.

Merritt, Marilyn, Ailie Cleghorn, and Jared O. Abagi. 1988. Dual translation and cultural congruence: Exemplary teaching practices in using English, Swahili, and mother-tongue in three Kenyan primary schools. In *Linguistic change & contact: Proceedings of the Sixteenth Annual Conference on New Ways of Analyzing Variation in Language*, ed. Kathleen Ferrara, Becky Brown, Keith Walters, and John Baugh, 232–39 (Vol. 30, *Texas Linguistics Forum*). Austin: Dept. of Linguistics, University of Texas.

Merritt, Marilyn, with Ailie Cleghorn, Jared O. Abagi, and Grace Bunyi. 1992. Socialising multilingualism—Determinants of codeswitching in Kenyan primary classrooms. *Journal of Multilingual and Multicultural Development* (guest editor: Carol Eastman) 13:103–21.

Michaels, Sarah. 1981. "Sharing time": Children's narrative styles and differential access to literacy. *Language in Society* 10:423–42.

———. 1986. Narrative presentations: An oral preparation for literacy with first graders. In *The social construction of literacy*, ed. Jenny Cook-Gumperz, 94–116. New York: Cambridge University Press.

———. 1991. The dismantling of narrative. In *Developing narrative structure*, ed. Allyssa McCabe and Carole Peterson, 303–51. Hillsdale, NJ: Erlbaum.

Michaels, Sarah, and James Collins. 1984. Oral discourse styles: Classroom interaction and the acquisition of literacy. In *Coherence in spoken and written discourse*, ed. Deborah Tannen, 219–44. Norwood, NJ: Ablex.

Milkie, Melissa. 1994. Social world approach to cultural studies: Mass media and gender in the adolescent peer group. *Journal of Contemporary Ethnography* 23:354–80.

Miller, Patrice M., Dorothy L. Danaher, and David Forbes. 1986. Sex-related strategies for coping with interpersonal conflict in children aged five and seven. *Developmental Psychology* 22:543–48.

Miller, Peggy. 1986. Teasing as language socialization and verbal play in a white working-class community. In *Language socialization across cultures*, ed. Bambi B. Schieffelin and Elinor Ochs, 199–212. New York: Cambridge University Press.

Milroy, James, and Lesley Milroy. 1991. *Authority in language*, 2nd edition. London: Routledge.

Milroy, Lesley. 1980. *Language and social networks*. Oxford: Basil Blackwell.

Mishler, Elliott. 1979. "Wou' you trade cookies with the popcorn?" The talk of trades among six year olds. In *Language, children, and society*, ed. Olga Garnica and Martha L. King, 221–36. New York: Pergamon Press.

Mitchell-Kernan, Claudia, and Keith T. Kernan. 1977. Pragmatics of directive choice among children. In *Child discourse*, ed. Susan Ervin-Tripp and Claudia Mitchell-Kernan, 189–208. New York: Academic Press.

Montalvo, Braulio. 1972. Home-school conflict and the Puerto Rican child. *Social Casework* 4.

Morgan, Marcyliena. 1995. No woman no cry: The linguistic representation of African American women. In *Cultural performances: Proceedings of the Third Berkeley Women and Language Conference*, ed. Mary Bucholtz, Kira Hall, and Birch Moonwomon, 525–41. Berkeley: Berkeley Women and Language Group, University of Californa.

Mukhopadhyay, C., and P. Higgins. 1988. Anthropological studies of women's status revisited: 1977–1987. *Annual Review of Anthropology* 17:461–95.

Mumby, Dennis, and Cynthia Stohl. 1991. Power and discourse in organization studies: Absence and the dialectic of control. *Discourse and Society* 2:313–32.

Noblet, George. 1993. Power and caring. *American Educational Research Journal* 30:23–38.

Ntshangase, Dumisani K. 1995. Indaba yami i-straight: Language and language practices in Soweto. In *Language and social history*, ed. Rajend Mesthrie. Cape Town, South Africa: David Philip.

Ochs, Elinor. 1979a. Planned and unplanned discourse. In *Discourse and syntax*, ed. Talmy Givon, 51–80. New York: Academic Press.

———. 1979b. Transcription as theory. In *Developmental pragmatics*, ed. Elinor Ochs and Bambi Schieffelin, 43–72. New York: Academic Press.

———. 1986. Introduction. In *Language socialization across cultures*, ed. Bambi B. Schieffelin and Elinor Ochs, 1–13. New York: Cambridge University Press.

———. 1988. *Culture and language development: Language acquisition and language socialization in a Samoan village*. New York: Cambridge University Press.

———. 1992. Constructing social identity: An invitation to applied linguistics. Keynote address to the American Association for Applied Linguistics, Seattle, February.

———. 1993. Constructing social identity: A language socialization perspective. *Research on Language and Social Interaction* 26:287–306.

Ochs, Elinor, Sally Jacoby, and Patrick Gonzales. 1994. Interpretive journeys: How physicists talk and travel through graphic space. *Configurations* 1:151–71.

Ochs, Elinor, and Bambi B. Schieffelin, eds. 1979. *Developmental pragmatics*. New York: Academic Press.

Ochs, Elinor, Carolyn Taylor, Dina Rudolph, and Ruth Smith. 1992. Storytelling as a theory-building activity. *Discourse Processes* 15:37–72.

O'Connor, Mary Catherine, and Sarah Michaels. 1993. Aligning academic task and participation status through revoicing: Analysis of a classroom discourse strategy. *Anthropology and Education Quarterly* 24:318–35.

Ogbu, John. 1981. On origins of human competence: A cultural ecological perspective. *Child Development* 52:413–29.

———. 1988. Cultural diversity and human development. In *Black children and poverty: A developmental perspective*, ed. D. T. Slaughter, 11–28. (New Directions for Child Development, No. 42, Winter). San Francisco: Jossey Bass.

Oliver, Pam. 1991. "What do girls know anyway?": Rationality, gender and social control. *Feminism and Psychology* 1:339–60.

Olivier de Sardan, Jean Pierre. 1995. *Anthropologie et developpement: Essai en socio-anthropologie du changement social*. Paris: Karthala.

Ong, Walter J. 1982. *Orality and literacy: The technologizing of the word*. London: Methuen.

Osuna, Juan. 1949. *A history of education in Puerto Rico*. Rio Piedras: Editorial de la Universidad de Puerto Rico.

Parker, Mike, and Jane Slaughter. 1988. *Choosing sides: Unions and the team concept*. Boston: South End Press.

Peters, Tom. 1988. *Thriving on chaos*. New York: Alfred Knopf.

Peterson, Carole, and Allyssa McCabe. 1988. The connective *and* as discourse glue. *First Language* 8:19–28.

———. 1991. Linking children's connective use and narrative macrostructure. In *Developing narrative structure*, ed. Allyssa McCabe and Carole Peterson, 29–53. Hillsdale, NJ: Erlbaum.

Philips, Susan U. 1993. *The invisible culture: Communication in classroom and community on the Warm Springs Indian Reservation*, 2nd ed. Prospect Heights, IL: Waveland Press.

Piaget, Jean. 1965. *The moral judgment of the child*. New York: Free Press.

Piestrup, Ann M. 1973. Black dialect interference and accommodation of reading instruction in first grade (Language-Behavior Research Laboratory Monograph No. 4). Berkeley: University of California.

Pinker, Steven. 1994. *The language instinct: How the mind creates language*. New York: William Morrow.

Polanyi, Livia. 1989. *Telling the American story*. Cambridge, MA: MIT Press.

Pomerantz, Anita. 1984. Agreeing and disagreeing with assessments: Some features of preferred/dispreferred turn shapes. In *Structures of social action: Studies in conversation analysis*, ed. J. M. Atkinson and J. Heritage, 57–101. New York: Cambridge University Press.

Poplack, Shana. 1981. Syntactic structure and social function of code–switching. In *Latino language and communicative behavior*, ed. Richard Duran, 169–84. Norwood, NJ: Ablex.

Postman, Neil. 1992. *Technopoly: The surrender of culture to technology*. New York: Alfred Knopf.

Pousada, Alicia, and Shana Poplack. 1982. No case for convergence: The Puerto Rican Spanish verb system in a language contact situation. In *Bilingual education for Hispanic students in the United States*, ed. Joshua A. Fishman and Gary Keller, 207–40. New York: Teachers College Press.

Rampton, M. B. H. 1991. Interracial Panjabi in a British adolescent peer group. *Language in Society* 20:391–422.

———. 1995. *Crossing: Language and ethnicity among adolescents*. New York: Longman.

Reichman, Rachel. 1990. Communication and mutual engagement. In *Conversational organization and its development*, ed. Bruce Dorval, 23–48. Norwood, NJ: Ablex.

Reid, E. 1978. Social and stylistic variation in the speech of children: Some evidence from Edinburgh. In *Sociolinguistic patterns in British English*, ed. Peter Trudgill, 158–71. London: Edward Arnold.

Rickford, John R., and Faye McNair-Knox. 1994. Addressee- and topic-influenced style shift: A quantitative sociolinguistic study. In *Sociolinguistic perspectives on register*, ed. Douglas Biber and Edward Finegan, 235–76. New York: Oxford University Press.

Rizzo, Thomas A. 1992. The role of conflict in children's friendship development. *New Directions for Child Development* 58 (Winter): 93–111.

Robins, Kikanza Nuri, and T. Jean Adenika. 1987. Informal conversation topics among urban Afro-American women. In *Women and language in transition*, ed. Joyce Penfield, 180–95. Albany, NY: SUNY Press.

Rodriguez, Clara. 1980. Puerto Ricans: Between black and white. In *The Puerto Rican struggle: Essays on survival in the United States*, ed. Clara Rodriguez, Virginia Sanchez, and Jose Alers, 20–30. New York: Puerto Rican Migration Consortium.

Rogoff, Barbara. 1994. Developing understanding of the idea of communities of learners. *Mind, Culture, and Activity* 1:209–29.

Romaine, Suzanne. 1984. *The language of children and adolescents: The acquisition of communicative competence.* Oxford: Basil Blackwell.

Rosaldo, Renato. 1989. *Culture and truth: The remaking of social analysis.* Boston: Beacon Press.

Rosebery, Anne S., Beth Warren, and F. Conant. 1992. Appropriating scientific discourse: Findings from language minority classrooms. *Journal of the Learning Sciences* 2:61–94.

Rubagumya, Casmir M., ed. 1993. *Teaching and researching language in African classrooms.* Clevedon, England: Multilingual Matters.

Rushdie, Salman. 1990. *Haroun and the sea of stories.* London: Penguin Books.

Rymer, Jone. 1993. Collaboration and conversation in learning communities: The discipline and the classroom. In *Professional communication: The social perspective*, ed. Nancy Blyler and Charlotte Thralls, 179–95. Newbury Park, CA: Sage.

Rymer, Russ. 1993. *Genie: A scientific tragedy.* New York: Harper Collins.

Sachs, Jacqueline. 1987. Preschool boys' and girls' language use in pretend play. In *Language, gender and sex in comparative perspective*, ed. Susan U. Philips, Susan Steele, and Christine Tanz, 178–88. New York: Cambridge University Press.

Sachs, Jacqueline, and J. Devin. 1976. Young children's use of age-appropriate speech styles in social interaction and role-playing. *Journal of Child Language* 3:81–98.

Sacks, Harvey. 1987/1973. On the preferences for agreement and contiguity in sequences in conversation. In *Talk and social organisation*, ed. Graham Button and John R. E. Lee, 54–69. Clevedon, England: Multilingual Matters.

———. 1992a. Adjacency pairs: Scope of operation. In *Lectures on conversation, Vol. 2*, ed. Gail Jefferson, 521–32. Oxford: Basil Blackwell.

———. 1992b. *Lectures on conversation, Vol. 1*, ed. Gail Jefferson. Oxford: Basil Blackwell.

Sacks, Harvey, Emanuel A. Schegloff, and Gail Jefferson. 1974. A simplest systematics for the organization of turn-taking for conversation. *Language* 50:696–735.

Sansom, Bernard. 1982. The sick who do not speak. *Semantic Anthropology.* A.S.A. Monograph 22:183–96. London: Academic Press.

Sapir, Edward. 1956. Linguistics as a "science." In *Culture, language and personality*, ed. George Mandelbaum. Berkeley: University of California Press.

Sattel, Jack W. 1983. Men, inexpressiveness, and power. In *Language, gender and society*, ed. Barrie Thorne, Cheris Kramarae, and Nancy Henley, 118–24. Rowley, MA: Newbury House.

Schank, Roger C., and Robert P. Abelson. 1977. *Scripts, plans, goals and understanding: An inquiry into human knowledge structures.* Hillsdale, NJ: Erlbaum.

Schegloff, Emanuel A. 1984. On some gestures' relation to talk. In *Structures of social action*, ed. J. Maxwell Atkinson and John Heritage, 266–96. New York: Cambridge University Press.

———. 1992. On talk and its institutional occasions. In *Talk at work: Interaction in institutional settings*, ed. Paul Drew and John Heritage, 101–34. New York: Cambridge University Press.

Schegloff, Emanuel A., Gail Jefferson, and Harvey Sacks. 1977. The preference for self-correction in the organization of repair in conversation. *Language* 53:361–82.

Schieffelin, Bambi B. 1990. *The give and take of everyday life: Language socialization of Kaluli children.* New York: Cambridge University Press.

Schieffelin, Bambi B., and Elinor Ochs, eds. 1986. *Language socialization across cultures.* New York: Cambridge University Press.

Schiffrin, Deborah. 1984. Jewish argument as sociability. *Language in Society* 13:311–35.

———. 1987. *Discourse markers*. New York: Cambridge University Press.

———. 1990. The management of a co-operative self during argument: The role of opinions and stories. In *Conflict talk: Sociolinguistic investigations of arguments in conversations*, ed. Allen D. Grimshaw, 241–59. New York: Cambridge University Press.

———. 1993. "Speaking for another" in sociolinguistic interviews: Alignments, identities, and frames. In *Framing in discourse*, ed. Deborah Tannen, 231–63. New York: Oxford University Press.

Schleppegrell, Mary J. 1991. Paratactic *because*. *Journal of Pragmatics* 16:323–37.

———. 1992. Subordination and linguistic complexity. *Discourse Processes* 15:117–31.

Schuster, I., and J. Hartz-Karp. 1986. Kinder, kueche, kibbutz: Women's aggression and status quo maintenance in a small scale community. *Anthropological Quarterly* 59:191–99.

Schutz, Alfred. 1970. *On phenomenology and social relations*. Chicago: University of Chicago Press.

Scollon, Ron, and Suzanne B. K. Scollon. 1981. *Narrative, literacy and face in interethnic communication*. Norwood, NJ: Ablex.

———. 1984. Cooking it up and boiling it down: Abstracts in Athabaskan children's story retellings. In *Coherence in spoken and written discourse*, ed. Deborah Tannen, 173–97. Norwood, NJ: Ablex.

Scott, Cheryl M. 1984. Adverbial connectivity in conversations of children 6 to 12. *Journal of Child Language* 11:423–52.

Scott, James C. 1985. *Weapons of the weak: Everyday forms of peasant resistance*. New Haven, CT: Yale University Press.

Scott, Kesho Yvonne. 1991. *The habit of surviving*. New York: Ballantine.

Shantz, Carolyn U., and Willard W. Hartup. 1992. Conflict and development: An introduction. In *Conflict in child and adolescent development*, ed. Carolyn U. Shantz and Willard W. Hartup, 1–11. New York: Cambridge University Press.

Sheldon, Amy. 1992. Conflict talk: Sociolinguistic challenges to self-assertion and how young girls meet them. *Merrill Palmer Quarterly* 38:95–117.

———. 1993. Pickle fights: Gendered talk in preschool disputes. In *Gender and conversational interaction*, ed. Deborah Tannen, 83–106. New York: Oxford University Press.

Shuman, Amy. 1986. *Storytelling rights: The uses of oral and written texts by urban adolescents*. New York: Cambridge University Press.

———. 1993. "Get outa my face": Entitlement and authoritative discourse. In *Responsibility and evidence in oral discourse*, ed. Jane H. Hill and Judith T. Irvine, 135–60. New York: Cambridge University Press.

Shuy, Roger, and Peg Griffin. 1981. What they do at school any day: Studying functional language. In *Children's oral communication skills*, ed. W. P. Dickson. New York: Academic Press.

Shuy, Roger, Walt Wolfram, and William K. Riley. 1967. *Linguistic correlates of social stratification in Detroit*. Final Report, Project 6-1347. Washington, DC: Office of Education.

Silva-Corvalán, Carmen. 1989. Past and present perspectives on language change in U.S. Spanish. *International Journal of the Sociology of Language* (Special issue: *U.S. Spanish: The language of Latinos*, ed. I. Wherritt and O. Garcia) 79:53–66.

Simich, Carmen. 1984. A sociolinguistic investigation of the structure of sixth grade science and art lessons with particular attention to Verification-of-Learning activities. Ph.D. dissertation, Georgetown University.

Simich-Dudgeon, Carmen, and Lynn McCreedy. 1988. Managing topics, tasks, and students: How teachers produce coherence in classroom discourse. Presentation at the Annual Meeting of the American Educational Research Association, New Orleans.

Sinclair, J., and M. Coulthard. 1975. *Towards an analysis of discourse: The English used by teachers and pupils*. London: Oxford University Press.

Smitherman, Geneva. 1986. *Talkin and testifyin: The language of Black America*, 2nd ed. Detroit: Wayne State University Press.

Sprott, Richard A. 1992. Children's use of discourse markers in disputes: Form-function relations and discourse in child language. *Discourse Processes* 15:423–39.

Stafford, Barbara Maria. 1994. *Artful science: Enlightenment entertainment and the eclipse of visual education*. Cambridge, MA: MIT Press.

Stanley, Louise. 1984. How the social science research process discriminates against women. In *Is higher education fair to women?*, ed. S. Acker and D. Warren-Piper, 189–207. Surrey, England: Srhe & Nfer-Nelson.

Stevens, Wallace. 1954. *The collected poems*. New York: Vintage Books.

Streeck, Jurgen. 1985. *Social order in child communication: A study in microethnography*. Philadelphia: John Benjamins.

———. 1993. Gesture as communication I: Its coordination with gaze and speech. *Communication Monographs* 60:275–99.

Sutton-Smith, Brian. 1979. The play of girls. In *Becoming female*, ed. Claire B. Kopp and Martha Kirkpatrick, 229–57. New York: Plenum.

Tajfel, Henri. 1978. *Differentiation between social groups*. London: Academic Press.

Tannen, Deborah. 1982a. Ethnic style in male-female conversation. In *Language and social identity*, ed. John J. Gumperz, 217–31. New York: Cambridge University Press.

———. 1982b. The oral/literate continuum in discourse. In *Spoken and written language: Exploring orality and literacy*, ed. Deborah Tannen, 1–16. Norwood, NJ: Ablex.

———. 1984. *Conversational style: Analyzing talk among friends*. Norwood, NJ: Ablex.

———. 1989. *Talking voices: Repetition, dialogue, and imagery in conversational discourse*. New York: Cambridge University Press.

———. 1990a. Gender differences in conversational coherence: Physical alignment and topical cohesion. In *Conversational organization and its development*, ed. Bruce Dorval, 167–206. Norwood, NJ: Ablex.

———. 1990b. *You just don't understand: Women and men in conversation*. New York: William Morrow.

———, ed. 1993a. *Framing in discourse*. New York: Oxford University Press.

———, ed. 1993b. *Gender and conversational interaction*. New York: Oxford University Press.

———. 1993c. What's in a frame?: Surface evidence for underlying expectations. In *Framing in discourse*, ed. Deborah Tannen, 14–56. New York: Oxford University Press.

Tannen, Deborah, and Cynthia Wallat. 1993. Interactive frames and knowledge schemas in interaction: Examples from a medical examination/interview. In *Framing in discourse*, ed. Deborah Tannen, 57–76. New York: Oxford University Press.

Taussig, Michael. 1993. *Mimesis and alterity*. New York: Routledge.

Taylor, Hanni. 1989. *Standard English, Black English, and bidialectalism: A controversy*. New York: Peter Lang.

Thakerar, Jitendra N., Howard Giles, and Jenny Cheshire. 1982. Psychological and linguistic parameters of speech accommodation theory. In *Advances in the social psychology of language*, ed. Colin Fraser and Klaus R. Scherer, 205–55. New York: Cambridge University Press.

Tharp, Roland, and Ronald Gallimore. 1988. *Rousing minds to life: Teaching, learning, and schooling in social context*. New York: Cambridge University Press.

Theberge, Christine, and John Rickford. 1989. Preterit *had* in the BEV of elementary school children. Paper presented at the 18th Annual Conference on New Ways of Analyzing Variation, Duke University. Under review for American Speech.

Thompson, Jim. 1993. *Positive coaching: Building character and self-esteem through sports.* Dubuque, IA: Brown and Benchmark.

Thorne, Barrie. 1986. Girls and boys together . . . but mostly apart: Gender arrangements in elementary school. In *Relationships and development*, ed. Willard W. Hartup and Zick Rubin, 167–84. Hillsdale, NJ: Erlbaum.

———. 1993. *Gender play: Girls and boys in school.* New Brunswick, NJ: Rutgers University Press.

Tobin, Lesley. 1996. Car wrecks, baseball caps, and man-to-man defense: The personal narratives of adolescent males. *College English* 18:158–75.

Troemel-Ploetz, Senta. 1992. The construction of conversational equality by women. In *Locating power: Proceedings of the Second Berkeley Women and Language Group*, ed. Kira Hall, Mary Bucholtz, and Birch Moonwomon, 581–89. Berkeley: Berkeley Women and Language Group, University of California.

Tuyay, Sabrina, Louise Jennings, and Carol Dixon. 1995. Classroom discourse and opportunities to learn: An ethnographic study of knowledge construction in a bilingual third-grade classroom. *Discourse Processes* 19:75–110.

U.S. Commission on Civil Rights. 1976. *Puerto Ricans in the continental United States: An uncertain future.* Washington, DC.

Vygotsky, L. S. 1978. *Mind in society: The development of higher psychological processes.* Cambridge, MA: Harvard University Press.

Walsh, Catherine E. 1991. *Pedagogy and the struggle for voice: Issues of language, power, and schooling for Puerto Ricans.* New York: Bergin and Garvey.

Watson, Karen Ann. 1975. Transferable communicative routines: Strategies and group identity in two speech events. *Language in Society* 4:53–72.

Watson-Gegeo, Karen Ann, and Stephen T. Boggs. 1977. From verbal play to talk story: The role of routines in speech events among Hawaiian children. In *Child Discourse*, ed. Susan Ervin-Tripp and Claudia Mitchell-Kernan, 67–90. New York: Academic Press.

Weber, Elizabeth G. 1982. Going, going, gone: Verb forms in baseball sportscasting. M.A. thesis, University of California, Los Angeles.

Weinrich, Uriel. 1968. *Languages in contact.* The Hague: Mouton.

Weinstein, Eugene A., and Paul Deutschberger. 1963. Some dimensions of altercasting. *Sociometry* 26:454–66.

Wertsch, James V. 1991. *Voices of the mind: A sociocultural approach to mediated action.* Cambridge, MA: Harvard University Press.

West, Candace, and Donald Zimmerman. 1983. Small insults: A study of interruptions in cross-sex conversations betwen unacquainted persons. In *Language, gender and society*, ed. Barrie Thorne, Cheris Kramarae, and Nancy Henley, 102–17. Rowley, MA: Newbury House.

White, Geoffrey M., and Karen Ann Watson-Gegeo. 1990. Disentangling discourse. In *Disentangling: Conflict discourse in pacific societies*, ed. Karen Ann Watson-Gegeo and Geoffrey M. White, 3–49. Stanford: Stanford University Press.

White, Sheida. 1989. Backchannels across cultures: A study of Americans and Japanese. *Language in Society* 18:59–76.

Whiting, Beatrice, and Carolyn Pope Edwards. 1973. A cross-cultural analysis of sex differences in the behavior of children aged three through eleven. *Journal of Social Psychology* 91:171–88.

Wilkinson, Louis Cherry, ed. 1982. *Communicating in the classroom.* New York: Academic Press.

Williams, Brett. 1988. *Upscaling downtown: Stalled gentrification in Washington, D.C.* Ithaca, NY: Cornell University Press.

Wittgenstein, Ludwig. 1958. *Philosophical investigations*, ed. G. E. M. Anscombe and R. Rhees, trans. G. E. M. Anscombe, 2nd ed. Oxford: Basil Blackwell.

Wolfram, Walt. 1970. Sociolinguistic implications for educational sequencing. In *Teaching standard English in the inner city*, ed. Ralph W. Fasold and Roger W. Shuy. Washington, DC: Center for Applied Linguistics.

———. 1974a. The relationship of southern white speech to Vernacular Black English. *Language* 50:498–527.

———. 1974b. Sociolinguistic aspects of assimilation (Puerto Rican English in New York City). Arlington, VA: Center for Applied Linguistics.

———. 1983. Test interpretation and sociolinguistic differences. *Topics in Language Disorders* 3:21–34.

———. 1991. *Dialects and American English.* Englewood Cliffs, NJ: Prentice Hall.

Wolfram, Walt, Carolyn Temple Adger, and Donna Christian. In press. *Dialects in schools and communities.* Mahwah, NJ: Erlbaum.

Wolfram, Walt, and Ralph W. Fasold. 1974. *The study of social dialects in American English.* Englewood Cliffs, NJ: Prentice-Hall.

Yaeger-Dror, Malcah. 1986. Intonational prominence on negatives in English. *Language and Speech* 28:197–230.

Youssef, Valerie. 1993. Children's linguistic choices: Audience design and societal norms. *Language in Society* 22:257–74.

Zentella, Ana Celia. 1981a. Hablamos los dos. We speak both: Growing up bilingual in El Barrio. Ph.D. dissertation, University of Pennsylvania.

———. 1981b. Language variety among Puerto Ricans. In *Language in the USA*, ed. Charles A. Ferguson and Shirley Brice Heath, 218–38. New York: Cambridge University Press.

———. 1982. Spanish and English in contact in the United States. *Word* 33:41–57.

———. 1985. The fate of Spanish in the United States: The Puerto Rican experience. In *The language of inequality*, ed. Nessa Wolfson and Joan Manes, 41–59. Berlin: Mouton.

———. 1987. Language and female identity in the Puerto Rican community. In *Women and language in transition.* ed. Joyce Penfield, 167–79. Albany, NY: SUNY Press.

———. 1990. Lexical leveling in four New York City Spanish dialects: Linguistic and social factors. *Hispania* 73:1094–105.

———. 1997. *Growing up bilingual: Puerto Rican children in New York City.* Cambridge, MA: Blackwell.

Index